CW01628294

THE METHODIST WORSHIP BOOK

METHODIST PUBLISHING HOUSE
PETERBOROUGH, ENGLAND

© 1999 Trustees for Methodist Church Purposes

First published 1999

The Methodist Worship Book is available in the following editions:

Standard full text, English, ISBN 1 85852 116 5

Presentation Editions
Bound in Blue, ISBN 1 85852 119 X
Bound in Red, ISBN 1 85852 120 3
Bound in Green, ISBN 1 85852 121 1

additionally there is a
Large Print edition, printed in black only, ISBN 1 85852 118 1

and a
Bilingual English/Welsh edition, ISBN 1 85852 117 3

The contents of this book have been authorized by the Methodist Conference for use in the Methodist Church. They may not be reproduced either in whole or in part, whether for sale or otherwise, by any method without the consent of the Methodist Publishing House, 20 Ivatt Way, Peterborough PE3 7PG England.

Printed in Great Britain by St Ives (Peterborough) Ltd and bound by Hunter & Foulis Limited, Edinburgh.

CONTENTS

PREFACE

The Church is called to offer worship to the glory and praise of God. From the earliest days of the Church, Christian people have gathered together for this purpose as 'a holy priesthood to offer spiritual sacrifices acceptable to God through Jesus Christ' and to 'proclaim the mighty acts' of God (1 Peter 2:5, 9).

All true worship is God-centred. As we acknowledge the mystery and glory of the eternal God, Father, Son and Holy Spirit, we are moved to offer our praise and to confess our sins, confident of God's mercy and forgiveness. God's acts of grace and love in creation and salvation are recounted and celebrated, and we respond with thanksgiving, intercession and the offering of our lives.

Worship is a gracious encounter between God and the Church. God speaks to us, especially through scripture read and proclaimed and through symbols and sacraments. We respond, chiefly through hymns and prayers and acts of dedication. Worship is the work of the whole people of God: a congregation is not an audience or a group of spectators. Those who lead worship are called to encourage and, with the help of the Holy Spirit, to enable the whole Body of Christ to participate fully. Such participation may include personal testimony and the use of the creative arts.

The Methodist Worship Book is the latest in a succession of Methodist service books which can be traced back to John Wesley's **The Sunday Service** (1784). The orders of worship printed here are the fruit of a long process of drafting and revision. They take account of recent liturgical and ecumenical developments throughout the world as well as distinctively Methodist traditions of worship. This book, like its predecessor, **The Methodist Service Book** (1975), is authorized by the

Conference as a standard for Methodist worship. The words of the 1975 Preface still apply: 'These forms are not intended to curb creative freedom, but rather to provide norms for its guidance.' Within our heritage, both fixed forms and freer expressions of worship have been, and should continue to be, valued.

In the years that have elapsed since the publication of **The Methodist Service Book** there have been many requests for the provision of a wider range of services and other worship material. This book is therefore more extensive than any of its predecessors. It is hoped that its rich and comprehensive nature will help to enhance and renew the worship of the Methodist people. Yet worship is not a matter of words alone. It involves not only what we say but also what we do and who we are. May these services be used to the honour and praise of God and may our prayer, as we use them, accord with the words of Charles Wesley:

While in the heavenly work we join,
Thy glory be our whole design,
  Thy glory, not our own.

GENERAL DIRECTIONS

1 Some directions in these services, for example those concerning standing or kneeling, may cause difficulty for some people. All should be encouraged to participate in worship in whatever ways are most appropriate to them.

2 Notices, if not printed, may be given before the service or at some other suitable point.

3 The term 'hymn' in these services means a Psalm, hymn or other spiritual song.

4 Though there are indications in the services of appropriate points at which hymns may be sung, it is not necessary to sing a hymn at every such point.

5 There should normally be only one collection of money during a service. If there are to be two collections, one of them should be taken as the people enter or leave.

6 All biblical references in this book are to **The New Revised Standard Version (Anglicized Edition)** of the Bible. Adaptations may be needed when other translations are used.

DAILY PRAYER

INTRODUCTION

From the time of the early Church, many Christians have followed the practice of offering daily prayer and praise to God, often at specified hours. In so doing we express the praise which is God's due from all creation and are united in worship with all God's people on earth and in heaven. In the Christian tradition daily prayer has taken many forms. In **The Book of Common Prayer**, the first version of which appeared in 1549, five of the eight daily acts of prayer, used in monasteries, were simplified and reduced to two, Morning and Evening Prayer.

Prayer in the Morning and ***Prayer in the Evening*** may be used for daily personal or corporate devotion but are not intended as the basis for public worship on Sundays. Hymns, prayers, psalms and scripture readings are suggested in the services, but ***Prayer in the Morning*** and ***Prayer in the Evening*** may be used in conjunction with other Bible reading schemes and devotional resources. Some may find objects such as a cross or candles helpful when saying Daily Prayer.

SENTENCES OF SCRIPTURE

Advent

Then will the glory of the Lord be revealed
and all will see it together.

Wait for the Lord; be strong and brave
and put your hope in the Lord.

Christmas

The Word became flesh; he lived among us,
and we have seen his glory,
the glory as of the Father's only Son,
full of grace and truth.

Epiphany

From the rising of the sun to its setting
my name is great among the nations,
says the Lord of hosts.

Lent

Because Christ has passed through the time of suffering,
he is able to help those in time of trial.

Rend your hearts and not your garments.
Return to the Lord, your God,
for he is gracious and merciful.

Passiontide

Jesus said:
'Anyone who wants to be a follower of mine
must renounce self,
and take up the cross and follow me.'

Eastertide

Alleluia! Christ is risen!
He is risen indeed! Alleluia!

Ascensiontide

Praise and honour, glory and might,
to him who sits on the throne
and to the Lamb, for ever.

Pentecost

God's love has been poured into our hearts
through the Holy Spirit who has been given to us.

Come, Holy Spirit,
and renew the face of the earth.

Trinity

Holy, holy, holy is the Lord of hosts:
the whole earth is full of his glory.

John the Baptist

There appeared a man named John.
He was sent from God,
and came as a witness
to testify to the light.

Mary the mother of our Lord

Mary said:
'Here am I, the servant of the Lord;
let it be with me according to your word.'

Apostles or Evangelists

We have seen for ourselves
and we are witnesses,
that the Father has sent the Son
to be the Saviour of the world.

All Saints (1 November) or any saint

You have come to Mount Zion
and to the city of the living God,
and to the assembly of the firstborn
who are enrolled in heaven.

You that are righteous, rejoice in the Lord
and praise his holy name.

At the time of or on the anniversary of a death

The Lamb who is at the centre of the throne
will be their shepherd
and will guide them to springs of the water of life;
and God will wipe away every tear from their eyes.

Times of trouble

God is our refuge and our stronghold,
a timely help in trouble.

Christian unity

There is one body and one Spirit,
just as there is one hope
held out in God's call to you;
one Lord, one faith, one Baptism,
one God and Father of all,
who is over all and through all and in all.

PRAYER IN THE MORNING

1 O Lord, open our lips,
and we shall praise your name.

2 In Eastertide:

Alleluia! Christ is risen!
He is risen indeed! Alleluia!

In other seasons or on other occasions, an appropriate sentence from pages 2-4 may be said.

3 One of these sentences:

Sunday

Holy, holy, holy is the Lord of hosts:
the whole earth is full of his glory.

Monday

God has sent into our hearts
the Spirit of his Son, crying,
'Abba! Father!'

Tuesday

There is one body and one Spirit,
just as there is one hope
held out in God's call to you.

Wednesday

The Lord is in his holy temple;
let all the earth be silent in his presence.

Thursday

May the words of my mouth
and the thoughts of my mind
be acceptable to you,
Lord, my rock and my redeemer.

Friday

God was in Christ
reconciling the world to himself,
and has entrusted us with the message of reconciliation.

Saturday

Send out your light and truth to be my guide;
let them lead me to your holy hill,
to your dwelling-place.

4 Glory to the Father, and to the Son,
and to the Holy Spirit:
as it was in the beginning, is now,
and shall be for ever. Amen.

5 Prayers of penitence, if desired

6 EITHER ***Venite*** (Psalm 95)

Come, let us sing to the Lord
and rejoice in the Rock, our Saviour.
Let us come and give thanks in his presence,
and greet him with songs of praise.

The Lord is a great God,
a king supreme over all;
in his hands are the depths of the earth,
and the mountain heights are his;
the sea is his – he made it –
and the dry land was formed by his hands.

Come, let us kneel and adore,
let us worship the Lord our maker.

He is our God and we are his people,
the flock he leads with his hand.

Glory to the Father, and to the Son,
and to the Holy Spirit:
as it was in the beginning, is now,
and shall be for ever. Amen.

OR this or some other hymn:

Christ, whose glory fills the skies,
Christ, the true, the only Light,
Sun of Righteousness, arise,
Triumph o'er the shades of night;
Dayspring from on high, be near;
Day-star, in my heart appear.

Dark and cheerless is the morn
Unaccompanied by thee;
Joyless is the day's return,
Till thy mercy's beams I see,
Till they inward light impart,
Glad my eyes and warm my heart.

Visit then this soul of mine:
Pierce the gloom of sin and grief;
Fill me, radiancy divine,
Scatter all my unbelief;
More and more thyself display,
Shining to the perfect day.

7 The Prayer of the Morning

This or some other prayer:

Blessèd are you, Lord our God,
Giver of life,
Father, Son and Holy Spirit.
At the opening of this day
you call us out of darkness
into your marvellous light.
Blessèd are you for ever and ever. **Amen.**

8 One of the following, or a Psalm selected freely or according to some other scheme:

Sunday	Psalm	8
Monday	Psalm	67
Tuesday	Psalm	98
Wednesday	Psalm	121
Thursday	Psalm	145
Friday	Psalm	146
Saturday	Psalm	148

OR Psalm 63:1-4

O God, you are my God, I seek you,
my soul thirsts for you;
my flesh faints for you,
as in a dry and weary land
where there is no water.
So I have looked upon you in the sanctuary,
beholding your power and glory.
Because your steadfast love is better than life,
my lips will praise you.
So I will bless you as long as I live;
I will lift up my hands
and call on your name.

9 Either one of the following or a reading from scripture selected freely or according to some other scheme:

Sunday

Hear, O Israel: the Lord is our God, the Lord alone. You shall love the Lord your God with all your heart, and with all your soul, and with all your might. Keep these words that I am commanding you today in your heart. Recite them to your children and talk about them when you are at home and when you are away, when you lie down and when you rise.

Deuteronomy 6:4-7

Monday

Thus says God, the Lord,
who created the heavens and stretched them out,
who spread out the earth and what comes from it,
who gives breath to the people upon it
and spirit to those who walk in it:
I am the Lord, I have called you in righteousness,
I have taken you by the hand and kept you;
I have given you as a covenant to the people,
a light to the nations,
to open the eyes that are blind,
to bring out the prisoners from the dungeon,
from the prison those who sit in darkness.
I am the Lord, that is my name.

Isaiah 42:5-8*a*

Tuesday

Once you were darkness, but now in the Lord you are light. Live as children of light – for the fruit of the light is found in all that is good and right and true. Try to find out what is pleasing to the Lord. Take no part in the unfruitful works of darkness, but instead expose them. For it is shameful even to mention what such people do secretly; but everything exposed by the light becomes visible, for everything that becomes visible is light. Therefore it says,

'Sleeper, awake!
Rise from the dead,
and Christ will shine on you.'

Ephesians 5:8-14

Wednesday

Jesus called his disciples and said to them, 'You know that among the Gentiles those whom they recognize as their rulers lord it over them, and their great ones are tyrants over them. But it is not so among you; but whoever wishes to become great among you must be your servant, and whoever wishes to be first among you must be slave of all. For the Son of Man came not to be served but to serve, and to give his life a ransom for many.'

Mark 10:42-45

Thursday

Happy are those who find wisdom,
and those who get understanding,
for her income is better than silver,
and her revenue better than gold.
She is more precious than jewels,
and nothing you desire can compare with her.
Long life is in her right hand;
in her left hand are riches and honour.
Her ways are ways of pleasantness,
and all her paths are peace.
She is a tree of life to those who lay hold of her;
those who hold her fast are called happy.
The Lord by wisdom founded the earth;
by understanding he established the heavens;
by his knowledge the deeps broke open,
and the clouds drop down the dew.

Proverbs 3:13-20

Friday

Christ suffered for you, leaving you an example, so that you should follow in his steps.

'He committed no sin,
and no deceit was found in his mouth.'

When he was abused, he did not return abuse; when he suffered, he did not threaten; but he entrusted himself to the one who judges justly. He himself bore our sins in his body on the cross, so that, free from sins, we might live for righteousness; by his wounds you have been healed. For you were going astray like sheep, but now you have returned to the shepherd and guardian of your souls.

1 Peter 2:21*b*-25

Saturday

Jesus said: 'I give you a new commandment, that you love one another. Just as I have loved you, you also should love one another. By this everyone will know that you are my disciples, if you have love for one another.'

John 13:34-35

10 One of the following, or some other canticle:

Benedictus (The Song of Zechariah)

Blessèd be the Lord, the God of Israel,
who has come to his people and set them free.

**The Lord has raised up for us a mighty Saviour,
born of the house of his servant David.**

Through the holy prophets, God promised of old
to save us from our enemies,
from the hands of all who hate us,
to show mercy to our forebears,
and to remember his holy covenant.

**This was the oath God swore to our father Abraham:
to set us free from the hands of our enemies,
free to worship him without fear,
holy and righteous before him,
all the days of our life.**

And you, child, shall be called the prophet of the Most High,
for you will go before the Lord to prepare his way,
to give his people knowledge of salvation
by the forgiveness of their sins.

**In the tender compassion of our God
the dawn from heaven shall break upon us,
to shine on those who dwell in darkness and the shadow of death,
and to guide our feet into the way of peace.**

Glory to the Father, and to the Son,
and to the Holy Spirit:
**as it was in the beginning, is now,
and shall be for ever. Amen.**

Te Deum Laudamus (A Song of the Church)

We praise you, O God,
we acclaim you as Lord;

**all creation worships you,
the Father everlasting.**

To you all angels, all the powers of heaven,
the cherubim and seraphim, sing in endless praise:

**Holy, holy, holy Lord,
God of power and might,
heaven and earth are full of your glory.**

The glorious company of apostles praise you.
The noble fellowship of prophets praise you.
The white-robed army of martyrs praise you.
Throughout the world the holy Church acclaims you:

**Father, of majesty unbounded,
your true and only Son,
worthy of all praise,
the Holy Spirit, advocate and guide.**

You, Christ, are the king of glory,
the eternal Son of the Father.
When you took our flesh to set us free
you humbly chose the Virgin's womb.

**You overcame the sting of death
and opened the kingdom of heaven to all believers.**

You are seated at God's right hand in glory.
We believe that you will come to be our judge.

**Come then, Lord, and help your people,
bought with the price of your own blood,
and bring us with your saints to glory everlasting.**

Save your people, Lord, and bless your inheritance.
Govern and uphold them now and always.

Day by day we bless you.
We praise your name for ever.

Keep us today, Lord, from all sin.
Have mercy on us, Lord, have mercy.

Lord, show us your love and mercy,
for we put our trust in you.

In you, Lord, is our hope:
let us never be put to shame.

11 These or some other prayers:

Let us offer our prayer
with all God's people
through Jesus Christ our Lord
who ever lives to pray for us.
  We pray for the needs of the world . . .
  We pray for the Church . . .
  We pray for all in trouble or distress . . .
  We pray for all who make a new beginning today . . .

Other petitions may follow.

Silent prayer

God of compassion and mercy,
listen to our prayer.
May what we ask in Jesus Christ your Son
be done according to his word, who said,
  'Ask, and you will receive,
  seek, and you will find,
  knock, and the door will be opened to you.'
To you, merciful God,
through your Son,
in the lifegiving Spirit,
be glory and praise for ever. **Amen.**

12 The Lord's Prayer

EITHER

We say together the prayer that Jesus gave us:

**Our Father in heaven,
hallowed be your Name,
your kingdom come,
your will be done,
on earth as in heaven.
Give us today our daily bread.
Forgive us our sins
as we forgive those who sin against us.
Save us from the time of trial
and deliver us from evil.
For the kingdom, the power and the glory are yours,
now and for ever. Amen.**

OR

As our Saviour taught his disciples, we pray:

**Our Father, who art in heaven,
hallowed be thy Name;
thy kingdom come;
thy will be done;
on earth as it is in heaven.
Give us this day our daily bread.
And forgive us our trespasses,
as we forgive those who trespass against us.
And lead us not into temptation;
but deliver us from evil.
For thine is the kingdom, the power, and the glory,
for ever and ever. Amen.**

13 Lord our God,
as with all creation
we offer you the life of this new day,
give us grace to love and serve you
to the praise of Jesus Christ our Lord. **Amen.**

14 Let us bless the Lord.
Thanks be to God.

PRAYER IN THE EVENING

1 Be swift, O God, to save us.
Come quickly, Lord, to help us.

2 In Eastertide:

Alleluia! Christ is risen!
He is risen indeed! Alleluia!

In other seasons or on other occasions, an appropriate sentence from pages 2-4 may be said.

3 One of these sentences:

Sunday

There is one body and one Spirit,
just as there is one hope
held out in God's call to you.

Monday

It is good to give thanks to the Lord,
to sing psalms to your name, O Most High.

Tuesday

From the rising of the sun to its setting
may the Lord's name be praised.

Wednesday

God was in Christ
reconciling the world to himself,
and has entrusted us with the message of reconciliation.

Thursday

God has sent into our hearts
the Spirit of his Son, crying,
'Abba! Father!'

Friday

Holy, holy, holy is the Lord of hosts:
the whole earth is full of his glory.

Saturday

May my prayer be like incense set before you,
and the lifting of my hands
like the evening offering.

4 Glory to the Father, and to the Son,
and to the Holy Spirit:
as it was in the beginning, is now,
and shall be for ever. Amen.

5 This or some other prayer of penitence may be said:

Most merciful God,
we confess to you
before the whole company of heaven
that we have sinned
in thought, word and deed,
and in what we have failed to do.
Forgive us our sins,
heal us by your Spirit
and raise us to new life in Christ. Amen.

If we confess our sins,
God is faithful and just,
and will forgive our sins,
and cleanse us from all unrighteousness.

Amen. Thanks be to God.

6 EITHER ***Jubilate*** (Psalm 100)

Cry out to the Lord, all the earth;
serve the Lord with gladness;
come into his presence with songs of joy.

Be assured that the Lord is God;
he has made us for himself.
We are his own, his people,
the sheep who feed on his pasture.

Come into his gates with thanksgiving,
enter his courts with praise;
give thanks to him and bless his name.

Truly the Lord is good:
his love endures for ever,
and from age to age he is faithful.

Glory to the Father, and to the Son,
and to the Holy Spirit:
as it was in the beginning, is now,
and shall be for ever. Amen.

OR this or some other hymn:

Hail, gladdening Light, of his pure glory poured
Who is the immortal Father, heavenly, blest,
Holiest of holies, Jesus Christ our Lord!

Now we are come to the sun's hour of rest;
The lights of evening round us shine;
We hymn the Father, Son and Holy Spirit divine.

Worthiest art thou at all times to be sung
With undefilèd tongue,
Son of our God, giver of life, alone;
Therefore in all the world thy glories, Lord, they own.

7 The Prayer of the Evening

EITHER

A God and Father of all,
as this day ends
we offer up its hours in praise to you.
As we take our rest,
unite us, by your Spirit,
in praise of Christ our Lord,
the Alpha and Omega,
the First and Last,
in whom we make our prayer. **Amen.**

OR

B O God, in whom there is no darkness,
with whom the night is as the day:
enlighten us by your presence,
that waking or sleeping
we may dwell in your peace,
in Jesus Christ our Lord. **Amen.**

8 One of the following, or a Psalm selected freely or according to some other scheme:

Sunday	Psalm	34
Monday	Psalm	84
Tuesday	Psalm	91
Wednesday	Psalm	96
Thursday	Psalm	103
Friday	Psalm	115
Saturday	Psalm	116

OR Psalm 134

**Come, bless the Lord,
all you, his servants,
who minister night after night
in the house of the Lord.
Lift up your hands towards the sanctuary
and bless the Lord.
May the Lord, maker of heaven and earth,
bless you from Zion!**

9 Either one of the following or a reading from scripture selected freely or according to some other scheme:

Sunday

A week later the disciples were again in the house, and Thomas was with them. Although the doors were shut, Jesus came and stood among them and said, 'Peace be with you.' Then he said to Thomas, 'Put your finger here and see my hands. Reach out your hand and put it in my side. Do not doubt but believe.' Thomas answered him, 'My Lord and my God!' Jesus said to him, 'Have you believed because you have seen me? Blessed are those who have not seen and yet have come to believe.'

Now Jesus did many other signs in the presence of his disciples, which are not written in this book. But these are written so that you may come to believe that Jesus is the Messiah, the Son of God, and that through believing you may have life in his name.

John 20:26-31

Monday

Seek the Lord while he may be found,
call upon him while he is near;
let the wicked forsake their way,
and the unrighteous their thoughts;
let them return to the Lord,
that he may have mercy on them,
and to our God, for he will abundantly pardon.
For my thoughts are not your thoughts,
nor are your ways my ways, says the Lord.
For as the heavens are higher than the earth,
so are my ways higher than your ways
and my thoughts than your thoughts.

Isaiah 55:6-9

Tuesday

Jesus said:
'Blessed are the poor in spirit, for theirs is the kingdom of heaven.
'Blessed are those who mourn, for they will be comforted.
'Blessed are the meek, for they will inherit the earth.
'Blessed are those who hunger and thirst for righteousness, for they will be filled.
'Blessed are the merciful, for they will receive mercy.
'Blessed are the pure in heart, for they will see God.
'Blessed are the peacemakers, for they will be called children of God.
'Blessed are those who are persecuted for righteousness' sake, for theirs is the kingdom of heaven.
'Blessed are you when people revile you and persecute you and utter all kinds of evil against you falsely on my account. Rejoice and be glad, for your reward is great in heaven, for in the same way they persecuted the prophets who were before you.'

Matthew 5:3-12

Wednesday

I appeal to you therefore, brothers and sisters, by the mercies of God, to present your bodies as a living sacrifice, holy and acceptable to God, which is your spiritual worship. Do not be conformed to this world, but be transformed by the renewing of your minds, so that you may discern what is the will of God – what is good and acceptable and perfect.

Romans 12:1-2

Thursday

Jesus said: 'Which one of you, having a hundred sheep and losing one of them, does not leave the ninety-nine in the wilderness and go after the one that is lost until he finds it? When he has found it, he lays it on his shoulders and rejoices. And when he comes home, he calls together his friends and neighbours, saying to them, "Rejoice with me, for I have found my sheep that was lost." Just so, I tell you, there will be more joy in heaven over one sinner who repents than over ninety-nine righteous people who need no repentance.

'Or what woman having ten silver coins, if she loses one of them, does not light a lamp, sweep out the house, and search carefully until she finds it? When she has found it, she calls together her friends and neighbours, saying, "Rejoice with me, for I have found the coin that I had lost." Just so, I tell you, there is joy in the presence of the angels of God over one sinner who repents.'

Luke 15:4-10

Friday

Jesus said: 'This is my commandment, that you love one another as I have loved you. No one has greater love than this, to lay down one's life for one's friends. You are my friends if you do what I command you. I do not call you servants any longer, because the servant does not know what the master is doing; but I have called you friends, because I have made known to you everything that I have heard from my Father. You did not choose me but I chose you. And I appointed you to go and bear fruit, fruit that will last, so that the Father will give you whatever you ask him in my name. I am giving you these commands so that you may love one another.'

John 15:12-17

Saturday

The angel showed me the river of the water of life, bright as crystal, flowing from the throne of God and of the Lamb through the middle of the street of the city. On either side of the river is the tree of life with its twelve kinds of fruit, producing its fruit each month; and the leaves of the tree are for the healing of the nations. Nothing accursed will be found there any more. But the throne of God and of the Lamb will be in it, and his servants will worship him; they will see his face, and his name will be on their foreheads. And there will be no more night; they need no light of lamp or sun, for the Lord God will be their light, and they will reign for ever and ever.

Revelation 22:1-5

10 One of the following, or some other canticle:

Magnificat (The Song of Mary)

My soul proclaims the greatness of the Lord,
my spirit rejoices in God my Saviour,
who has looked with favour on his lowly servant.

From this day all generations will call me blessèd:
the Almighty has done great things for me
and holy is his name.

God has mercy on those who fear him,
from generation to generation.

The Lord has shown strength with his arm
and scattered the proud in their conceit,
casting down the mighty from their thrones
and lifting up the lowly.

God has filled the hungry with good things
and sent the rich away empty.

He has come to the aid of his servant Israel,
to remember the promise of mercy,
the promise made to our forebears,
to Abraham and his children for ever.

Glory to the Father, and to the Son,
and to the Holy Spirit:
as it was in the beginning, is now,
and shall be for ever. Amen.

Nunc Dimittis (The Song of Simeon)

Now, Lord, you let your servant go in peace:
your word has been fulfilled.

My own eyes have seen the salvation
which you have prepared in the sight of every people:

a light to reveal you to the nations
and the glory of your people Israel.

Glory to the Father, and to the Son,
and to the Holy Spirit:
as it was in the beginning,
is now, and shall be for ever. Amen.

11 These or some other prayers:

Christ, through whom all things were made,
sustain all creation.

Christ, exalted in the lowest and the least,
give us humility.

Christ, present in the poor and the oppressed,
fill us with compassion.

Christ, forsaken in the hungry and the homeless,
minister to them through our hands.

Christ, present where two or three are gathered,
be known among us.

Christ, present in word, sacrament and sign,
grant us your peace.

12 The Lord's Prayer

EITHER

We say together the prayer that Jesus gave us:

**Our Father in heaven,
hallowed be your Name,
your kingdom come,
your will be done,
on earth as in heaven.
Give us today our daily
bread.
Forgive us our sins
as we forgive those who
sin against us.
Save us from the time of
trial
and deliver us from evil.
For the kingdom, the
power and the glory
are yours,
now and for ever. Amen.**

OR

As our Saviour taught his disciples, we pray:

**Our Father, who art in
heaven,
hallowed be thy Name;
thy kingdom come;
thy will be done;
on earth as it is in heaven.
Give us this day our
daily bread.
And forgive us our
trespasses,
as we forgive those who
trespass against us.
And lead us not into
temptation;
but deliver us from evil.
For thine is the kingdom,
the power, and the
glory,
for ever and ever. Amen.**

13 Lord our God,
at the ending of this day,
and in the darkness and silence of this night,
cover us with healing and forgiveness,
that we may take our rest in peace;
through Jesus Christ our Lord. **Amen.**

14 EITHER

A We will lie down in peace and take our rest;
for you alone, Lord, make us dwell in safety.

OR

B Let us bless the Lord.
Thanks be to God.

15 The following may be said:

May the souls of the faithful,
through the mercy of God,
rest in peace and rise in glory. **Amen.**

MORNING, AFTERNOON, OR EVENING SERVICES

INTRODUCTION

Most acts of worship in the Methodist Church are preaching services, consisting mainly of hymns, prayers, scripture readings and a sermon. The early Methodist preaching services were meant to be supplementary to worship in the Parish Church and there was a great emphasis on the sermon. In recent years, more attention has been given to the shape of the Christian Year, the systematic reading of scripture, different types of prayer, a wider variety of musical resources, and greater congregational participation.

The two services which follow are complete orders of worship for use at any time. They may also be regarded as models on which other forms may be based. They share a common fourfold structure of Preparation, Ministry of the Word, Response and Dismissal, developed in two slightly different ways. Those leading prayer may pray in their own words or use other resources. It is always important, especially in all-age worship, to use language which is appropriate for the particular congregation. Some additional material is included here for the various sections of the service, including some appropriate for seasons of the Christian Year. Other material in the book – notably the prayers of intercession in the various services of ***Holy Communion*** – is also suitable for use in this type of service.

Guidance for Ordering a Morning, Afternoon, or Evening Service follows the ***Second Service***.

FIRST SERVICE

THE PREPARATION

1 From Easter to Pentecost:

Alleluia! Christ is risen!
He is risen indeed! Alleluia!

At other times:

This is the day that the Lord has made.
We will rejoice and be glad in it!

or a sentence from pages 52-55 or another sentence of scripture

2 Hymn

3 Prayer of approach

Let us pray.

Silence

EITHER

A Loving God, we have come to worship you.

**Help us to remember that you are here with us.
May we pray to you in faith,
sing your praise with gratitude,
and listen to your word with eagerness;
through Christ our Lord. Amen.**

OR

B Holy God,
holy and strong,
holy and immortal:
have mercy on us.
**Holy God,
holy and strong,
holy and immortal:
have mercy on us.**

Silence

Eternal God, source of all blessing,
help us to worship you
with all our heart and mind and strength;
for you alone are God,
Father, Son and Holy Spirit,
for ever and ever. **Amen.**

4 Prayer of adoration

Let us praise God.

Silence

EITHER

A Holy God,
to you alone belong glory, honour and praise.
We join with the hosts of heaven as we worship.
You alone are worthy of adoration from every mouth,
and every tongue shall sing your praise.
You create the earth by your power;
you save the human race in your mercy,
and renew it through your grace.
To you, loving God,
Father, Son and Holy Spirit,
be all glory, honour and praise
now and for ever. **Amen.**

OR

B Praise be to you, O God,
the maker of the universe,
by whose wisdom we are created and sustained.

Praise be to you, O God,
the Father of our Lord Jesus Christ,
by whose love we are redeemed and forgiven.

Praise be to you, O God,
the source of all holiness,
**by whose Spirit we are made whole
and brought to perfection.**

**Praise be to you, O God,
Source of all being,
Eternal Word and Holy Spirit,
as it was in the beginning, is now
and shall be for ever. Amen.**

5 Prayer of confession and declaration of forgiveness

EITHER

A Let us confess our sins.

Silence

Loving God,

**we have sinned against you
in what we have thought, said and done.
We have not loved you with our whole heart;
we have not loved our neighbours as ourselves.
We are truly sorry
and turn away from what is wrong.
Forgive us for the sake of your Son,
Jesus Christ our Lord. Amen.**

Silence

Christ Jesus came into the world to save sinners.
This is his gracious word:
'Your sins are forgiven.'

Amen. Thanks be to God.

OR

B Let us confess our sins to God.

Silence

For our foolishness
and our thoughtless use of the gifts of your creation,
Lord, have mercy.

Lord, have mercy.

For our neglect of you,
and our failure to care for others,
Christ, have mercy.

Christ, have mercy.

For our selfishness in prayer
and our carelessness in worship,
Lord, have mercy.

Lord, have mercy.

Silence

Here is good news for all who put their trust in Christ.
Jesus says: 'Your sins are forgiven.'

Amen. Thanks be to God.

OR

C If we say that we have no sin,
we deceive ourselves
and the truth is not in us.
If we confess our sins,
God, who is faithful and just,
will forgive our sins
and cleanse us from all unrighteousness.

Let us confess our sins.

Silence

God of truth and love,

**be merciful to us,
as we claim your promised forgiveness
through Jesus Christ our Lord.**

God, who is faithful and just,
assures us of pardon and peace.

Amen. Thanks be to God.

6 The collect of the day or another suitable prayer

7 The Lord's Prayer may be said here or at no. 15 or no. 17.

8 Hymn or song or canticle of praise

THE MINISTRY OF THE WORD

9 Two or three readings from scripture

After each reading, the reader may say:

Thanks be to God.

and the people may respond: **Amen.**

There may be psalms, canticles, hymns or periods of silence between the readings.

10 Sermon

11 Affirmation of Faith

Let us confess the faith of the Church.

**We believe in God the Father,
who made the world.
We believe in Jesus Christ, his Son,
who redeemed humankind.
We believe in the Holy Spirit,
who gives life to the people of God.**

12 Hymn

THE RESPONSE

13 Prayers of thanksgiving

EITHER

A Let us give thanks to God.

For the love of our Father, the Maker of all,
the giver of all good things:
let us bless the Lord.

Thanks be to God.

For the world's beauty and the changing seasons,
and for the life that we have been given:
let us bless the Lord.

Thanks be to God.

For Jesus Christ our Saviour,
who lived and worked among us:
let us bless the Lord.

Thanks be to God.

For his suffering and death on the cross
and his resurrection to new life:
let us bless the Lord.

Thanks be to God.

For his rule over all things
and his presence in the world:
let us bless the Lord.

Thanks be to God.

For the Holy Spirit, the giver of life,
who teaches and guides us:
let us bless the Lord.

Thanks be to God.

For the grace of the Spirit
in the work of the Church
and the life of the world:
let us bless the Lord.

Thanks be to God. Amen.

OR

B We praise you, eternal God,
for the world which you have created
and for our place in it.

May you be praised for ever and ever.

You have given us life that we may love and serve you
and though we have resisted your purpose and misused your gift,
you have not left us in our sin,
but have sent your Son Jesus Christ to be our Saviour.

May you be praised for ever and ever.

We thank you that for us he became human,
died on the cross, rose from the dead, and ascended into heaven,
where he reigns in glory and prays for us.

May you be praised for ever and ever.

We thank you that you have sent your Holy Spirit,
to bring us to freedom and to new life in Christ.

May you be praised for ever and ever.

Seasonal or other thanksgivings such as those on pages 55-57 may be included here.

Therefore with all your Church
on earth and in heaven,
we give you our thanks and praise.

**We dedicate ourselves to you;
strengthen us by your Spirit to do your will,
and bring us with all your saints
to the glory of your kingdom;
through Jesus Christ our Lord. Amen.**

14 Prayers of intercession

EITHER

A The leader may make special biddings for prayer.

Silence

Blessèd are you, eternal God,
to be praised and glorified for ever.

Hear us as we pray for your holy catholic Church:
make us all one, that the world may believe.

Grant that every member of the Church may truly and humbly serve you:
that the life of Christ may be revealed in us.

Strengthen all who minister in Christ's name:
give them courage to proclaim your Gospel.

Inspire and lead those who hold authority in the nations of the world:
guide them and all people in the way of justice and peace.

Make us alive to the needs of our community:
help us to share each other's joys and burdens.

Look with kindness on our homes and families:
grant that your love may grow in our hearts.

Inspire us to have compassion on those who suffer from
sickness, grief or trouble:
in your presence may they find their strength.

We remember those who have died:
Father, into your hands we commend them.

We praise you for all your saints
who have entered your eternal glory:
bring us all to share in your heavenly kingdom.

Silence

Heavenly Father,
you have promised to hear
what we ask in the name of your Son:
we pray you to accept and answer our prayers,
not as we ask in our ignorance,
nor as we deserve in our sinfulness,
but as you know and love us in your Son,
Jesus Christ our Lord. **Amen.**

OR

B God our Father,
grant us the help of your Spirit
in our prayers for the salvation of all people.

We pray for the Church throughout the world
for this church and all its members
for . . .
that in faith and unity
we may be constantly renewed by your Holy Spirit
for mission and service.

Lord, in your mercy,
hear our prayer.

We pray for the peoples of the world
for the leaders of the nations
for . . .
that they may seek justice, freedom and peace for all.

Lord, in your mercy,
hear our prayer.

We pray for our country
for those who have authority and influence
for . . .
that all may serve one another
in wisdom, honesty and compassion.

Lord, in your mercy,
hear our prayer.

We pray for those among whom we live and work
for all our neighbours
for . . .
that we may so use your gifts
that together we may find joy in your creation.

Lord, in your mercy,
hear our prayer.

We pray for all in sorrow, need, anxiety or sickness
for . . .
for . . .
that in their weakness they may know your strength,
and in despair find hope.

Lord, in your mercy,
hear our prayer.

In you, Father,
we are one family on earth and in heaven.
We remember in your presence
those who have died . . .
giving thanks especially for those
who have revealed to us your grace in Christ.

Help us to follow the example of your saints in light
and bring us with them
to the fullness of your eternal joy;
through Jesus Christ our Lord. **Amen.**

OR an appropriate prayer of intercession from ***Holy Communion*** may be said.

15 The Lord's Prayer may be said here or at no. 17, if it has not already been said.

EITHER

We say together the prayer that Jesus gave us:

Our Father in heaven,
hallowed be your Name,
your kingdom come,
your will be done,
on earth as in heaven.
Give us today our daily bread.
Forgive us our sins
as we forgive those who sin against us.
Save us from the time of trial
and deliver us from evil.
For the kingdom, the power and the glory are yours,
now and for ever. Amen.

OR

As our Saviour taught his disciples, we pray:

Our Father, who art in heaven,
hallowed be thy Name;
thy kingdom come;
thy will be done;
on earth as it is in heaven.
Give us this day our daily bread.
And forgive us our trespasses,
as we forgive those who trespass against us.
And lead us not into temptation;
but deliver us from evil.
For thine is the kingdom, the power, and the glory,
for ever and ever. Amen.

16 Offering and prayer of dedication

The gifts of the people are presented.

EITHER

A God of all goodness and grace,
receive the gifts we offer;
and grant that our whole life
may give you glory and praise;
through Christ our Lord. **Amen.**

OR

B Let us pray.

Gracious God, accept these gifts,
and with them our lives,
to be used in your service;
through Jesus Christ our Lord. Amen.

17 The Lord's Prayer, if it has not already been said

THE DISMISSAL

18 Hymn

19 EITHER

A A seasonal introduction to the blessing from pages 57-59 may be said.

The blessing of God,
the Father, the Son and the Holy Spirit,
be among *you/us* and remain with *you/us* always. **Amen.**

OR

B We say together:

The love of the Father enfold us,
the wisdom of the Son enlighten us,
the fire of the Spirit enflame us;
and the blessing of God, the Three in One,
be upon us and abide with us now and for ever. Amen.

20 Go in peace to love and serve the Lord.
In the name of Christ. Amen.

SECOND SERVICE

THE PREPARATION

1 From Easter to Pentecost:

Alleluia! Christ is risen!
He is risen indeed! Alleluia!

At other times:

This is the day that the Lord has made.
We will rejoice and be glad in it!

or a sentence from pages 52-55 or another sentence of scripture

2 Hymn

3 Prayer of approach

EITHER

A Lord our God,

**eternal and wonderful,
wholly to be trusted:
you give life to all;
you help those who come to you
and give hope to those who call on you.
Set our hearts and minds at peace,
that we may bring our prayers to you
with confidence and joy;
through Jesus Christ our Lord. Amen.**

OR

B Gracious God,
as we rejoice in the gift of this new day,
may the light of your presence
set our hearts on fire with love for you,
now and for ever. **Amen.**

4 Prayer of adoration

EITHER

A Blessèd are you, Lord our God:
in your love you create all things out of nothing
through your eternal Word.
We glorify and adore you.

Blessèd are you, Lord our God:
in your love you redeemed the world
through our Lord Jesus Christ.
We glorify and adore you.

Blessèd are you, Lord our God:
in your love you empower your people
through the gift of the Holy Spirit.
We glorify and adore you. Amen.

OR

B Eternal God and Father,
you are the source of all life,
the fount of all wisdom,
the well-spring of all grace.
Your days are without end,
your loving mercies without number.
We depend on you:
and we remember your goodness to us
and to those who have gone before us.

We tell your story in every generation:
God of Abraham, Isaac and Jacob,
God of Sarah, Rebekah and Rachel,
God and Father of our Lord Jesus Christ,
God of a pilgrim people, your Church.
You are our God,
ahead of us, leading us,
guiding us and calling us;
you are the Lord God,
the all-wise, the all-compassionate.

To you we lift up our hearts
and we worship you,
one God for ever and ever. Amen.

5 The collect of the day or another suitable prayer

6 The Lord's Prayer may be said here or at no. 16.

7 Hymn or song or canticle of praise

THE MINISTRY OF THE WORD

8 Two or three readings from scripture

After each reading, the reader may say:

Thanks be to God.

and the people may respond: **Amen.**

There may be psalms, canticles, hymns or periods of silence between the readings.

9 Sermon

THE RESPONSE

10 Prayer of confession and declaration of forgiveness

EITHER

A Let us make our confession to God.

Silence

Holy God,

we confess that we have rebelled against you
and broken your law of love;
we have not loved our neighbours
nor heard the cry of the needy.
Forgive us, we pray,
and free us for joyful obedience;
through Jesus Christ our Lord. Amen.

In Christ we are set free.
Through Christ we are forgiven.

Amen. Thanks be to God.

OR

B Let us call to mind our sinfulness.

Silence

Loving God, Father of all,
have mercy on us.

Jesus Christ, Son of God,
have mercy on us.

Holy Spirit, Lord of life,
have mercy on us.

Silence, after which the leader says:

I confess to God and to you
that I have sinned in thought, word and deed;
may God have mercy on me.

May God grant you pardon,
forgiveness of all your sins,
time to amend your life,
and the grace and comfort of his Holy Spirit. Amen.

Silence, after which the people say:

We confess to God and to you
that we have sinned in thought, word and deed;
may God have mercy on us.

May God grant you pardon,
forgiveness of all your sins,
time to amend your life,
and the grace and comfort of his Holy Spirit. **Amen.**

11 The Peace

All stand.

Christ is our peace.
In the one body we are reconciled to God and to one another.

The peace of the Lord be always with you.
And also with you.

The people may greet one another in the name of Christ.

12 Offering and prayer of dedication

The gifts of the people are presented.

EITHER

A Everything in heaven and earth comes from you, O Lord,
and of your own we give you.

May you be praised for ever. Amen.

OR

B Generous God,
out of your providing
we bring these gifts from our daily living.
May the use of our gifts
and the offering of our lives
be for your glory;
through Jesus Christ our Lord. **Amen.**

13 Hymn

14 Prayers of thanksgiving

EITHER

A We thank you, O God,
for you are gracious.
You have loved us from the beginning of time
and you remember us in times of trouble and of joy.

Your mercy endures for ever.

We thank you, O God,
for you came to us in Jesus Christ,
who has redeemed the world
and saves us from our sins.

Your mercy endures for ever.

We thank you, O God,
for you have sent your Holy Spirit,
who comforts us and leads us into all truth.

Your mercy endures for ever. Amen.

OR

B Blessèd are you, Holy God,
creator, redeemer and life-giver;
you have spoken the world into being
and filled it with wonder and beauty.

For every blessing we have received
we give you thanks and praise.

Blessèd are you, Holy God,
for people of every language and culture
and for the rich variety you give to life.

For every blessing we have received
we give you thanks and praise.

Blessèd are you, Holy God,
for Jesus Christ our Saviour,
truly divine and truly human,
living and dying for us,
and going before us into heaven.

For every blessing we have received
we give you thanks and praise.

Blessèd are you, Holy God,
for your Spirit,
the fire of love burning in our hearts,
bringing us to faith,
and calling us to holiness
in the Church and in the world.

For every blessing we have received
we give you thanks and praise.

Seasonal or other thanksgivings such as those on pages 55-57 may be included here.

Therefore, Holy God,
all glory be given to you,
Father, Son and Holy Spirit. **Amen.**

15 These or some other prayers of intercession:

EITHER

A Let us pray for all people everywhere
according to their need.

Let us pray
for the Church of Christ throughout the world
for its unity in Christ
for the fulfilment of its mission
for all ministers of the gospel
for all Christians here in . . .

Silence

Strengthen your Church
in the service of Christ;
that we and all who confess your name
may be united in your truth,
live together in your love,
and reveal your glory in the world.

Lord, in your mercy,
hear our prayer.

Let us pray
for all the nations and peoples of the world
for all who serve the common good
for our own country and government
for all in authority
for all those involved in . . .

Silence

Give wisdom to all in authority;
direct this and every nation
in the ways of justice and of peace;
that we may honour one another,
and seek the common good.

Lord, in your mercy,
hear our prayer.

Let us pray
for those we know and love
for the local community
for our families and friends
for. . .

Silence

Give grace to us,
to our families and friends,
and to all our neighbours,
that we may serve Christ in one another,
and love as he loves us.

Lord, in your mercy,
hear our prayer.

Let us pray
  for all who suffer
  for the sick
  for those who mourn
  for those without faith
  for those who serve the needy
  for . . .

Silence

Comfort and heal all those who suffer
in body, mind or spirit;
give them courage and hope in their troubles;
and bring them the joy of your salvation.

Lord, in your mercy,
hear our prayer.

Let us remember all who have died,
giving thanks especially
for those who have died in the faith of Christ.

Silence

We commend all people to your unfailing love,
that in them your will may be fulfilled;
and we rejoice at the faithful witness
of your saints in every age,
praying that we may share with them
in your eternal kingdom.

Lord, in your mercy,
hear our prayer.

**Merciful Father,
accept these prayers for the sake of your Son,
our Saviour Jesus Christ. Amen.**

OR

B The leader may make special biddings for prayer.

In peace let us pray to the Lord.

Lord, have mercy.

For the peace that is from above
and for our salvation,
let us pray to the Lord:

Lord, have mercy.

For the peace of the whole world,
and for the life and unity of the Church,
let us pray to the Lord:

Lord, have mercy.

That we may worship God
in spirit and in truth,
let us pray to the Lord:

Lord, have mercy.

For all ministers of the Church
and the whole company of God's people,
let us pray to the Lord:

Lord, have mercy.

For the governments of the nations
that they may seek justice and peace for all people,
let us pray to the Lord:

Lord, have mercy.

For our own country and local community,
let us pray to the Lord:

Lord, have mercy.

For the sick, for the afflicted and for prisoners,
let us pray to the Lord:

Lord, have mercy.

For ourselves
that we may truly serve him who called us
out of darkness into his marvellous light,
let us pray to the Lord:

Lord, have mercy.

That, with all who have served God and are now at rest,
we may enter into the fullness of unending joy,
let us pray to the Lord:

Lord, have mercy.

Almighty God,
to whom our needs are known before we ask,
help us to ask only what accords with your will;
and those good things which we dare not
or in our blindness cannot ask,
grant us for the sake of your Son,
Jesus Christ our Lord. **Amen.**

16 The Lord's Prayer, if it has not already been said

EITHER

We say together the prayer
that Jesus gave us:

**Our Father in heaven,
hallowed be your Name,
your kingdom come,
your will be done,
on earth as in heaven.
Give us today our daily
bread.
Forgive us our sins
as we forgive those who
sin against us.**

OR

As our Saviour taught his
disciples, we pray:

**Our Father, who art in
heaven,
hallowed be thy Name;
thy kingdom come;
thy will be done;
on earth as it is in heaven.
Give us this day our
daily bread.
And forgive us our
trespasses,**

Save us from the time of trial
and deliver us from evil.
For the kingdom, the power and the glory are yours,
now and for ever. Amen.

as we forgive those who trespass against us.
And lead us not into temptation;
but deliver us from evil.
For thine is the kingdom, the power, and the glory,
for ever and ever. Amen.

THE DISMISSAL

17 Hymn

18 EITHER

A A seasonal introduction to the blessing from pages 57-59 may be said.

The blessing of God,
the Father, the Son and the Holy Spirit,
be among *you/us* and remain with *you/us* always. **Amen.**

OR

B The Lord give strength to his people.
The Lord bless his people with peace. **Amen.**

19 **We go into the world**
to walk in God's light,
to rejoice in God's love
and to reflect God's glory. Amen.

GUIDANCE FOR ORDERING A MORNING, AFTERNOON, OR EVENING SERVICE

THE PREPARATION

The leader and people gather in God's name.
Notices may be given and news items may be shared.
Acts of approach and praise are offered in song and prayer.
A prayer of penitence is followed by an assurance of God's forgiveness.

There may be a brief introduction to the service or a short prayer reflecting the season or festival.

THE MINISTRY OF THE WORD

The scriptures are read, including a passage from the New Testament.
God's word is proclaimed and shared in songs, hymns, music, dance and other art forms, in a sermon, or in comment, discussion and in silence.

The Peace may be shared and introduced with an appropriate sentence of scripture.

THE RESPONSE

Prayers of thanksgiving are offered for God's gift of creation and redemption in Christ through the Holy Spirit.
Prayers are offered for the Church, for the world and for those in need, and a remembrance may be made of those who have died.
The Lord's Prayer is said, unless it has been said earlier.

The leader and people dedicate themselves to God in prayer.
The offerings of the people may be placed on the Lord's table.

THE DISMISSAL

A final act of praise is followed by words of blessing and dismissal, or 'The Grace' is said.

RESOURCE MATERIAL

OPENING SENTENCES

Advent

The glory of the Lord shall be revealed
and all people shall see it.

Salvation is nearer to us now
than when we became believers.

Christmas

A child has been born for us, a Son given to us.

The Word became flesh and lived among us
and we have seen his glory.

Epiphany

Arise, shine; for your light has come,
and the glory of the Lord has risen upon you.

From the rising of the sun to its setting
my name is great among the nations,
says the Lord.

Lent

The sacrifice acceptable to God
is a broken spirit;
a broken and contrite heart, O God,
you will not despise.

To the Lord our God belong mercy and forgiveness,
though we have rebelled against him.

Passiontide

Christ died for all
so that those who live
might live no longer for themselves
but for him who died and was raised for them.

Christ himself bore our sins
in his body on the cross,
so that, free from sins,
we might live for righteousness;
by his wounds you have been healed.

Christ suffered for sin once for all,
the righteous for the unrighteous,
in order to bring you to God.

Eastertide

Alleluia! Christ is risen!
He is risen indeed! Alleluia!

Ascensiontide

Praise and honour, glory and might,
to him who sits on the throne
and to the Lamb, for ever.

Pentecost

God's love has been poured into our hearts
through the Holy Spirit who has been given to us.

Trinity

By day and by night around the throne they sing:
Holy, holy, holy is the Lord God almighty:
who was, and is, and is to come.

Harvest

The earth is the Lord's and all that is in it.

Let the heavens be glad
and let the earth rejoice.

In ordinary seasons

God is our refuge and strength,
a very present help in trouble.

Worship the Lord in the beauty of holiness;
let the whole earth stand in awe.

Make a joyful noise to the Lord, all the earth.
Worship the Lord with gladness;
come into his presence with singing.

Give thanks to the Lord, call on his name;
proclaim his deeds to the people.

Our help is in the name of the Lord,
who made heaven and earth.

Seek the Lord while he may be found,
call upon him while he is near.

Jesus said: 'Know that I am with you always,
to the end of time.'

God is Spirit
and those who worship him
must worship in spirit and truth.

If anyone is in Christ, there is a new creation:
the old order has gone;
a new order has already begun.

You are worthy, our Lord and God,
to receive glory and honour and power,
for you created all things,
and by your will they existed and were created.

Hallelujah!
For the Lord our God the Almighty reigns.
Let us rejoice and exult and give God the glory.

SEASONAL MATERIAL FOR PRAYERS OF THANKSGIVING

Advent

And now we give you thanks
because in Christ's coming among us
the day of deliverance has dawned,
and through him you will make all things new.

Christmas and Epiphany

And now we give you thanks
because in Christ
the light which shines for all
has come into the world,
and has become one with us
that we may become one with you.

And now we give you thanks
because in coming to dwell among us,
Christ revealed the radiance of your glory
and brought us out of darkness
into your own marvellous light.

Lent

And now we give you thanks because Christ,
though tempted in every way as we are,
did not sin;
through him therefore we may triumph over evil
and grow in grace.

Passiontide

And now we give you thanks
because out of love for us
Christ accepted death
and, lifted high on the cross,
drew the whole world to himself.
The tree of shame became the tree of glory;
where life was lost there life has been restored.

Eastertide

And now we give you thanks
because you raised Christ to life,
triumphant over death,
and exalted him in glory.
By his victory over death,
the reign of sin is ended,
a new age has dawned,
a broken world is restored
and we are made whole once more.

Ascensiontide

And now we give you thanks
because you have highly exalted Christ
and given him the name which is above every name:
at the name of Jesus every knee shall bow
and every tongue confess that he is Lord.

Pentecost

And now we give you thanks
because by the Holy Spirit
you lead us into all truth,
and give us the power to serve you
as a royal priesthood
and to take the joy of the gospel
into all the world.

Trinity

And now we give you thanks
because you have revealed your glory
as the glory of your Son and of the Holy Spirit:
three persons equal in majesty,
undivided in splendour,
yet one Lord, one God,
ever to be worshipped.

All Saints

And now we give you thanks
for all your saints
who heard your call to holiness
and obeyed the heavenly vision.
We rejoice in their company with us
on our pilgrimage.

SEASONAL INTRODUCTIONS TO THE BLESSING

Advent

Christ the Sun of Righteousness shine on *you/us*
and scatter the darkness from before *you/us*;
and the blessing . . .

Christmas and Epiphany

Christ the Son of God, born of Mary,
fill *you/us* with his grace to trust his promises;
and the blessing . . .

Christ the Son of God
gladden *your/our* hearts
with the good news of his kingdom;
and the blessing . . .

Lent

Christ give *you/us* grace to grow in holiness,
to deny *yourselves/ourselves*,
to take up *your/our* cross and follow him;
and the blessing . . .

Passiontide

Christ crucified draw *you/us* to himself,
that *you/we* may find in him
a sure ground for faith,
a firm support for hope
and the assurance of sins forgiven;
and the blessing . . .

Eastertide

God the Father,
by whose glory Christ was raised from the dead,
strengthen *you/us*
to walk with him in his risen life;
and the blessing . . .

God, who through the resurrection
of our Lord Jesus Christ
has given us the victory,
give *you/us* joy and peace in *your/our* faith;
and the blessing . . .

Ascensiontide

Christ our King
make *you/us* faithful and strong to do his will
that *you/we* may reign with him in glory;
and the blessing . . .

Pentecost

The Spirit of truth lead *you/us* into all truth,
give *you/us* grace to confess
that Jesus Christ is Lord,
and to proclaim the word and works of God;
and the blessing . . .

Trinity

God the Holy Trinity
make *you/us* strong in faith and love,
defend *you/us* on every side,
and guide *you/us* in truth and peace;
and the blessing . . .

All Saints

God give *you/us* grace to follow his saints
in faith and hope and love;
and the blessing . . .

Christian unity

Christ the Good Shepherd,
who laid down his life for the sheep,
draw *you/us* and all who hear his voice
to be one people within one fold;
and the blessing . . .

ENTRY INTO THE CHURCH

INTRODUCTION

Baptism marks entry into the One Holy Catholic and Apostolic Church, of which the Methodist Church is part. In Confirmation, those who have been baptized declare their faith in Christ and are strengthened by the Holy Spirit for continuing discipleship.

Baptism

Christian Baptism is always administered with water in the name of the Father, the Son and the Holy Spirit. From its earliest days the Church has believed that this sacrament was commanded by Christ as the divinely appointed means of initiation into the Christian community and therefore a person can be baptized only once.

Baptism shows the love of God for all people, displayed supremely in the self-giving of Jesus Christ, and demonstrates all that Christ has won for us through his death and resurrection. Baptism makes plain that, before and without any response on our part, Christ died for us. The Methodist Church, like most branches of the Christian Church, administers the sacrament to both adults and young children.

Water, the central symbol of Baptism, speaks to us – among other things – of being washed clean and of making a new beginning. God's offer of new life in Christ invites us to respond, challenges us to discipleship and calls us to the life of faith in the Church and in the world. Such discipleship is possible only with the help of God's Holy Spirit. Since Baptism is also entry into a community of faith it involves the support and encouragement of other members of that community. For this reason, Baptism normally takes place in a service of public worship.

Baptism marks a new relationship with the Church of Christ. It is a rite of initiation, the ritual beginning of a journey of faith.

Confirmation and Reception into Membership

The service of Confirmation and Reception into Membership marks a significant point along the journey of faith which starts with Baptism.

Confirmation reminds us that we are baptized and that God continues to be at work in our lives: we respond by affirming that we belong to Christ and to the whole people of God. At a Service of Confirmation, baptized Christians are also received into membership of the Methodist Church and take their place as such in a local congregation.

Although the Baptism of young children and the Baptism of those who are able to answer for themselves often occur separately, there are occasions when both are to happen, and on such occasions Confirmation and Reception into Membership will normally take place. Five services are provided, which allow for a number of different circumstances, as explained in the **NOTES** which precede the services.

THE BAPTISM OF THOSE WHO ARE ABLE TO ANSWER FOR THEMSELVES, AND OF YOUNG CHILDREN, WITH CONFIRMATION AND RECEPTION INTO MEMBERSHIP

NOTES

1 This service is used when **both** *those* who *are* able to answer for *themselves* **and** *young children* are to be baptized.

2 Normally those who have been baptized when they are able to answer for themselves should be confirmed and received into membership immediately, and the service provides for this, though provision is also made for the possibility that the Confirmation and Reception may be deferred.

3 When this service includes the Confirmation and Reception into membership of *those* baptized who *have* answered for *themselves*, it may also include the Confirmation and Reception of *persons* baptized on a previous occasion.

4 The Sacrament of Baptism is normally administered during an act of public worship, most appropriately a celebration of ***Holy Communion***. When the service includes Confirmation, it always takes place during a celebration of Holy Communion, following the sermon.

5 When the service is used for Baptism without Confirmation, it is preferable that it follow the sermon, but it may be used before the Ministry of the Word.

6 If candles are to be given to the newly-baptized, they may be lit from the Easter Candle (see page 265) or some other candle lit at the beginning of the service.

7 Prayers for those who have been baptized (and confirmed), and, as appropriate, for their families, should be included in the prayers of intercession.

8 The minister shall ensure that a certificate of Baptism is given to each newly-baptized person, or, in the case of *young children*, to the *parents*, during or after the service. A certificate of Confirmation may be given to each newly-confirmed person during or after the service.

---

1 Hymn

THE DECLARATION

2 Sisters and brothers,
Baptism is a gift of God.
It declares to each of us
the love and grace of God.

In this sacrament we celebrate
the life of Christ laid down for us,
the Holy Spirit poured out on us,
and the living water offered to us.
God claims and cleanses us,
rescues us from sin,
and raises us to new life.
He plants us into the Church of Christ
and sustains and strengthens us
with the power of the Spirit.

Although we do not deserve these gifts of grace,
or fully understand them,
God offers them to all,
and, through Christ, invites us to respond.

We recall the words of the risen Christ:

'All authority in heaven and on earth has been given to me.
Go therefore and make disciples of all nations,
baptizing them in the name of the Father
and of the Son and of the Holy Spirit,
and teaching them to obey everything that I have commanded you.
And remember, I am with you always, to the end of the age.'

On the day of Pentecost, Peter preached the Gospel of Christ's resurrection. Those who heard the message asked what they should do. Peter told them:

'Repent, and be baptized, every one of you,
in the name of Jesus Christ
so that your sins may be forgiven;
and you will receive the gift of the Holy Spirit.
For the promise is for you,
for your children,
and for all who are far away,
everyone whom the Lord our God calls.'

THE REQUEST FOR BAPTISM

3 The *candidates* for Baptism who *are* able to answer for *themselves stand.*

The minister says to *them*:

N and N (N), having heard these things, how do you respond to the offer of God's grace?

Answer: I thank God, and ask to be baptized.

4 The *parents* (and *godparents*) of the *children* to be baptized *stand.*

The minister says to the *parents*:

A and B (A), having heard these things, how do you respond to the offer of God's grace?

Answer:

We/I thank God, and ask that *our/my child/children* be baptized.

5 If a candidate is to give personal testimony to God's grace, this may be done here.

THE THANKSGIVING OVER THE WATER

6 All stand.

Except where a baptistry is to be used, water is poured into the font, in the sight of the people.

The candidates for Baptism and the *parents* (and *godparents*) gather round or near the font or baptistry.

The minister stands at the font or baptistry and says:

Gracious God, we thank you
for your gifts of water and the Holy Spirit,
for your sustaining, cleansing, and life-giving power.

From the beginning
your grace has been made known
through water and the Spirit.

Your Spirit moved over the waters at creation
and you led your people to freedom through a parted sea.
In the fullness of time you sent Jesus.
He was baptized in the waters of the Jordan
and anointed with the Holy Spirit.
He passed through the deep waters of death
and lives for evermore.
He offers living water
and the gift of the Holy Spirit.

The minister may extend her/his hands over the water.

Pour out your Holy Spirit
that those baptized in this water
may die to sin,
be raised with Christ,
and be born to new life in the family of your Church.
We ask this through Jesus Christ our Lord. **Amen.**

7 Hymn

THE AFFIRMATION OF FAITH

8 The people remain standing.

The minister says to the *candidates* for Baptism able to answer for *themselves*, to the *parents* (and *godparents*) and to any *candidates* for Confirmation who *are* already baptized:

Do you turn away from evil and all that denies God?

Answer: By the grace of God, I do.

Do you turn to God,
trusting in Jesus Christ as Lord and Saviour,
and in the Holy Spirit as Helper and Guide?

Answer: By the grace of God, I do.

9 The minister says to everyone present:

Do you believe and trust in God the Father?

**I believe in God, the Father almighty,
creator of heaven and earth.**

Do you believe and trust in God the Son?

**I believe in Jesus Christ,
God's only Son, our Lord,
who was conceived by the Holy Spirit,
born of the Virgin Mary,
suffered under Pontius Pilate,**

was crucified, died, and was buried;
he descended to the dead.
On the third day he rose again,
he ascended into heaven,
he is seated at the right hand of the Father,
and he will come again to judge the living and the dead.

Do you believe and trust in God the Holy Spirit?

I believe in the Holy Spirit,
the holy catholic Church,
the communion of saints,
the forgiveness of sins,
the resurrection of the body,
and the life everlasting. Amen.

THE BAPTISM

10 The minister says to each candidate able to answer for herself/himself:

What is your name?

Each candidate responds with her/his Christian name(s).

11 The minister says to the *parents* of each child:

What name have you given this child?

The *parents respond* with the Christian name(s) of the child.

12 The minister may say to those to be baptized:

N and N,
for you Jesus Christ came into the world;
for you he lived and showed God's love;
for you he suffered death on the Cross;
for you he triumphed over death,
rising to newness of life;
for you he prays at God's right hand:
all this for you,
before you could know anything of it.

In your Baptism,
the word of Scripture is fulfilled:
'We love, because God first loved us.'

13 The minister pours water generously and visibly three times on the bowed head of each candidate able to answer for herself/himself, or dips her/him in water three times, once at the mention of each Person of the Holy Trinity, saying:

N, I baptize you
in the Name of the Father,
and of the Son,
and of the Holy Spirit. **Amen.**

By Baptism, God has received you into the Church.

The minister makes the sign of the cross on the forehead of each newly-baptized person, saying:

N, I sign you with the cross, the sign of Christ.

14 The minister, taking each child into her/his arms, pours water generously and visibly on the child's head, or dips the child in water three times, once at the mention of each Person of the Holy Trinity, saying:

N, I baptize you
in the Name of the Father,
and of the Son,
and of the Holy Spirit. **Amen.**

By Baptism, God has received you into the Church.

The minister makes the sign of the cross on the forehead of each newly-baptized child, saying:

N, I sign you with the cross, the sign of Christ.

15 The people sit.

A lighted candle may be given to each of the newly-baptized or, in the case of *infants*, to *their parents* or *godparents*.

The minister, or a representative of the local church, says to the newly-baptized:

Receive this light,
for you belong to Christ,
the Light of the world.

Christ is your Light and your Way.

May you grow and live in the faith of Christ. Amen.

16 The newly-baptized *stand* facing the people or, in the case of *infants*, *are* shown to the people.

All say or sing:

**The Lord bless you and keep you;
the Lord make his face to shine on you
and be gracious to you;
the Lord look on you with kindness
and give you peace. Amen.**

THE BAPTISMAL PROMISES

17 *Those* who *have* answered for *themselves sit.*

The *parents* (and *godparents*) of the newly-baptized *children stand.*

The minister says to the *parents*:

A and B (A), I ask you now to respond to God's love and grace to your *children* by making these promises.

Will you love *these* your *children*,
committing *yourselves* to care for *them*
in body, mind and spirit?

Answer: With God's help *we* will.

Will you, therefore,
ensure that *they are* nurtured
in the faith and life of the Christian community?

Answer: With God's help *we* will.

Will you set before *them* a Christian example,
that through your prayers, words and deeds,
they may learn the way of Christ?

Answer: With God's help *we* will.

18 If there *are godparents*, the minister says to *them*:

C and D (C),
will you help *these parents*
to nurture *their children* in the Christian faith?

Answer: With God's help *we* will.

If, in exceptional circumstances and for good reason, the Confirmation of *those* newly-baptized who *have* answered for *themselves* is to be delayed, the service continues from no. 31.

---

19 All stand. The minister says to the people:

Members of the body of Christ, we rejoice that *these children have* been baptized.

Will you so maintain the Church's life of worship and service that *they* may grow in grace and in the knowledge and love of God and of his Son Jesus Christ our Lord?

With God's help we will.

THE REQUEST FOR CONFIRMATION

20 The minister says to the newly-baptized *candidates* for Confirmation, and to any *candidates* for Confirmation who *have* been baptized on a previous occasion:

N and N (N),
God has constantly been at work in your life
and, at your Baptism into Christ,
offered you the gifts of his grace.
In this moment
God offers to strengthen you by his Spirit
and invites you to respond.

Answer: I thank God, and ask to be confirmed.

THE CONFIRMATION

21 The people remain standing. *Those* who *are* to be confirmed *kneel*.

The minister, extending her/his hands towards the *candidates*, says:

By your power and grace, Lord,
strengthen *these* your *servants,*
that *they* may live as *faithful disciples* of Jesus Christ.
Increase in *them* your gifts of grace,
and fill *them* with your Holy Spirit:
  the Spirit of wisdom and understanding;
  the Spirit of discernment and inner strength;
  the Spirit of knowledge, holiness, and awe.

22 The minister lays her/his hand upon the head of each candidate, saying:

Lord, confirm your servant *N* by your Holy Spirit
that *she/he* may continue yours for ever. **Amen.**

THE RECEPTION AND WELCOME

23 *Those* newly-confirmed *stand.* The minister says to *them*:

N and N (N),
we receive and welcome you
as *members* of the Methodist Church,
and of the church in this place.

24 The minister and a representative of the local church extend the hand of fellowship to each newly-confirmed person.

THE PROMISES OF THOSE NEWLY-CONFIRMED

25 The minister says to *those* newly-confirmed:

N and N (N),
I ask you now to respond to God's love and grace
by making these promises.

Will you commit yourself to the Christian life of worship and service, and be open to the renewing power of God?

Answer: **With God's help I will.**

Will you seek the strength of God's Spirit as you accept the cost of following Jesus Christ in your daily life?

Answer: **With God's help I will.**

Will you witness, by word and deed, to the good news of God in Christ, and so bring glory to God?

Answer: **With God's help I will.**

THE PROMISE OF THE PEOPLE

26 The minister says to the people:

Members of the Body of Christ, we rejoice that *these,* our *sisters and brothers, have* been baptized and confirmed.

Will you so maintain the Church's life of worship and service that *they* may grow in grace and in the knowledge and love of God and of his Son Jesus Christ our Lord?

With God's help we will.

27 The people sit.

A Bible or some other book may be given.

Certificates of Baptism and Confirmation, as appropriate, may be given.

28 The minister says:

Let us pray.

Generous God,
touch us again
with the fire of your Spirit
and renew in us all
the grace of our Baptism;
that we may profess the one true faith
and live in love and unity
with all who are baptized into Christ. Amen.

29 Hymn

30 The service continues from the prayers of intercession in any appropriate order for Holy Communion. That for ***The Day of Pentecost and Times of Renewal in the Life of the Church*** (page 174) is especially suitable.

When no one is to be confirmed the service continues as follows after no. 18:

THE BAPTISMAL PROMISES

31 *Those* newly-baptized who *have* answered for *themselves stand*. The minister says to *them*:

N and N (N),
I ask you now to respond to God's love and grace
by making these promises.

Will you commit yourself to the Christian life of worship and service, and be open to the renewing power of God?

Answer: With God's help I will.

Will you seek the strength of God's Spirit as you accept the cost of following Jesus Christ in your daily life?

Answer: With God's help I will.

Will you witness, by word and deed, to the good news of God in Christ, and so bring glory to God?

Answer: With God's help I will.

THE PROMISE OF THE PEOPLE

32 The people stand. The minister says to them:

Members of the body of Christ, we rejoice that *these*, our *sisters and brothers, have* been baptized.

Will you so maintain the Church's life of worship and service that they may grow in grace and in the knowledge and love of God and of his Son Jesus Christ our Lord?

With God's help we will.

33 A Bible or some other book may be given.

A certificate of Baptism may be given.

34 The minister says:

Let us pray.

**Generous God,
touch us again
with the fire of your Spirit
and renew in us all
the grace of our Baptism;
that we may profess the one true faith
and live in love and unity
with all who are baptized into Christ. Amen.**

35 The Lord's Prayer, if it is not said at some other point in the service

EITHER

We say together the prayer that Jesus gave us:

**Our Father in heaven,
hallowed be your Name,
your kingdom come,
your will be done,
on earth as in heaven.
Give us today our daily
bread.
Forgive us our sins
as we forgive those who
sin against us.
Save us from the time of
trial
and deliver us from evil.
For the kingdom, the
power and the glory
are yours,
now and for ever. Amen.**

OR

As our Saviour taught his disciples, we pray:

**Our Father, who art in
heaven,
hallowed be thy Name;
thy kingdom come;
thy will be done;
on earth as it is in heaven.
Give us this day our
daily bread.
And forgive us our
trespasses,
as we forgive those who
trespass against us.
And lead us not into
temptation;
but deliver us from evil.
For thine is the kingdom,
the power, and the
glory,
for ever and ever. Amen.**

36 Hymn

37 The service continues.

THE BAPTISM OF THOSE WHO ARE ABLE TO ANSWER FOR THEMSELVES, WITH CONFIRMATION AND RECEPTION INTO MEMBERSHIP

NOTES

1 This service is used when **only** *those* who *are* able to answer for *themselves are* to be baptized.

2 Normally those who have been baptized when they are able to answer for themselves should be confirmed and received into membership immediately, and the service provides for this, though provision is also made for the possibility that the Confirmation and Reception may be deferred.

3 When this service includes the Confirmation and Reception into Membership of *those* baptized who *have* answered for *themselves*, it may also include the Confirmation and Reception of *persons* baptized on a previous occasion.

4 The Sacrament of Baptism is normally administered during an act of public worship, most appropriately a celebration of ***Holy Communion***. When the service includes Confirmation, it always takes place during a celebration of Holy Communion, following the sermon.

5 When the service is used for Baptism without Confirmation, it is preferable that it follow the sermon, but it may be used before the Ministry of the Word.

6 If *candles* are to be given to the newly-baptized, *they* may be lit from the Easter Candle (see page 265) or some other candle lit at the beginning of the service.

7 Prayers for *those* who *have* been baptized (and confirmed), and, as appropriate, for *their families*, should be included in the prayers of intercession.

8 The minister shall ensure that a certificate of Baptism is given to each newly-baptized person during or after the service. A certificate of Confirmation may be given to each newly-confirmed person during or after the service.

---

1 Hymn

THE DECLARATION

2 Sisters and brothers,
Baptism is a gift of God.
It declares to each of us
the love and grace of God.

In this sacrament we celebrate
the life of Christ laid down for us,
the Holy Spirit poured out on us,
and the living water offered to us.
God claims and cleanses us,
rescues us from sin,
and raises us to new life.
He plants us into the Church of Christ
and sustains and strengthens us
with the power of the Spirit.

Although we do not deserve these gifts of grace,
or fully understand them,
God offers them to all,
and, through Christ, invites us to respond.

We recall the words of the risen Christ:

'All authority in heaven and on earth has been given to me.
Go therefore and make disciples of all nations,
baptizing them in the name of the Father
and of the Son and of the Holy Spirit,
and teaching them to obey everything that I have commanded you.
And remember, I am with you always, to the end of the age.'

On the day of Pentecost, Peter preached the Gospel of Christ's resurrection. Those who heard the message asked what they should do. Peter told them:

'Repent, and be baptized, every one of you,
in the name of Jesus Christ
so that your sins may be forgiven;
and you will receive the gift of the Holy Spirit.
For the promise is for you,
for your children,
and for all who are far away,
everyone whom the Lord our God calls.'

THE REQUEST FOR BAPTISM

3 The *candidates* for Baptism *stand.*

The minister says to *them*:

N and N (N), having heard these things, how do you respond to the offer of God's grace?

Answer: I thank God, and ask to be baptized.

4 If a candidate is to give personal testimony to God's grace, this may be done here.

THE THANKSGIVING OVER THE WATER

5 All stand.

Except where a baptistry is to be used, water is poured into the font, in the sight of the people.

The *candidates stand* round or near the font or baptistry.

The minister stands at the font or baptistry and says:

Gracious God, we thank you
for your gifts of water and the Holy Spirit,
for your sustaining, cleansing, and life-giving power.

From the beginning
your grace has been made known
through water and the Spirit.

Your Spirit moved over the waters at creation
and you led your people to freedom through a parted sea.
In the fullness of time you sent Jesus.
He was baptized in the waters of the Jordan
and anointed with the Holy Spirit.
He passed through the deep waters of death
and lives for evermore.
He offers living water
and the gift of the Holy Spirit.

The minister may extend her/his hands over the water.

Pour out your Holy Spirit
that *those/the one* baptized in this water
may die to sin,
be raised with Christ,
and be born to new life in the family of your Church.
We ask this through Jesus Christ our Lord. **Amen.**

6 Hymn

THE AFFIRMATION OF FAITH

7 The people remain standing.

The minister says to the *candidates*:

Do you turn away from evil and all that denies God?

Answer: By the grace of God, I do.

Do you turn to God,
trusting in Jesus Christ as Lord and Saviour,
and in the Holy Spirit as Helper and Guide?

Answer: By the grace of God, I do.

8 The minister says to everyone present:

Do you believe and trust in God the Father?

**I believe in God, the Father almighty,
creator of heaven and earth.**

Do you believe and trust in God the Son?

**I believe in Jesus Christ,
God's only Son, our Lord,
who was conceived by the Holy Spirit,
born of the Virgin Mary,
suffered under Pontius Pilate,
was crucified, died, and was buried;
he descended to the dead.
On the third day he rose again,
he ascended into heaven,
he is seated at the right hand of the Father,
and he will come again to judge the living and the dead.**

Do you believe and trust in God the Holy Spirit?

**I believe in the Holy Spirit,
the holy catholic Church,
the communion of saints,
the forgiveness of sins,
the resurrection of the body,
and the life everlasting. Amen.**

THE BAPTISM

9 The minister says to each candidate:

What is your name?

Each candidate responds with her/his Christian name(s).

10 The minister may say to the *candidates*:

N and N (N),
for you Jesus Christ came into the world;
for you he lived and showed God's love;

for you he suffered death on the Cross;
for you he triumphed over death,
rising to newness of life;
for you he prays at God's right hand:
  all this for you,
  before you could know anything of it.
In your Baptism,
the word of Scripture is fulfilled:
'We love, because God first loved us.'

11 The minister pours water generously and visibly three times on the bowed head of each candidate, or dips her/him in water three times, once at the mention of each Person of the Holy Trinity, saying:

N, I baptize you
in the Name of the Father,
and of the Son,
and of the Holy Spirit. **Amen.**

By Baptism, God has received you into the Church.

The minister makes the sign of the cross on the forehead of each newly-baptized person, saying:

N, I sign you with the cross, the sign of Christ.

12 The people sit.

A lighted candle may be given to each newly-baptized person.

The minister, or a representative of the local church, says to *them*:

Receive this light,
for you belong to Christ,
the Light of the world.

Christ is your Light and your Way.

May you grow and live in the faith of Christ. Amen.

13 *Those* newly-baptized *stand* facing the people.

All say or sing:

The Lord bless you and keep you;
the Lord make his face to shine on you
and be gracious to you;
the Lord look on you with kindness
and give you peace. Amen.

If, in exceptional circumstances and for good reason, the Confirmation of *those* newly-baptized is to be delayed, the service continues from no. 25.

THE REQUEST FOR CONFIRMATION

14 Any *candidates* for Confirmation who *have* been baptized on a previous occasion *stand.*

The minister says to *all* the *candidates* for Confirmation:

N and N (N),
God has constantly been at work in your life
and, at your Baptism into Christ,
offered you the gifts of his grace.
In this moment
God offers to strengthen you by his Spirit
and invites you to respond.

Answer: I thank God, and ask to be confirmed.

THE CONFIRMATION

15 The people stand. *Those* who *are* to be confirmed *kneel.*

The minister, extending her/his hands towards the *candidates*, says:

By your power and grace, Lord,
strengthen *these* your *servants*,
that *they* may live as *faithful disciples* of Jesus Christ.
Increase in *them* your gifts of grace,
and fill *them* with your Holy Spirit:
the Spirit of wisdom and understanding;
the Spirit of discernment and inner strength;
the Spirit of knowledge, holiness, and awe.

16 The minister lays her/his hand upon the head of each candidate, saying:

Lord, confirm your servant *N* by your Holy Spirit
that *she/he* may continue yours for ever. **Amen.**

THE RECEPTION AND WELCOME

17 *Those* newly-confirmed *stand.* The minister says to *them*:

N and N (N),
we receive and welcome you
as *members* of the Methodist Church,
and of the church in this place.

18 The minister and a representative of the local church extend the hand of fellowship to each newly-confirmed person.

THE PROMISES OF THOSE NEWLY-CONFIRMED

19 The minister says to *those* newly-confirmed:

N and N (N),
I ask you now to respond to God's love and grace
by making these promises.

Will you commit yourself to the Christian life of worship and service, and be open to the renewing power of God?

Answer: With God's help I will.

Will you seek the strength of God's Spirit as you accept the cost of following Jesus Christ in your daily life?

Answer: With God's help I will.

Will you witness, by word and deed, to the good news of God in Christ, and so bring glory to God?

Answer: With God's help I will.

THE PROMISE OF THE PEOPLE

20 The minister says to the people:

Members of the body of Christ, we rejoice that *these,* our *sisters and brothers*, *have* been baptized and confirmed.

Will you so maintain the Church's life of worship and service that *they* may grow in grace and in the knowledge and love of God and of his Son Jesus Christ our Lord?

With God's help we will.

21 The people sit.

A Bible or some other book may be given.

Certificates of Baptism and Confirmation, as appropriate, may be given.

22 The minister says:

Let us pray.

Generous God,
touch us again
with the fire of your Spirit
and renew in us all
the grace of our Baptism;
that we may profess the one true faith
and live in love and unity
with all who are baptized into Christ. Amen.

23 Hymn

24 The service continues from the prayers of intercession in any appropriate order for Holy Communion. That for ***The Day of Pentecost and Times of Renewal in the Life of the Church*** (page 174) is especially suitable.

When no one is to be confirmed the service continues as follows after no. 13:

THE BAPTISMAL PROMISES

25 The minister says to *those* newly-baptized:

N and N (N),
I ask you now to respond to God's love and grace
by making these promises.

Will you commit yourself to the Christian life of worship and service, and be open to the renewing power of God?

Answer: With God's help I will.

Will you seek the strength of God's Spirit as you accept the cost of following Jesus Christ in your daily life?

Answer: With God's help I will.

Will you witness, by word and deed, to the good news of God in Christ, and so bring glory to God?

Answer: With God's help I will.

THE PROMISE OF THE PEOPLE

26 The people stand. The minister says to them:

Members of the body of Christ, we rejoice that *these*, our *sisters and brothers*, *have* been baptized.

Will you so maintain the Church's life of worship and service that *they* may grow in grace and in the knowledge and love of God and of his Son Jesus Christ our Lord?

With God's help we will.

27 The people sit.

A Bible or some other book may be given.

A certificate of Baptism may be given.

28 The minister says:

Let us pray.

Generous God,
touch us again
with the fire of your Spirit
and renew in us all
the grace of our Baptism;
that we may profess the one true faith
and live in love and unity
with all who are baptized into Christ. Amen.

29 The Lord's Prayer, if it is not said at some other point in the service

EITHER

We say together the prayer that Jesus gave us:

Our Father in heaven,
hallowed be your Name,
your kingdom come,
your will be done,
on earth as in heaven.
Give us today our daily bread.
Forgive us our sins
as we forgive those who sin against us.
Save us from the time of trial
and deliver us from evil.
For the kingdom, the power and the glory are yours,
now and for ever. Amen.

OR

As our Saviour taught his disciples, we pray:

Our Father, who art in heaven,
hallowed be thy Name;
thy kingdom come;
thy will be done;
on earth as it is in heaven.
Give us this day our daily bread.
And forgive us our trespasses,
as we forgive those who trespass against us.
And lead us not into temptation;
but deliver us from evil.
For thine is the kingdom, the power, and the glory,
for ever and ever. Amen.

30 Hymn

31 The service continues.

THE BAPTISM OF YOUNG CHILDREN

NOTES

1 This service is used when **only** *young children are* to be baptized.

2 The Sacrament of Baptism is normally administered during an act of public worship. It is preferable that it follow the sermon, but it may be used before the Ministry of the Word.

3 If *candles* are to be given to the newly-baptized, *they* may be lit from the Easter Candle (see page 265) or some other candle lit at the beginning of the service.

4 Prayers for *those* who have been baptized, and for *their families*, should be included in the prayers of intercession.

5 The minister shall ensure that a certificate of Baptism is given to the *parents* of each newly-baptized child during or after the service.

---

1 Hymn

THE DECLARATION

2 Sisters and brothers,
Baptism is a gift of God.
It declares to each of us
  the love and grace of God.

In this sacrament we celebrate
  the life of Christ laid down for us,
  the Holy Spirit poured out on us,
  and the living water offered to us.
God claims and cleanses us,
rescues us from sin,
and raises us to new life.

He plants us into the Church of Christ
and sustains and strengthens us
with the power of the Spirit.

Although we do not deserve these gifts of grace,
or fully understand them,
God offers them to all,
and, through Christ, invites us to respond.

We recall the words of the risen Christ:

'All authority in heaven and on earth has been given to me.
Go therefore and make disciples of all nations,
baptizing them in the name of the Father
and of the Son and of the Holy Spirit,
and teaching them to obey everything that I have commanded you.
And remember, I am with you always, to the end of the age.'

On the day of Pentecost, Peter preached the Gospel of Christ's resurrection. Those who heard the message asked what they should do. Peter told them:

'Repent, and be baptized, every one of you,
in the name of Jesus Christ
so that your sins may be forgiven;
and you will receive the gift of the Holy Spirit.
For the promise is for you,
for your children,
and for all who are far away,
everyone whom the Lord our God calls.'

THE REQUEST FOR BAPTISM

3 The *parents* (and *godparents*) of the *children* to be baptized *stand.*

The minister says to the *parents*:

A and B (A), having heard these things, how do you respond to the offer of God's grace?

Answer:

We/I thank God, and ask that *our/my child/children* be baptized.

THE THANKSGIVING OVER THE WATER

4 All stand.

Except where a baptistry is to be used, water is poured into the font, in the sight of the people.

The *parents* (and *godparents*) *gather* round or near the font or baptistry.

The minister stands at the font or baptistry and says:

Gracious God, we thank you
for your gifts of water and the Holy Spirit,
for your sustaining, cleansing, and life-giving power.

From the beginning
your grace has been made known
through water and the Spirit.

Your Spirit moved over the waters at creation
and you led your people to freedom through a parted sea.
In the fullness of time you sent Jesus.
He was baptized in the waters of the Jordan
and anointed with the Holy Spirit.
He passed through the deep waters of death
and lives for evermore.
He offers living water
and the gift of the Holy Spirit.

The minister may extend her/his hands over the water.

Pour out your Holy Spirit
that *those/the one* baptized in this water
may die to sin,
be raised with Christ,
and be born to new life in the family of your Church.
We ask this through Jesus Christ our Lord. **Amen.**

5 Hymn

THE AFFIRMATION OF FAITH

6 The people remain standing.

The minister says to the *parents* (and *godparents*):

Do you turn away from evil and all that denies God?

Answer: By the grace of God, I do.

Do you turn to God,
trusting in Jesus Christ as Lord and Saviour,
and in the Holy Spirit as Helper and Guide?

Answer: By the grace of God, I do.

7 The minister says to everyone present:

EITHER

A Do you believe and trust in God the Father?

**I believe in God, the Father almighty,
creator of heaven and earth.**

Do you believe and trust in God the Son?

**I believe in Jesus Christ,
God's only Son, our Lord,
who was conceived by the Holy Spirit,
born of the Virgin Mary,
suffered under Pontius Pilate,
was crucified, died, and was buried;
he descended to the dead.**

On the third day he rose again,
he ascended into heaven,
he is seated at the right hand of the Father,
and he will come again to judge the living and the dead.

Do you believe and trust in God the Holy Spirit?

I believe in the Holy Spirit,
the holy catholic Church,
the communion of saints,
the forgiveness of sins,
the resurrection of the body,
and the life everlasting. Amen.

OR

B We say together:

We believe in God the Father,
who made the world.
We believe in Jesus Christ, his Son,
who redeemed humankind.
We believe in the Holy Spirit,
who gives life to the people of God.

THE BAPTISM

8 The minister says to the *parents* of each child:

What name have you given this child?

The *parents respond* with the Christian name(s) of the child.

9 The minister may say to *those* to be baptized:

N and N (N),
for you Jesus Christ came into the world;
for you he lived and showed God's love;
for you he suffered death on the Cross;
for you he triumphed over death,
rising to newness of life;

for you he prays at God's right hand:
all this for you,
before you could know anything of it.
In your Baptism,
the word of Scripture is fulfilled:
'We love, because God first loved us.'

10 The minister, taking each child into her/his arms, pours water generously and visibly on the child's head, or dips the child in water three times, once at the mention of each Person of the Holy Trinity, saying:

N, I baptize you
in the Name of the Father,
and of the Son,
and of the Holy Spirit. **Amen.**

By Baptism, God has received you into the Church.

The minister makes the sign of the cross on the forehead of each child, saying:

N, I sign you with the cross, the sign of Christ.

11 The people sit.

A lighted candle may be given to the *parents* or *godparents* of each child.

The minister, or a representative of the local church, says to the *children*:

N and N (N),
receive this light,
for you belong to Christ,
the Light of the world.

Christ is your Light and your Way.

May you grow and live in the faith of Christ. Amen.

12 The newly-baptized *children are* shown to the people.

All say or sing:

**The Lord bless you and keep you;
the Lord make his face to shine on you
and be gracious to you;
the Lord look on you with kindness
and give you peace. Amen.**

THE BAPTISMAL PROMISES

13 The *parents* (and *godparents*) *stand.*

The minister says to the *parents*:

A and B (A), I ask you now to respond to God's love and grace to your *children* by making these promises.

Will you love *these* your *children,*
committing *yourselves* to care for *them*
in body, mind and spirit?

Answer: With God's help *we* will.

Will you, therefore,
ensure that *they are* nurtured
in the faith and life of the Christian community?

Answer: With God's help *we* will.

Will you set before *them* a Christian example,
that through your prayers, words and deeds,
they may learn the way of Christ?

Answer: With God's help *we* will.

14 If there *are godparents*, the minister says to *them*:

C and D (C),
will you help *these parents*
to nurture *their children* in the Christian faith?

Answer: With God's help *we* will.

THE PROMISE OF THE PEOPLE

15 The people stand. The minister says to them:

Members of the body of Christ, we rejoice that *these,* our *sisters and brothers, have* been baptized.

Will you so maintain the Church's life of worship and service that *they* may grow in grace and in the knowledge and love of God and of his Son Jesus Christ our Lord?

With God's help we will.

16 The people sit.

A Bible or some other book may be given.

A certificate of Baptism may be given.

17 The minister says:

Let us pray.

Generous God,
touch us again
with the fire of your Spirit
and renew in us all
the grace of our Baptism;
that we may profess the one true faith
and live in love and unity
with all who are baptized into Christ. Amen.

18 The Lord's Prayer, if it is not said at some other point in the service

EITHER

We say together the prayer that Jesus gave us:

Our Father in heaven,
hallowed be your Name,
your kingdom come,
your will be done,
on earth as in heaven.
Give us today our daily bread.
Forgive us our sins
as we forgive those who sin against us.
Save us from the time of trial
and deliver us from evil.
For the kingdom, the power and the glory are yours,
now and for ever. Amen.

OR

As our Saviour taught his disciples, we pray:

Our Father, who art in heaven,
hallowed be thy Name;
thy kingdom come;
thy will be done;
on earth as it is in heaven.
Give us this day our daily bread.
And forgive us our trespasses,
as we forgive those who trespass against us.
And lead us not into temptation;
but deliver us from evil.
For thine is the kingdom, the power, and the glory,
for ever and ever. Amen.

19 Hymn

20 The service continues.

CONFIRMATION AND RECEPTION INTO MEMBERSHIP

NOTES

1 This service is used when *persons* baptized on a previous occasion *are* to be confirmed and received into membership.

2 It takes place during a celebration of ***Holy Communion***, following the sermon.

3 This service is not suitable for use when any *candidates* for Confirmation and Reception *are* to be baptized. In those circumstances, ***The Baptism of those who are able to answer for themselves, and of Young Children, with Confirmation and Reception into Membership*** (page 62) or ***The Baptism of those who are able to answer for themselves, with Confirmation and Reception into Membership*** (page 76), as appropriate, should be used.

4 Prayers for *those* who *have* been confirmed, and, as appropriate, for *their families*, should be included in the prayers of intercession.

5 A certificate of Confirmation may be given to each newly-confirmed person during or after the service.

---

1 Hymn

THE DECLARATION

2 Sisters and brothers,
by grace,
through the sign and seal of Baptism,
and in the power of the Holy Spirit,
we become God's people, the Church.

In Confirmation we are strengthened by the Holy Spirit
that we may remain in Christ for ever
as his faithful servants and witnesses.

3 Let us pray.

Living God,
may all who are baptized into Christ
be sustained by the Holy Spirit,
that through lives of faith and love
your grace may be known
and your name honoured;
through Jesus Christ our Lord. **Amen.**

THE REQUEST FOR CONFIRMATION

4 The *candidates stand.*

The minister says to *them*:

N and N (N),
at your Baptism into Christ,
God offered you the gifts of his grace
and has constantly been at work in your life.
In this moment
God offers to strengthen you by his Spirit
and invites you to respond.

Answer: I thank God, and ask to be confirmed.

5 If a candidate is to give personal testimony to God's grace, this may be done here.

THE AFFIRMATION OF FAITH

6 The minister says to the *candidates*:

Do you turn away from evil and all that denies God?

Answer: By the grace of God, I do.

Do you turn to God,
trusting in Jesus Christ as Lord and Saviour,
and in the Holy Spirit as Helper and Guide?

Answer: By the grace of God, I do.

7 *The people stand.*

The minister says to everyone present:

Do you believe and trust in God the Father?

**I believe in God, the Father almighty,
creator of heaven and earth.**

Do you believe and trust in God the Son?

**I believe in Jesus Christ,
God's only Son, our Lord,
who was conceived by the Holy Spirit,
born of the Virgin Mary,
suffered under Pontius Pilate,
was crucified, died, and was buried;
he descended to the dead.
On the third day he rose again,
he ascended into heaven,
he is seated at the right hand of the Father,
and he will come again to judge the living and the dead.**

Do you believe and trust in God the Holy Spirit?

**I believe in the Holy Spirit,
the holy catholic Church,
the communion of saints,
the forgiveness of sins,
the resurrection of the body,
and the life everlasting. Amen.**

8 *Hymn*

THE CONFIRMATION

9 The people remain standing. *Those* who *are* to be confirmed *kneel.*

The minister, extending her/his hands towards the *candidates*, says:

By your power and grace, Lord,
strengthen *these* your *servants*,
that *they* may live as *faithful disciples* of Jesus Christ.
Increase in *them* your gifts of grace,
and fill *them* with your Holy Spirit:
  the Spirit of wisdom and understanding;
  the Spirit of discernment and inner strength;
  the Spirit of knowledge, holiness, and awe.

10 The minister lays her/his hand upon the head of each candidate, saying:

Lord, confirm your servant *N* by your Holy Spirit
that *she/he* may continue yours for ever. **Amen.**

THE RECEPTION AND WELCOME

11 *Those* newly-confirmed *stand.* The minister says to *them*:

N and N (N),
we receive and welcome you
as *members* of the Methodist Church,
and of the church in this place.

12 The minister and a representative of the local church extend the hand of fellowship to each newly-confirmed person.

THE PROMISES OF THOSE NEWLY-CONFIRMED

13 The minister says to *those* newly-confirmed:

N and N (N),
I ask you now to respond to God's love and grace
by making these promises.

Will you commit yourself to the Christian life of worship and service, and be open to the renewing power of God?

Answer: With God's help I will.

Will you seek the strength of God's Spirit as you accept the cost of following Jesus Christ in your daily life?

Answer: With God's help I will.

Will you witness, by word and deed, to the good news of God in Christ, and so bring glory to God?

Answer: With God's help I will.

THE PROMISE OF THE PEOPLE

14 The minister says to the people:

Members of the body of Christ, we rejoice that *these*, our *sisters and brothers*, *have* been confirmed.

Will you so maintain the Church's life of worship and service that *they* may grow in grace and in the knowledge and love of God and of his Son Jesus Christ our Lord?

With God's help we will.

15 The people sit.

A Bible or some other book may be given.

A certificate of Confirmation may be given.

16 The minister says:

Let us pray.

Generous God,
touch us again
with the fire of your Spirit
and renew us by your grace,
that we may profess the one true faith
and live in love and unity
with all who follow Christ. Amen.

17 Hymn

18 The service continues from the prayers of intercession in any appropriate order for Holy Communion. That for ***The Day of Pentecost and Times of Renewal in the Life of the Church*** (page 174) is especially suitable.

THE BAPTISM OF YOUNG CHILDREN WITH CONFIRMATION AND RECEPTION INTO MEMBERSHIP

NOTES

1 This service is used when *young children are* to be baptized **and** *persons* previously baptized *are* to be confirmed and received into membership.

2 It takes place during a celebration of ***Holy Communion***, following the sermon.

3 This service is not suitable for use when any *candidates* for Confirmation and Reception *are* to be baptized. In those circumstances, ***The Baptism of those who are able to answer for themselves, and of Young Children, with Confirmation and Reception into Membership*** (page 62) should be used.

4 If *candles* are to be given to the newly-baptized, *they* may be lit from the Easter Candle (see page 265) or some other candle lit at the beginning of the service.

5 Prayers for *those* who *have* been baptized, and for *those* who *have* been confirmed, and, as appropriate, for *their families*, should be included in the prayers of intercession.

6 The minister shall ensure that a certificate of Baptism is given to the *parents* of each newly-baptized child during or after the service. A certificate of Confirmation may be given to each newly-confirmed person during or after the service.

BAPTISM

1 Hymn

THE DECLARATION

2 Sisters and brothers,
Baptism is a gift of God.
It declares to each of us
the love and grace of God.

In this sacrament we celebrate
the life of Christ laid down for us,
the Holy Spirit poured out on us,
and the living water offered to us.
God claims and cleanses us,
rescues us from sin,
and raises us to new life.
He plants us into the Church of Christ
and sustains and strengthens us
with the power of the Spirit.

Although we do not deserve these gifts of grace,
or fully understand them,
God offers them to all,
and, through Christ, invites us to respond.

We recall the words of the risen Christ:

> 'All authority in heaven and on earth has been given to me.
> Go therefore and make disciples of all nations,
> baptizing them in the name of the Father
> and of the Son and of the Holy Spirit,
> and teaching them to obey everything that I have commanded you.
> And remember, I am with you always, to the end of the age.'

On the day of Pentecost, Peter preached the Gospel of Christ's resurrection. Those who heard the message asked what they should do. Peter told them:

'Repent, and be baptized, every one of you,
in the name of Jesus Christ
so that your sins may be forgiven;
and you will receive the gift of the Holy Spirit.
For the promise is for you,
for your children,
and for all who are far away,
everyone whom the Lord our God calls.'

THE REQUEST FOR BAPTISM

3 The *parents* (and *godparents*) of the *children* to be baptized *stand*.

The minister says to the *parents*:

A and B (A), having heard these things, how do you respond to the offer of God's grace?

Answer:

We/I thank God, and ask that *our/my child/children* be baptized.

THE THANKSGIVING OVER THE WATER

4 All stand.

Except where a baptistry is to be used, water is poured into the font, in the sight of the people.

The *parents* (and *godparents*) *gather* round or near the font or baptistry.

The minister stands at the font or baptistry and says:

Gracious God, we thank you
for your gifts of water and the Holy Spirit,
for your sustaining, cleansing, and life-giving power.

From the beginning
your grace has been made known
through water and the Spirit.

Your Spirit moved over the waters at creation
and you led your people to freedom through a parted sea.
In the fullness of time you sent Jesus.
He was baptized in the waters of the Jordan
and anointed with the Holy Spirit.
He passed through the deep waters of death
and lives for evermore.
He offers living water
and the gift of the Holy Spirit.

The minister may extend her/his hands over the water.

Pour out your Holy Spirit
that *those/the one* baptized in this water
may die to sin,
be raised with Christ,
and be born to new life in the family of your Church.
We ask this through Jesus Christ our Lord. **Amen.**

5 Hymn

THE AFFIRMATION OF FAITH

6 The people remain standing.

The minister says to the *parents* (and *godparents*) and to *those* who *are* to be confirmed:

Do you turn away from evil and all that denies God?

Answer: By the grace of God, I do.

Do you turn to God,
trusting in Jesus Christ as Lord and Saviour,
and in the Holy Spirit as Helper and Guide?

Answer: By the grace of God, I do.

7 The minister says to everyone present:

Do you believe and trust in God the Father?

**I believe in God, the Father almighty,
creator of heaven and earth.**

Do you believe and trust in God the Son?

**I believe in Jesus Christ,
God's only Son, our Lord,
who was conceived by the Holy Spirit,
born of the Virgin Mary,
suffered under Pontius Pilate,
was crucified, died, and was buried;
he descended to the dead.
On the third day he rose again,
he ascended into heaven,
he is seated at the right hand of the Father,
and he will come again to judge the living and the dead.**

Do you believe and trust in God the Holy Spirit?

**I believe in the Holy Spirit,
the holy catholic Church,
the communion of saints,
the forgiveness of sins,
the resurrection of the body,
and the life everlasting. Amen.**

THE BAPTISM

8 The minister says to the *parents* of each child:

What name have you given this child?

The *parents respond* with the Christian name(s) of the child.

9 The minister may say to *those* to be baptized:

N and N (N),
for you Jesus Christ came into the world;
for you he lived and showed God's love;
for you he suffered death on the Cross;
for you he triumphed over death,
rising to newness of life;
for you he prays at God's right hand:
all this for you,
before you could know anything of it.
In your Baptism,
the word of Scripture is fulfilled:
'We love, because God first loved us.'

10 The minister, taking each child into her/his arms, pours water generously and visibly on the child's head, or dips the child in water three times, once at the mention of each Person of the Holy Trinity, saying:

N, I baptize you
in the Name of the Father,
and of the Son,
and of the Holy Spirit. **Amen.**

By Baptism, God has received you into the Church.

The minister makes the sign of the cross on the forehead of each child, saying:

N, I sign you with the cross, the sign of Christ.

11 The people sit.

A lighted candle may be given to the *parents* or *godparents* of each child.

The minister, or a representative of the local church, says to the *children*:

N and N (N),
receive this light,
for you belong to Christ,
the Light of the world.

Christ is your Light and your Way.

May you grow and live in the faith of Christ. Amen.

12 The newly-baptized *children are* shown to the people.

All say or sing:

**The Lord bless you and keep you;
the Lord make his face to shine on you
and be gracious to you;
the Lord look on you with kindness
and give you peace. Amen.**

THE BAPTISMAL PROMISES

13 The *parents* (and *godparents*) *stand.*

The minister says to the *parents*:

A and B (A), I ask you now to respond to God's love and grace to your *children* by making these promises.

Will you love *these* your *children,*
committing *yourselves* to care for *them*
in body, mind and spirit?

Answer: With God's help *we* will.

Will you, therefore,
ensure that *they are* nurtured
in the faith and life of the Christian community?

Answer: With God's help *we* will.

Will you set before *them* a Christian example,
that through your prayers, words and deeds,
they may learn the way of Christ?

Answer: With God's help *we* will.

14 If there *are godparents*, the minister says to *them*:

C and D (C),
will you help *these parents*
to nurture *their children* in the Christian faith?

Answer: With God's help *we* will.

15 The people stand. The minister says to them:

Members of the body of Christ, we rejoice that *these,* our *sisters and brothers, have* been baptized.

Will you so maintain the Church's life of worship and service that *they* may grow in grace and in the knowledge and love of God and of his Son Jesus Christ our Lord?

With God's help we will.

CONFIRMATION

THE DECLARATION

16 The people sit.

The minister says:

Sisters and brothers,
by grace,
through the sign and seal of Baptism,
and in the power of the Holy Spirit,
we become God's people, the Church.
In Confirmation we are strengthened by the Holy Spirit
that we may remain in Christ for ever
as his faithful servants and witnesses.

17 Let us pray.

Living God,
may all who are baptized into Christ
be sustained by the Holy Spirit,
that through lives of faith and love
your grace may be known
and your name honoured;
through Jesus Christ our Lord. **Amen.**

THE REQUEST FOR CONFIRMATION

18 The *candidates* for Confirmation *stand.*

The minister says to *them*:

N and N (N),
at your Baptism into Christ,
God offered you the gifts of his grace
and has constantly been at work in your life.
In this moment
God offers to strengthen you by his Spirit
and invites you to respond.

Answer: I thank God, and ask to be confirmed.

19 If a candidate is to give personal testimony to God's grace, this may be done here.

THE CONFIRMATION

20 The people stand. *Those* who *are* to be confirmed *kneel.*

The minister, extending her/his hands towards the *candidates*, says:

By your power and grace, Lord,
strengthen *these* your *servants,*
that *they* may live as *faithful disciples* of Jesus Christ.

Increase in *them* your gifts of grace,
and fill *them* with your Holy Spirit:
the Spirit of wisdom and understanding;
the Spirit of discernment and inner strength;
the Spirit of knowledge, holiness, and awe.

21 The minister lays her/his hand upon the head of each candidate, saying:

Lord, confirm your servant *N* by your Holy Spirit
that *she/he* may continue yours for ever. **Amen.**

THE RECEPTION AND WELCOME

22 *Those* newly-confirmed *stand*. The minister says to *them*:

N and N (N),
we receive and welcome you
as *members* of the Methodist Church,
and of the church in this place.

23 The minister and a representative of the local church extend the hand of fellowship to each newly-confirmed person.

THE PROMISES OF THOSE NEWLY-CONFIRMED

24 The minister says to *those* newly-confirmed:

N and N (N),
I ask you now to respond to God's love and grace
by making these promises.

Will you commit yourself to the Christian life of worship and service, and be open to the renewing power of God?

Answer: With God's help I will.

Will you seek the strength of God's Spirit as you accept the cost of following Jesus Christ in your daily life?

Answer: With God's help I will.

Will you witness, by word and deed, to the good news of God in Christ, and so bring glory to God?

Answer: With God's help I will.

THE PROMISE OF THE PEOPLE

25 The minister says to the people:

Members of the body of Christ, we rejoice that *these,* our *sisters and brothers, have* been confirmed.

Will you so maintain the Church's life of worship and service that *they* may grow in grace and in the knowledge and love of God and of his Son Jesus Christ our Lord?

With God's help we will.

26 The people sit.

A Bible or some other book may be given.

A certificate of Confirmation may be given.

27 The minister says:

Let us pray.

Generous God,
touch us again
with the fire of your Spirit
and renew us by your grace,
that we may profess the one true faith
and live in love and unity
with all who follow Christ. Amen.

28 Hymn

29 The service continues from the prayers of intercession in any appropriate order for Holy Communion. That for ***The Day of Pentecost and Times of Renewal in the Life of the Church*** (page 174) is especially suitable.

ORDERS OF SERVICE FOR HOLY COMMUNION

INTRODUCTION

Holy Communion, or the Lord's Supper, is the central act of Christian worship, in which the Church responds to our Lord's command, 'Do this in remembrance of me' (1 Corinthians 11:24-25).

Many of the themes of John and Charles Wesley's **Hymns on the Lord's Supper** (1745) are reflected in present-day ecumenical understanding of this sacrament. In communion with the people of God in heaven and on earth, we give thanks for God's mighty acts in creation and redemption, represented supremely in the life, death and resurrection of Jesus Christ. In this means of grace, the Church joyfully celebrates the presence of Christ in its midst, calls to mind his sacrifice and, in the power of the Holy Spirit, is united with him as the Body of Christ. At the Lord's table, Christ's disciples share bread and wine, the tokens of his dying love and the food for their earthly pilgrimage, which are also a foretaste of the heavenly banquet, prepared for all people. Those who gather around the table of the Lord are empowered for mission: apostles, sent out in the power of the Spirit, to live and work to God's praise and glory. One of the keynotes of the Methodist revival was John Wesley's emphasis on 'The Duty of Constant Communion' and it is still the duty and privilege of members of the Methodist Church to share in this sacrament. The Methodist Conference has encouraged local churches to admit baptized children to communion. Those who are communicants and belong to other Churches whose discipline so permits are also welcome as communicants in the Methodist Church.

The services of ***Holy Communion*** in this book are set out, after the initial 'The Gathering of the People of God', under the two historic headings, 'The Ministry of the Word' and 'The Lord's Supper'. The hinge point between the two is normally the sharing of the Peace. The shape of the Lord's Supper follows the record in scripture of Jesus' characteristic sharing with his disciples, especially after the final meal on the night before the crucifixion. His seven actions with the bread and wine (four with the bread, three with the wine) were taken up in the Church's tradition as a fourfold shape: Taking, Giving Thanks, Breaking and Sharing. In the Great Thanksgiving, the service of praise offered by God's people on earth is joined with the praises of the heavenly host, praising God, Father, Son and Holy Spirit. This Eucharistic Prayer (the word 'Eucharist', derived from a Greek word which means 'Thanksgiving', is increasingly accepted by Christians of all traditions as one of the names for this sacrament) is Trinitarian both in its structure and in its focus.

In this book, complete orders for ***Holy Communion*** have been provided for the major festivals and seasons, offering a wide range of seasonal language and imagery throughout each service. This also has the practical advantage that each service is complete in itself so that there is no need to turn to different parts of the book to find additional material. There are three orders for use in Ordinary Seasons (that is, when it is not a particular season or festival). Other sections of **The Methodist Worship Book** provide eucharistic prayers for certain specific occasions.

NOTES

1 The basic elements of each service are marked by the symbol *. Other sections may be omitted.

2 The term 'presiding minister' in these services means a presbyter or a person with an authorisation from the Conference to preside at the Lord's Supper. The presiding minister should begin and end the service. She/he should also greet the people at the Peace and preside over the fourfold Eucharistic action by taking the bread and wine, leading the Great Prayer of Thanksgiving, breaking the bread, and presiding over the sharing of the bread and wine. Other people may be invited to share in other parts of the service.

3 Several other services in this book are designed to take place within the context of ***Holy Communion***. The **NOTES** for those services indicate the most appropriate places for their insertion into the service of ***Holy Communion***.

4 In some churches it is customary to stand for the reading of the Gospel.

5 The juice of the grape shall be used.

6 What remains of the elements should be reverently consumed, or otherwise reverently disposed of, at the end of the service.

HOLY COMMUNION FOR ADVENT

NOTE

An Advent ceremony, such as the lighting of Advent candles, may be included after either no. 1 or no. 7, or at some other appropriate place.

THE GATHERING OF THE PEOPLE OF GOD

* 1 The presiding minister says:

Grace and peace to you
from God our Father and the Lord Jesus Christ.
Blessèd are those who will come
from east and west, from north and south,
to feast in the kingdom of God.

2 Hymn

3 God of all glory,
you brought the universe into existence,
and raised up witnesses
to your greatness and love.
We praise and adore you.
Grant that by the inspiration of your Holy Spirit
we may worship and serve you,
and praise your holy name;
through Christ our Lord. **Amen.**

4 The commandments of the Lord Jesus may be read.

Our Lord Jesus Christ said: 'The first commandment is, "Hear, O Israel: the Lord our God, the Lord is one; you shall love the Lord your God with all your heart, and with all your soul, and with all your mind, and with all your strength." The second is this, "You shall love your neighbour as yourself." There is no other commandment greater than these.' 'I give you a new commandment, that you love one another. Just as I have loved you, you also should love one another.'

Amen. Lord, have mercy.

* 5 The presiding minister says:

Let us confess our sins to God,
trusting in his mercy and forgiveness.

Holy and forgiving God,
we have sinned against you and each other
in thought and word and deed.
We have turned from your life-giving word,
and ignored the message of those you sent.
We are unprepared for the coming of your Son.
Have mercy upon us and forgive us,
that strengthened by your love
we may serve you more faithfully;
through Jesus Christ our Lord. Amen.

Silence

'I am making all things new,' says the Lord.

This is Christ's gracious word:

'Your sins are forgiven.'

Amen. Thanks be to God.

* 6 The collect of the day, or this or some other prayer:

God of mercy and power,
whose Son rules over all,
grant us so to live in obedience to your holy will,
that at his appearing
we may be raised to eternal life;
through Jesus Christ our Lord. **Amen.**

The collect of the Advent season (page 523) may also be said.

7 Hymn

OR *Benedictus*

Blessèd be the Lord, the God of Israel,
who has come to his people and set them free.

**The Lord has raised up for us a mighty Saviour,
born of the house of his servant David.**

Through the holy prophets, God promised of old
to save us from our enemies,
from the hands of all who hate us,
to show mercy to our forebears,
and to remember his holy covenant.

**This was the oath God swore to our father Abraham:
to set us free from the hands of our enemies,
free to worship him without fear,
holy and righteous before him,
all the days of our life.**

And you, child, shall be called the prophet of the
Most High,
for you will go before the Lord to prepare his way,
to give his people knowledge of salvation
by the forgiveness of their sins.

**In the tender compassion of our God
the dawn from heaven shall break upon us,
to shine on those who dwell in darkness and
the shadow of death,
and to guide our feet into the way of peace.**

Glory to the Father, and to the Son,
and to the Holy Spirit:
**as it was in the beginning, is now,
and shall be for ever. Amen.**

OR ***Magnificat***

My soul proclaims the greatness of the Lord,
my spirit rejoices in God my Saviour,
who has looked with favour on his lowly servant.

**From this day all generations will call me blessèd:
the Almighty has done great things for me
and holy is his name.**

God has mercy on those who fear him,
from generation to generation.

**The Lord has shown strength with his arm
and scattered the proud in their conceit,
casting down the mighty from their thrones
and lifting up the lowly.**

God has filled the hungry with good things
and sent the rich away empty.

**He has come to the aid of his servant Israel,
to remember the promise of mercy,
the promise made to our forebears,
to Abraham and his children for ever.**

Glory to the Father, and to the Son,
and to the Holy Spirit:
**as it was in the beginning, is now,
and shall be for ever. Amen.**

THE MINISTRY OF THE WORD

* Either two or three readings from scripture follow, the last of which is the Gospel.

8 Old Testament reading

9 A Psalm or portion of a Psalm may be said or sung.

10 Epistle

11 Hymn

*12 A reading from the Gospel according to . . .

Hear the Gospel of Christ.
Glory to Christ our Saviour.

The Gospel is read.

This is the Gospel of Christ.
Praise to Christ our Lord.

*13 Sermon

14 Hymn

*15 These or some other prayers of intercession:

Let us pray.

In joyful expectation of his coming to reign
we pray to our Lord, saying,
Come, Lord Jesus.

Come, Lord Jesus.

Come to your world as King of the nations.
We pray for . . .
Before you rulers will stand in silence.
Come, Lord Jesus.

Come, Lord Jesus.

Come to your Church as Lord and Judge.
We pray for . . .
Help us to live in the light of your coming
and give us a longing to do your will.
Come, Lord Jesus.

Come, Lord Jesus.

Come to your people
as Saviour and bearer of pain.
We pray for . . .
Enfold us all in your love and mercy,
wipe away the tears of failure, fear and distress,
and set us free to serve you for ever.
Come, Lord Jesus.

Come, Lord Jesus.

Come to us from heaven
with power and great glory,
and lift us up to meet you,
where with all your saints and angels,
we will live with you for ever.
Come, Lord Jesus.

Come, Lord Jesus. Amen.

16 Silence

THE LORD'S SUPPER

17 EITHER

Let us pray.

We do not presume
to come to this your table,
merciful Lord,
trusting in our own
righteousness,
but in your manifold
and great mercies.
We are not worthy
so much as to gather up
the crumbs under your
table.
But you are the same Lord
whose nature is always to
have mercy.
Grant us therefore,
gracious Lord,
so to eat the flesh
of your dear Son Jesus
Christ,
and to drink his blood,
that we may evermore
dwell in him
and he in us. Amen.

OR

We say together:

Lord, we come to your
table,
trusting in your mercy
and not in any goodness
of our own.
We are not worthy
even to gather up
the crumbs under your
table,
but it is your nature
always to have mercy,
and on that we depend.
So feed us
with the body and blood
of Jesus Christ, your Son,
that we may for ever
live in him and he in us.
Amen.

18 The Peace

All stand.

May the God of peace make you holy
and keep you free from every fault
as you wait in joyful hope
for the coming of our Lord Jesus Christ.

The peace of the Lord be always with you.
And also with you.

The people may greet one another in the name of Christ.

THE PREPARATION OF THE GIFTS

19 Hymn

*20 The offerings of the people are presented. Bread and wine are brought to the table (or if already on the table are uncovered). The presiding minister takes the bread and wine and prepares them for use.

THE THANKSGIVING

*21 All stand.

The presiding minister leads the great prayer of thanksgiving:

The Lord be with you.
And also with you.

Lift up your hearts.
We lift them to the Lord.

Let us give thanks to the Lord our God.
It is right to give our thanks and praise.

God of all glory and light of our salvation,
we offer you thanks and praise
through Jesus Christ your Son our Lord.

By your living Word
you called all things into being,
breathed into life the desire of your heart
and shaped us in your own likeness.
Though we rejected your love,
you did not give us up
or cease to fashion our salvation.
You made a covenant to be our God,
spoke to us through the prophets,
and prepared the way for our redemption.

We praise you that in the fullness of time
you sent your only Son Jesus Christ.

The Lord of eternity,
announced by angels and born of Mary,
he became incarnate,
fulfilling the promise of your salvation.

And so we offer our praise
with all your people, on earth and in heaven.
With the full chorus of your creation,
we proclaim the glory of your name:

**Holy, holy, holy Lord,
God of power and might.
Heaven and earth are full of your glory.
Hosanna in the highest.
Blessèd is he who comes in the name of the Lord.
Hosanna in the highest.**

We praise you, Lord God, King of the universe,
through our Lord Jesus Christ,
who, on the night in which he was betrayed,
took bread, gave thanks, broke it,
and gave it to his disciples, saying,
'Take this and eat it.
This is my body given for you.
Do this in remembrance of me.'

In the same way, after supper,
he took the cup, gave thanks,
and gave it to them, saying,
'Drink from it all of you.
This is my blood of the new covenant,
poured out for you and for many,
for the forgiveness of sins.
Do this, whenever you drink it,
in remembrance of me.'

**Christ has died.
Christ is risen.
Christ will come in glory.
He is Alpha and Omega,
the beginning and the end;
the King of kings, and Lord of lords.**

Recalling his death and resurrection,
and in obedience to his command,
we celebrate the offering of his eternal sacrifice,
until he comes again.

Through him, our Priest and King,
accept us as a living sacrifice,
a people for your praise.

Generous and holy God,
pour out your Spirit
that these gifts of bread and wine
may be for us the body and blood of Christ.

Refashion us in your image
that we may be found ready
at the coming of our Lord Jesus Christ.

Blessing and honour and glory and power
be yours, O Lord, for ever and ever. Amen.

*22 The Lord's Prayer

EITHER

We say together the prayer
that Jesus gave us:

Our Father in heaven,
hallowed be your Name,
your kingdom come,
your will be done,
on earth as in heaven.
Give us today our daily bread.
Forgive us our sins
as we forgive those who sin against us.
Save us from the time of trial
and deliver us from evil.
For the kingdom, the power and the glory are yours,
now and for ever. Amen.

OR

As our Saviour taught his
disciples, we pray:

Our Father, who art in heaven,
hallowed be thy Name;
thy kingdom come;
thy will be done;
on earth as it is in heaven.
Give us this day our daily bread.
And forgive us our trespasses,
as we forgive those who trespass against us.
And lead us not into temptation;
but deliver us from evil.
For thine is the kingdom, the power, and the glory,
for ever and ever. Amen.

THE BREAKING OF THE BREAD

*23 The presiding minister breaks the bread in the sight of the people in silence, or saying:

The bread we break is a sharing in the body of Christ.

The cup we take is a sharing in the blood of Christ.

Happy are those who share the banquet.

OR

Like those that look for the morning
so our souls wait for the Lord.

Be known to us, Lord, in the breaking of the bread.

*24 Silence, all seated or kneeling

THE SHARING OF THE BREAD AND WINE

*25 The presiding minister, those assisting with the distribution, and the people receive, according to local custom.

The presiding minister may say these or other words of invitation:

The true bread of heaven gives life to the world.
Come, all who are hungry, come and eat.
Come, all who are thirsty, come and drink.

*26 Words such as the following are said during the distribution:

The body of Christ keep you in eternal life. **Amen.**

The blood of Christ keep you in eternal life. **Amen.**

27 During the distribution there may be appropriate music.

*28 The elements that remain are covered with a white cloth.

PRAYERS AND DISMISSAL

29 Silence

30 Let us pray.

**We thank you, Lord,
for feeding us with the bread of heaven
and the cup of salvation.
Keep us in your grace
and at the coming of Christ in glory
bring us with your saints
into the life of your kingdom. Amen.**

31 Hymn

32 The presiding minister says:

Christ the Sun of Righteousness
shine upon *you/us*
and prepare *your/our* hearts and souls
to meet him when he comes in glory;
and the blessing of God,
the Father, the Son and the Holy Spirit,
be *yours/ours*, now and always. **Amen.**

*33 The presiding minister says:

The day of the Lord is surely coming.
Be faithful in worship,
unwavering in hope,
fervent in the work of God's kingdom
and all the more as you see the Day drawing near.

Amen. Come, Lord Jesus.

HOLY COMMUNION
FOR CHRISTMAS AND EPIPHANY

NOTE

This service is intended for use between midnight on Christmas Eve and the Sunday after Epiphany inclusive.

THE GATHERING OF THE PEOPLE OF GOD

* 1 The presiding minister says:

Great and wonderful are the things
the Lord our God has done for us.
The people who walked in darkness
have seen a great light.

2 Hymn

3 In the silence and stillness
let us open our hearts and lives to God,
that we may be prepared for his coming
as Light and Word, as Bread and Wine.

Silence

4 The presiding minister says:

We say together:

Loving God,
you have searched us and known us,
our blindness, our frailties,
our fears and our selfishness.
In sorrow we confess
that we have sinned against you
and disobeyed your command to love.
Forgive us,
for the sake of your Son, Jesus Christ,
who became like us
that we might become like him. Amen.

The true light that gives light to everyone
has come into the world.
To all who receive him,
he gives power to become children of God.
This is Christ's gracious word:

'Your sins are forgiven.'
Amen. Thanks be to God.

* 5 The collect of the day, or this or some other prayer:

Ever-living God,
whose glory was revealed
in the Word made flesh,
may we, who have seen such splendour
in the coming of your Son,
be true witnesses to your self-giving love in the world;
through Jesus Christ our Lord,
who is alive and reigns with you,
in the unity of the Holy Spirit,
one God, now and for ever. **Amen.**

6 EITHER ***Glory to God in the highest***

Glory to God in the highest,
and peace to God's people on earth.

Lord God, heavenly King,
almighty God and Father,
we worship you, we give you thanks,
we praise you for your glory.

Lord Jesus Christ, only Son of the Father,
Lord God, Lamb of God,
you take away the sin of the world:
have mercy on us.
You are seated at the right hand of the Father:
receive our prayer.

For you alone are the Holy One,
you alone are the Lord,
you alone are the Most High, Jesus Christ,
with the Holy Spirit,
in the glory of God the Father. Amen.

OR *A Song of the Incarnation*

The grace of God has dawned upon the world
with healing for all.
The people who walked in darkness
have seen a great light:
Light has dawned upon us,
dwellers in a land as dark as death.
For a child has been born for us,
a son given to us.

God is love;
and his love was disclosed to us in this,
that he sent his only Son into the world to bring us life.
We know how generous our Lord Jesus Christ has been:
he was rich, yet for our sake he became poor,
so that through his poverty we might become rich.

God has spoken to us in the Son
whom he has made heir to the whole universe.
The Word became flesh and came to dwell among us.
We saw his glory,
such glory as befits the Father's only Son,
full of grace and truth.

THE MINISTRY OF THE WORD

* Either two or three readings from scripture follow, the last of which is the Gospel.

7 Old Testament reading

8 A Psalm or portion of a Psalm may be said or sung.

9 Epistle

10 Hymn

*11 A reading from the Gospel according to . . .

Hear the Gospel of Christ.
Glory to Christ our Saviour.

The Gospel is read.

This is the Gospel of Christ.
Praise to Christ our Lord.

*12 Sermon

13 Hymn

*14 These or some other prayers of intercession:

Let us pray.

Unlooked for,
Christ comes.

To shepherds,
watching their sheep through the long, dark night,
he comes with the glory of the angels' song
and in the humility of the manger.

Silence

Loving God, we pray for our community . . .
In the midst of our everyday lives, surprise us with glimpses of the glorious, humble love at the heart of existence.

Lord, come to your people.
In your mercy set us free.

Searched for,
Christ comes.

To the wise and powerful,
star-led to Bethlehem, seeking a king,
he comes, child of Mary,
crowned with meekness,
worthy of every gift.

Silence

Loving God, we pray for the leaders of the world . . . Guide them with your light to the true wisdom of justice and peace, of freedom and respect for every human life.

Lord, come to your people.
In your mercy set us free.

Longed for,
Christ comes.

To Anna and Simeon,
whose days are lived in faithful expectation,
he comes, a new life to the old,
a living prophecy of hope.

Silence

Loving God, we pray for the Church in all the world . . . Unite us by your Spirit, and make us faithful witnesses to the hope we have in you.

Lord, come to your people.
In your mercy set us free.

Prayed for,
Christ comes.

To men and women, girls and boys,
crying out in darkness, pain and loneliness,
he comes, baptized, at one with us,
our Saviour, healer and friend.

Silence

Loving God, we pray for those whose lives are hard and painful or whose existence is sorrowful, bitter or empty . . . In their need, may they know your healing touch, reaching out to comfort, strengthen and restore.

Lord, come to your people.
In your mercy set us free.

Unlooked for and searched for,
longed for and prayed for,
loving God, you come to us now
as you have come to your people in every age.
We thank you for all who have reflected the light of Christ.
Help us to follow their example
and bring us with them to eternal life;
through Jesus Christ our Lord. **Amen.**

*15 The Lord's Prayer

EITHER

We say together the prayer that Jesus gave us:

**Our Father in heaven,
hallowed be your Name,
your kingdom come,
your will be done,
on earth as in heaven.
Give us today our daily bread.
Forgive us our sins
as we forgive those who sin against us.
Save us from the time of trial
and deliver us from evil.
For the kingdom, the power and the glory are yours,
now and for ever. Amen.**

OR

As our Saviour taught his disciples, we pray:

**Our Father, who art in heaven,
hallowed be thy Name;
thy kingdom come;
thy will be done;
on earth as it is in heaven.
Give us this day our daily bread.
And forgive us our trespasses,
as we forgive those who trespass against us.
And lead us not into temptation;
but deliver us from evil.
For thine is the kingdom, the power, and the glory,
for ever and ever. Amen.**

16 The Peace

All stand.

Glory to God in the highest,
and on earth peace to all in whom he delights.

The peace of the Lord be always with you.
And also with you.

The people may greet one another in the name of Christ.

17 The Nicene Creed

All stand.

Let us profess the faith of the Church.

**We believe in one God,
the Father, the Almighty,
maker of heaven and earth,
of all that is, seen and unseen.**

**We believe in one Lord, Jesus Christ,
the only Son of God,
eternally begotten of the Father,
God from God, Light from Light,
true God from true God,
begotten, not made,
of one Being with the Father;
through him all things were made.**

**For us and for our salvation
he came down from heaven,
was incarnate of the Holy Spirit and the Virgin Mary
and became truly human.
For our sake he was crucified under Pontius Pilate;
he suffered death and was buried.
On the third day he rose again
in accordance with the Scriptures;
he ascended into heaven
and is seated at the right hand of the Father.**

He will come again in glory to judge the living and the dead,
and his kingdom will have no end.

We believe in the Holy Spirit, the Lord, the giver of life,
who proceeds from the Father and the Son,
who with the Father and the Son is worshipped and glorified,
who has spoken through the prophets.
We believe in one holy catholic and apostolic Church.
We acknowledge one Baptism for the forgiveness of sins.
We look for the resurrection of the dead,
and the life of the world to come. Amen.

THE LORD'S SUPPER

THE PREPARATION OF THE GIFTS

18 Hymn

*19 The offerings of the people are presented. Bread and wine are brought to the table (or if already on the table are uncovered). The presiding minister takes the bread and wine and prepares them for use.

20 Lord and Giver of every good thing,
we bring to you
bread and wine for our communion,
lives and gifts for your kingdom,
all for transformation through your grace and love,
made known in Jesus Christ our Saviour. **Amen.**

THE THANKSGIVING

*21 All stand.

The presiding minister leads the great prayer of thanksgiving:

The Lord be with you.
And also with you.

Lift up your hearts.
We lift them to the Lord.

Let us give thanks to the Lord our God.
It is right to give our thanks and praise.

Father, it is our joy and delight,
our reason for being,
to offer you thanks and praise.

All your actions show wisdom and love.
Through your Word you spoke creation into existence
and made us in your image and likeness.
When we disobeyed you and drew away from you,
you did not leave us in darkness
but sent your Son, the Word made flesh,
to be the light of the world.

Emptying himself of all but love,
he was born of Mary,
shared our human nature and died on the cross.

Yet you have raised him from death to eternal life;
and through him you have sent your holy and
life-giving Spirit
to make us your people, a people of light,
to reflect your glory in all the earth.

And so with angels and archangels
and all the heavenly choir
we join in the unending hymn of praise:

Holy, holy, holy Lord,
God of power and might.
Heaven and earth are full of your glory.
Hosanna in the highest.
Blessèd is he who comes in the name of the Lord.
Hosanna in the highest.

Holy and redeeming God,
we see your grace and truth in Jesus Christ our Lord,
who, on the night in which he was betrayed,
took bread, gave thanks, broke it,
and gave it to his disciples, saying,
'Take this and eat it.
This is my body given for you.
Do this in remembrance of me.'

In the same way, after supper,
he took the cup, gave thanks,
and gave it to them, saying,
'Drink from it all of you.
This is my blood of the new covenant,
poured out for you and for many,
for the forgiveness of sins.
Do this, whenever you drink it,
in remembrance of me.'

Christ is born.
The Saviour has come.
God is with us.

And so, Father, we remember and celebrate
all that Christ has done for us.
Send your Holy Spirit
that these gifts of bread and wine
may be for us the body and blood of Christ.

Through him we give ourselves to you.
May your Spirit draw us together
in the one body of Christ,
that we may have life in all its fullness,
live in your love,
and fill creation with a song of never-ending praise.

We ask this through your Son,
Jesus Christ our Lord.

**Through him, with him, and in him,
in the unity of the Holy Spirit,
all honour and glory be given to you,
almighty Father,
throughout all ages. Amen.**

THE BREAKING OF THE BREAD

*22 The presiding minister breaks the bread in the sight of the people in silence, or saying:

Christ is the bread of life.
Christ is the light of the world.

**God here among us,
light in the midst of us,
bring us light and life.**

*23 Silence, all seated or kneeling

THE SHARING OF THE BREAD AND WINE

*24 The presiding minister, those assisting with the distribution, and the people receive, according to local custom.

The presiding minister may say these or other words of invitation:

Christ is the true bread from heaven.
Whoever eats this bread will live for ever.

Draw near with faith.

*25 Words such as the following are said during the distribution:

The body of Christ given for you. **Amen.**

The blood of Christ shed for you. **Amen.**

26 During the distribution there may be appropriate music.

*27 The elements that remain are covered with a white cloth.

PRAYERS AND DISMISSAL

28 Silence

29 Let us pray.

**Father of all,
we give you thanks and praise,
that when we were still far off
you met us in your Son and brought us home.
Dying and living,
he declared your love, gave us grace, and opened the gate of glory.
May we who share Christ's body live his risen life;
we who drink his cup bring life to others;
we whom the Spirit lights give light to the world.
Keep us firm in the hope that you have set before us,
so we and all your children shall be free,
and the whole earth live to praise your name;
through Jesus Christ our Lord. Amen.**

30 Hymn

31 The presiding minister says:

May he, who by his incarnation
gathered into one things earthly and heavenly,
fill *your/our* lives with his light and joy and peace;
and the blessing of God,
the Father, the Son and the Holy Spirit,
remain with *you/us* always. **Amen.**

*32 The presiding minister says:

We go in the peace of Christ.

Thanks be to God.

HOLY COMMUNION
FOR ASH WEDNESDAY
(or for the First Sunday in Lent)

NOTES

1 This service is intended primarily for use on Ash Wednesday. Where this is not possible it may be used on the First Sunday in Lent.

2 The ceremony of ashes, a sign of repentance and a symbol of mortality, is an option within the service and, when included, is optional for members of the congregation.

3 It is customary, but not essential, to produce the ashes by burning the palm crosses of the previous year. This may be done before or during the service. The ashes should be placed in a bowl on or near the communion table.

THE GATHERING OF THE PEOPLE OF GOD

* 1 The presiding minister says:

Grace and peace to you from God our Father
and the Lord Jesus Christ.

2 Hymn

* 3 Sisters and brothers in Christ, since early days Christians have observed with great devotion the time of our Lord's passion, death and resurrection. It is the custom of the Church to prepare for this by a season of penitence and self-denial.

At first, this season of Lent was observed by those being prepared for Baptism at Easter and by those seeking restoration to the Church's fellowship. In the course of time, all Christians were invited to keep these days carefully, to take to heart the call to repentance, to receive the assurance of forgiveness proclaimed in the Gospel, and so to grow in faith and devotion to our Lord.

In the name of Christ, therefore, I invite you to observe this holy season of Lent, by prayer, self-denial and charitable giving; by self-examination and repentance; and by reading and meditating on God's word.

4 *Saviour of the World*

Jesus, Saviour of the world,
come to us in your mercy:
we look to you to save and help us.

By your cross and your life laid down
you set your people free:
we look to you to save and help us.

When they were ready to perish
you saved your disciples:
we look to you to come to our help.

In the greatness of your mercy
loose us from our chains:
forgive the sins of all your people.

Make yourself known
as our saviour and mighty deliverer:
save and help us that we may praise you.

Come now and dwell with us, Lord Christ Jesus:
hear our prayer and be with us always.

And when you come in your glory:
make us to be one with you
and to share the life of your kingdom.

* 5 This or some other Lenten collect:

Let us pray.

Almighty and merciful God,
you hate nothing that you have made,
and forgive the sins of all who are penitent.
Create in us new and contrite hearts,
so that when we turn to you
and confess our sins
we may receive
your full and perfect forgiveness;
through Jesus Christ our Lord. **Amen.**

THE MINISTRY OF THE WORD

* In addition to the Psalm, either two or three readings from scripture follow, the last of which is the Gospel.

6 Old Testament reading

* 7 Psalm 51 is said or sung:

**Have mercy on me, O God,
in your constant love;
in the fullness of your mercy
blot out my offences.
Wash away all my guilt,
and cleanse me from my sin.
Create in me a clean heart, O God,
and renew a right spirit within me.
Give me the joy of your help again
and strengthen me with a willing spirit.**

8 Epistle

9 Hymn

*10 A reading from the Gospel according to . . .

Hear the Gospel of Christ.
Glory to Christ our Saviour.

The Gospel is read.

This is the Gospel of Christ.
Praise to Christ our Lord.

*11 Sermon

12 The Ten Commandments

Hear the commandments
which God has given to his people:

I am the Lord your God;
you shall have no other gods besides me.

You shall not idolize anything God has made.

You shall not dishonour
the name of the Lord your God.

Remember the Lord's Day and keep it holy.

Lord, have mercy on us:
and turn our hearts to delight in your law.

Honour your father and your mother.

You shall not murder.

You shall not commit adultery.

You shall not steal.

You shall not give false evidence.

You shall not set your heart
on anything that is your neighbour's.

Lord, have mercy on us:
and turn our hearts to delight in your law.

THE ACT OF PENITENCE

*13 Silence

14 Let us pray.

Holy and merciful God,
we confess to you,
and to one another,
in communion with all the saints,
that we have sinned through our own fault
in thought, and word, and deed;
in what we have done
and in what we have failed to do.

We have not loved you with all our heart, soul, mind and strength.
We have not loved our neighbours as ourselves.
We have not loved one another as Christ has loved us.
We have not forgiven others as we have been forgiven.
We have grieved your Holy Spirit.

Lord, have mercy.
Christ, have mercy.

We confess to you, O God, all our past unfaithfulness:
the pride, hypocrisy and impatience of our lives,
our self-indulgence and our exploitation of other people.

Lord, have mercy.
Christ, have mercy.

We confess our preoccupation with worldly goods and comforts,
and our envy of others.

Lord, have mercy.
Christ, have mercy.

We confess our blindness to human need and suffering,
our indifference to injustice and cruelty,
our misuse and pollution of creation,
and our lack of concern for the generations to come.

Lord, have mercy.
Christ, have mercy.

We confess our negligence in prayer and worship,
and our failure to commend the faith that is in us.

Lord, have mercy.
Christ, have mercy.

*15 Silence

16 If there is to be an ashing ceremony, the presiding minister says:

Let us pray.

Almighty God,
you create us from the dust of the earth.
Let these ashes be for us
a sign of our repentance
and a symbol of our mortality.
May we always remember
that by your grace alone
we are given eternal life;
through Jesus Christ our Lord. **Amen.**

In the name of Christ,
I invite you to receive on your forehead
the sign of the cross.

The presiding minister first receives the sign of the cross in ash from an assistant. Those who wish come forward. At each signing these words are said:

Remember that you are dust and to dust you shall return.

Turn away from sin and be faithful to Christ.

During the ashing silence may be kept or there may be appropriate music.

*17 The presiding minister says:

EITHER

The almighty and most
merciful God
grant you pardon,
forgiveness of all your sins,
time for true repentance
and amendment of life,
and the grace and comfort
of the Holy Spirit. **Amen.**

OR

May almighty God
have mercy on us,
forgive us our sins,
and keep us in life eternal.
Amen.

*18 The service continues from no. 15 in ***Holy Communion for Lent and Passiontide*** (page 152).

HOLY COMMUNION
FOR LENT AND PASSIONTIDE

THE GATHERING OF THE PEOPLE OF GOD

* 1 The presiding minister says:

Grace and peace to you from God our Father
and the Lord Jesus Christ.

2 Hymn

3 The commandments of the Lord Jesus may be read.

Our Lord Jesus Christ said: 'The first commandment is, "Hear, O Israel: the Lord our God, the Lord is one; you shall love the Lord your God with all your heart, and with all your soul, and with all your mind, and with all your strength." The second is this, "You shall love your neighbour as yourself." There is no other commandment greater than these.' 'I give you a new commandment, that you love one another. Just as I have loved you, you also should love one another.'

Amen. Lord, have mercy.

* 4 The presiding minister says:

Let us pray.

Lord, you are steadfast in your love
and infinite in your mercy;
you welcome sinners
and invite them to be your guests.
We confess our sins,
trusting in you to forgive us.

Silence

We have yielded to temptation and sinned:

Lord, have mercy.
Lord, have mercy.

We have turned from our neighbours in their need:

Christ, have mercy.
Christ, have mercy.

We have resisted your word in our hearts:

Lord, have mercy.
Lord, have mercy.

EITHER

The almighty and most
merciful God
grant you pardon,
forgiveness of all your sins,
time for true repentance
and amendment of life,
and the grace and comfort
of the Holy Spirit. **Amen.**

OR

May almighty God
have mercy on us,
forgive us our sins,
and keep us in life eternal.
Amen.

* 5 The collect of the day, or one of the following or some other prayer:

Until the Fifth Sunday in Lent:

Almighty God,
whose Son Jesus Christ
fasted forty days in the wilderness
and was tempted as we are, yet without sin:
give us grace to discipline ourselves
in obedience to your Spirit;
and, as you know our weakness,
so may we know your power to save;
through Jesus Christ our Lord. **Amen.**

From the Fifth Sunday in Lent:

Most merciful God,
who by the death and resurrection
of your Son Jesus Christ
delivered and saved the world:
grant that by faith in him
who suffered on the cross,
we may triumph in the power of his victory;
through Jesus Christ our Lord. **Amen.**

6 Hymn or ***Saviour of the World***

Jesus, Saviour of the world,
come to us in your mercy:
we look to you to save and help us.

By your cross and your life laid down
you set your people free:
we look to you to save and help us.

When they were ready to perish
you saved your disciples:
we look to you to come to our help.

In the greatness of your mercy
loose us from our chains:
forgive the sins of all your people.

Make yourself known
as our saviour and mighty deliverer:
save and help us that we may praise you.

Come now and dwell with us, Lord Christ Jesus:
hear our prayer and be with us always.

And when you come in your glory:
make us to be one with you
and to share the life of your kingdom.

THE MINISTRY OF THE WORD

* Either two or three readings from scripture follow, the last of which is the Gospel.

7 Old Testament reading

8 A Psalm or portion of a Psalm may be said or sung.

9 Epistle

10 Hymn

*11 A reading from the Gospel according to . . .

Hear the Gospel of Christ.
Glory to Christ our Saviour.

The Gospel is read.

This is the Gospel of Christ.
Praise to Christ our Lord.

*12 Sermon

13 Affirmation of Faith: The Apostles' Creed

All stand.

I believe in God, the Father almighty,
creator of heaven and earth.

I believe in Jesus Christ,
God's only Son, our Lord,
who was conceived by the Holy Spirit,
born of the Virgin Mary,
suffered under Pontius Pilate,
was crucified, died, and was buried;
he descended to the dead.
On the third day he rose again,
he ascended into heaven,
he is seated at the right hand of the Father,
and he will come to judge the living and the dead.

I believe in the Holy Spirit,
the holy catholic Church,
the communion of saints,
the forgiveness of sins,
the resurrection of the body,
and the life everlasting. Amen.

14 Hymn

*15 These or some other prayers of intercession:

Let us pray for the Church of God throughout the world, for . . . and for . . .

Lord, hear us.
Lord, graciously hear us.

Let us pray for those who have power and influence and for all who govern the nations, for . . . and for . . .

Lord, hear us.
Lord, graciously hear us.

Let us pray for the powerless, for all victims of famine and war, and for all who strive for justice and peace, for . . . and for . . .

Lord, hear us.
Lord, graciously hear us.

Let us pray for the afflicted and sorrowful and for all who need our prayers, for . . . and for . . .

Lord, hear us.
Lord, graciously hear us.

Let us remember before God those who have passed from this life in faith and obedience, giving thanks for . . . and for . . .

Lord, hear us.
Lord, graciously hear us.

Eternal God,
through the self-offering of your Son
you have filled our lives with your presence.
Help us in our sufferings and trials
and strengthen us in our weakness;
through Jesus Christ our Lord. **Amen.**

THE LORD'S SUPPER

16 The Peace

All stand.

In Christ, God was pleased to reconcile to himself all things, whether on earth or in heaven, by making peace through his blood which was shed on the cross.

The peace of the Lord be always with you.
And also with you.

THE PREPARATION OF THE GIFTS

17 Hymn

*18 The offerings of the people are presented. Bread and wine are brought to the table (or if already on the table are uncovered). The presiding minister takes the bread and wine and prepares them for use.

THE THANKSGIVING

*19 All stand.

The presiding minister leads the great prayer of thanksgiving:

The Lord be with you.
And also with you.

Lift up your hearts.
We lift them to the Lord.

Let us give thanks to the Lord our God.
It is right to give our thanks and praise.

Blessing and praise belong to you,
gracious and eternal God.

Through your living Word
you created all things,
the majesty of the heavens
and the glory of the earth.
In your wisdom and goodness
you have made all people
in your image and likeness.

Therefore with saints and angels
and with all creation
we lift up our voices
to proclaim the glory of your name:

Holy, holy, holy Lord,
God of power and might,
heaven and earth are full of your glory.
Hosanna in the highest.
Blessèd is he who comes in the name of the Lord.
Hosanna in the highest.

Holy and gracious God,
we give you thanks and praise
that in the fullness of time
you gave your only Son
to share our human nature
and to be tempted in every way as we are,
yet without sin;
to set his face resolutely towards Jerusalem
and to be lifted high upon the cross,
that he might draw all creation to himself.

When the hour of his glory came,
and loving his own to the end,
he sat with them at supper,
took bread and, after giving thanks to you,
he broke it and gave it to his disciples, saying,
'Take, eat. This is my body which is for you.
Do this in remembrance of me.'

In the same way
he took the cup after supper, saying,
'Drink from this, all of you;
this cup is the new covenant in my blood.
Do this, whenever you drink it,
in remembrance of me.'

Dying, you destroyed our death.
Rising, you restored our life.
Lord Jesus, come in glory.

In obedience to his command
we recall his suffering and death,
his resurrection and ascension,
and we look for his coming in glory.

Send your Holy Spirit
that these gifts of bread and wine
may be for us the body and blood of Christ.

In union with Christ's offering for us,
we offer ourselves as a holy and living sacrifice.
Unite us in love and peace with all your people
until, with the whole company of heaven,
we are brought into the presence of your eternal glory,
through Jesus Christ our Lord.

Through him, with him, and in him,
in the unity of the Holy Spirit,
all honour and glory are yours,
almighty Father, now and for ever. Amen.

*20 The Lord's Prayer

EITHER

We say together the prayer that Jesus gave us:

**Our Father in heaven,
hallowed be your Name,
your kingdom come,
your will be done,
on earth as in heaven.
Give us today our daily bread.
Forgive us our sins
as we forgive those who sin against us.
Save us from the time of trial
and deliver us from evil.
For the kingdom, the power and the glory are yours,
now and for ever. Amen.**

OR

As our Saviour taught his disciples, we pray:

**Our Father, who art in heaven,
hallowed be thy Name;
thy kingdom come;
thy will be done;
on earth as it is in heaven.
Give us this day our daily bread.
And forgive us our trespasses,
as we forgive those who trespass against us.
And lead us not into temptation;
but deliver us from evil.
For thine is the kingdom, the power, and the glory,
for ever and ever. Amen.**

THE BREAKING OF THE BREAD

*21 The presiding minister breaks the bread in the sight of the people in silence, or saying:

The bread we break is a sharing in the body of Christ.
Christ is the Bread of Life.

The presiding minister may lift the cup in silence, or saying:

The cup we take is a sharing in the blood of Christ.
Christ is the true Vine.

*22 Silence, all seated or kneeling

23 **Jesus, Lamb of God, have mercy on us.**
Jesus, bearer of our sins, have mercy on us.
Jesus, redeemer of the world, grant us peace.

24 EITHER

Let us pray.

We do not presume
to come to this your table,
merciful Lord,
trusting in our own righteousness,
but in your manifold and great mercies.
We are not worthy
so much as to gather up the crumbs under your table.
But you are the same Lord
whose nature is always to have mercy.
Grant us therefore, gracious Lord,
so to eat the flesh
of your dear Son Jesus Christ,
and to drink his blood,
that we may evermore dwell in him
and he in us. Amen.

OR

We say together:

Lord, we come to your table,
trusting in your mercy
and not in any goodness of our own.
We are not worthy
even to gather up the crumbs under your table,
but it is your nature
always to have mercy,
and on that we depend.
So feed us
with the body and blood
of Jesus Christ, your Son,
that we may for ever
live in him and he in us.
Amen.

THE SHARING OF THE BREAD AND WINE

*25 The presiding minister, those assisting with the distribution, and the people receive, according to local custom.

The presiding minister may say these or other words of invitation:

EITHER

Receive this holy sacrament
of the body and blood of Christ
and feed on the Lamb of God
with reverence and with faith.

OR

Come to this sacred table,
not because you must but because you may;
come, not to declare that you are righteous,
but that you desire to be true disciples of our Lord Jesus Christ:
come, not because you are strong,
but because you are weak;
not because you have any claim on heaven's rewards,
but because in your frailty and sin
you stand in constant need of heaven's mercy and help.

*26 Words such as the following are said during the distribution:

The body of Christ given for you. **Amen.**

The blood of Christ shed for you. **Amen.**

*27 The elements that remain are covered with a white cloth.

PRAYERS AND DISMISSAL

28 Silence

29 **Gracious God,
we thank you that you have nourished us
with the bread of life
and with the cup of salvation.
May we who have received this sacrament
be strengthened in your service;
we who have sung your praises
live in your glory;
and we who have known
the greatness of your love
see you face to face in your kingdom;
through Jesus Christ our Lord. Amen.**

30 Hymn

31 The presiding minister says:

The God of all grace
who has called *you/us* to eternal glory in Christ,
make *you/us* perfect,
confirming and strengthening *you/us;*
and to him be the power for ever and ever. **Amen.**

The almighty and merciful Lord,
the Father, the Son and the Holy Spirit,
bless *you/us* and keep *you/us*,
now and always. **Amen.**

*32 The presiding minister says:

Go in peace to love and serve the Lord.

In the name of Christ. Amen.

HOLY COMMUNION FOR THE EASTER SEASON (including ASCENSIONTIDE)

THE GATHERING OF THE PEOPLE OF GOD

* 1 The presiding minister says:

Alleluia! Christ is risen!
He is risen indeed! Alleluia!

or, from the Sixth Sunday of Easter:

Alleluia! The Lord reigns!
Let the earth rejoice! Alleluia!

2 Hymn

3 Let us pray.

Glory to you, O God:
you raised Jesus from the grave,
bringing us victory over death
and giving us eternal life.

Glory to you, O Christ:
for us and for our salvation
you overcame death
and opened the gate to everlasting life.

Glory to you, O Holy Spirit:
you lead us into the truth
and breathe new life into us.

Glory to you, Father, Son and Holy Spirit,
now and for ever. **Amen.**

4 The presiding minister says:

If we have fallen into despair,
Lord, forgive us.

If we have failed to hope in you,
Lord, forgive us.

If we have been fearful of death,
Lord, forgive us.

If we have forgotten the victory of Christ,
Lord, forgive us.

Silence

May the living God
raise *you/us* from despair,
give *you/us* victory over sin
and set *you/us* free in Christ. **Amen.**

* 5 The collect

On Easter Day:

Lord of all life and power,
who through the mighty resurrection of your Son
overcame the old order of sin and death
to make all things new in him:
grant that we, being dead to sin
and alive to you in Jesus Christ,
may reign with him in glory;
to whom with you in the unity of the Holy Spirit
be praise and honour, glory and might,
now and in all eternity. **Amen.**

On other days of the Easter season before the Sixth Sunday of Easter, the collect of the day, or this or some other prayer:

Almighty God,
of your own free goodness and mercy
you have created us,
and through the resurrection
of your only-begotten Son
you have given us hope;
guard us by your love
and, in your wisdom, keep us in eternal life;
through Jesus Christ our Lord. **Amen.**

From the Sixth Sunday of Easter to the Saturday before Pentecost, the collect of the day, or this or some other prayer:

Almighty God,
you have exalted your only Son, Jesus Christ,
with great triumph to your kingdom in heaven.
Mercifully give us faith
to know that, as he promised,
he abides with us on earth to the end of time,
who is alive and reigns
with you and the Holy Spirit,
one God now and for ever. **Amen.**

* 6 EITHER ***Glory to God in the highest***

**Glory to God in the highest,
and peace to God's people on earth.**

**Lord God, heavenly King,
almighty God and Father,
we worship you, we give you thanks,
we praise you for your glory.**

**Lord Jesus Christ, only Son of the Father,
Lord God, Lamb of God,
you take away the sin of the world:
have mercy on us.
You are seated at the right hand of the Father:
receive our prayer.**

**For you alone are the Holy One,
you alone are the Lord,
you alone are the Most High, Jesus Christ,
with the Holy Spirit,
in the glory of God the Father. Amen.**

OR (before the Sixth Sunday of Easter) ***A Song of Resurrection***

Christ our Passover has been sacrificed for us,
so let us celebrate the feast,

not with the old leaven
of corruption and wickedness,
but with the unleavened bread
of sincerity and truth.

Christ once raised from the dead dies no more;
death has no more dominion over him.

In dying, he died to sin once for all;
In living, he lives to God.

See yourselves therefore as dead to sin
and alive to God in Jesus Christ our Lord.

Christ has been raised from the dead;
the firstfruits of those who sleep.

For as by one man came death,
by another has come also the resurrection of the dead.

For as in Adam all die,
even so in Christ shall all be made alive.

Glory to the Father, and to the Son,
and to the Holy Spirit:
as it was in the beginning, is now,
and shall be for ever. Amen.

OR (from the Sixth Sunday of Easter) ***A Song of Christ's Glory***

Christ Jesus was in the form of God,
but he did not cling to equality with God.

**He emptied himself,
taking the form of a servant,
and was born in our human likeness.
Being found in human form,
he humbled himself
and became obedient unto death,
even death on a cross.
Therefore, God has highly exalted him,
and bestowed on him the name above every name,
that at the name of Jesus every knee shall bow,
in heaven and on earth and under the earth,
and every tongue confess that Jesus Christ is Lord,
to the glory of God the Father.**

OR a hymn

THE MINISTRY OF THE WORD

* Either two or three readings from scripture follow, the last of which is the Gospel.

7 Reading from Acts or Old Testament reading

8 A Psalm or portion of a Psalm may be said or sung.

9 Epistle

10 Hymn

*11 A reading from the Gospel according to . . .

Alleluia! Hear the Gospel of Christ.
Glory to Christ our Saviour. Alleluia!

The Gospel is read.

Alleluia! This is the Gospel of Christ.
Praise to Christ our Lord. Alleluia!

*12 Sermon

13 Hymn

*14 These or some other prayers of intercession:

In the power of the resurrection we offer our prayers to God.

Let us pray.

Remember, O Lord, in your love
the Church throughout the world . . .
those recently baptized and confirmed . . .
those who minister to others . . .

Silence

May your whole Church know your power and be a sign that Christ is risen.

Lord of life,
hear us in your love.

Remember in your love the world you have made . . .
those who seek a fair and proper use of the world's resources . . .
those who strive for justice and peace among the nations . . .

Silence

May the whole earth be transformed by mercy and rejoice in hope.

Lord of life,
hear us in your love.

Remember in your love those who suffer . . .
the victims of violence and injustice . . .
those who mourn . . .

Silence

May all in need find comfort, strength and freedom in the living Christ.

Lord of life,
hear us in your love.

Remember in your love those who have died:
those who have confessed the faith
and those whose faith is known to you alone.

Silence

May all your children receive grace and light according to their needs and come at last to share with all the saints in life eternal.

Lord of life,
hear us in your love.

Gracious God, we ask these prayers through Jesus Christ, our risen Lord and Saviour. **Amen.**

*15 The Lord's Prayer

EITHER

We say together the prayer that Jesus gave us:

**Our Father in heaven,
hallowed be your Name,
your kingdom come,
your will be done,
on earth as in heaven.
Give us today our daily bread.
Forgive us our sins
as we forgive those who sin against us.
Save us from the time of trial
and deliver us from evil.
For the kingdom, the power and the glory are yours,
now and for ever. Amen.**

OR

As our Saviour taught his disciples, we pray:

**Our Father, who art in heaven,
hallowed be thy Name;
thy kingdom come;
thy will be done;
on earth as it is in heaven.
Give us this day our daily bread.
And forgive us our trespasses,
as we forgive those who trespass against us.
And lead us not into temptation;
but deliver us from evil.
For thine is the kingdom, the power, and the glory,
for ever and ever. Amen.**

16 The Nicene Creed

All stand.

Let us profess the faith of the Church.

**We believe in one God,
the Father, the Almighty,
maker of heaven and earth,
of all that is, seen and unseen.**

**We believe in one Lord, Jesus Christ,
the only Son of God,
eternally begotten of the Father,
God from God, Light from Light,
true God from true God,
begotten, not made,
of one Being with the Father;
through him all things were made.
For us and for our salvation
he came down from heaven,
was incarnate of the Holy Spirit and the Virgin Mary
and became truly human.
For our sake he was crucified under Pontius Pilate;
he suffered death and was buried.
On the third day he rose again
in accordance with the Scriptures;
he ascended into heaven
and is seated at the right hand of the Father.
He will come again in glory to judge the living and the dead,
and his kingdom will have no end.**

**We believe in the Holy Spirit, the Lord, the giver of life,
who proceeds from the Father and the Son,
who with the Father and the Son is worshipped and glorified,
who has spoken through the prophets.
We believe in one holy catholic and apostolic Church.
We acknowledge one Baptism for the forgiveness of sins.
We look for the resurrection of the dead,
and the life of the world to come. Amen.**

THE LORD'S SUPPER

*17 The Peace

All stand.

The risen Christ came and stood among his disciples and said: 'Peace be with you!'

Then they were glad when they saw the Lord.

Alleluia! The peace of the risen Christ be always with you.
And also with you. Alleluia!

The people may greet one another in the name of the risen Lord.

THE PREPARATION OF THE GIFTS

18 Hymn

*19 The offerings of the people are presented. Bread and wine are brought to the table (or if already on the table are uncovered).

The presiding minister takes the bread and lifts it in the sight of the people, saying:

Here is bread, God's good gift.
It will become for us the bread of life.

The presiding minister takes the cup and lifts it in the sight of the people, saying:

Here is wine, God's good gift.
It will become for us the cup of salvation.

THE THANKSGIVING

*20 All stand.

The presiding minister leads the great prayer of thanksgiving:

The Lord be with you.
And also with you.

Lift up your hearts.
We lift them to the Lord.

Let us give thanks to the Lord our God.
It is right to give our thanks and praise.

Blessing and honour, glory and power,
are rightly yours, all-gracious God.
By your creative word
you brought the world to birth;
in your generous love
you made the human family,
that we might see your glory
and live for ever in your presence.

**Blessing and honour, glory and power,
are rightly yours, all-gracious God.**

When we wandered from you in our sin
you sought us with your steadfast love
and did not give us up.
In the fullness of time you sent your Son
to be our Saviour and Deliverer.
Made of flesh and blood, he lived our life
and died our death upon the cross.
Death could not hold him
and now he reigns at your right hand.

**Blessing and honour, glory and power,
are rightly yours, all-gracious God.**

Therefore with angels and archangels
and all the company of heaven
we bless and praise your glorious name, saying:

Holy, holy, holy Lord,
God of power and might,
Heaven and earth are full of your glory.
Hosanna in the highest.
Blessèd is he who comes in the name of the Lord.
Hosanna in the highest.

Blessèd indeed is the Lord Jesus Christ
who, at supper with his friends,
took bread and gave you thanks,
broke it, gave it to them and said:
'Take this, all of you, and eat it.
This is my body given for you.
Do this in remembrance of me.'

When supper was ended,
he took the cup and gave you thanks,
gave it to them, and said:
'Drink from it all of you.
This is my blood of the new covenant,
poured out for you and for everyone,
for the forgiveness of sins.
Do this in remembrance of me.'

Dying, you destroyed our death.
Rising, you restored our life.
Lord Jesus, come in glory.

Therefore, Father,
we celebrate this Passover of gladness;
for as in Adam all die,
even so in Christ shall all be made alive.
Accept, through him, our great high priest,
this, our sacrifice of praise.

Send your Holy Spirit
that these gifts of bread and wine
may be for us the body and the blood of Christ.
Gather us, who share this feast,
into the kingdom of your glory
that with all your people in every time and place
we may praise and worship you for ever;
through Jesus Christ our Lord,

**by whom and with whom
in the unity of the Holy Spirit,
all honour and glory are yours,
heavenly Father, now and always. Amen.**

THE BREAKING OF THE BREAD

*21 The presiding minister breaks the bread in the sight of the people in silence, or saying:

Alleluia! Christ our Passover is sacrificed for us.
Therefore let us keep the feast. Alleluia!

OR, after the Sixth Sunday of Easter:

The things of God for God's holy people.

**Jesus Christ is holy;
Jesus Christ is Lord.
Glory to God the Father.**

*22 Silence, all seated or kneeling

THE SHARING OF THE BREAD AND WINE

*23 The presiding minister, those assisting with the distribution, and the people receive, according to local custom.

The presiding minister may say these or other words of invitation:

We meet the risen Christ in the breaking of the bread.

Draw near with faith.

*24 Words such as the following are said during the distribution:

The body of Christ keep you in eternal life. **Amen.**

The blood of Christ keep you in eternal life. **Amen.**

25 During the distribution there may be appropriate music.

*26 The elements that remain are covered with a white cloth.

PRAYERS AND DISMISSAL

*27 Silence

28 Let us pray.

EITHER

A **God of our salvation,
we thank you for our communion with the risen Christ
and with all who love him in earth and heaven.
We pray that, strengthened by his grace,
we may serve you faithfully all our days;
through Jesus Christ our Lord. Amen.**

OR

B **Lord our God, we give you thanks
because you have delivered us from the power of darkness
and brought us into the kingdom of your Son.
Grant that, as by his resurrection
we are brought to new life,
so by his continued reign in us
we may be brought to eternal joy;
through the same Christ our Lord. Amen.**

29 Hymn

30 The presiding minister says:

EITHER (before the Sixth Sunday of Easter)

A God the Father,
by whose glory Christ was raised from the dead,
strengthen *you/us*
to walk with him in his risen life;
and may almighty God bless *you/us*,
the Father, the Son and the Holy Spirit. **Amen.**

OR (from the Sixth Sunday of Easter)

B Christ our King
make *you/us* faithful and strong to do his will
that *you/we* may reign with him in glory;
and may almighty God bless *you/us*,
the Father, the Son and the Holy Spirit. **Amen.**

*31 The presiding minister says:

Alleluia!
Go in joy and peace to love and serve the Lord.

In the name of Christ. Alleluia!

HOLY COMMUNION
FOR THE DAY OF PENTECOST
and Times of Renewal in the Life of the Church

THE GATHERING OF THE PEOPLE OF GOD

* 1 The presiding minister says:

God declares:
I will pour out my Spirit on all flesh.
Then everyone who calls on the name of the Lord shall be saved.

2 Hymn

3 Let us pray.

Come, Holy Spirit,
fill the hearts of your faithful people,
and kindle in us the fire of your love;
through Jesus Christ our Lord. Amen.

4 The presiding minister says:

Let us confess our sins to God.

Silence

Gracious and holy God,
we confess that we have sinned
against you and against our neighbour.
Your Spirit gives light,
but we have preferred darkness;
your Spirit gives wisdom,
but we have been foolish;
your Spirit gives power,
but we have trusted in our own strength.
For the sake of Jesus Christ, your Son,
forgive our sins,
and enable us by your Spirit
to serve you in joyful obedience,
to the glory of your Name. Amen.

There is now no condemnation
for those who live in union with Christ Jesus;
for the law of the Spirit of life
has set us free from the law of sin and death.

Amen. Thanks be to God.

* 5 The collect of the day, or this or some other prayer:

Faithful God,
you fulfilled the promise of Easter
by sending your Holy Spirit
and opening the way of eternal life
to all the human race.
Keep us in the unity of your Spirit,
that every tongue may tell of your glory;
through Jesus Christ our Lord,
who is alive and reigns with you,
in the unity of the Holy Spirit,
one God, now and for ever. **Amen.**

6 Hymn or ***Glory to God in the highest***

**Glory to God in the highest,
and peace to God's people on earth.**

**Lord God, heavenly King,
almighty God and Father,
we worship you, we give you thanks,
we praise you for your glory.**

**Lord Jesus Christ, only Son of the Father,
Lord God, Lamb of God,
you take away the sin of the world:
have mercy on us.
You are seated at the right hand of the Father:
receive our prayer.**

**For you alone are the Holy One,
you alone are the Lord,
you alone are the Most High, Jesus Christ,
with the Holy Spirit,
in the glory of God the Father. Amen.**

THE MINISTRY OF THE WORD

* Either two or three readings from scripture follow, the last of which is the Gospel.

7 Old Testament reading or, on the Day of Pentecost, a reading from Acts.

8 A Psalm or portion of a Psalm may be said or sung.

9 Epistle

10 Hymn

*11 A reading from the Gospel according to . . .

Hear the Gospel of Christ.
Glory to Christ our Saviour.

The Gospel is read.

This is the Gospel of Christ.
Praise to Christ our Lord.

*12 Sermon

13 There may be a time of quiet reflection or testimony.

*14 These or some other prayers of intercession:

Gracious God,
whose Spirit helps us in our weakness
and guides us in our prayers,
we pray for the Church and for the world
in the name of Jesus Christ.

Renew the life and faith of the Church;
strengthen our witness;
and make us one in Christ . . .
Grant that we and all who confess that Christ is Lord
may be faithful in your service
and filled with the Spirit,
that the world may be turned to you.

Lord, in your mercy,
hear our prayer.

Guide the nations
in the ways of justice, liberty and peace;
and help them to seek
the unity and welfare of all people . . .
Give to all in authority
wisdom to know and strength to do what is right.

Lord, in your mercy,
hear our prayer.

Comfort those in sorrow;
heal the sick in body or in mind
and deliver the oppressed . . .
Grant us compassion for all who suffer,
and help us so to carry one another's burdens
that we may fulfil the law of Christ.

Lord, in your mercy,
hear our prayer.

Receive our thanks and praise
for all who have served you faithfully here on earth,
and especially those who have revealed to us
your grace in Christ . . .
May we and all your people
share the life and joy of your kingdom;
through Jesus Christ our Lord. **Amen.**

15 The Peace

All stand.

We are the Body of Christ.

In the one Spirit
we were all baptized into one body.
Let us therefore keep the unity of the Spirit
in the bond of peace.

The peace of the Lord be always with you.
And also with you.

The people may greet one another in the name of Christ.

16 The Nicene Creed

All stand.

Let us profess the faith of the Church.

**We believe in one God,
the Father, the Almighty,
maker of heaven and earth,
of all that is, seen and unseen.**

**We believe in one Lord, Jesus Christ,
the only Son of God,
eternally begotten of the Father,
God from God, Light from Light,
true God from true God,
begotten, not made,
of one Being with the Father;
through him all things were made.
For us and for our salvation
he came down from heaven,
was incarnate of the Holy Spirit and the Virgin Mary
and became truly human.**

**For our sake he was crucified under Pontius Pilate;
he suffered death and was buried.
On the third day he rose again
in accordance with the Scriptures;
he ascended into heaven
and is seated at the right hand of the Father.
He will come again in glory to judge the living and the dead,
and his kingdom will have no end.**

**We believe in the Holy Spirit, the Lord, the giver of life,
who proceeds from the Father and the Son,
who with the Father and the Son is worshipped and glorified,
who has spoken through the prophets.**

We believe in one holy catholic and apostolic Church.
We acknowledge one Baptism for the forgiveness of sins.
We look for the resurrection of the dead,
and the life of the world to come. Amen.

THE LORD'S SUPPER

THE PREPARATION OF THE GIFTS

17 Hymn

*18 The offerings of the people are presented. Bread and wine are brought to the table (or if already on the table are uncovered). The presiding minister takes the bread and wine and prepares them for use.

THE THANKSGIVING

*19 All stand.

The presiding minister leads the great prayer of thanksgiving:

The Lord be with you.
And also with you.

Lift up your hearts.
We lift them to the Lord.

Let us give thanks to the Lord our God.
It is right to give our thanks and praise.

It is indeed right,
it is our duty and our joy,
gracious and holy Father,
always and everywhere to give you thanks.

In the beginning
your Spirit swept across the face of the waters,
bringing order and beauty out of chaos.
You formed us in your image
and breathed into us the breath of life.

Though we turned away from you,
your love remained steadfast,
and you sent your only Son Jesus Christ
to be the Saviour of the world.

At his Baptism in the Jordan
he was anointed by your Spirit
and revealed as your beloved Son.
In the power of the Spirit
he was sent to preach good news to the poor,
to proclaim release to the captives
and recovery of sight to the blind,
to set at liberty those who are oppressed,
and to announce that the time had come
when you would save your people.

Sharing our human nature,
he died on the cross.
Raised again in glory,
he lives for ever to pray for us.
By the gift of the Spirit,
whom you have sent in his name,
you bring to completion the work of your Son,
leading us into all truth,
making us a people for your praise
and giving us power to proclaim the Gospel
in all the world.

And so, with all the faithful of every time and place,
we join with choirs of angels in the eternal hymn:

Holy, holy, holy Lord,
God of power and might,
heaven and earth are full of your glory.
Hosanna in the highest.
Blessèd is he who comes in the name of the Lord.
Hosanna in the highest.

On the night before he died,
the Lord Jesus took bread and gave you thanks.
He broke it, and gave it to his disciples, saying,
'Take, eat. This is my body, given for you.
Do this in remembrance of me.'

After supper, he took the cup of wine.
He gave thanks, and gave it to them, saying,
'Drink from it, all of you.
This is my blood of the new covenant,
poured out for all people
for the forgiveness of sins.
Do this in remembrance of me.'

And so,
in remembrance of all his mighty acts,
we offer you these gifts,
and with them ourselves
as a holy, living sacrifice.

You send forth your Spirit.
You bind us in love.
You renew the face of the earth.

Pour out your Holy Spirit
that these gifts of bread and wine
may be for us the body and blood of Christ.
Unite us with him and with one another
in mission to all the world;
and bring us with the whole creation
to your heavenly kingdom.

Through Christ, with Christ, in Christ,
in the unity of the Holy Spirit,
all blessing and honour and glory and power
be yours for ever and ever. Amen.

*20 The Lord's Prayer

EITHER

We say together the prayer that Jesus gave us:

Our Father in heaven,
hallowed be your Name,
your kingdom come,
your will be done,
on earth as in heaven.
Give us today our daily bread.
Forgive us our sins
as we forgive those who sin against us.
Save us from the time of trial
and deliver us from evil.
For the kingdom, the power and the glory are yours,
now and for ever. Amen.

OR

As our Saviour taught his disciples, we pray:

Our Father, who art in heaven,
hallowed be thy Name;
thy kingdom come;
thy will be done;
on earth as it is in heaven.
Give us this day our daily bread.
And forgive us our trespasses,
as we forgive those who trespass against us.
And lead us not into temptation;
but deliver us from evil.
For thine is the kingdom, the power, and the glory,
for ever and ever. Amen.

THE BREAKING OF THE BREAD

*21 The presiding minister breaks the bread in the sight of the people in silence, or saying:

On the Day of Pentecost:

Alleluia! Christ our Passover is sacrificed for us.
Therefore let us keep the feast. Alleluia!

At other times:

We break this bread to share in the body of Christ.

Though we are many, we are one body,
because we all share in one bread.

*22 Silence, all seated or kneeling

THE SHARING OF THE BREAD AND WINE

*23 The presiding minister, those assisting with the distribution, and the people receive, according to local custom.

The presiding minister may say these or other words of invitation:

Receive this holy sacrament
of the body and blood of Christ,
and feed on the Lamb of God
with reverence and with faith.

*24 Words such as the following are said during the distribution:

The body of Christ keep you in eternal life. **Amen.**

The blood of Christ keep you in eternal life. **Amen.**

25 During the distribution there may be appropriate music.

*26 The elements that remain are covered with a white cloth.

PRAYERS AND DISMISSAL

27 Silence

28 Let us pray.

**God of power,
may the boldness of your Spirit transform us,
may the gentleness of your Spirit lead us,
and may the gifts of your Spirit equip us
to serve and worship you
now and always. Amen.**

29 Hymn

30 The presiding minister says:

The Spirit of truth lead *you/us* into all truth,
give *you/us* grace to confess that Jesus Christ is Lord,
and to proclaim the word and works of God;
and the blessing of God,
Spirit, Son and Father,
remain with *you/us* always. **Amen.**

*31 The presiding minister says:

We go into the world in the power of the Spirit
to fulfil our high calling as servants of Christ.

Thanks be to God. Amen.

HOLY COMMUNION
DURING ORDINARY SEASONS
(First Service)

NOTE

This service is intended for use (1) in the period which follows the Sunday after Epiphany and precedes Ash Wednesday and (2) in the period which follows the Day of Pentecost and precedes the First Sunday of Advent.

THE GATHERING OF THE PEOPLE OF GOD

* 1 The presiding minister reads a sentence of scripture.

2 Hymn

3 Let us pray.

Almighty God,
to whom all hearts are open,
all desires known,
and from whom no secrets are hidden:
cleanse the thoughts of our hearts
by the inspiration of your Holy Spirit,
that we may perfectly love you,
and worthily magnify your holy Name;
through Christ our Lord. Amen.

* 4 The presiding minister says:

Let us confess our sins to God.

Most merciful God,
we confess that we have sinned against you
in thought and word and deed.
We have not loved you with our whole heart.
We have not loved our neighbours as ourselves.

Silence

In your mercy,

forgive what we have been,
help us to amend what we are,
and direct what we shall be;
that we may delight in your will
and walk in your ways;
through Jesus Christ our Lord. Amen.

If we confess our sins,
God is faithful and just
and will forgive our sins,
and cleanse us from all unrighteousness.
Amen. Thanks be to God.

* 5 The collect of the day, or this or some other prayer:

Gracious God,
whose love for the world is revealed in your Son our
Saviour:
grant that he may live in our hearts by faith,
and be proclaimed in our lives by love;
through the same Jesus Christ our Lord,
to whom with you and the Holy Spirit
be glory and praise, now and for ever. **Amen.**

6 ***Glory to God in the highest***, a hymn, or some other canticle of praise

Glory to God in the highest,
and peace to God's people on earth.

Lord God, heavenly King,
almighty God and Father,
we worship you, we give you thanks,
we praise you for your glory.

Lord Jesus Christ, only Son of the Father,
Lord God, Lamb of God,
you take away the sin of the world:
have mercy on us.
You are seated at the right hand of the Father:
receive our prayer.

For you alone are the Holy One,
you alone are the Lord,
you alone are the Most High, Jesus Christ,
with the Holy Spirit,
in the glory of God the Father. Amen.

THE MINISTRY OF THE WORD

* Either two or three readings from scripture follow, the last of which is the Gospel.

7 Old Testament reading

8 A Psalm or portion of a Psalm may be said or sung.

9 Epistle

10 Hymn

*11 A reading from the Gospel according to . . .

Hear the Gospel of Christ.
Glory to Christ our Saviour.

The Gospel is read.

This is the Gospel of Christ.
Praise to Christ our Lord.

*12 Sermon

13 Hymn

*14 These or some other prayers of intercession:

Let us pray.

God, most gracious and most holy,
grant us the help of your Spirit
as we pray for the Church and the world.

We pray for the Church in every land . . .
for this church and for other local churches . . .
that we may worship and serve you
with reverence and joy.

Silence

Lord, hear us.
Lord, graciously hear us.

We pray for the peoples of the world . . .
and for the leaders of the nations . . .
that all may work together for justice and peace.

Silence

Lord, hear us.
Lord, graciously hear us.

We pray for those who are ill or distressed . . .
for the lonely and the bereaved . . .
and for those in any other need or trouble . . .
that they may be comforted and sustained.

Silence

Lord, hear us.
Lord, graciously hear us.

Father, we remember before you
all your servants who have died in the faith of Christ . . .

We pray that we too may lead faithful and godly lives in this world,
and finally share with all the saints in everlasting joy;
through Jesus Christ our Lord. **Amen.**

*15 The Lord's Prayer

EITHER

We say together the prayer that Jesus gave us:

Our Father in heaven,
hallowed be your Name,
your kingdom come,
your will be done,
on earth as in heaven.
Give us today our daily bread.
Forgive us our sins
as we forgive those who sin against us.
Save us from the time of trial
and deliver us from evil.
For the kingdom, the power and the glory are yours,
now and for ever. Amen.

OR

As our Saviour taught his disciples, we pray:

Our Father, who art in heaven,
hallowed be thy Name;
thy kingdom come;
thy will be done;
on earth as it is in heaven.
Give us this day our daily bread.
And forgive us our trespasses,
as we forgive those who trespass against us.
And lead us not into temptation;
but deliver us from evil.
For thine is the kingdom, the power, and the glory,
for ever and ever. Amen.

16 The Peace

All stand.

We are the Body of Christ.

In the one Spirit
we were all baptized into one body.
Let us therefore keep the unity of the Spirit
in the bond of peace.

The peace of the Lord be always with you.
And also with you.

The people may greet one another in the name of Christ.

17 The Nicene Creed

All stand.

Let us profess the faith of the Church.

**We believe in one God,
the Father, the Almighty,
maker of heaven and earth,
of all that is, seen and unseen.**

**We believe in one Lord, Jesus Christ,
the only Son of God,
eternally begotten of the Father,
God from God, Light from Light,
true God from true God,
begotten, not made,
of one Being with the Father;
through him all things were made.
For us and for our salvation
he came down from heaven,
was incarnate of the Holy Spirit and the Virgin Mary
and became truly human.
For our sake he was crucified under Pontius Pilate;
he suffered death and was buried.
On the third day he rose again
in accordance with the Scriptures;
he ascended into heaven
and is seated at the right hand of the Father.
He will come again in glory to judge the living and the dead,
and his kingdom will have no end.**

**We believe in the Holy Spirit, the Lord, the giver of life,
who proceeds from the Father and the Son,
who with the Father and the Son is worshipped and glorified,
who has spoken through the prophets.
We believe in one holy catholic and apostolic Church.**

We acknowledge one Baptism for the forgiveness of sins.
We look for the resurrection of the dead,
and the life of the world to come. Amen.

THE LORD'S SUPPER

THE PREPARATION OF THE GIFTS

18 Hymn

*19 The offerings of the people are presented. Bread and wine are brought to the table (or if already on the table are uncovered). The presiding minister takes the bread and wine and prepares them for use.

20 Lord and Giver of every good thing,
we bring to you
bread and wine for our communion,
lives and gifts for your kingdom,
all for transformation through your grace and love,
made known in Jesus Christ our Saviour. **Amen.**

THE THANKSGIVING

*21 All stand.

The presiding minister leads the great prayer of thanksgiving:

The Lord be with you.
And also with you.

Lift up your hearts.
We lift them to the Lord.

Let us give thanks to the Lord our God.
It is right to give our thanks and praise.

We praise you, gracious Father,
our Maker and Sustainer.
You created the heavens and the earth
and formed us in your own image.
Though we sinned against you,
your love for us was constant,
and you sent your Son Jesus Christ
to be the Saviour of the world.

Sharing our human nature,
he was born of Mary
and baptized in the Jordan.
He proclaimed your kingdom, by word and deed,
and was put to death upon the cross.
You raised him from the dead;
you exalted him in glory;
and through him you have sent your Holy Spirit,
calling us to be your people,
a community of faith.

ON TRINITY SUNDAY

And now we give you thanks
because you have revealed your glory
as the glory of your Son and of the Holy Spirit:
three persons equal in majesty,
undivided in splendour,
yet one Lord, one God,
ever to be worshipped.
(And so . . .)

ON ALL SAINTS DAY (or for any saint)

And now we give you thanks
for the glorious pledge of the hope of our calling
which you have given us in your saints;
that, following their example
and strengthened by their fellowship,
we may run with perseverance
the race that is set before us,
and with them receive the unfading crown of glory.
(And so . . .)

And so, with angels and archangels
and all the choirs of heaven,
we join in the triumphant hymn:

Holy, holy, holy Lord,
God of power and might,
heaven and earth are full of your glory.
Hosanna in the highest.
Blessèd is he who comes in the name of the Lord.
Hosanna in the highest.

Holy God, we praise you
that on the night in which he was betrayed
our Saviour Christ took bread
and gave you thanks.
He broke it, and gave it to his disciples, saying,
'Take, eat. This is my body, given for you.
Do this in remembrance of me.'

After supper, he took the cup of wine,
gave thanks, and gave it to them, saying,
'Drink from it, all of you.
This is my blood of the new covenant,
poured out for all people
for the forgiveness of sins.
Do this in remembrance of me.'

Remembering, therefore, his death and resurrection,
and proclaiming his eternal sacrifice,
we offer ourselves to you in praise and thanksgiving,
as we declare the mystery of faith:

Christ has died.
Christ is risen.
Christ will come again.

Send down your Holy Spirit
that these gifts of bread and wine
may be for us the body and blood of Christ.
Unite us with him for ever
and bring us with the whole creation
to your eternal kingdom.

Through Christ, with Christ, in Christ,
in the power of the Holy Spirit,
we worship you in songs of everlasting praise.
Blessing and honour and glory and power
be yours for ever and ever. Amen.

THE BREAKING OF THE BREAD

*22 The presiding minister breaks the bread in the sight of the people in silence, or saying:

EITHER

We break this bread to share in the body of Christ.

Though we are many, we are one body,
because we all share in one bread.

OR

The gifts of God for the people of God.
May Jesus Christ be praised!

*23 Silence, all seated or kneeling

24 EITHER

A Jesus, Lamb of God,
have mercy on us.
Jesus, bearer of our sins,
have mercy on us.
Jesus, redeemer of the world,
grant us peace.

OR

B Jesus is the Lamb of God
who takes away the sin of the world.
Happy are those who are called to his supper.

Lord, I am not worthy to receive you,
but only say the word and I shall be healed.

OR

C Let us pray.

We do not presume
to come to this your table, merciful Lord,
trusting in our own righteousness,
but in your manifold and great mercies.
We are not worthy
so much as to gather up the crumbs under your table.
But you are the same Lord
whose nature is always to have mercy.
Grant us therefore, gracious Lord,
so to eat the flesh of your dear Son Jesus Christ
and to drink his blood,
that we may evermore dwell in him
and he in us. Amen.

OR

D We say together:

**Lord, we come to your table,
trusting in your mercy
and not in any goodness of our own.
We are not worthy
even to gather up the crumbs under your table,
but it is your nature always to have mercy,
and on that we depend.
So feed us with the body and blood
of Jesus Christ, your Son,
that we may for ever live in him
and he in us. Amen.**

THE SHARING OF THE BREAD AND WINE

*25 The presiding minister, those assisting with the distribution, and the people receive, according to local custom.

The presiding minister may say these or other words of invitation:

Jesus said: 'I am the bread of life.
Those who come to me shall not hunger
and those who believe in me shall never thirst.'

Draw near with faith.

*26 Words such as the following are said during the distribution:

The body of Christ keep you in eternal life. **Amen.**

The blood of Christ keep you in eternal life. **Amen.**

27 During the distribution there may be appropriate music.

*28 The elements that remain are covered with a white cloth.

PRAYERS AND DISMISSAL

29 Silence

30 Let us pray.

**We thank you, Lord,
that you have fed us in this sacrament,
united us with Christ,
and given us a foretaste of the heavenly banquet
prepared for all people. Amen.**

31 This or some other hymn:

**Love's redeeming work is done,
Alleluia!
Fought the fight, the battle won;
Alleluia!
Vain the stone, the watch, the seal;
Alleluia!
Christ has burst the gates of hell;
Alleluia!**

**Soar we now where Christ has led,
Alleluia!
Following our exalted Head;
Alleluia!
Made like him, like him we rise;
Alleluia!
Ours the cross, the grave, the skies;
Alleluia!**

32 The presiding minister says:

The blessing of God,
the Father, the Son and the Holy Spirit,
remain with *you/us* always. **Amen.**

*33 The presiding minister says:

Go in peace in the power of the Spirit
to live and work to God's praise and glory.

Thanks be to God. Amen.

HOLY COMMUNION
DURING ORDINARY SEASONS
(Second Service)

NOTES

1 This service is intended for use (1) in the period which follows the Sunday after Epiphany and precedes Ash Wednesday and (2) in the period which follows the Day of Pentecost and precedes the First Sunday of Advent.

2 Musical settings other than those printed may be used.

THE GATHERING OF THE PEOPLE OF GOD

* 1 The presiding minister says:

God's grace and peace are with us.
Let our hearts be filled with joy.

2 Hymn

* 3 The presiding minister says:

Let us pray.

**God of mercy,
your love for us is strong,
but our love for you is weak.
You call us to follow Jesus,
but we are slow to obey.
You care for all that you have made,
but we ignore the needs of others
and misuse your creation.
We are sorry for our sins.
Forgive us,
and help us to please you
by the way we live;
through Jesus Christ our Lord. Amen.**

God is love
and forgives our sins through Jesus. **Amen.**

* 4 The collect of the day, or this or some other prayer:

Generous God,
you gave your Son for the life of the whole world.
Give us the joy of knowing the risen Christ,
and let your Holy Spirit guide us,
that we may love and serve you on earth
and live with you for ever in heaven;
through Jesus Christ our Lord. **Amen.**

5 Hymn or one of these versions of ***Glory to God*** or some other act of praise

A

B **Glory to God in the highest,**
and peace to God's people on earth.

Lord God, heavenly King,
almighty God and Father,
we worship you, we give you thanks,
we praise you for your glory.

Lord Jesus Christ, only Son of the Father,
Lord God, Lamb of God,
you take away the sin of the world:
have mercy on us.
You are seated at the right hand of the Father:
receive our prayer.

For you alone are the Holy One,
you alone are the Lord,
you alone are the Most High, Jesus Christ,
with the Holy Spirit,
in the glory of God the Father. Amen.

THE MINISTRY OF THE WORD

* Either two or three readings from scripture follow, the last of which is the Gospel.

6 Old Testament reading

7 A Psalm or portion of a Psalm may be said or sung.

8 Epistle

9 Hymn or Alleluia

*10 A reading from the Gospel according to . . .

Hear the Gospel of Christ.
Glory to Christ our Saviour.

The Gospel is read.

This is the Gospel of Christ.
Praise to Christ our Lord.

*11 Sermon

12 EITHER

A The Nicene Creed

All stand.

Let us profess the faith of the Church.

We believe in one God,
the Father, the Almighty,
maker of heaven and earth,
of all that is, seen and unseen.

We believe in one Lord, Jesus Christ,
the only Son of God,
eternally begotten of the Father,
God from God, Light from Light,
true God from true God,
begotten, not made,
of one Being with the Father;
through him all things were made.
For us and for our salvation
he came down from heaven,
was incarnate of the Holy Spirit and the Virgin Mary
and became truly human.
For our sake he was crucified under Pontius Pilate;
he suffered death and was buried.

On the third day he rose again
in accordance with the Scriptures;
he ascended into heaven
and is seated at the right hand of the Father.
He will come again in glory to judge the living and the dead,
and his kingdom will have no end.

We believe in the Holy Spirit, the Lord, the giver of life,
who proceeds from the Father and the Son,
who with the Father and the Son is worshipped and glorified,
who has spoken through the prophets.
We believe in one holy catholic and apostolic Church.
We acknowledge one Baptism for the forgiveness of sins.
We look for the resurrection of the dead,
and the life of the world to come. Amen.

OR

B An Affirmation of Faith

All stand.

Do you believe and trust in God the Father
who has created the universe?

We believe and trust in God the Father.

Do you believe and trust in Jesus, the Son of God,
who has redeemed the world?

We believe and trust in God the Son.

Do you believe and trust in the Holy Spirit,
who gives life to the people of God?

We believe and trust in God the Holy Spirit.

*13 Prayers of intercession

for the universal Church,
for peace and justice in the world,
for those in authority,
for the concerns of the local community,
for those who suffer;
thanksgiving for the departed.

A sung or spoken versicle and response may conclude each section.

THE LORD'S SUPPER

14 The Peace

All stand.

Our Lord Jesus Christ said:
'I leave you peace, my peace I give to you.'

The peace of the Lord be always with you.
And also with you.

The people may greet one another in the name of Christ.

THE PREPARATION OF THE GIFTS

15 Hymn

*16 The offerings of the people are presented. Bread and wine are brought to the table (or if already on the table are uncovered). The presiding minister takes the bread and wine and prepares them for use.

THE THANKSGIVING

*17 All stand.

The presiding minister leads the great prayer of thanksgiving:

The Lord be with you.
And also with you.

Lift up your hearts.
We lift them to the Lord.

Let us give thanks to the Lord our God.
It is right to give our thanks and praise.

God our Father and our Mother,
we give you thanks and praise
for all that you have made,
for the stars in their splendour
and the world in its wonder
and for the glorious gift of human life.
With the saints and angels in heaven
we praise your holy name.

EITHER

A **Holy, holy, holy Lord,**
God of power and might,
heaven and earth are full of your glory.
Hosanna in the highest.
Blessèd is he who comes in the name of the Lord.
Hosanna in the highest.

OR

B

Holy God, you go on loving us
even when we turn away from you.
You sent your Son Jesus
who healed those who were sick,
wept with those who were sad,
and forgave sinners.
To show the world your love
he died for all upon the cross
and you raised him up in glory.

On the night before Jesus died,
he had supper with his disciples.
He took bread,
thanked you, as we are thanking you,
broke the bread,
and gave it to them, saying,
'Take, eat. This is my body, given for you.
Do this to remember me.'

Jesus the Lord says, I am the bread,
the bread of life for the world am I.

After supper, he took a cup of wine,
thanked you,
and gave it to his disciples, saying,
'Drink from it, all of you.
This cup is the new covenant in my blood.
It will be shed for you and for all people
for the forgiveness of sins.
Do this to remember me.'

Jesus the Lord says, I am the vine,
the true and fruitful vine am I.

And so, God of love,
we remember that Jesus died and rose again
to make all things new.
Through his offering for us all,
we offer our whole life to you in thanks and praise.

Send your Holy Spirit
that these gifts of bread and wine
may be for us Christ's saving body and blood.
May this same Spirit unite us
with all your people on earth and in heaven.

Bring us at last
to live in your glory with all your saints,
that we may praise you for ever,
through Jesus your Son,
in the fellowship of the Holy Spirit.

This or some other doxology ending with **Amen** is sung or said:

All glory to the Father be,
the Spirit and the Son:
all glory to the One in Three
while endless ages run.
Alleluia! Amen.

*18 The Lord's Prayer

EITHER

We say together the prayer that Jesus gave us:

Our Father in heaven,
hallowed be your Name,
your kingdom come,
your will be done,
on earth as in heaven.
Give us today our daily bread.
Forgive us our sins
as we forgive those who sin against us.
Save us from the time of trial
and deliver us from evil.
For the kingdom, the power and the glory are yours,
now and for ever. Amen.

OR

As our Saviour taught his disciples, we pray:

Our Father, who art in heaven,
hallowed be thy Name;
thy kingdom come;
thy will be done;
on earth as it is in heaven.
Give us this day our daily bread.
And forgive us our trespasses,
as we forgive those who trespass against us.
And lead us not into temptation;
but deliver us from evil.
For thine is the kingdom, the power, and the glory,
for ever and ever. Amen.

THE BREAKING OF THE BREAD

*19 The presiding minister breaks the bread in the sight of the people in silence, or saying:

The bread we break is a sharing in the body of Christ.
Christ is the Bread of life.

The presiding minister may lift the cup in silence, or saying:

The cup of blessing for which we give thanks
is a sharing in the blood of Christ.
Christ is the true Vine.

*20 Silence, all seated or kneeling

21 Jesus, Lamb of God,
have mercy on us.
Jesus, bearer of our sins,
have mercy on us.
Jesus, redeemer of the world,
grant us peace.

THE SHARING OF THE BREAD AND WINE

*22 The presiding minister, those assisting with the distribution, and the people receive, according to local custom.

Appropriate words of invitation may be said.

*23 Words such as the following are said during the distribution:

The body of Christ, given for you. **Amen.**

The blood of Christ, shed for you. **Amen.**

24 During the distribution there may be appropriate music.

*25 The elements that remain are covered with a white cloth.

PRAYERS AND DISMISSAL

26 Silence

27 Let us pray.

God of glory,
we have seen with our eyes
and touched with our hands
the bread of heaven.
Strengthen us in our life together
that we may grow in love
for you and for each other;
through Jesus Christ our Lord. Amen.

28 Hymn

29 The presiding minister says:

The blessing of God,
the Father, the Son and the Holy Spirit,
be upon *you/us*, now and always. **Amen.**

*30 The presiding minister says:

Go in peace to love and serve the Lord.

In the name of Christ. Amen.

HOLY COMMUNION
DURING ORDINARY SEASONS
(Third Service)

NOTE

This service is intended for use (1) in the period which follows the Sunday after Epiphany and precedes Ash Wednesday and (2) in the period which follows the Day of Pentecost and precedes the First Sunday of Advent.

THE GATHERING OF THE PEOPLE OF GOD

* 1 The presiding minister says:

The grace of the Lord Jesus Christ,
and the love of God,
and the fellowship of the Holy Spirit,
be with you all. **Amen.**

2 Hymn

3 Let us pray.

Give us, O God, a vision of your glory,
that we may worship you in spirit and in truth,
and offer the praise of glad and thankful hearts;
through Christ our Lord. Amen.

* 4 The presiding minister says:

Let us call to mind our sins.

Silence

Lord Jesus, you came into the world to save sinners:

Lord, have mercy.
Lord, have mercy.

We have brought sorrow and hurt to you,
to others and to ourselves:

Christ, have mercy.
Christ, have mercy.

You give yourself to heal and renew us,
and to bring us strength:

Lord, have mercy.
Lord, have mercy.

EITHER

May almighty God
have mercy on us,
forgive us our sins,
and keep us in life eternal.
Amen.

OR

Know that your sins
are forgiven
through Jesus Christ,
our Saviour,
and rejoice in his goodness
and grace.
Amen.
Thanks be to God.

* 5 The collect of the day, or this or some other prayer:

God, the source of all wisdom,
you teach us in your word
that love is the fulfilling of the law:
grant that we may love you with all our heart
and our neighbours as ourselves;
through Jesus Christ our Lord. **Amen.**

6 Hymn or ***You are Worthy*** or a short time of praise

You are worthy, our Lord and God;
to receive glory and honour and power,
for you have created all things:
and by your will they were created and have their being.

**You are worthy, O Christ,
for you were slain:
and with your blood
you redeemed the human race for God,
and have chosen us to be a holy priesthood
from every people and nation.
To the One who is seated on the throne
and to the Lamb:
be blessing and honour, glory and might,
for ever and ever. Amen.**

THE MINISTRY OF THE WORD

* Either two or three readings from scripture follow, the last of which is the Gospel.

7 Old Testament reading

8 A Psalm or portion of a Psalm may be said or sung.

9 Epistle

10 Hymn

*11 A reading from the Gospel according to . . .

Hear the Gospel of Christ.
Glory to Christ our Saviour.

The Gospel is read.

This is the Gospel of Christ.
Praise to Christ our Lord.

*12 Sermon

13 There may be a time of quiet reflection or testimony.

14 Hymn

*15 These or some other prayers of intercession:

In faith let us pray to God our Father,
in the name of his Son, Jesus Christ,
and in the power of the Holy Spirit.

God of love, we pray for the life of your Church throughout the world . . . May every congregation be a community of love and every Christian a witness to your grace. Renew all who worship in this place that we may be a living fellowship in your Spirit and serve our neighbourhood.

Your kingdom come.
Your will be done.

God of mercy, we pray for the life of the world . . . and for those who exercise power . . . Show us how to live as members of the human family; to reject the ways of war; to bear each other's burdens and to work together for justice and peace.

Your kingdom come.
Your will be done.

God of compassion, we pray for those who are ill or anxious at home or in hospital . . . We pray for those whose lives are filled with fear and despair . . . Draw near with your saving love and bring healing and hope.

Your kingdom come.
Your will be done.

God of glory, we rejoice in the communion of saints; we remember all who have faithfully lived and all who have died in Christian hope, especially . . . Help us to follow their example and bring us with them into the fullness of your eternal joy.

Your kingdom come.
Your will be done.

Merciful God,
you have prepared for those who love you
such good things as pass our understanding;
pour into our hearts such love towards you
that we, loving you above all things,
may obtain your promises,
which exceed all that we can desire;
through Jesus Christ our Lord. **Amen.**

THE LORD'S SUPPER

16 The Peace

All stand.

Our Lord Jesus Christ said to the apostles:
'I leave you peace, my peace I give to you.'

The peace of the Lord be always with you.
And also with you.

The people may greet one another in the name of Christ.

THE PREPARATION OF THE GIFTS

17 Hymn

*18 The offerings of the people are presented. Bread and wine are brought to the table (or if already on the table are uncovered). The presiding minister takes the bread and wine and prepares them for use.

THE THANKSGIVING

*19 All stand.

The presiding minister leads the great prayer of thanksgiving:

The Lord be with you.
And also with you.

Lift up your hearts.
We lift them to the Lord.

Let us give thanks to the Lord our God.
It is right to give our thanks and praise.

It is indeed right, always and everywhere,
to give thanks to you, the true and living God.
Endless is your mercy and eternal is your reign.
All creation rejoices in your radiant splendour.

You made a covenant with your people
and declared your purpose of justice and love.
When all things were ready,
you sent your Son to be our Saviour.
In words and deeds he proclaimed your kingdom,
and obeyed your will even to death on the cross.

Through his mighty resurrection
he overcame sin and death
to set the whole creation free.

Therefore with saints and angels
and with all the choirs of heaven,
we join in the song of eternal praise:

Holy, holy, holy Lord,
God of power and might,
heaven and earth are full of your glory.
Hosanna in the highest.
Blessèd is he who comes in the name of the Lord.
Hosanna in the highest.

We praise you, Father,
that on the night in which he was betrayed,
our Lord Jesus took bread and gave thanks,
broke it, and gave it to his disciples, saying,
'Take and eat. This is my body, given for you.
Do this in remembrance of me.'

After supper, he took the cup, gave thanks,
and gave it for all to drink, saying,
'This cup is the new covenant of my blood,
shed for you and for all people
for the forgiveness of sin.
Do this in remembrance of me.'

As often as we eat this bread and drink this cup
we proclaim the Lord's death until he comes.

Therefore, gracious God,
with this bread and this cup
we remember that our Lord offered his life for us.

Believing the witness of his resurrection and ascension,
we look for his coming in glory,
and our sharing in his great and promised feast.

Amen. Come, Lord Jesus.

Send now, we pray, your Holy Spirit,
that these gifts of bread and wine
may be for us the body and blood of Christ
and that we may live to your praise and glory
with all your saints in light.

Amen. Come, Holy Spirit.

Join our prayers
and the prayers of all your people
on earth and in heaven
with the intercession of Christ,
our great high priest,

through whom, with whom, and in whom,
in the unity of the Holy Spirit,
all worship and honour are yours,
almighty God and Father,
for ever and ever. Amen.

*20 The Lord's Prayer

EITHER

We say together the prayer that Jesus gave us:

Our Father in heaven,
hallowed be your Name,
your kingdom come,
your will be done,
on earth as in heaven.
Give us today our daily bread.
Forgive us our sins
as we forgive those who sin against us.
Save us from the time of trial
and deliver us from evil.
For the kingdom, the power and the glory are yours,
now and for ever. Amen.

OR

As our Saviour taught his disciples, we pray:

Our Father, who art in heaven,
hallowed be thy Name;
thy kingdom come;
thy will be done;
on earth as it is in heaven.
Give us this day our daily bread.
And forgive us our trespasses,
as we forgive those who trespass against us.
And lead us not into temptation;
but deliver us from evil.
For thine is the kingdom, the power, and the glory,
for ever and ever. Amen.

THE BREAKING OF THE BREAD

*21 The presiding minister breaks the bread in the sight of the people in silence, or saying:

The bread we break is a sharing in the body of Christ.
Christ is the Bread of Life.

The presiding minister may lift the cup in silence, or saying:

The cup we take is a sharing in the blood of Christ.
Christ is the True Vine.

*22 Silence, all seated or kneeling

23 ***Lamb of God*** or some other short hymn or song on a similar theme

Jesus, Lamb of God,
have mercy on us.
Jesus, bearer of our sins,
have mercy on us.
Jesus, redeemer of the world,
grant us peace.

THE SHARING OF THE BREAD AND WINE

*24 The presiding minister, those assisting with the distribution, and the people receive, according to local custom.

The presiding minister may say these or other words of invitation:

Jesus is the Lamb of God
who takes away the sin of the world.
Happy are those who are called to his supper.

Receive the body of Christ which was given for you
and the blood of Christ which was shed for you,
and feed on him in your hearts,
by faith with thanksgiving.

*25 Words such as the following are said during the distribution:

The body of Christ. **Amen.**

The blood of Christ. **Amen.**

26 During the distribution there may be appropriate music.

*27 The elements that remain are covered with a white cloth.

PRAYERS AND DISMISSAL

28 Silence

29 Let us pray.

**We praise you, God,
for the bread of heaven
and the cup of salvation
which you give for the life of the world.
With this food for our journey
bring us with your saints
to the feast of your glory. Amen.**

30 Hymn

31 The presiding minister says:

EITHER

The Lord bless you and
keep you;
the Lord make his face to
shine on you
and be gracious to you;
the Lord look on you with
kindness
and give you peace. **Amen.**

OR

God be gracious to us
and bless us,
and make his face to shine
upon us. **Amen.**

*32 The presiding minister says:

Go in peace to love and serve the Lord.

In the name of Christ. Amen.

GUIDANCE FOR ORDERING A SERVICE OF HOLY COMMUNION

THE GATHERING OF THE PEOPLE OF GOD

The presiding minister and the people gather in God's name.
Notices may be given and news items may be shared.
Acts of approach and praise are offered in song and prayer.
A prayer of penitence is followed by an assurance of God's forgiveness.

There may be a brief introduction to the service.
A short prayer reflecting the season or festival is offered.

THE MINISTRY OF THE WORD

The scriptures are read, concluding with a passage from the Gospels.
God's word is proclaimed and shared in songs, hymns, music, dance and other art forms, in a sermon, or in comment, discussion and in silence.

Prayers are offered for the Church, for the world and for those in need; a remembrance is made of those who have died; and the Lord's Prayer may be said.

THE LORD'S SUPPER

The Peace is introduced by an appropriate sentence of scripture and may be shared by the presiding minister and the people.

The offerings of the people may be placed on the Lord's table.

The presiding minister takes the bread and wine and prepares them for use.

The presiding minister leads the great prayer of thanksgiving:

> The people are invited to offer praise to God.
> There is thanksgiving
> for creation,
> for God's self-revelation,
> for the salvation of the world through Christ,
> and for the gift of the Holy Spirit,
> with special reference to the season or festival.
>
> God's glory may be proclaimed in a version of 'Holy, holy, holy'.
>
> The story of the institution of the Lord's Supper is told.
> Christ's death and resurrection are recalled.
> God is asked to receive the worshippers' sacrifice of praise.
>
> There is prayer for the coming of the Holy Spirit that the gifts of bread and wine may be, for those who are participating, the body and blood of Christ.
>
> The worshippers, offering themselves in service to God, ask to be united in communion with all God's people on earth and in heaven.
>
> The prayer concludes with all honour and glory being given to God, the Father, the Son and the Holy Spirit, the people responding with a loud '**Amen**'.

The Lord's Prayer is said, if it has not been said earlier.

The presiding minister breaks the bread in silence, or saying an appropriate sentence.

The presiding minister and people receive communion, after which the elements that remain are covered.

PRAYERS AND DISMISSAL

A short prayer is offered in which the worshippers thank God for the communion and look forward to the final feast in God's kingdom.

There may be a time of praise.

The presiding minister says a blessing and sends the people out to live to God's praise and glory.

HOLY COMMUNION IN A HOME OR A HOSPITAL

NOTES

1 This service is a celebration of ***Holy Communion*** and should be distinguished from the order for ***Extended Communion***, during which elements already set aside at a previous celebration of ***Holy Communion*** are received.

2 For pastoral reasons, it may sometimes be desirable to give communion by dipping the bread lightly in the wine or to give only the bread or the wine. Bread dipped in wine is given with the words, 'The body and blood of Christ, given for you'.

3 If necessary, the words printed in **bold** type may be said by the presiding minister alone.

---

1 The peace of the Lord be always with you.
And also with you.

2 Let us pray.

Almighty God,
to whom all hearts are open,
all desires known,
and from whom no secrets are hidden:
cleanse the thoughts of our hearts
by the inspiration of your Holy Spirit,
that we may perfectly love you,
and worthily magnify your holy Name;
through Christ our Lord. Amen.

3 Let us confess our sins to God.

Most merciful God,
we have sinned in thought, word and deed,
and in what we have left undone.
For the sake of your Son, Jesus Christ,
have mercy on us and forgive us,
that we may serve you in newness of life,
to the glory of your name. Amen.

God our Father,
who forgives all who truly repent,
have mercy on *you/us,*
pardon and deliver *you/us* from all *your/our* sins,
confirm and strengthen *you/us* in all goodness,
and keep *you/us* in eternal life;
through Jesus Christ our Lord. **Amen.**

* 4 The collect of the day or some other prayer

* 5 One or more short readings from scripture, including a passage from the Gospels

6 A brief exposition may be given.

7 A short act of intercession

* 8 The Lord's Prayer

EITHER

We say together the prayer that Jesus gave us:

Our Father in heaven,
hallowed be your Name,
your kingdom come,
your will be done,
on earth as in heaven.
Give us today our daily bread.
Forgive us our sins
as we forgive those who sin against us.

OR

As our Saviour taught his disciples, we pray:

Our Father, who art in heaven,
hallowed be thy Name;
thy kingdom come;
thy will be done;
on earth as it is in heaven.
Give us this day our daily bread.
And forgive us our trespasses,

Save us from the time of trial
and deliver us from evil.
For the kingdom, the power and the glory are yours,
now and for ever. Amen.

as we forgive those who trespass against us.
And lead us not into temptation;
but deliver us from evil.
For thine is the kingdom, the power, and the glory,
for ever and ever. Amen.

* 9 The presiding minister takes the bread and wine and prepares them for use.

*10 The presiding minister leads the great prayer of thanksgiving:

The Lord be with you.
And also with you.

Lift up your hearts.
We lift them to the Lord.

Let us give thanks to the Lord our God.
It is right to give our thanks and praise.

Father, almighty and everliving God,
it is right to give you thanks and praise
at all times and in all places.
With angels and archangels
and with all your people on earth and in heaven,
we proclaim your glorious name,
evermore praising you and saying:

Holy, holy, holy Lord,
God of power and might,
heaven and earth are full of your glory.
Hosanna in the highest.
Blessèd is he who comes in the name of the Lord.
Hosanna in the highest.

Holy and blessèd God,
you have created all things
and made us in your own image.
When we had fallen into sin
you gave your only Son Jesus Christ
to suffer death upon the cross for our redemption,
making there the one perfect sacrifice
for the sins of the whole world.

On the night that he was betrayed he took bread;
and when he had given you thanks,
he broke it, and gave it to his disciples, saying,
'Take, eat. This is my body which is given for you.
Do this in remembrance of me.'

In the same way, after supper, he took the cup;
and when he had given you thanks,
he gave it to them, saying,
'Drink this, all of you.
This is my blood of the new covenant
which is shed for you and for many
for the forgiveness of sins.
Do this, as often as you drink it,
in remembrance of me.'

Therefore, Father,
we do as Christ your Son commanded;
we remember his passion and death,
we celebrate his resurrection and ascension,
and we look for the coming of his kingdom.

Accept through him
this our sacrifice of praise and thanksgiving;
and grant that by the power of your life-giving Spirit,
we who eat and drink these holy gifts
may share in the body and blood of Christ
and be united with all your people
on earth and in heaven;

through the same Jesus Christ our Lord,
by whom, and with whom,
in the unity of the Holy Spirit,
all honour and glory are yours,
almighty Father,
for ever and ever. **Amen.**

*11 The presiding minister breaks the bread in silence, or saying:

The bread we break is a sharing in the body of Christ.

The cup we take is a sharing in the blood of Christ.

*12 Silence

13 EITHER

Let us pray.

**We do not presume
to come to this your table,
merciful Lord,
trusting in our own
righteousness,
but in your manifold
and great mercies.
We are not worthy
so much as to gather up
the crumbs under your
table.
But you are the same Lord
whose nature is always to
have mercy.
Grant us therefore,
gracious Lord,
so to eat the flesh
of your dear Son Jesus
Christ,
and to drink his blood,
that we may evermore
dwell in him
and he in us. Amen.**

OR

We say together:

**Lord, we come to your
table,
trusting in your mercy
and not in any goodness
of our own.
We are not worthy
even to gather up
the crumbs under your
table,
but it is your nature
always to have mercy,
and on that we depend.
So feed us
with the body and blood
of Jesus Christ, your Son,
that we may for ever
live in him and he in us.
Amen.**

*14 Bread and wine are given with these or similar words:

The body of our Lord Jesus Christ, given for you. **Amen.**

The blood of our Lord Jesus Christ, shed for you. **Amen.**

15 Silence

16 EITHER

A Let us pray.

We thank you, Lord,
that you have fed us in this sacrament,
united us with Christ,
and given us a foretaste of the heavenly banquet
prepared for all people. Amen.

OR

B Lord our God,
you have strengthened us for our journey
with Christ, the Living Bread.
Bring us to be with you in glory
that with angels and archangels
and all the company of heaven
we may praise you for ever. **Amen.**

*17 The peace of God
which passes all understanding,
keep *your/our* hearts and minds
in the knowledge and love of God
and of his Son, Jesus Christ our Lord;
and the blessing of God,
the Father, the Son and the Holy Spirit,
remain with *you/us* always. **Amen.**

EXTENDED COMMUNION

NOTES

1 This service is an act of worship during which the participants receive elements previously set apart at a service of ***Holy Communion***.

2 This service may be led by a presbyter, or by a deacon stationed in the circuit, or by a lay person with an authorisation from the Conference to preside at the Lord's Supper, or by a lay person duly prepared and trained for the purpose who has been so appointed by the local Church Council in accordance with Standing Orders.

3 The setting apart of bread and wine in the service of public worship takes place when all have communicated. That which is set apart should be placed in a home communion set or other suitable vessels provided by the Church Council, before the cloth is placed over the rest of the elements, and should be taken from the communion table to a safe place where it can be kept until the time when it is to be taken to a home or hospital.

4 It is desirable that communion in a home or hospital using this Order should be given on the same day as the bread and wine have been set apart. When it is known that this will not be possible and there will be some delay, consideration should be given to the setting apart of some of the bread in the form of wafers for use in the home or hospital.

5 For pastoral reasons, it may sometimes be desirable to give communion by dipping the bread lightly in the wine or to give only the bread or the wine. Bread dipped in wine is given with the words, 'The body and blood of Christ, given for you'.

6 If necessary, the words printed in **bold** type may be said by the leader alone.

7 The scripture reading(s) at no. 7 may appropriately be selected from among those which were used at the service of Holy Communion at which the elements were set apart.

* 1 The bread and wine are reverently set out.

* 2 Grace to you and peace from God our Father
and the Lord Jesus Christ. **Amen.**

3 The following may be said:

The Church of God, to which we belong, has taken bread and wine and given thanks over them according to our Lord's command. I bring these holy gifts that you may share in the communion of his body and blood. The bread and wine which we share in this service come from a celebration of the Lord's Supper at *N* . . . Church on *(date)*. We who are many are one body, because we all share in one bread.

4 Let us pray.

Almighty God,
to whom all hearts are open,
all desires known,
and from whom no secrets are hidden:
cleanse the thoughts of our hearts
by the inspiration of your Holy Spirit,
that we may perfectly love you,
and worthily magnify your holy Name;
through Christ our Lord. Amen.

5 Let us confess our sins to God.

Most merciful God,
we have sinned in thought, word and deed,
and in what we have left undone.
For the sake of your Son, Jesus Christ,
have mercy on us and forgive us,
that we may serve you in newness of life,
to the glory of your name. Amen.

God our Father, who forgives all who truly repent,
have mercy on *you/us,*
pardon and deliver *you/us* from all *your/our* sins,
confirm and strengthen *you/us* in all goodness,

and keep *you/us* in eternal life;
through Jesus Christ our Lord. **Amen.**

* 6 God our Father,
we come to this feast which you have prepared,
as guests whom you have invited:
may we receive the bread of eternal life
which you provide for our healing and strength;
through Christ our Lord. **Amen.**

* 7 One or more short readings from scripture, including a passage from the Gospels

8 A brief exposition may be given.

9 These or some other prayers of thanksgiving and intercession may be said:

We praise you, God our Father,
for creating all things
and for sending your Son Jesus Christ
to be our Saviour.
We give you thanks
for the outpouring of your Holy Spirit,
for our life together in your Church
and for our calling to serve you in the world.
Yours, Lord, is the greatness and the power,
the majesty and the splendour,
now and for ever. **Amen.**

Let us pray for the whole Church of God in Christ Jesus,
and for peace and justice throughout the world.

Appropriate concerns may be mentioned here, and may include reference to the life of the local church.

Lord God, make your ways known upon earth,
and your saving power among all peoples.

Renew your Church in holiness,
and help us to serve you with joy.

Guide the leaders of this and every nation,
that justice may prevail throughout the world.

Bless and strengthen the sick and the suffering,
and grant us your salvation.

Make us one with the apostles and martyrs,
and bring us with your saints to glory everlasting.

We ask these prayers in the name of our Lord and Saviour Jesus Christ. **Amen.**

*10 The Lord's Prayer

EITHER

We say together the prayer that Jesus gave us:

**Our Father in heaven,
hallowed be your Name,
your kingdom come,
your will be done,
on earth as in heaven.
Give us today our daily bread.
Forgive us our sins
as we forgive those who sin against us.
Save us from the time of trial
and deliver us from evil.
For the kingdom, the power and the glory are yours,
now and for ever. Amen.**

OR

As our Saviour taught his disciples, we pray:

**Our Father, who art in heaven,
hallowed be thy Name;
thy kingdom come;
thy will be done;
on earth as it is in heaven.
Give us this day our daily bread.
And forgive us our trespasses,
as we forgive those who trespass against us.
And lead us not into temptation;
but deliver us from evil.
For thine is the kingdom, the power, and the glory,
for ever and ever. Amen.**

11 EITHER

Let us pray.

We do not presume
to come to this your table,
merciful Lord,
trusting in our own
righteousness,
but in your manifold
and great mercies.
We are not worthy
so much as to gather up
the crumbs under your
table.
But you are the same Lord
whose nature is always to
have mercy.
Grant us therefore,
gracious Lord,
so to eat the flesh
of your dear Son Jesus
Christ,
and to drink his blood,
that we may evermore
dwell in him
and he in us. Amen.

OR

We say together:

Lord, we come to your
table,
trusting in your mercy
and not in any goodness
of our own.
We are not worthy
even to gather up
the crumbs under your
table,
but it is your nature
always to have mercy,
and on that we depend.
So feed us
with the body and blood
of Jesus Christ, your Son,
that we may for ever
live in him and he in us.
Amen.

*12 These or other words of invitation:

Receive this holy sacrament in remembrance that Christ died for you, and feed on him in your heart by faith with thanksgiving.

Bread and wine are given with these or similar words:

The body of Christ, given for you. **Amen.**

The blood of Christ, shed for you. **Amen.**

13 EITHER

A Let us pray.

We thank you, Lord,
that you have fed us in this sacrament,
united us with Christ,
and given us a foretaste of the heavenly banquet
prepared for all people. Amen.

OR

B Lord our God,
you have strengthened us for our journey
with Christ, the Living Bread.
Bring us to be with you in glory
that with angels and archangels
and all the company of heaven
we may praise you for ever. **Amen.**

*14 The peace of God
which passes all understanding,
keep *your/our* hearts and minds
in the knowledge and love of God
and of his Son, Jesus Christ our Lord;
and the blessing of God,
the Father, the Son and the Holy Spirit,
remain with *you/us* always. **Amen.**

HOLY WEEK SERVICES

INTRODUCTION

The observance of Holy Week originated in celebrations by early Christians in the places where the Passion events occurred. Down the centuries the universal Church continued to remember these events. In the services of Holy Week, we are invited to identify and be united with Christ in his sufferings so that we may share his risen life. So, for example, the procession on the Second Sunday of the Passion (Palm Sunday) is not just a reminder of what happened in the past. Rather, it is an act of praise to Christ and an expression of the worshippers' own willingness to follow in his way – the way of humble love (the triumphal entry), of mutual love (the foot-washing commandment), of obedient love (Gethsemane), of victorious, self-giving love (Good Friday), culminating in the celebration of love which is stronger than death (Easter Day).

PALM SUNDAY
(The Second Sunday of the Passion)

INTRODUCTION

The main act of worship on this day should have two distinct features: a celebration of Christ's triumphal entry into Jerusalem (traditionally by means of a procession) and, more importantly, an extended proclamation of and meditation on the Passion story (traditionally by the reading of the Passion from one of the Synoptic Gospels).

NOTES

1 The congregation assembles in a suitable place away from the church building, and goes in procession to the church building. Where this is not possible, all is done inside the church building, and if possible some or all of the congregation take part in the procession.

2 The people bring palm or other branches, or palm crosses, or are given them as they arrive.

3 The Passion narrative may be read by more than one person. When it is read in full, the sermon may be omitted.

4 In a service of ***Holy Communion***, or one of the ***Morning, Afternoon or Evening Services***, nos. 1-5 below take the place of the Gathering of the People of God or the Preparation.

---

1 Hosanna to the Son of David!
Hosanna in the highest!

Blessèd is he who comes in the name of the Lord.
Hosanna in the highest!

Sisters and brothers in Christ, during Lent we have been preparing for the celebration of our Lord's death and resurrection. Today we begin this solemn celebration in union with Christians throughout the world. Our Lord Jesus Christ entered Jerusalem in triumph to complete his work as our Saviour; to be rejected, to suffer and die, and to be raised from the dead.

Let us go with him in faith and love, so that, united with him in his sufferings, we may share his risen life.

2 This prayer may be said over the palms:

Let us pray.

God our Saviour,
whose Son entered Jerusalem as Messiah to suffer and die:
may these palms be for us a sign of his victory;
may we who carry them ever hail him as king
and follow him in the way that leads to eternal life.
With all the faithful,
may we enter the new Jerusalem in triumph;
through Jesus Christ our Lord,
who is alive and reigns with you,
in the unity of the Holy Spirit,
one God, now and for ever. **Amen.**

3 A reading from the Gospel according to . . .

Hear the Gospel of Christ.
Glory to Christ our Saviour.

The Gospel is read:

Year A: Matthew 21:1-11
Year B: Mark 11:1-11 *or* John 12:12-16
Year C: Luke 19:28-40

This is the Gospel of Christ.
Praise to Christ our Lord.

4 During the procession the following or another hymn may be sung:

All glory, laud, and honour
To thee, Redeemer, King,
To whom the lips of children
Made sweet hosannas ring!

Thou art the King of Israel,
Thou David's royal Son.
Who in the Lord's name comest,
The King and Blessèd One.

The company of angels
Are praising thee on high,
And mortal men and all things
Created make reply.

The people of the Hebrews
With palms before thee went;
Our praise and prayer and anthems
Before thee we present.

To thee before thy Passion
They sang their hymns of praise;
To thee now high exalted
Our melody we raise.

Thou didst accept their praises;
Accept the prayers we bring,
Who in all good delightest,
Thou good and gracious King.

Do thou direct our footsteps
Upon our earthly way,
And bring us by thy mercy
To heaven's eternal day.

Within that blessèd City
Thy praises may we sing,
And ever raise hosannas
To our most loving King.

5 This or some other prayer:

Let us pray.

Eternal God,
in your tender love towards the human race
you sent your Son our Saviour Jesus Christ
to take our flesh and to suffer death upon a cross.
Grant that we may follow the example of his great humility,
and share in the glory of his resurrection;
through the same Jesus Christ our Lord. **Amen.**

6 The service continues from the Ministry of the Word with readings from scripture which focus on the Passion. When the Passion Gospel is read, it may be introduced with the words:

The Passion of our Lord Jesus Christ according to . . .

At the end, the narrator may say:

This is the Passion of the Lord.

MAUNDY THURSDAY

INTRODUCTION

The word 'Maundy' is derived from the first words of the traditional Latin anthem '*Mandatum novum do vobis*' ('A new commandment I give to you', John 13:34). A re-enactment of the foot-washing scene also became central to the Maundy Thursday liturgy.

The celebration of Holy Communion on this day should be marked by joyful thanksgiving for Christ's gift of this sacrament to his Church. In the words and actions which may follow the Lord's Supper, a more sombre mood prevails.

In some churches it is customary on Maundy Thursday to remove all vessels, cloths, books and furnishings from the sanctuary as a sign of the desolation of Gethsemane.

After the main Maundy Thursday service *A Prayer Vigil* may be held as a response to our Lord's invitation to watch and pray; or ***A Service of Light and Darkness*** may be held.

NOTES

1 The basic elements of the service are marked by the symbol *. Other sections may be omitted.

2 If foot-washing is to be included in the service, it may take one of three forms. Either the minister may wash the feet of twelve members of the congregation, or a small group may wash each other's feet in turn, or the first and second forms may be used together.

3 When there is ***A Service of Light and Darkness***, the number of candles to be lit is one fewer than the number of readings. Following each reading, except the last, a candle is extinguished. The last candle, the Christ candle, is extinguished at the end of the penultimate reading (the death of Christ). Apart from a light for the reader, the building is in darkness for the final reading.

THE GATHERING OF THE PEOPLE OF GOD

* 1 The presiding minister says:

On this night, our Lord Jesus Christ said:
'A new commandment I give to you,
that you love each other, as I have loved you.'

2 Hymn

* 3 The presiding minister says:

Let us confess our sins to God and ask him to cleanse us.

Father eternal, giver of light and grace,
we have sinned against you,
against our neighbour,
and against each other,
in thought, word and deed,
in the evil we have done
and in the good we have not done,
through ignorance, through weakness,
through our own deliberate fault.
We have wounded your love
and marred your image within us.
We are sorry and ashamed
and repent of all our sins.
For the sake of your Son Jesus Christ,
who died for us,
forgive us all that is past
and lead us out of darkness
to walk as children of light. Amen.

This is the message we have heard from him and proclaim
to you,
that God is light and in him is no darkness at all.
If we walk in the light, as he is in the light,
we have fellowship with one another,
and the blood of Jesus his Son cleanses us from all sin.

This is Christ's gracious word:
'Your sins are forgiven.'

Amen. Thanks be to God.

4 *Glory to God in the highest*

Glory to God in the highest,
and peace to God's people on earth.

Lord God, heavenly King,
almighty God and Father,
we worship you, we give you thanks,
we praise you for your glory.

Lord Jesus Christ, only Son of the Father,
Lord God, Lamb of God,
you take away the sin of the world:
have mercy on us.
You are seated at the right hand of the Father:
receive our prayer.

For you alone are the Holy One,
you alone are the Lord,
you alone are the Most High, Jesus Christ,
with the Holy Spirit,
in the glory of God the Father. Amen.

* 5 Let us pray.

God our Father,
you have invited us to share in the supper
which your Son gave to his Church.
Nourish us, we pray, by his presence,
and unite us in his love;
who is alive and reigns with you,
in the unity of the Holy Spirit,
one God, now and for ever. **Amen.**

THE MINISTRY OF THE WORD

* 6 Old Testament reading: Exodus 12:1-4 (5-10) 11-14

7 Psalm 116:1-2, 12-19

* 8 Epistle: 1 Corinthians 11:23-26

9 Hymn

*10 A reading from the Gospel according to John.

Hear the Gospel of Christ.
Glory to Christ our Saviour.

The Gospel, John 13:1-17, 31*b*-35, is read.

This is the Gospel of Christ.
Praise to Christ our Lord.

*11 Sermon

12 The service may continue with the washing of feet. Otherwise, the service continues from no. 15.

THE WASHING OF FEET

13 The presiding minister says:

Let us pray.

Gracious God,
your Son Jesus Christ girded himself with a towel
and washed the feet of his disciples.
Give us the will to be the servants of others
as he was the servant of all,
who gave up his life and died for us,
yet lives and reigns with you and the Holy Spirit,
one God, now and for ever. **Amen.**

14 Those who are to have their feet washed move to the front. Water is poured over their feet, which are dried with a towel. During the foot-washing there may be appropriate music. Those who have had their feet washed return to their places.

*15 These or some other prayers of intercession:

Let us pray.

Father, on this night, the night on which he was betrayed, your Son Jesus Christ washed his disciples' feet and said that they ought to wash one another's feet.

We commit ourselves to follow his example of love and service.

Lord, hear us.
Lord, humble us.

On this night, Jesus prayed for his disciples to be one.

We pray for the unity of your Church . . .

Lord, hear us.
Lord, unite us.

On this night, Jesus prayed for those who were to believe in him.

We pray for the mission of your Church . . .

Lord, hear us.
Lord, renew our zeal.

On this night, Jesus commanded his disciples to love, but suffered rejection himself.

We pray for those who are rejected and unloved . . .

Lord, hear us.
Lord, fill us with your love.

On this night, Jesus reminded his disciples that if the world hated them it first hated him.

We pray for those who are persecuted for their faith . . .

Lord, hear us.
Lord, increase our faith.

On this night, Jesus told his disciples that he was going to prepare a place for them.

We remember in your presence all who have died . . .
and those who have been bereaved . . .

Lord, hear us.
Lord, renew our hope and trust in you.

*16 The Lord's Prayer

EITHER

We say together the prayer that Jesus gave us:

**Our Father in heaven,
hallowed be your Name,
your kingdom come,
your will be done,
on earth as in heaven.
Give us today our daily bread.
Forgive us our sins
as we forgive those who sin against us.
Save us from the time of trial
and deliver us from evil.
For the kingdom, the power and the glory are yours,
now and for ever. Amen.**

OR

As our Saviour taught his disciples, we pray:

**Our Father, who art in heaven,
hallowed be thy Name;
thy kingdom come;
thy will be done;
on earth as it is in heaven.
Give us this day our daily bread.
And forgive us our trespasses,
as we forgive those who trespass against us.
And lead us not into temptation;
but deliver us from evil.
For thine is the kingdom, the power, and the glory,
for ever and ever. Amen.**

THE LORD'S SUPPER

*17 The Peace

All stand.

On this night,
our Lord Jesus Christ said to his disciples:
'Peace I leave with you; my peace I give to you.'

The peace of the Lord be always with you.
And also with you.

The people may greet one another in the name of Christ.

THE PREPARATION OF THE GIFTS

18 Hymn

*19 The offerings of the people are presented. Bread and wine are brought to the table (or if already on the table are uncovered). The presiding minister takes the bread and wine and prepares them for use.

THE THANKSGIVING

*20 All stand.

*21 The presiding minister leads the great prayer of thanksgiving:

The Lord be with you.
And also with you.

Lift up your hearts.
We lift them to the Lord.

Let us give thanks to the Lord our God.
It is right to give our thanks and praise.

Lord our God,
you brought everything into existence,
and created us in your own image and likeness.
When in our sin we turned from you,
you did not leave us in darkness.

On the night of the Passover
you delivered your chosen people.
In the wilderness you fed them
with bread from heaven
and led them to the promised land.

In your enduring love,
you sent your Son to be our Saviour.
By his life and death
and his rising from the tomb,
you offer to all the gift of eternal life.
Through him
you sent your Holy Spirit
to be with your people for ever.

In communion with your faithful servants
in every time and place
we join with all creation in the eternal hymn:

Holy, holy, holy Lord,
God of power and might,
heaven and earth are full of your glory.
Hosanna in the highest.
Blessèd is he who comes in the name of the Lord.
Hosanna in the highest.

God of grace and mercy,
we remember how,
on this night in which he was betrayed,
our Lord Jesus Christ took bread
and gave you thanks;
he broke it and gave it to his disciples, saying,
'Take this, all of you, and eat it.
This is my body given for you.
Do this in remembrance of me.'

After supper he took the cup;
he gave you thanks and gave it to them, saying,
'Drink from it, all of you.
This is my blood of the new covenant,
shed for you and for many
for the forgiveness of sins.
Do this in remembrance of me.'

Dying, you destroyed our death.
Rising, you restored our life.
Lord Jesus, come in glory.

Therefore, Father,
with this bread and this cup,
we share this paschal mystery
in remembrance of Christ your Son,
and we offer our lives to serve you.
Send your Spirit of life and power
that these gifts of bread and wine
may be for us the body and blood of Christ.

By that same Spirit
may we be made worthy to live for you
and to tell of your saving power.

Give grace to us
that our words and deeds may not betray you,
but that we may love one another
as your Son commanded.

Remember, Lord,
all whom you have called to serve you in your holy
Church,
and all who offer themselves for the life of the world.

Unite us at the table in your kingdom
with all who have faithfully served you.

We offer our prayer
through Jesus Christ our Lord,

**to whom, with you and the Holy Spirit,
belong endless praise and eternal blessing,
now and through all ages. Amen.**

THE BREAKING OF THE BREAD

*22 The presiding minister breaks the bread in the sight of the people in silence, or saying:

We break this bread to share in the body of Christ.

**Though we are many, we are one body,
because we all share in one bread.**

*23 Silence, all seated or kneeling

THE SHARING OF THE BREAD AND WINE

*24 The presiding minister, those assisting with the distribution, and the people receive, according to local custom.

The presiding minister may say these or other words of invitation:

Jesus is the Lamb of God
who takes away the sin of the world.
Happy are those who are called to his supper.

**Lord, I am not worthy to receive you,
but only say the word and I shall be healed.**

*25 Words such as the following are said during the distribution:

The body of Christ, given for you. **Amen.**

The blood of Christ, shed for you. **Amen.**

26 During the distribution this or some other hymn may be sung:

Sing, my tongue, the Saviour's glory,
Of his cross the mystery sing;
Lift on high the wondrous trophy,
Tell the triumph of the King:
He, the world's Redeemer, conquers
Death, through death now vanquishing.

On the night of that last supper
Seated with his chosen band,
He, the paschal victim eating,
First fulfils the law's command,
Then as food to his disciples
Gives himself with his own hand.

Word made flesh! His word life-giving,
Gives his flesh our meat to be,
Bids us drink his blood, believing,
Through his death, we life shall see:
Blessèd they who thus receiving
Are from death and sin set free.

Low in adoration bending,
Now our hearts our God revere;
Faith her aid to sight is lending,
Though unseen the Lord is near;
Ancient types and shadows ending,
Christ our paschal Lamb is here.

Praise for ever, thanks and blessing,
Thine, O gracious Father, be;
Praise be thine, O Christ, who bringest
Life and immortality;
Praise be thine, thou quickening Spirit,
Praise through all eternity.

*27 The elements that remain are covered with a white cloth.

PRAYERS AND DISMISSAL

28 Silence

29 Let us pray.

**Gracious God,
we thank you for the gift of this sacrament
in which we remember Jesus Christ your Son.
May we who revere this sacred mystery
know and reveal in our lives
the fruits of his redemption;
who is alive and reigns with you
in the unity of the Holy Spirit,
one God, now and for ever. Amen.**

30 Hymn

If ***A Service of Light and Darkness*** is to follow, the candles are lit.

31 The service may continue with ***The Gospel of the Watch*** or ***A Service of Light and Darkness***. Either may be followed by ***The Stripping of the Communion Table***, or ***A Prayer Vigil***, or both.

Otherwise, the service concludes with these words:

When the disciples had sung a hymn
they went out to the Mount of Olives.

Jesus prayed to his Father:

'If it is possible,
take this cup of suffering from me;
yet not my will but yours be done.'

Christ was obedient to the point of death,
even death on a cross.

32 All leave in silence.

THE GOSPEL OF THE WATCH

33 The lighting in the church is dimmed.

34 The Gospel is read:

Year A: Matthew 26:30-75
Year B: Mark 14:26-72
Year C: Luke 22:39-65

35 All leave in silence, or the service continues from no. 42 or no. 44.

A SERVICE OF LIGHT AND DARKNESS

36 The lighting in the church is dimmed.

37 God is light, in whom there is no darkness at all.
Jesus Christ is the light of the world.

And this is the judgement,
that the light has come into the world,
and we loved darkness rather than light.

38 The service continues with the readings in the table on page 254, which may be adapted, provided that the penultimate reading always recounts the death of Christ.

39 Following each reading, except the last, a candle is extinguished and a period of silence is kept. After each reading or group of readings a prayer is said and a hymn or verses of a hymn may be sung (from memory if there is not enough light).

40 May Jesus Christ,
who for our sake became obedient unto death,
even death on a cross,
keep you and strengthen you
this night and for ever. **Amen.**

Go in peace.

41 All leave in silence, or the service continues from no. 42 or no. 44.

THE STRIPPING OF THE COMMUNION TABLE

42 The communion linen and vessels, service and hymn books are removed from the communion table in an unhurried and dignified manner. Articles such as pulpit falls, hangings, banners, candlesticks and other decorations may also be removed. This may be done in silence or during the reading of Psalm 22.

43 All leave in silence, or the service continues from no. 44.

A PRAYER VIGIL

44 Prayers, readings and other sources for meditation may be provided to enable the congregation to 'watch and pray'.

45 All leave in silence.

Reading	Year A Matthew	Year B Mark	Year C Luke
1	26:30-35	14:26-31	22:24-27
2	26:36-46	14:32-42	22:28-30
3	26:47-56	14:43-52	22:31-34
4	26:57-68	14:53-65	22:35-38
5	26:69-75	14:66-72	22:39-46
6	27:1-2	15:1-5	22:47-53
7	27:3-10	15:6-15	22:54-62
8	27:11-14	15:16-20	22:63-65
9	27:15-23	15:21	22:66-71
10	27:24-26	15:22-24	23:1-7
11	27:27-31	15:25-32	23:8-12
12	27:32-37	15:33-34	23:13-25
13	27:38-44	15:35-37	23:26-31
14	27:45-46	15:38-47	23:32-43
15	27:47-50		23:44-46
16	27:51-61		23:47-56

GOOD FRIDAY

NOTES

1 Adequate provision should be made for silent prayer and meditation. It is appropriate that the service should begin and end in silence and that musical instruments should be used only to support the singing.

2 The Passion narrative may be read by more than one person. When it is read in full, the sermon may be omitted.

3 If the material at no. 13 is used, the words are read by two alternate voices or groups, the congregation responding '**Holy God . . .**'.

4 An evening service on Good Friday may take the form of ***A Service of Light and Darkness*** (see pages 252-253).

THE MINISTRY OF THE WORD

1 Silence

2 Let us pray.

Gracious and eternal God,
look with mercy on this your family,
for which our Lord Jesus Christ
was content to be betrayed
and given up into the hands of sinners
and to suffer death upon the cross;
who is alive and glorified with you,
in the unity of the Holy Spirit,
one God, now and for ever. **Amen.**

3 Old Testament reading: Isaiah 52:13 - 53:12

4 Silence

5 Psalm 22

6 Epistle: Hebrews 10:16-25 *or* Hebrews 4:14-16; 5:7-9

7 Silence

8 Hymn

9 The Passion of our Lord Jesus Christ according to John.

The Gospel, John 18:1 - 19:42, is read.

This is the Passion of the Lord.

10 Silence

11 Sermon

THE PROCLAMATION OF THE CROSS

12 Hymn

During the singing of this hymn, a wooden cross may be carried to the front of the church.

13 The following may be said:

Hear the Reproaches of God,
the Father, the Son and the Holy Spirit.

1: My people, what have I done to you?
How have I offended you? Answer me!

Holy God,
holy and strong,
holy and immortal:
have mercy on us.

2: I delivered you from the hand of Pharaoh,
but you delivered me up to be crucified.

1: My people, what have I done to you?
How have I offended you? Answer me!

2: My presence was with you in the pillar of cloud,
but you could not watch with me one hour.

1: My people, what have I done to you?
How have I offended you? Answer me!

2: I opened the sea to lead you out from slavery,
but you opened my side with a spear.

1: My people, what have I done to you?
How have I offended you? Answer me!

Holy God,
holy and strong,
holy and immortal:
have mercy on us.

2: I sustained you with manna in the wilderness,
but you shared my bread and deserted me.

1: My people, what have I done to you?
How have I offended you? Answer me!

2: I saved you from thirst with water from the rock,
but in my thirst you gave me vinegar to drink.

1: My people, what have I done to you?
How have I offended you? Answer me!

2: I struck down your enemies before you,
but you struck my head with a reed.

1: My people, what have I done to you?
How have I offended you? Answer me!

Holy God,
holy and strong,
holy and immortal:
have mercy on us.

2: I planted you as my fairest vine,
but you yielded only bitterness.

1: My people, what have I done to you?
How have I offended you? Answer me!

2: I gave you a royal sceptre,
but you gave me a crown of thorns.

1: My people, what have I done to you?
How have I offended you? Answer me!

2: I raised you to the height of majesty,
but you have raised me high on a cross.

1: My people, what have I done to you?
How have I offended you? Answer me!

Holy God,
holy and strong,
holy and immortal:
have mercy on us.

14 Silence

15 Let the same mind be in you that was in Christ Jesus,
who humbled himself
and became obedient to the point of death,
even death on a cross.

We praise and adore you, O Christ:
by your cross and precious blood
you have redeemed us.

Worthy is the Lamb, the Lamb that was slain,
to receive all power and wealth,
wisdom and might,
honour and glory and praise!

We praise and adore you, O Christ:
by your cross and precious blood
you have redeemed us.

You are worthy, O Christ, for you were slain,
and by your blood you purchased for God
saints from every tribe and language, people and nation;
you have made them a royal house,
to serve God as priests,
and they shall reign upon earth.

We praise and adore you, O Christ:
by your cross and precious blood
you have redeemed us.

To him who loves us
and has freed us from our sins by his blood,

to him be glory and dominion
for ever and ever. Amen.

16 Hymn

THE INTERCESSIONS

17 God sent his Son into the world,
not to condemn the world,
but that, through him, the world might be saved.

Let us therefore pray to our heavenly Father
for people everywhere according to their need.

For the Church of God throughout the world,
for those preparing for Baptism,
and for all who suffer for the sake of Christ,
that God will confirm his people in faith,
strengthen them in love,
and preserve them in peace;
let us pray to the Lord.

Lord, have mercy.

Silence

Almighty and everlasting God,
by your Spirit the whole body of the Church
is governed and sanctified.
Hear the prayers we offer
for all your faithful people;
that in their vocation and ministry
each may serve you in holiness and truth
to the glory of your name;
through Jesus Christ our Saviour. **Amen.**

For the nations of the world and their leaders,
for our own country and those who govern us,
and for all who work for reconciliation,
that by God's help
we may live in justice, peace and freedom;
let us pray to the Lord.

Lord, have mercy.

Silence

God of peace,
whose will is to restore all things
in your beloved Son, the king of all:
govern the hearts and minds of those in authority,
and bring the families of the nations,
divided and torn apart by the ravages of sin,
to be subject to his just and gentle rule;

who is alive and reigns with you,
in the unity of the Holy Spirit,
one God, now and for ever. **Amen.**

For God's covenant people, Israel,
whom he called to be his own
and for all who seek to live by the light of God's truth,
that, with them, God will grant us grace
to live in faithfulness
and to grow in the love of his name;
let us pray to the Lord.

Lord, have mercy.

Silence

Eternal God,
bless all who look to Abraham
as the father of faith.
Set us free from prejudice, blindness,
and hardness of heart,
that in accordance with your will and guided by your truth
our life together may be for the glory of your name;
we ask this through Jesus Christ our Lord. **Amen.**

For all who lack faith
and for those who are hostile to it,
that God will open their hearts to the truth
and lead them to faith and obedience;
let us pray to the Lord.

Lord, have mercy.

Silence

God our redeemer,
who called your Church to witness
that you were in Christ
reconciling the world to yourself:

help us so to proclaim the good news of your love
that all who hear it may be reconciled to you;
through him who died for us and rose again
and reigns with you and the Holy Spirit,
one God, now and for ever. **Amen.**

For all who suffer:
for victims of violence, injustice and abuse,
for the lonely, the bereaved, and those without hope,
for the sick, the dying, and all who care for them,
that, in his mercy, God will sustain them
with the knowledge of his presence;
let us pray to the Lord.

Lord, have mercy.

Silence

Gracious God,
the comfort of all who sorrow,
the strength of all who suffer,
hear the prayers of your children
who cry out to you in their need.
In their afflictions show them your mercy,
and give us, we pray, the strength to serve them,
for the sake of him who suffered for us,
your Son Jesus Christ our Lord. **Amen.**

Remembering those who have died,
all whose lives have ended in loneliness,
and all who have offered their lives for the sake of others,
and remembering the saints and martyrs of every generation,
that we also, inspired by their example,
may have grace to glorify Christ;
let us pray to the Lord.

Lord, have mercy.

Silence

Almighty and everlasting God,
whose Son Jesus Christ is the resurrection and the life:
set his passion, cross and death
between your judgement and our souls,
now and in the hour of our death,
and bring us, with the whole creation,
to the light and glory of your kingdom;
through Jesus Christ our Lord. **Amen.**

18 The Lord's Prayer

EITHER

We say together the prayer that Jesus gave us:

Our Father in heaven,
hallowed be your Name,
your kingdom come,
your will be done,
on earth as in heaven.
Give us today our daily bread.
Forgive us our sins
as we forgive those who sin against us.
Save us from the time of trial
and deliver us from evil.
For the kingdom, the power and the glory are yours,
now and for ever. Amen.

OR

As our Saviour taught his disciples, we pray:

Our Father, who art in heaven,
hallowed be thy Name;
thy kingdom come;
thy will be done;
on earth as it is in heaven.
Give us this day our daily bread.
And forgive us our trespasses,
as we forgive those who trespass against us.
And lead us not into temptation;
but deliver us from evil.
For thine is the kingdom, the power, and the glory,
for ever and ever. Amen.

19 Hymn

20 EITHER

A Most merciful God,
who by the death and resurrection
of your Son Jesus Christ,
delivered and saved the world:
grant that by faith in him who suffered on the cross
we may triumph in the power of his victory;
through Jesus Christ our Lord. **Amen.**

OR

B Almighty God,
whose most dear Son went not up to joy
but first he suffered pain,
and entered not into glory before he was crucified:
mercifully grant that we, walking in the way of the cross,
may find it to be the way of life and peace;
through Jesus Christ our Lord. **Amen.**

21 There is no blessing or dismissal.

All leave in silence.

THE EASTER VIGIL

INTRODUCTION

The Easter Vigil is derived from the great vigils on Holy Saturday during which the early Christians waited in hope and expectancy to begin the celebration of the resurrection. On this occasion, candidates were presented for Baptism. The service consisted of prayer, readings recalling the mighty acts of God, and the lighting of the Easter Candle signifying the triumph of the risen Lord and his presence among his people.

NOTES

1 ***The Easter Vigil*** should begin after sunset on Easter Eve and before sunrise on Easter Day.

2 An Easter Candle is a large candle which is traditionally lit for all services during the great fifty days of Easter and may be lit for Baptisms and funerals during the following year. Transfers for the Easter Candle can be obtained from appropriate suppliers. The symbols shown are the cross, A and Ω (Alpha and Omega), which remind us that Christ is the first and the last, the numerals of the current year which remind us that the Lord of all ages is present here and now, and the five 'nails' to represent the 'five bleeding wounds he bears, received on Calvary'.

3 When a number of congregations come together for this service only one Easter Candle should be used. If Easter Candles are to be taken back to other churches, they should be lit from the first candle at the end of the service.

4 One of the traditional diaconal roles is the carrying of the Easter Candle and the saying of the first text at no. 12 and the text at no. 13. If there is a deacon in the circuit, it is fitting that she/he be invited to exercise this ministry.

5 The Easter Candle may be prepared at no. 6, the presiding minister saying:

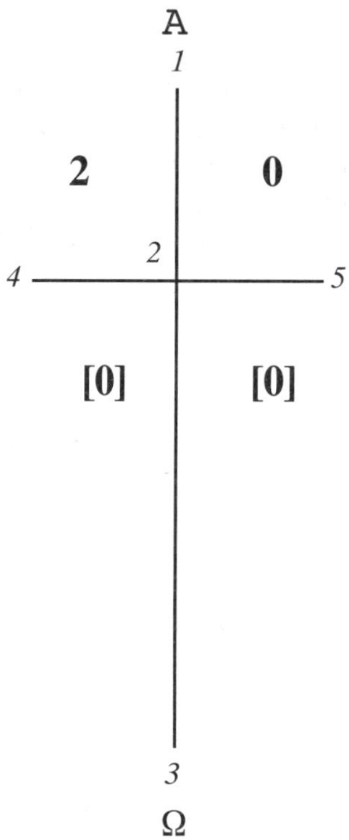

(as she/he traces the vertical arm of the cross, 1-3)

Christ, yesterday and today

(as she/he traces the horizontal arm of the cross, 4-5)

the beginning and the end,

(as she/he traces the alpha above the cross)

Alpha

(as she/he traces the omega below the cross)

and Omega;

(as she/he traces the first digit of the year in the upper left corner of the cross)

his are all times

(as she/he traces the second digit in the upper right corner of the cross)

and ages;

(as she/he traces the third digit in the lower left corner of the cross)

to him be glory and dominion,

(as she/he traces the fourth digit in the lower right corner of the cross)

for ever and ever. **Amen.**

Five nails may be inserted into the Candle at the four points and the intersection of the cross as the presiding minister says:

(1) By his holy
(2) and glorious wounds
(3) may Christ our Lord
(4) guard us
(5) and keep us. **Amen.**

6 Each member of the congregation should be provided with a small candle and some form of protection against the hot wax. Non-drip candles are recommended. The candles are lit during the Service of Light and may be extinguished at no. 14.

THE VIGIL

1 The lights, except one for reading, are switched off.

2 The presiding minister says:

Sisters and brothers in Christ, on this most holy night in which our Lord Jesus Christ passed over from death to life, we gather in vigil, prayer and celebration.

This is the Passover of the Lord, in which through word and sacrament we share in his victory over death.

3 At least three of the following sets of Old Testament readings, psalms or canticles, and collects are read here or at no. 17. Set D should always be used.

For each psalm or canticle, an optional refrain has been provided. When a refrain is used it is announced by the reader and said or sung before and after, and at appropriate points during, the psalm or canticle.

A Genesis 1:1 - 2:4*a*

Psalm 136:1-9, 23-26

Refrain

Christ is the image of the invisible God,
through whom all things were made.

Collect

Let us pray.

Almighty God,
you wonderfully created us
and still more wonderfully redeemed us.
Bring us to those lasting joys
which you have prepared for us
through the sacrifice of Christ our Passover;
who lives and reigns with you and the Holy Spirit,
one God, now and for ever. **Amen.**

B Genesis 7:1-5, 11-18; 8:6-18; 9:8-13

Psalm 46

Refrain

In Baptism we died to sin.
In Christ we are raised to life.

Collect

Let us pray.

Faithful God,
in the waters of the flood
you pronounced judgement on sin
and proclaimed the steadfastness of your covenant love.
Grant that we, who have been baptized in your name,
being rescued from sin,
may rejoice in your mercy;
through Christ our Lord. **Amen.**

Silence

C Genesis 22:1-18

Psalm 16

Refrain

God so loved the world
that he gave his only Son.

Collect

Let us pray.

God and Father of all who believe in you,
you promised Abraham that he would become
the father of many nations,
and through the death and resurrection of Christ
you fulfil that promise.
May we joyfully accept your invitation
to the new life of grace;
through Jesus Christ our Lord. **Amen.**

Silence

D Exodus 14:10-31; 15:20-21

Canticle: Exodus 15:1*b*-13, 17-18

Refrain

Christ our Passover is sacrificed for us.
Therefore let us keep the feast.

Collect

Let us pray.

Redeemer God,
you heard the cry of your people
and sent Moses your servant
to lead them out of slavery.

Free us from the tyranny of sin and death
and, by the leading of your Spirit,
bring us to our promised land;
through Jesus Christ our Lord. **Amen.**

Silence

E Isaiah 55:1-11

Canticle: Isaiah 12:2-6

Refrain

All who come to Christ will never hunger.
All who believe in Christ will never thirst.

Collect

Let us pray.

God our Father and Provider,
whose Son has given his flesh for the life of the world:
sustain your pilgrim Church on its journey
with the word of life and the bread of heaven.
Draw us nearer to him in whose name we gather,
that, following his way of sacrificial love,
we may come to the banquet of eternal life;
through Jesus Christ our Lord. **Amen.**

Silence

F Baruch 3:9-15, 32 - 4:4 *or* Proverbs 8:1-8, 19-21; 9:4*b*-6

Psalm 19

Refrain

Christ is the wisdom of God.
Christ has the words of eternal life.

Collect

Let us pray.

God Most High,
whose eternal Word chose a dwelling among us,
that we might live in your presence:
grant us a spirit of wisdom
to know how rich is the glory you have given us,
and how great is the hope to which we are
called in the Word made flesh;
who is alive and reigns with you
in the unity of the Holy Spirit,
one God for ever and ever. **Amen.**

Silence

G Ezekiel 36:24-28

Psalms 42; 43

Refrain

Christ gives the living water.
Christ is the fountain of eternal life.

Collect

Let us pray.

Gracious God,
you give the water of eternal life
through Jesus Christ your Son.
May we always turn to you,
the spring of life and source of goodness;
through the same Jesus Christ our Lord. **Amen.**

Silence

H Ezekiel 37:1-14

Psalm 143

Refrain

Christ is the resurrection and the life.
Those who believe in Christ shall never die.

Collect

Let us pray.

Grant, Lord,
that we who are baptized into the death
of your Son our Saviour Jesus Christ
may continually put to death our evil desires
and be buried with him;
that through the grave and gate of death
we may pass to our joyful resurrection;
through the merits of him
who died and was buried and rose again for us,
your Son Jesus Christ our Lord. **Amen.**

Silence

I Zephaniah 3:14-20

Psalm 98

Refrain

Where, O death, is your victory?
Where, O death, is your sting?

Collect

Let us pray.

God of all holiness,
your promises stand unshaken through all generations
and you lift up all who are burdened and brought low.
Renew our hope in you,
as we wait for the coming in glory of Jesus Christ,
our Judge and our Saviour,
who lives and reigns with you and the Holy Spirit,
one God, world without end. **Amen.**

Silence

THE SERVICE OF LIGHT

4 The people stand.

5 The presiding minister, the deacon or other person carrying the Easter Candle, and the assistants carrying small candles go in silent procession to the entrance of the church. All turn to face the Easter Candle.

6 The Easter Candle may be prepared.

7 The presiding minister lights the Easter Candle and says:

May the light of Christ, rising in glory,
banish all darkness from our hearts and minds. **Amen.**

8 The person carrying the Easter Candle raises it and says:

Christ our Light.
Thanks be to God.

9 The procession moves to the centre of the church. The person carrying the Easter Candle again raises it and, in a louder voice, says:

Christ our Light.
Thanks be to God.

10 The assistants' candles are lit from the Easter Candle and the procession moves to the front of the church. The person carrying the Easter Candle again raises it and, in a still louder voice, says:

Christ our Light.
Thanks be to God.

11 The people's candles are lit from the assistants' candles and the Easter Candle is placed near the font. When all the candles are lit, the person who carried the Easter Candle says:

Alleluia! Christ is risen!
He is risen indeed. Alleluia!

12 EITHER

A the person who carried the Easter Candle says:

Rejoice, heavenly powers! Sing, choirs of angels!
Exult, all creation around God's throne!
Jesus Christ, our King, is risen!
Sound the trumpet of salvation!

Rejoice, O earth, in shining splendour,
radiant in the brightness of your King!
Christ has conquered! Glory fills you!
Darkness vanishes for ever!

Rejoice, O Mother Church! Exult in glory!
The risen Saviour shines upon you!
Let this place resound with joy,
echoing the mighty song of all God's people!

OR

B all sing:

Sing, choirs of heaven! Let saints and angels sing!
Around God's throne exult in harmony!
Now Jesus Christ is risen from the grave!
Salute your King in glorious symphony!

Sing, choirs of earth! Behold, your light has come!
The glory of the Lord shines radiantly!
Lift up your hearts, for Christ has conquered death!
The night is past; the day of life is here!

Sing, Church of God! Exult with joy outpoured!
The gospel trumpets tell of victory won!
Your Saviour lives: he's with you evermore!
Let all God's people shout the long Amen!

(Tune: WOODLANDS)

13 The person who carried the Easter Candle says:

The Lord be with you.
And also with you.

Lift up your hearts.
We lift them to the Lord.

Let us give thanks to the Lord our God.
It is right to give our thanks and praise.

It is truly right
that with full hearts and minds and voices
we should praise the unseen God
and his only Son, our Lord Jesus Christ,
who has ransomed us with his blood,
and reconciled us to the Father!

This is our Passover feast, when Christ, the true Lamb, is slain,
whose blood consecrates the homes of all believers.

This is the night when first God saved our ancestors:
he freed the people of Israel from their slavery
and led them dry-shod through the sea.

This is the night when Jesus Christ broke the chains of death
and rose triumphant from the grave.

Most blessed of all nights,
chosen by God to see Christ rising from the dead!

Of this night Scripture says:
'The night will be as clear as day:
it will become my light, my joy.'

The power of this holy night dispels all evil,
washes guilt away, restores lost innocence,
brings mourners joy;
it casts out hatred, brings us peace,
and humbles earthly pride.

Night truly blessed when heaven is wedded to earth
and all creation reconciled to God!

Therefore, heavenly Father,
in the joy of this night,
receive our evening sacrifice of praise,
your Church's solemn offering.

Accept this Easter candle,
a flame divided but undimmed,
a pillar of fire that glows to the honour of your name.

May Christ, the Morning Star which never sets,
find the flame of love still burning within us:
Christ, who came back from the dead,
Christ, who sheds his peaceful light on all the world,
Christ, who lives and reigns for ever and ever. **Amen.**

14 A fanfare may be played, cymbals clashed, bells rung, lights switched on and the people's candles put out.

15 **Glory to God in the highest,**
and peace to God's people on earth.

Lord God, heavenly King,
almighty God and Father,
we worship you, we give you thanks,
we praise you for your glory.

**Lord Jesus Christ, only Son of the Father,
Lord God, Lamb of God,
you take away the sin of the world:
have mercy on us.
You are seated at the right hand of the Father:
receive our prayer.**

**For you alone are the Holy One,
you alone are the Lord,
you alone are the Most High, Jesus Christ,
with the Holy Spirit,
in the glory of God the Father. Amen.**

16 The presiding minister says:

Let us pray.

Lord of all life and power,
who through the mighty resurrection of your Son
overcame the old order of sin and death
to make all things new in him:
grant that we, being dead to sin
and alive to you in Jesus Christ,
may reign with him in glory;
to whom with you in the unity of the Holy Spirit
be praise and honour, glory and might,
now and in all eternity. **Amen.**

17 All sit. If the Vigil has not already been kept, the material at no. 3 now follows.

18 O give thanks to the Lord for he is good;
his steadfast love endures for ever!
The Lord is my strength and my might,
he has become my salvation.

Alleluia! Alleluia! Alleluia!

The right hand of the Lord does valiantly;
the right hand of the Lord is exalted.
I shall not die, but I shall live,
and recount the deeds of the Lord.

Alleluia! Alleluia! Alleluia!

The stone that the builders rejected
has become the chief cornerstone.
This is the Lord's doing;
it is marvellous in our eyes.

Alleluia! Alleluia! Alleluia!

19 Epistle: Romans 6:3-11

20 Hymn

21 A reading from the Gospel according to . . .

Alleluia! Hear the Gospel of Christ.
Glory to Christ our Saviour. Alleluia!

The Gospel is read:

Year A: Matthew 28:1-10
Year B: Mark 16:1-8
Year C: Luke 24:1-12

Alleluia! This is the Gospel of Christ.
Praise to Christ our Lord. Alleluia!

22 Sermon

23 Hymn

THE REAFFIRMATION OF BAPTISM

24 All stand.

Sisters and brothers in Christ,
through the paschal mystery
we have been buried with Christ in Baptism,
so that we may rise with him to a new life.
Let us affirm the faith
in which we were baptized
and in which we live and grow.

I ask you, therefore:

Do you believe and trust in God the Father?

I believe in God, the Father almighty,
creator of heaven and earth.

Do you believe and trust in God the Son?

I believe in Jesus Christ,
God's only Son, our Lord,
who was conceived by the Holy Spirit,
born of the Virgin Mary,
suffered under Pontius Pilate,
was crucified, died, and was buried;
he descended to the dead.
On the third day he rose again,
he ascended into heaven,
he is seated at the right hand of the Father,
and he will come to judge the living and the dead.

Do you believe and trust in God the Holy Spirit?

I believe in the Holy Spirit,
the holy catholic Church,
the communion of saints,
the forgiveness of sins,
the resurrection of the body,
and the life everlasting. Amen.

25 Let us pray.

Lord God almighty,
the radiance of your glory lights up our hearts.
Enable us truly to understand
the waters in which we were cleansed,
the Spirit by which we were reborn,
and the blood by which we were redeemed;
that in our earthly pilgrimage
we may walk more closely
with our risen Saviour and Lord;
who is alive and reigns
with you and the Holy Spirit,
one God, now and for ever. **Amen.**

26 The service continues from no. 14 in ***Holy Communion for the Easter Season*** (page 165). The Nicene Creed is not said.

THE COVENANT SERVICE

INTRODUCTION

From the earliest days of the Methodist societies, John Wesley invited the Methodist people to renew their covenant relationship with God. Wesley drew much of his material for the service from seventeenth-century Puritans and subsequently made changes to it. The Wesleyan Conference revised it twice during the nineteenth century and other branches of Methodism had versions of it.

The Book of Offices (1936) included a form of ***The Covenant Service*** which quickly achieved great popularity. **The Methodist Service Book** (1975) version strengthened the link between the renewal of the covenant and the Holy Communion, but at the cost of losing some familiar and much loved passages. In the present service, some of these have been recast and restored, not least in the penitential section.

The present ***Covenant Service*** moves from praise of the Trinity to listening to the word in scripture, read and preached, and then follows a penitential approach to the words of the Covenant. Changes in the use and understanding of language have led to the provision of two forms of this part of the service. The first form is offered as a contemporary version of the Covenant Prayer; the second form is the more traditional text. In this form, the words, 'Put me to doing, put me to suffering', have raised difficulties for some people. These words do not mean that we ask God to make us suffer, but rather that we desire, by God's help, actively to do or patiently to accept whatever is God's will for us.

The emphasis of the whole service is on God's readiness to enfold us in generous love, not dependent on our deserving. Our response, also in love, springs with penitent joy from thankful recognition of God's grace. The covenant is not just a one-to-one transaction between individuals and God, but the act of the whole faith community. The prayers of intercession which follow emphasize our unity with all humanity. The service proceeds to the Lord's Supper, for which a special form has been provided to emphasize the continuity between word, response and sacrament. The service is meant to lead us, by a path both similar to and differing from that of normal Sunday worship, to that commitment which all worship seeks both to inspire and to strengthen.

NOTES

1 ***The Covenant Service*** should normally be held only once in each year.

2 At whatever time of day this service is held, it should be regarded as the principal service and used in full.

THE GATHERING OF THE PEOPLE OF GOD

1 Hymn

2 Let us pray.

Glory to the Father, the God of love,
who created us;
who continually preserves and sustains us;
who has loved us with an everlasting love,
and given us the light of the knowledge of his glory
in the face of Jesus Christ.

Blessèd be God for ever.

Glory to Jesus Christ our Saviour,
who, though he was rich,
yet for our sake became poor,
and was tested in every way as we are,
yet without sin;

who proclaimed the good news of the kingdom,
and was obedient to the point of death,
even death on a cross;
who was raised from the dead and is alive for ever,
and has opened the kingdom of heaven
to all who trust in him;
who is seated at God's right hand in glory,
and will come to be our judge.

Blessèd be God for ever.

Glory to the Holy Spirit,
the Lord, the giver of life,
by whom we are born into the family of God,
and made members of the body of Christ;
whose witness confirms us;
whose wisdom teaches us;
whose power enables us;
who will do for us more than we can ask or think.

Blessèd be God for ever.

To the one God, Father, Son and Holy Spirit,
be praise and glory for ever. **Amen.**

3 Silence

4 Collect

God of grace,
through the mediation of your Son,
you call us into a new covenant.
Help us therefore to draw near with faith
and join ourselves in a perpetual covenant with you;
through Jesus Christ our Lord. **Amen.**

THE MINISTRY OF THE WORD

5 A reading from the Law.

Exodus 24:3-11 *or* Deuteronomy 29:10-15 is read.

For the wisdom that guides us
we praise you, O God.

6 A reading from the Prophets.

Jeremiah 31:31-34 is read.

For the word that inspires us
we praise you, O God.

7 A reading from the Epistles.

Romans 12:1-2 is read.

For the truth that enlightens us
we praise you, O God.

8 Hymn

9 A reading from the Gospel according to . . .

Hear the Gospel of Christ.
Glory to Christ our Saviour.

The Gospel, John 15:1-10 *or* Mark 14:22-25, is read.

This is the Gospel of Christ.
Praise to Christ our Lord.

10 Sermon

11 Hymn

THE COVENANT

12 God made a covenant with the people of Israel, calling them to be a holy nation, chosen to bear witness to his steadfast love by finding delight in the law.

The covenant was renewed in Jesus Christ our Lord, in his life, work, death and resurrection. In him all people may be set free from sin and its power, and united in love and obedience.

In this covenant God promises us new life in Christ. For our part we promise to live no longer for ourselves but for God.

We meet, therefore, as generations have met before us, to renew the covenant which bound them and binds us to God.

Let us then seek forgiveness for the sin by which we have denied God's claim upon us.

13 Let us pray.

God of mercy, hear us as we confess our sins.

For the sin that has made us slow to learn from Christ,
reluctant to follow him,
and afraid to bear the cross:

Lord, have mercy,
Lord, forgive.

For the sin that has caused the poverty of our worship,
the formality and selfishness of our prayers,
our neglect of fellowship and the means of grace,
and our hesitating witness for Christ:

Lord, have mercy,
Lord, forgive.

For the sin that has led us to misuse your gifts,
evade our responsibilities,
and fail to be good stewards of your creation:

Lord, have mercy,
Lord, forgive.

For the sin that has made us unwilling to overcome evil
with good,
tolerant of injustice,
quick to condemn,
and selfish in sharing your love with others:

Lord, have mercy,
Lord, forgive.

Silence

Have mercy on me, O God,
in your constant love;
in the fullness of your mercy
blot out my offences.
Wash away all my guilt,
and cleanse me from my sin.
Create in me a clean heart, O God,
and renew a right spirit within me.
Give me the joy of your help again
and strengthen me with a willing spirit.

The presiding minister says:

If we confess our sins,
God is faithful and just,
and will forgive our sins,
and cleanse us from all unrighteousness.

Therefore to all who truly repent
this is his gracious word:
'Your sins are forgiven.'

Amen. Thanks be to God.

14 Hymn

Come, let us use the grace divine,
And all, with one accord,
In a perpetual cov'nant join
Ourselves to Christ the Lord:

Give up ourselves, through Jesu's power,
His name to glorify;
And promise, in this sacred hour,
For God to live and die.

The cov'nant we this moment make
Be ever kept in mind:
We will no more our God forsake,
Or cast his words behind.

We never will throw off his fear
Who hears our solemn vow;
And if thou art well pleased to hear,
Come down, and meet us now.

To each the cov'nant blood apply,
Which takes our sins away;
And register our names on high,
And keep us to that day.

15 The people remain standing and the presiding minister says:

EITHER

A Sisters and brothers in Christ,
let us again accept our place within this covenant
which God has made with us and with all who are called to be Christ's disciples.

This means that, by the help of the Holy Spirit,
we accept God's purpose for us,
and the call to love and serve God
in all our life and work.

Christ has many services to be done:
some are easy, others are difficult;
some bring honour, others bring reproach;
some are suitable to our natural inclinations and material
  interests,
others are contrary to both;
in some we may please Christ and please ourselves;
in others we cannot please Christ except by denying
  ourselves.
Yet the power to do all these things is given to us in Christ,
  who strengthens us.

Therefore let us make this covenant of God our own.
Let us give ourselves to him,
trusting in his promises and relying on his grace.

Eternal God,
in your faithful and enduring love
you call us to share in your gracious covenant in Jesus
  Christ.
In obedience we hear and accept your commands;
in love we seek to do your perfect will;
with joy we offer ourselves anew to you.
We are no longer our own but yours.

I am no longer my own but yours.
Your will, not mine, be done in all things,
  wherever you may place me,
  in all that I do
    and in all that I may endure;
  when there is work for me
    and when there is none;
  when I am troubled
    and when I am at peace.
Your will be done
  when I am valued
    and when I am disregarded;
  when I find fulfilment
    and when it is lacking;
  when I have all things,
    and when I have nothing.

I willingly offer
all I have and am
to serve you,
as and where you choose.

Glorious and blessèd God,
Father, Son and Holy Spirit,
you are mine and I am yours.
May it be so for ever.
Let this covenant now made on earth
be fulfilled in heaven. Amen.

OR

B Beloved in Christ,
let us again claim for ourselves
this covenant which God has made with his people,
and take upon us the yoke of Christ.

This means that we are content
that he appoint us our place and work,
and that he himself be our reward.

Christ has many services to be done:
some are easy, others are difficult;
some bring honour, others bring reproach;
some are suitable to our natural inclinations and material interests,
others are contrary to both;
in some we may please Christ and please ourselves;
in others we cannot please Christ except by denying ourselves.
Yet the power to do all these things is given to us in Christ, who strengthens us.

Therefore let us make this covenant of God our own.
Let us give ourselves to him,
trusting in his promises and relying on his grace.

Lord God, holy Father,
since you have called us through Christ
to share in this gracious covenant,
we take upon ourselves with joy the yoke of obedience
and, for love of you,
engage ourselves to seek and do your perfect will.
We are no longer our own but yours.

I am no longer my own but yours.
Put me to what you will,
rank me with whom you will;
put me to doing,
put me to suffering;
let me be employed for you
or laid aside for you,
exalted for you
or brought low for you;
let me be full,
let me be empty,
let me have all things,
let me have nothing;
I freely and wholeheartedly yield all things
to your pleasure and disposal.

And now, glorious and blessèd God,
Father, Son and Holy Spirit,
you are mine and I am yours.
So be it.
And the covenant now made on earth,
let it be ratified in heaven. Amen.

16 Silence, all seated

17 As we have entered this covenant not for ourselves alone, but as God's servants and witnesses, let us pray for the Church and for the world.

Loving God, hear us as we pray for your holy catholic Church:
make us all one, that the world may believe.

Inspire and lead all who govern and hold authority in the nations of the world:
establish justice and peace among all people.

Have compassion on all who suffer from any sickness, grief or trouble:
deliver them from their distress.

We praise you for all your saints who have entered your eternal glory:
bring us all to share in your heavenly kingdom.

Let us pray in silence for our own needs and for those of others . . .

Silence

Lord our God,
you have helped us by your grace
to make these prayers,
and you have promised through Christ our Lord
that when two or three agree in his name
you will grant what they ask.
Answer now your servants' prayers
according to their needs;
in this world grant that we may truly know you,
and in the world to come
graciously give us eternal life;
through Jesus Christ our Lord. **Amen.**

THE LORD'S SUPPER

18 The Peace

All stand.

The Lord has made an everlasting covenant of peace with his people.

The peace of the Lord be always with you.
And also with you.

The people may greet one another in the name of Christ.

THE PREPARATION OF THE GIFTS

19 Hymn

20 The offerings of the people are presented. Bread and wine are brought to the table (or if already on the table are uncovered). The presiding minister takes the bread and wine and prepares them for use.

THE THANKSGIVING

21 All stand.

The presiding minister leads the great prayer of thanksgiving:

The Lord be with you.
And also with you.

Lift up your hearts.
We lift them to the Lord.

Let us give thanks to the Lord our God.
It is right to give our thanks and praise.

God our Father, fountain of goodness,
creator of all that is,
you have made us in your own image.
You have given us life and reason,
and love for one another,
setting in our hearts a hunger for you.

In darkness you are our light,
in adversity and temptation our strength.
You bear patiently with our folly and sin,
granting us your law to guide us
and your prophets to renew our faith.

In the fullness of time
you came to us in love and mercy
in Jesus Christ, your living Word,
full of grace and truth.

He lived among us,
declaring your forgiveness
and revealing your wisdom
in works of mercy and in his word of power.
For us he suffered and died upon the cross,
by death destroying death.
You raised him from the dead
and exalted him to your right hand on high.
Through him you sent your Holy Spirit
to be the life and light of your people,
gathered together in every time and place
to glorify your holy name.

With them and all the company of heaven
we join in the unending hymn of praise:

Holy, holy, holy Lord,
God of power and might,
heaven and earth are full of your glory.
Hosanna in the highest.
Blessèd is he who comes in the name of the Lord.
Hosanna in the highest.

Holy God, pour out your Spirit
that these gifts of bread and wine
may be for us the body and blood
of your Son Jesus Christ our Lord,
who, on the night in which he was betrayed,
took bread, gave thanks, broke it,
and gave it to his disciples, saying,
'Take this and eat it.
This is my body given for you.
Do this in remembrance of me.'

In the same way, after supper,
he took the cup, gave thanks,
and gave it to them, saying,

'Drink from it, all of you.
This is my blood of the new covenant,
poured out for you and for many,
for the forgiveness of sins.
Do this, whenever you drink it,
in remembrance of me.'

Christ has died.
Christ is risen.
Christ will come again.

And so, Lord, we obey his command
with this bread and this cup,
by which we recall his death and resurrection,
the source of our life and salvation.
Grant that we, who share in this holy sacrament,
may be united by your Spirit
and grow into perfect love.

Bring us,
with those who have done your will in every age,
into the light of your presence
and the joy of your kingdom.

Through Christ, with Christ, in Christ,
in the power of the Holy Spirit,
we worship you in songs of everlasting praise.
Blessing and honour and glory and power
be yours for ever and ever. Amen.

22 The Lord's Prayer

EITHER

We say together the prayer that Jesus gave us:

Our Father in heaven,
hallowed be your Name,
your kingdom come,
your will be done,
on earth as in heaven.

OR

As our Saviour taught his disciples, we pray:

Our Father, who art in heaven,
hallowed be thy Name;
thy kingdom come;
thy will be done;

Give us today our daily bread.
Forgive us our sins
as we forgive those who sin against us.
Save us from the time of trial
and deliver us from evil.
For the kingdom, the power and the glory are yours,
now and for ever. Amen.

on earth as it is in heaven.
Give us this day our daily bread.
And forgive us our trespasses,
as we forgive those who trespass against us.
And lead us not into temptation;
but deliver us from evil.
For thine is the kingdom, the power, and the glory,
for ever and ever. Amen.

THE BREAKING OF THE BREAD

23 The presiding minister breaks the bread in the sight of the people in silence, or saying:

The things of God for God's holy people.

Jesus Christ is holy;
Jesus Christ is Lord.
Glory to God the Father.

24 Silence, all seated or kneeling

THE SHARING OF THE BREAD AND WINE

25 The presiding minister, those assisting with the distribution, and the people receive, according to local custom.

The presiding minister may invite the congregation to receive communion with these or similar words:

Jesus said: 'I am the bread of life.
Those who come to me shall not hunger
and those who believe in me shall never thirst.'

Draw near with faith.

26 Words such as the following are said during the distribution:

The body of Christ keep you in eternal life. **Amen.**

The blood of Christ keep you in eternal life. **Amen.**

27 During the distribution there may be appropriate music.

28 The elements that remain are covered with a white cloth.

PRAYERS AND DISMISSAL

29 Silence

30 Let us pray.

Faithful God,
with these holy gifts
you have fed and strengthened us
in Jesus Christ your Son.
Guide us on our way,
that with all your faithful people
we may come to share the feast
of your eternal kingdom;
through Jesus Christ our Lord. Amen.

31 Hymn

32 The presiding minister says:

The blessing of God,
the Father, the Son and the Holy Spirit,
be upon *you/us* and remain with *you/us* for ever. **Amen.**

33 The presiding minister says:

Go in peace to love and serve the Lord.

In the name of Christ. Amen.

ORDINATION SERVICES

INTRODUCTION

All Christians are called through their Baptism and by the hearing of God's word to ministry and service among the whole people of God and in the life of the world. Some are called and ordained to specific ministries. The Methodist Church has received and transmitted two orders of ministry, the presbyteral and the diaconal.

Presbyters, usually called Ministers, derive their origin from the presbyter/bishops of New Testament times. The development of the form in which the Methodist Church has received this office was influenced by the vocation and work of John and Charles Wesley, who were themselves presbyters in the Church of England. As the work of God progressed among the Methodist people, some of the preachers who were not already presbyters in the Church of England were ordained to celebrate the sacraments, to preach the word and to care for God's people.

More recently, the Methodist Diaconal Order has developed from the Wesley Deaconess Order into an order of ministry for both women and men. Deacons are ordained to a ministry of service and pastoral care and seek to equip God's people for service in the world. In the Methodist Church, diaconal ministry is an office in its own right rather than a step toward the office of presbyter. For both presbyters and deacons, ordination is to a permanent lifelong office of ministry.

At all Methodist ordinations, the President of the Conference or the President's deputy presides. Ordination is by prayer and the laying on of hands and takes place within the context of Holy Communion. The ordination prayer (no. 16 in each service) is in three parts. The first and third parts are said only once, but the second part, which accompanies the laying on of hands, is repeated for each ordinand, as God is asked to send the Holy Spirit upon the ordinand for the office and work of a presbyter or deacon.

In common with other churches, in the ordination of presbyters and deacons, the Methodist Church intends to ordain, not to a denomination, but to the presbyterate and the diaconate in the One Holy Catholic and Apostolic Church. It looks for the day when, in communion with the whole Church, such ministries are recognized and exercised in common.

THE ORDINATION OF PRESBYTERS, USUALLY CALLED MINISTERS

NOTE

When, in accordance with Standing Orders, *a candidate is* to be ordained before being received into Full Connexion, the words spoken at no. 11 are amended appropriately.

THE GATHERING OF THE PEOPLE OF GOD

1 Silence

2 All stand as those who are leading worship enter the church.

The President says:

O give thanks to the Lord, for he is good;
and his mercy endures for ever.

I welcome you all on this joyful occasion and greet you in the name of God.

The grace of the Lord Jesus Christ, and the love of God, and the fellowship of the Holy Spirit, be with you all.

And also with you.

3 This or some other hymn:

The Saviour, when to heaven he rose

4 All sit. The President says:

Let us pray.

Silence

God of all grace,
you call your Church to be a holy people
to the praise of your name.
In the power of your Spirit,
fill our hearts with your love
and our lives with your glory;
through Jesus Christ our Lord. **Amen.**

THE MINISTRY OF THE WORD

5 Old Testament reading: Isaiah 6:1-8

6 Epistle: Romans 12:1-18

7 This or some other hymn:

Ye servants of God, your Master proclaim

8 All remain standing.

A reading from the Gospel according to John.

Hear the Gospel of Christ.
Glory to Christ our Saviour.

The Gospel, John 20:19-29, is read.

This is the Gospel of Christ.
Praise to Christ our Lord.

9 All sit.

Sermon

10 The Nicene Creed

All stand.

Let us profess the faith of the Church.

**We believe in one God,
the Father, the Almighty,
maker of heaven and earth,
of all that is, seen and unseen.**

**We believe in one Lord, Jesus Christ,
the only Son of God,
eternally begotten of the Father,
God from God, Light from Light,
true God from true God,
begotten, not made,
of one Being with the Father;
through him all things were made.
For us and for our salvation
he came down from heaven,
was incarnate of the Holy Spirit and the Virgin Mary
and became truly human.
For our sake he was crucified under Pontius Pilate;
he suffered death and was buried.
On the third day he rose again
in accordance with the Scriptures;
he ascended into heaven
and is seated at the right hand of the Father.
He will come again in glory to judge the living and the dead,
and his kingdom will have no end.**

**We believe in the Holy Spirit, the Lord, the giver of life,
who proceeds from the Father and the Son,
who with the Father and the Son is worshipped and glorified,
who has spoken through the prophets.
We believe in one holy catholic and apostolic Church.
We acknowledge one Baptism for the forgiveness of sins.
We look for the resurrection of the dead,
and the life of the world to come. Amen.**

THE ORDINATION

THE PRESENTATION

11 All sit.

The Secretary presents the candidates to the President.

Madam/Mr President, I present to you these persons to be ordained presbyters. The Conference has received them into Full Connexion and resolved that they be ordained by prayer and the laying on of hands.

The Secretary reads the names of those to be ordained. Each candidate rises as her/his name is called, and remains standing.

12 The people stand and the President says:

Sisters and brothers in Christ, these are the persons whom we intend, in God's name, to ordain to the Ministry of Christ's holy Church in the Order of Presbyters.

Their call has been tested in preparation for this ministry and they have been found to be of sound learning and faithful to their vocation.

We ask you to declare your assent to their ordination.

Do you believe and trust that they are, by God's grace, worthy to be ordained?

The people acclaim:

They are worthy.

Will you uphold them in their ministry?

The people answer:

We will uphold them.

THE EXAMINATION

13 The people sit. The ordinands remain standing and the President says to them:

Beloved in Christ, the Church is God's holy people, the Body of Christ, the dwelling place of the Holy Spirit.

All who are received into the Church by Baptism are called to proclaim the mighty acts of God in Jesus Christ our Saviour, and to serve him in the Church and in the world.

God has called you into the Order of Presbyters among his people.

In his name you are

to preach by word and deed the Gospel of God's grace;
to declare God's forgiveness of sins to all who are penitent;
to baptize, to confirm
and to preside at the celebration of the sacrament of Christ's body and blood;
to lead God's people in worship, prayer and service;
to minister Christ's love and compassion;
to serve others, in whom you serve the Lord himself.

These things are your common duty and delight.
In them you are to watch over one another in love.

In all things, give counsel and encouragement
to those whom Christ entrusts to your care.
Pray without ceasing.
Work with joy in the Lord's service.
Let no one suffer hurt through your neglect.

This ministry will make great demands upon you and upon those close to you, yet in all this, the Holy Spirit will sustain you by his grace.

I now ask you to declare your lifelong commitment to this ministry:

Do you believe that God has called you to be a Minister of the Word and Sacraments in the universal Church?

Answer: I do.

Do you accept the Holy Scriptures as revealing all things necessary for salvation through Jesus Christ our Lord?

Answer: I do.

Do you believe the doctrines of the Christian faith as this Church has received them?

Answer: I do.

Will you accept our discipline, and work together with your sisters and brothers in the Church?

Answer: I will.

Will you be faithful in worship, in prayer, in the reading of the Holy Scriptures, and in those studies which will equip you for your ministry?

Answer: I will.

May God who has called you to this ministry give you grace and power to do his will; through Jesus Christ our Lord. **Amen.**

THE LITANY

14 The ordinands sit.

Let us pray.

All pray in silence.

On the peoples of the world
and the leaders of the nations,
gracious God,
pour out your Spirit.

On your holy Church throughout the world,
gracious God,
pour out your Spirit.

On all whom you have called to be ordained,
gracious God,
pour out your Spirit.

On all whom they serve in their ministry,
gracious God,
pour out your Spirit.

On their families and friends
and all who have helped and encouraged them,
gracious God,
pour out your Spirit.

Remember, O Lord, what you have wrought in us,
and not what we deserve;
and as you have called us to your service,
make us worthy of our calling;
through Jesus Christ our Lord. **Amen.**

THE ORDINATION

15 Hymn

**Come, Holy Ghost, our souls inspire,
And lighten with celestial fire;
Thou the anointing Spirit art,
Who dost thy sevenfold gifts impart:**

**Thy blessèd unction from above
Is comfort, life, and fire of love;
Enable with perpetual light
The dullness of our blinded sight:**

Anoint and cheer our soilèd face
With the abundance of thy grace;
Keep far our foes, give peace at home;
Where thou art guide no ill can come.

Teach us to know the Father, Son,
And thee, of both, to be but One;
That through the ages all along
This may be our endless song:

'Praise to thy eternal merit,
Father, Son, and Holy Spirit. Amen.'

16 The people sit. The ordinands kneel and the President, standing, says:

Lord our God,
we give you thanks and praise.
You are the light and life of your people in every age,
calling us to declare your acts of mercy and love.

You sent your Son Jesus Christ
to be our Saviour.
He called the apostles
to witness to his words and deeds,
his life, death and resurrection.
Through him you have made your Church
a royal priesthood for the glory of your name.
In the power of the Holy Spirit
you strengthen and shepherd your people,
by sending apostles and prophets,
pastors, evangelists and teachers,
in a succession of truth and grace.

By the same Spirit
you have called these your servants
to be Ministers in your Church.

Increase in them the gifts of your grace
for their life and ministry.

The prayer continues as the President lays her/his hands upon the head of each ordinand in turn, other ministers also laying their right hands on the ordinand.

The President says over each one:

Father, send the Holy Spirit upon *N* for the office and work of a Presbyter in your Church.

Each time the President says these words, all answer:

Amen.

When hands have been laid on all of them, the President continues:

Gracious God,
as you call and ordain these your servants to this ministry,
we ask you to fulfil in them the work you have begun.

Grant them unfailing love for those people among whom
you appoint them as pastors and teachers.

May they boldly proclaim your truth
and faithfully celebrate your sacraments.

Give them wisdom and patience
in their witness and service.
Sustain and strengthen them at all times,
giving faith and perseverance to all who believe in you
through their word.

May they be counted worthy at the last
to enter into the joy of their Lord.

We ask this through Jesus Christ our Lord,
who lives and reigns with you
in the unity of the Holy Spirit,
one God for ever and ever. **Amen.**

17 The Lord's Prayer

EITHER

We say together the prayer that Jesus gave us:

**Our Father in heaven,
hallowed be your Name,
your kingdom come,
your will be done,
on earth as in heaven.
Give us today our daily bread.
Forgive us our sins
as we forgive those who sin against us.
Save us from the time of trial
and deliver us from evil.
For the kingdom, the power and the glory are yours,
now and for ever. Amen.**

OR

As our Saviour taught his disciples, we pray:

**Our Father, who art in heaven,
hallowed be thy Name;
thy kingdom come;
thy will be done;
on earth as it is in heaven.
Give us this day our daily bread.
And forgive us our trespasses,
as we forgive those who trespass against us.
And lead us not into temptation;
but deliver us from evil.
For thine is the kingdom, the power, and the glory,
for ever and ever. Amen.**

THE GIVING OF THE BIBLE

18 The newly-ordained Ministers stand.

The Vice-President presents a Bible to each of them, saying:

N, receive this Bible
as a sign of the authority committed to you this day
to preach the word of God
and to celebrate the sacraments.

THE DECLARATION

19 All stand. The President says:

In the name of our Lord Jesus Christ I declare that you have been ordained as Presbyters of the one holy catholic and apostolic Church of Christ.

Remember your call.

Declare the Good News.
Celebrate the sacraments.
Serve the needy.
Minister to the sick.
Welcome the stranger.
Seek the lost.

Be shepherds to the flock of Christ.
As you exercise mercy, do not forget justice;
as you minister discipline, do not forget mercy;
that when Christ the Chief Shepherd comes in glory
he may count you among his faithful servants.

To God be the glory for ever. Amen.

20 The people may welcome the newly-ordained Ministers with applause.

THE LORD'S SUPPER

21 The Peace

All stand. The President says:

The peace of the Lord be always with you.
And also with you.

The people may greet one another in the name of Christ.

THE PREPARATION OF THE GIFTS

22 This or some other hymn:

Lord, enthroned in heavenly splendour

23 Bread and wine are brought to the table (or if already on the table are uncovered). The President takes the bread and wine and prepares them for use.

THE THANKSGIVING

24 All stand.

The President leads the great prayer of thanksgiving:

The Lord be with you.
And also with you.

Lift up your hearts.
We lift them to the Lord.

Let us give thanks to the Lord our God.
It is right to give our thanks and praise.

Lord our God, gracious and holy,
your power sustains all creation.
In love you create all things
and in mercy you redeem them.
From age to age you gather a people to serve you,
to proclaim your glory
and to reveal your presence in all the world.

In the fullness of time
you sent your Son, Jesus Christ,
the true Shepherd of your people;
in him we see your face and hear your word.
In compassion he restored us and made us whole,
laying down his life upon the cross
and freely offering himself for all.
You did not leave him in death
but raised him by your mighty power
to make all things new.

Through him you sent the Holy Spirit,
to lead your people into all truth,
calling from among us pastors and preachers
and teachers of your word.
With them and all your people on earth and in heaven
we join the ceaseless song of praise:

Holy, holy, holy Lord,
God of power and might,
heaven and earth are full of your glory.
Hosanna in the highest.
Blessèd is he who comes in the name of the Lord.
Hosanna in the highest.

Father, we give you praise
as we call to mind
how, at supper with his disciples,
your Son Jesus Christ took bread
and gave you thanks.
He broke it and gave it to them, saying,
'Take this, all of you, and eat it.
This is my body, given for you.
Do this in remembrance of me.'

After supper he took the cup.
He gave you thanks and gave it to them, saying,
'Drink this, all of you.
This is my blood of the new covenant,
shed for you and for all
for the forgiveness of sins.
Do this in remembrance of me.'

Christ has died.
Christ is risen.
Christ will come again.

Therefore, recalling Christ's offering of himself
and celebrating this feast of our redemption,
we offer ourselves to you
through Christ our great High Priest.

Send your Holy Spirit
that these gifts of bread and wine
may be for us the body and blood of Christ.

Remember, Lord, your Church throughout the world.
Send your Spirit upon us;
gather us into unity,
strengthen our faith
and sustain our hope.

Bring us, with all who place their hope in you,
to the promised feast in your kingdom,
where for ever we may offer you our praise,
through Jesus Christ our Lord,

through whom, with whom, and in whom,
in the unity of the Holy Spirit,
all honour and glory are yours,
now and for ever. Amen.

THE BREAKING OF THE BREAD

25 The President breaks the bread in the sight of the people in silence, or saying:

Christ is the true bread from heaven.
Christ gives life to the world.

THE SHARING OF THE BREAD AND WINE

26 All sit. The President, those assisting with the distribution, and the people receive.

The President may say these or other words of invitation:

Christ welcomes you to his table.
Draw near with faith.

27 Words such as the following are said during the distribution.

The body of Christ given for you. **Amen.**

The blood of Christ shed for you. **Amen.**

28 During the distribution there may be appropriate music.

29 The President covers what remains of the elements with a white cloth.

THE FINAL PRAYERS

30 Silence

31 Let us pray.

Lord our God,
strengthen the hands
that have received these holy gifts,
that we may faithfully serve you all our days;
through Jesus Christ our Lord. Amen.

32 This or some other hymn:

O thou who camest from above

33 All remain standing. The President says:

The almighty God bless *you/us,*
the Father, the Son and the Holy Spirit. **Amen.**

34 The President says:

Go in peace to love and serve the Lord.

In the name of Christ. Amen.

THE ORDINATION OF DEACONS

THE GATHERING OF THE PEOPLE OF GOD

1 Silence

2 All stand as those who are leading worship enter the church.

The President says:

O give thanks to the Lord, for he is good;
and his mercy endures for ever.

I welcome you all on this joyful occasion and greet you in the name of God.

The grace of the Lord Jesus Christ, and the love of God, and the fellowship of the Holy Spirit, be with you all.
And also with you.

3 This or some other hymn:

Ye servants of God, your Master proclaim

4 All sit. The President says:

Let us pray.

Silence

God of all grace,
you call your Church to be a holy people
to the praise of your name.
In the power of your Spirit,
fill our hearts with your love
and our lives with your glory;
through Jesus Christ our Lord. **Amen.**

THE MINISTRY OF THE WORD

5 Old Testament reading: Isaiah 61:1-4

6 Epistle: 1 Corinthians 12:27 - 13:13

7 This or some other hymn:

Lord God, your love has called us here

8 All remain standing.

A reading from the Gospel according to John.

Hear the Gospel of Christ.
Glory to Christ our Saviour.

The Gospel, John 13:1-17, is read.

This is the Gospel of Christ.
Praise to Christ our Lord.

9 All sit.

Sermon

10 The Nicene Creed

All stand.

Let us profess the faith of the Church.

We believe in one God,
the Father, the Almighty,
maker of heaven and earth,
of all that is, seen and unseen.

We believe in one Lord, Jesus Christ,
the only Son of God,
eternally begotten of the Father,

**God from God, Light from Light,
true God from true God,
begotten, not made,
of one Being with the Father;
through him all things were made.
For us and for our salvation
he came down from heaven,
was incarnate of the Holy Spirit and the Virgin Mary
and became truly human.
For our sake he was crucified under Pontius Pilate;
he suffered death and was buried.
On the third day he rose again
in accordance with the Scriptures;
he ascended into heaven
and is seated at the right hand of the Father.
He will come again in glory to judge the living and the dead,
and his kingdom will have no end.**

**We believe in the Holy Spirit, the Lord, the giver of life,
who proceeds from the Father and the Son,
who with the Father and the Son is worshipped and glorified,
who has spoken through the prophets.
We believe in one holy catholic and apostolic Church.
We acknowledge one Baptism for the forgiveness of sins.
We look for the resurrection of the dead,
and the life of the world to come. Amen.**

THE ORDINATION

THE PRESENTATION

11 All sit. The Warden of the Methodist Diaconal Order presents the candidates to the President.

Madam/Mr President, I present to you these persons to be ordained deacons. The Conference has received them into Full Connexion and resolved that they be ordained by prayer and the laying on of hands.

The Warden reads the names of those to be ordained. Each candidate rises as her/his name is called, and remains standing.

12 The people stand and the President says:

Sisters and brothers in Christ, these are the persons whom we intend, in God's name, to ordain to the Ministry of Christ's holy Church in the Order of Deacons.

Their call has been tested in preparation for this ministry and they have been found to be of sound learning and faithful to their vocation.

We ask you to declare your assent to their ordination.

Do you believe and trust that they are, by God's grace, worthy to be ordained?

The people acclaim:

They are worthy.

Will you uphold them in their ministry?

The people answer:

We will uphold them.

THE EXAMINATION

13 The people sit. The ordinands remain standing and the President says to them:

Beloved in Christ, the Church is God's holy people, the Body of Christ, the dwelling place of the Holy Spirit.

All who are received into the Church by Baptism are called to proclaim the mighty acts of God in Jesus Christ our Saviour, and to serve him in the Church and in the world.

God has called you into the Order of Deacons among his people.

In his name you are

to assist God's people in worship and prayer;
to hold before them the needs and concerns of the world;
to minister Christ's love and compassion;
to visit and support the sick and the suffering;
to seek out the lost and the lonely;
and to help those you serve to offer their lives to God.

Fulfil your calling as disciples of Jesus Christ, who came not to be served but to serve.

In all things, give counsel and encouragement
to all whom Christ entrusts to your care.
Pray without ceasing.
Work with joy in the Lord's service.
Let no one suffer hurt through your neglect.

This ministry will make great demands upon you and upon those close to you, yet in all this, the Holy Spirit will sustain you by his grace.

I now ask you to declare your lifelong commitment to this ministry:

Do you believe that God has called you to be a Deacon in the universal Church?

Answer: I do.

Do you accept the Holy Scriptures as revealing all things necessary for salvation through Jesus Christ our Lord?

Answer: I do.

Do you believe the doctrines of the Christian faith as this Church has received them?

Answer: I do.

Will you accept our discipline, and work together with your sisters and brothers in the Church?

Answer: I will.

Will you be faithful in worship, in prayer, in the reading of the Holy Scriptures and in those studies which will equip you for your ministry?

Answer: I will.

May God who has called you to this ministry give you grace and power to do his will; through Jesus Christ our Lord. **Amen.**

THE LITANY

14 The ordinands sit.

Let us pray.

All pray in silence.

The Warden of the Order leads the following litany:

On the peoples of the world
and the leaders of the nations,
gracious God,
pour out your Spirit.

On your holy Church throughout the world,
gracious God,
pour out your Spirit.

On all whom you have called to be ordained,
gracious God,
pour out your Spirit.

On all whom they serve in their ministry,
gracious God,
pour out your Spirit.

On their families and friends
and all who have helped and encouraged them,
gracious God,
pour out your Spirit.

Remember, O Lord, what you have wrought in us,
and not what we deserve;
and as you have called us to your service,
make us worthy of our calling;
through Jesus Christ our Lord. **Amen.**

THE ORDINATION

15 Hymn

**Come, Holy Ghost, our souls inspire,
And lighten with celestial fire;
Thou the anointing Spirit art,
Who dost thy sevenfold gifts impart:**

**Thy blessèd unction from above
Is comfort, life, and fire of love;
Enable with perpetual light
The dullness of our blinded sight:**

**Anoint and cheer our soilèd face
With the abundance of thy grace;
Keep far our foes, give peace at home;
Where thou art guide no ill can come.**

**Teach us to know the Father, Son,
And thee, of both, to be but One;
That through the ages all along
This may be our endless song:**

**'Praise to thy eternal merit,
Father, Son, and Holy Spirit. Amen.'**

16 The people sit. The ordinands kneel and the President, standing, says:

Lord our God,
we give you thanks and praise;
by your mighty power
you create all things in heaven and on earth for your glory.
In every age you gather your people
to obey your commands
and proclaim the greatness of your name.
You send messengers to recall them to your service,
reminding them of your love and faithfulness.

At the appointed time you sent your Son,
our Saviour Jesus Christ, the Word made flesh,
who lived among us, full of grace and truth.

Revealing your tender mercy
he healed and restored the sick
and comforted the broken and the lost.
In humility he washed the feet of his disciples,
calling us to follow his example as one who serves.

He suffered and died for us upon the cross,
bearing our sorrows and forgiving our sins.
By your mighty power
he broke the bonds of death and lives for ever,
calling us to serve you to the glory of your name.

Through him you sent your Spirit of truth and love
to guide and strengthen us.

By the same Spirit
you have called these your servants
to be Deacons in your Church.

Increase in them the gifts of your grace
for their life and ministry.

The prayer continues as the President lays her/his hands upon the head of each ordinand in turn. A deacon also lays her/his right hand on the ordinand.

The President says over each one:

Father, send the Holy Spirit upon *N* for the office and work of a Deacon in your Church.

Each time the President says these words, all answer:

Amen.

When hands have been laid on all of them, the President continues:

Gracious God,
as you call and ordain these your servants to this ministry,
we ask you to fulfil in them the work you have begun.

Give them wisdom and patience in their witness and service,
and unfailing love for those whom they serve.

May their lives reflect your glory
that they may be faithful examples to your people.

Guide and uphold them at all times
that with those whom they serve
they may rejoice in their ministry.

May they be counted worthy at the last
to enter into the joy of their Lord.

We ask this through Jesus Christ our Lord,
who lives and reigns with you,
in the unity of the Holy Spirit,
one God for ever and ever. **Amen.**

17 The Lord's Prayer

EITHER

We say together the prayer that Jesus gave us:

Our Father in heaven,
hallowed be your Name,
your kingdom come,
your will be done,
on earth as in heaven.
Give us today our daily bread.
Forgive us our sins
as we forgive those who sin against us.
Save us from the time of trial
and deliver us from evil.
For the kingdom, the power and the glory are yours,
now and for ever. Amen.

OR

As our Saviour taught his disciples, we pray:

Our Father, who art in heaven,
hallowed be thy Name;
thy kingdom come;
thy will be done;
on earth as it is in heaven.
Give us this day our daily bread.
And forgive us our trespasses,
as we forgive those who trespass against us.
And lead us not into temptation;
but deliver us from evil.
For thine is the kingdom, the power, and the glory,
for ever and ever. Amen.

THE GIVING OF THE BIBLE AND THE BADGE

18 The newly-ordained Deacons stand.

The Vice-President of the Conference presents a Bible to each of them, saying:

N, receive this Bible
as a sign of the ministry committed to you this day,
and witness to the Gospel by word and deed
in the Church and in the world.

19 The badge of the Methodist Diaconal Order is presented to each newly-ordained Deacon by a representative of the Order, who says:

Receive this badge
as a sign of the membership of the Order
to which you have been admitted by your ordination.

THE DECLARATION

20 All stand. The President says:

In the name of our Lord Jesus Christ I declare that you have been ordained as Deacons of the one holy catholic and apostolic Church of Christ.

You are to share fully in the life of your Order and to keep its discipline.

Remember your call.

Support the weak.
Bind up the broken.
Gather in the outcast.
Welcome the stranger.
Seek the lost.

So minister care that you make glad those whom you help in their need.
Let the concerns and sorrows of others be as your own.

May Christ your Master, when he comes in glory,
count you among his faithful servants.

To God be the glory for ever. Amen.

21 The people may welcome the newly-ordained Deacons with applause.

THE LORD'S SUPPER

22 The Peace

All stand. The President says:

The peace of the Lord be always with you.
And also with you.

The people may greet one another in the name of Christ.

THE PREPARATION OF THE GIFTS

23 This or some other hymn:

The Son of God proclaim

24 Bread and wine are brought to the table (or if already on the table are uncovered). The President takes the bread and wine and prepares them for use.

THE THANKSGIVING

25 All stand.

The President leads the great prayer of thanksgiving:

The Lord be with you.
And also with you.

Lift up your hearts.
We lift them to the Lord.

Let us give thanks to the Lord our God.
It is right to give our thanks and praise.

Lord our God,
your love and grace fill everything you have made.
In time and eternity your praise resounds
through earth and heaven.

From age to age you gather a people to serve you,
to proclaim your glory
and to reveal your presence in all the world.

In humility you came among us in Jesus Christ,
who brought the good news of the kingdom,
restoring the sick to health and the dead to life.

Taking the form of a servant,
he suffered and became obedient to death upon the cross.
You raised him from the dead,
breaking the power of death
and exalting him to your right hand on high.
Through him you sent your Spirit of life and power
into the hearts of the faithful,
filling the Church with your presence.

From among us you call those who serve you
with diverse gifts of ministry,
to build up your people in love.

With them and all your servants on earth and in heaven
we join the ceaseless song of praise:

Holy, holy, holy Lord,
God of power and might,
heaven and earth are full of your glory.
Hosanna in the highest.
Blessèd is he who comes in the name of the Lord.
Hosanna in the highest.

Father, we give you praise
as we call to mind
how, at supper with his disciples,
your Son Jesus Christ took bread
and gave you thanks.
He broke it and gave it to them, saying,
'Take this, all of you, and eat it.
This is my body, given for you.
Do this in remembrance of me.'

After supper he took the cup.
He gave you thanks and gave it to them, saying,
'Drink this, all of you.
This is my blood of the new covenant,
shed for you and for all
for the forgiveness of sins.
Do this in remembrance of me.'

Christ has died,
Christ is risen,
Christ will come again.

Therefore,
recalling Christ's offering of himself
and celebrating this feast of our redemption,
we offer ourselves to you
through Christ our great High Priest.

Send your Holy Spirit
that these gifts of bread and wine
may be for us the body and blood of Christ.

Remember, Lord, your Church throughout the world.
Send your Spirit upon us;
gather us into unity,
strengthen our faith
and sustain our hope.

Bring us, with all who place their hope in you,
to the promised feast in your kingdom,
where for ever we may offer you our praise,
through Jesus Christ our Lord,

through whom, with whom, and in whom,
in the unity of the Holy Spirit,
all honour and glory are yours,
now and for ever. Amen.

THE BREAKING OF THE BREAD

26 The President breaks the bread in the sight of the people in silence, or saying:

Christ is the true bread from heaven.
Christ gives life to the world.

THE SHARING OF THE BREAD AND WINE

27 All sit. The President, those assisting with the distribution, and the people receive.

The President may say these or other words of invitation:

Christ welcomes you to his table.
Draw near with faith.

28 Words such as the following are said during the distribution:

The body of Christ given for you. **Amen.**

The blood of Christ shed for you. **Amen.**

29 During the distribution there may be appropriate music.

30 The President covers what remains of the elements with a white cloth.

THE FINAL PRAYERS

31 Silence

32 Let us pray.

Lord our God,
strengthen the hands
that have received these holy gifts,
that we may faithfully serve you all our days;
through Jesus Christ our Lord. Amen.

33 This or some other hymn:

O thou who camest from above

34 All remain standing. The President says:

The almighty God bless *you/us*,
the Father, the Son and the Holy Spirit. **Amen.**

35 The Warden of the Order says:

Go in peace to love and serve the Lord.

In the name of Christ. Amen.

ADMISSION, COMMISSIONING AND WELCOME SERVICES

THE ADMISSION OF LOCAL PREACHERS

INTRODUCTION

John Wesley recognized that some lay people were called to preach the Gospel and he appointed them to this work. Methodist Local Preachers are called by God and trained to lead God's people in worship. After their initial training and approval by the Circuit Meeting, they are admitted during an act of worship to the office and work of a Local Preacher. The office of a Local Preacher is a permanent one, to which a person is admitted only once.

NOTES

1 ***The Admission of Local Preachers*** is a circuit service at which the Superintendent Minister should normally preside. It should normally take place during a celebration of ***Holy Communion*** and whenever possible it should take place on a Sunday.

2 Local Preachers should be invited to take part in appropriate sections of the service, such as readings, sermon, intercessions, and the distribution of Holy Communion.

3 The readings for the day should be read on the First Sunday of Advent, Easter Day, Ascension Day, the Day of Pentecost, Trinity Sunday and All Saints' Day.

THE PREPARATION

1 The Superintendent says:

The Lord gave the word,
and great was the company of the preachers.

In this act of worship, we are to admit *N and N (N)*
to the office and ministry of a Local Preacher.

2 Hymn

3 Glory to you,
Father, Son and Holy Spirit:
in company with all the saints
we proclaim your greatness and your majesty.

Glory to you, now and for ever. Amen.

4 The Superintendent says:

In silence let us call to mind our sins.

Silence

Holy God,
we confess that we have failed to be your faithful people.
We have not listened to your word,
responded to your call,
or loved our neighbours.
Forgive us, we pray,
and free us for joyful obedience;
through Jesus Christ our Lord. Amen.

Merciful God,
grant to your people pardon and peace;
through Christ our Lord. **Amen.**

5 This collect, which may be preceded or followed by the collect of the day:

Lord our God,
as we rejoice in the ministry of preaching,
let the Gospel of your Son come to us,
not in words alone, but in power and love;
that through our life and witness
the world may believe;
through Christ our Lord. **Amen.**

THE MINISTRY OF THE WORD

6 One of the following or the Old Testament reading for the day:

Exodus 3:1-7, 10-12
Isaiah 52:7-12
Isaiah 55:6-11

7 Hymn or Psalm

8 One of the following or the Epistle for the day:

2 Corinthians 5:14-20
Ephesians 4:7-8, 11-16
James 1:16-25

9 Hymn

10 A reading from the Gospel according to . . .

Hear the Gospel of Christ.
Glory to Christ our Saviour.

One of the following or the Gospel for the day is read:

Matthew 25:14-29
Luke 4:14-24
John 12:20-26

This is the Gospel of Christ.
Praise to Christ our Lord.

11 Sermon

12 Hymn

THE ADMISSION

THE PRESENTATION

13 *Those* to be admitted as Local Preachers *move* to the front of the church. The Secretary of the Local Preachers' Meeting presents *those* to be admitted to the Superintendent, saying:

Madam/Mr Superintendent, I present to you *N and N (N)*. The Church has examined *their* knowledge, competence and conviction. On the recommendation of the Local Preachers' Meeting, *they have* been approved by the Circuit Meeting for admission to the office and ministry of a Local Preacher.

THE PREFACE

14 The Superintendent says:

The Church of Christ exists to glorify God the Father, who has revealed the way of salvation in the life, ministry and victory of Christ, and has given the Holy Spirit to inspire Christian proclamation and preaching.

From the early days of Methodism, God has called lay people to lead worship and prayer, and to preach the Gospel. In every generation since, women and men have responded to this call and have been admitted as Local Preachers.

Local Preachers are called to be worthy in character, to lead God's people in prayer and praise, and to share in the Church's mission in the whole world.

N and N (N), yours is a responsibility rooted in the word of God. You will bring the message of salvation to all, in season and out of season. As you lead worship, and offer good news to others, your own life will be shaped and transformed.

THE QUESTIONS

15 The Superintendent says to *those* to be admitted:

N and N (N), do you believe that you are called by God to the office and ministry of a Local Preacher?

Answer: I do so believe.

Will you be faithful in prayer and in the reading and study of the Scriptures, and will you preach nothing contrary to the doctrines of the Methodist Church?

Answer: With God's help, I will.

Will you accept our discipline and work together with your sisters and brothers in the Church?

Answer: With God's help, I will.

Will you make yourself available to lead worship, attend the Local Preachers' Meeting and develop your skills and studies?

Answer: With God's help, I will.

Will you seek to fashion your life according to the way of Christ and in all things seek to promote, not your own glory, but the glory of the Lord?

Answer: With God's help, I will.

May the God of all grace uphold you in the service to which you are called. **Amen.**

THE ADMISSION

16 The Superintendent addresses the Local Preachers present and says:

The admission of *N and N (N)* as *Local Preachers* in the Methodist Church will bring *them* into membership of the Local Preachers' Meeting to which you belong. I invite you, as Local Preachers, to stand as *they are* admitted, and thereby to re-affirm your own ministry.

The Local Preachers stand.

17 The Superintendent says to the people:

I invite you all to stand.

The people stand.

Let us pray.

Blessed are you, gracious God,
our creator and our redeemer.
In Christ, you offer redemption
and fullness of life.
In every generation you call men and women
to speak your word and proclaim your glory.
We thank you that *these* your *servants*
have responded to your call
to be *Local Preachers* in your Church.

Give your Holy Spirit to *N and N (N),*
whom we now admit to the office and ministry of a Local Preacher,
that *they* may fulfil *their* calling.
Grant *them* the assurance of faith,
that *they* may abound in hope
and be rooted and grounded in love,
to the praise of Jesus Christ our Lord,
to whom with you and your Holy Spirit,
belong glory and honour, now and for ever. **Amen.**

18 The Superintendent or a Local Preacher presents a Bible to each new Local Preacher. The Superintendent says:

Receive this Bible as a sign of your authority to preach the Gospel and lead God's people in worship and praise.

19 The Superintendent says to the people:

N and N (N) have been admitted to the office and ministry of a Local Preacher in the Methodist Church.

Will you support *them* with your prayers,
faithfully share in the worship *they lead*
and receive through *them* the word of God?

We will.

20 The people sit. The Secretary of the Local Preachers' Meeting or another Local Preacher reads the President's letter and gives a copy to each new Local Preacher.

21 The hand of fellowship is then given to each new Local Preacher by the Superintendent and the Secretary of the Local Preachers' Meeting.

22 The newly-admitted Local *Preachers* may be invited to speak about *their* calling.

23 If the Lord's Supper is to be celebrated, the service continues from the prayers of intercession in an appropriate seasonal or Ordinary Seasons service of ***Holy Communion***. Otherwise, the service continues with prayers of thanksgiving and intercession from ***Morning, Afternoon, or Evening Services***, or some other prayers of thanksgiving and intercession.

THE COMMISSIONING OF LAY WORKERS

INTRODUCTION

Lay Workers are appointed to a variety of ministries, remunerated or unremunerated, full-time or part-time, in Circuit or District appointments.

This Commissioning Service is intended to be sufficiently adaptable for use in these varying circumstances.

NOTES

1 ***The Commissioning of Lay Workers*** should normally take place during a celebration of ***Holy Communion***.

2 This service is intended for the Commissioning of a Lay Worker in a Circuit or District appointment. In the case of a District appointment, it will be necessary to adapt nos. 10, 12, 13 and 14.

THE GATHERING OF THE PEOPLE OF GOD

1 Hymn

2 This collect, which may be preceded or followed by the collect of the day:

Eternal God, in your love
you pour out upon us gifts of your Spirit
for the service of the Gospel:
look now on your *servant, N,*
whom we are to commission in your Name,
that *she/he* and all your people
may make your grace and glory known to the world;
through Jesus Christ our Lord. **Amen.**

THE MINISTRY OF THE WORD

3 The Old Testament reading for the day or one of the following:

Isaiah 55:6-13
Jeremiah 1:4-10

4 A Psalm or portion of a Psalm may be said or sung.

5 The Epistle for the day or one of the following:

Ephesians 4:7-16
Colossians 4:2-6

6 Hymn

7 A reading from the Gospel according to . . .

Hear the Gospel of Christ.
Glory to Christ our Saviour.

The Gospel for the day is read, or one of the following:

Luke 6:20-26
Luke 10:1-2
Luke 10:38-42

This is the Gospel of Christ.
Praise to Christ our Lord.

8 Sermon

9 Hymn

THE COMMISSIONING

10 All stand.

The presiding minister says to the people:

Sisters and brothers, I present to you *N*, who *is* to serve as *a* Lay *Worker* in this *Circuit.*

The work to which *N is* appointed is particularly concerned with . . .

Here the presiding minister will indicate in a phrase the duties to be carried out by the Lay *Worker*.

N, we rejoice that you are now to exercise *this ministry* within the life and mission of the Church. In your work you will be strengthened by the Holy Spirit.

Do you believe that you are called by God to serve as *a* Lay *Worker* in this *Circuit*?

Answer: I do.

Will you accept the discipline of the Church, and work with us in its mission and ministry?

Answer: With God's help I will.

Will you be faithful in worship, in prayer and in reading the Holy Scriptures?

Answer: With God's help I will.

11 The presiding minister says:

Let us pray.

Faithful God, we thank you
that *N has* offered *herself/himself*
as *a* Lay *Worker* in your Church.
Uphold *her/him* by your love
and enable *her/him* by your Spirit,
that through *her/his* ministry
your Church may be strengthened
and your name may be glorified;
through Jesus Christ our Lord. **Amen.**

12 A *Circuit Steward* says to the people:

Sisters and brothers,
will you welcome *N*,
and will you offer *her/him*
your friendship, support and prayers
as we join together in the work
to which God has called us?

With God's help, we will.

13 *A representative* of the local *church* with which the Lay *Worker* will be mainly involved may say:

I welcome you in the name of . . . *Church*.

14 Welcomes may then be given by *circuit* and ecumenical representatives, civic leaders and other appropriate persons.

15 Each newly-appointed Lay Worker may reply briefly in her/his own words and/or as follows:

I thank you for your welcome.
I will work with you and pray for you.

16 These or some other prayers of intercession:

Let us pray.

In faith we pray to God,
who is more ready to hear than we are to ask.

Let us pray for the whole Church of God,
that, rejoicing in our richness and variety,
we may seek peace and unity
and be constantly renewed for mission and service.

Silence

The Lord hears our prayer.
Thanks be to God.

Let us pray for the churches of our Circuit and District,
that, rejoicing in our common heritage,
we may strengthen each other and be built up in love.

Silence

The Lord hears our prayer.
Thanks be to God.

Let us pray for the life of the world,
that, rejoicing in our common humanity,
we may reject the ways of war and conflict
and work together for justice and peace.

Silence

The Lord hears our prayer.
Thanks be to God.

Let us rejoice in the communion of saints,
that, strengthened by their faithful example,
we may follow the way of Christ
and live to God's praise and glory.

Silence

The Lord hears our prayer.
Thanks be to God.

Give us wisdom, Lord, to know your will,
and courage to do it.
May our words declare your love
and may our compassion give substance to our words;
through Jesus Christ our Lord. **Amen.**

17 The Lord's Prayer

EITHER

We say together the prayer that Jesus gave us:

**Our Father in heaven,
hallowed be your Name,
your kingdom come,
your will be done,
on earth as in heaven.
Give us today our daily bread.
Forgive us our sins
as we forgive those who sin against us.
Save us from the time of trial
and deliver us from evil.
For the kingdom, the power and the glory are yours,
now and for ever. Amen.**

OR

As our Saviour taught his disciples, we pray:

**Our Father, who art in heaven,
hallowed be thy Name;
thy kingdom come;
thy will be done;
on earth as it is in heaven.
Give us this day our daily bread.
And forgive us our trespasses,
as we forgive those who trespass against us.
And lead us not into temptation;
but deliver us from evil.
For thine is the kingdom, the power, and the glory,
for ever and ever. Amen.**

THE LORD'S SUPPER

18 The Peace

All stand.

We are the Body of Christ.

**In the one Spirit
we were all baptized into one body.
Let us therefore keep the unity of the Spirit
in the bond of peace.**

The peace of the Lord be always with you.
And also with you.

The people may greet one another in the name of Christ.

19 The service continues from the Preparation of the Gifts. Any appropriate order may be used, but that for ***The Day of Pentecost and Times of Renewal in the Life of the Church*** (page 174) is especially suitable.

If the Lord's Supper is not celebrated, the service concludes as follows:

20 Hymn

21 Offering and prayer of dedication

22 This or some other prayer of thanksgiving:

Let us pray.

Generous God,
from whom comes every good and perfect gift,
we thank you for your mercies:
for your goodness that has created us,
your grace that has sustained us,
your patience that has borne with us,
and your love that has redeemed us.
We thank you for Jesus Christ your Son:
for his humble birth and his holy life,
his ministry of love and care,
his suffering and death,
his resurrection, and his eternal reign.

We thank you for the Holy Spirit:
for the gifts of the Spirit poured out on the Church,
for our life together of worship and service,
and our calling to make disciples
and to serve Christ in our neighbours.

In the power of the Spirit,
we offer ourselves again to you
as a living sacrifice to your praise and glory;
through Jesus Christ our Lord. Amen.

23 Hymn

24 The presiding minister says:

May the God of love
stir up in us the gifts of his grace
and sustain each of us
in our discipleship and service;
and the blessing of God,
the Father, the Son and the Holy Spirit,
remain with *you/us* for ever. **Amen.**

THE ANNUAL COMMISSIONING OF PASTORAL VISITORS AND CLASS LEADERS

INTRODUCTION

John Wesley appointed Class Leaders to meet regularly with groups (classes) of members, to encourage them in their spiritual development. Class meetings still take place in some churches, though many churches now appoint Pastoral Visitors who exercise pastoral responsibility for a group of people without meeting them formally in class. It is appropriate that this Service of Commissioning should take place annually.

NOTE

The Annual Commissioning of Pastoral Visitors and Class Leaders should normally take place after the sermon during a celebration of ***Holy Communion***.

---

1 This or some other prayer:

Merciful God,
you renew the strength
of all who wait upon you.
Fill us with your Holy Spirit,
that, in serving others,
we may always be true to Christ,
our Lord and our Redeemer,
who lives and reigns with you and the Holy Spirit,
one God, now and for ever. **Amen.**

THE PREFACE

2 The minister says:

Today we commission *those* who *offer themselves* for service as *Pastoral Visitors and Class Leaders* in the Methodist Church.

We are the Body of Christ:

each of us is a member of it.

There is one ministry of Christ:

in this ministry we all share.

There are different ways of serving God:

it is the same Lord whom we serve.

It is the tradition of the Methodist Church that within our community we offer pastoral care to one another. In order that this ministry may be fulfilled, the Church appoints Pastoral Visitors and Class Leaders.

It is their privilege and responsibility, in the name of Christ and on behalf of the whole Church:

to pray regularly for those in their care;
to share in their joys;
and to give comfort and support in time of sorrow and need.

In all these things, they will seek for themselves and for those in their care a deepening experience of God's grace in Christ.

Without God's help no one can exercise this ministry; but the Holy Spirit has been given to us, and is our Helper and Counsellor.

THE COMMISSIONING

3 *Those* to be commissioned *move* to the front of the church as *their names are* read. The minister then says:

Sisters and brothers, do you believe that you are called by God through the Church to the work of pastoral care?

Answer: I do so believe.

Relying on God's grace, will you endeavour to fulfil this ministry?

Answer: With God's help, I will.

The minister says:

Let us pray.

We thank you, gracious God,
that you have sent Jesus Christ your Son
to be our Shepherd and Saviour.
Give to *these* your *servants*
the power of the Holy Spirit
for this work and ministry;
through Jesus Christ our Lord. **Amen.**

4 The people stand. The minister says to them:

Members of the Body of Christ, will you encourage *these Pastoral Visitors and Class Leaders* in *their* ministry and support *them* with your prayers?

With God's help, we will.

5 The minister gives the hand of fellowship to each Pastoral Visitor and Class Leader.

6 The minister may give to the *Pastoral Visitors and Class Leaders* the tickets of membership for those in *their* care.

7 The service continues.

THE ANNUAL COMMISSIONING OF WORKERS WITH CHILDREN AND YOUNG PEOPLE

INTRODUCTION

Work with children and young people has long been valued and emphasized in the Methodist Church. Some people are trained and commissioned to devote particular attention to this work. This service may be used when new Workers with Children and Young People are commissioned, but it is primarily intended as an Annual Commissioning Service for all such Workers within a local church.

NOTES

1 ***The Annual Commissioning of Workers with Children and Young People*** should normally take place after the sermon during a celebration of ***Holy Communion***.

2 It is desirable that the children and young people of the church should be present.

---

1 This or some other prayer:

From our earliest days, O God,
you call us by name.
Make our ears attentive to your voice
and our spirits eager to respond,
that, having heard your word in Jesus,
we may draw others to be his disciples.
We ask this through Jesus Christ our Lord. **Amen.**

THE PREFACE

2 The minister says:

Today we commission *those* who *offer themselves* for service as *Workers* with Children and Young People in the Methodist Church.

We are the Body of Christ:

each of us is a member of it.

There is one ministry of Christ:

in this ministry we all share.

There are different ways of serving God:

it is the same Lord whom we serve.

When children are baptized, we promise so to maintain the Church's life of worship and service that they may grow in grace and in the knowledge and love of God and of his Son Jesus Christ our Lord. The Christian nurture of children and young people is thus the responsibility of the whole Church. In order that this ministry may be fulfilled, the Methodist Church appoints Workers with Children and Young People.

It is their privilege and responsibility, in the name of Christ:

to pray regularly for those in their care;
to offer, by word and deed, a Christian example;
and to guide them in their journey of faith.

In all these things, they will seek for themselves and for those in their care a deepening experience of God's grace in Christ.

Without God's help no one can exercise this ministry; but the Holy Spirit has been given to us, and is our Helper and Counsellor.

THE COMMISSIONING

3 *Those* to be commissioned *move* to the front of the church as *their names are* read. *They* may be led from *their places* by a child or young person. The minister then says:

Sisters and brothers, do you believe that you are called by God through the Church to work with children and young people?

Answer: I do so believe.

Will you be diligent in preparation and continue to equip yourself for this ministry?

Answer: With God's help, I will.

4 A child or young person, or the minister, says:

Let us pray.

Loving God, we thank you for *those* who *have* responded to your call. We pray that your Holy Spirit may inspire *them* as *they undertake* this ministry in your name.

By *their* encouragement and example, may *they* enable others to discover new life in Christ. Amen.

5 The people stand. The minister says to them:

Members of the Body of Christ, will you encourage in *their* ministry *these Workers* with Children and Young People, and support *them* with your prayers?

With God's help, we will.

6 The minister gives the hand of fellowship to each Worker with Children and Young People.

7 The service continues.

THE COMMISSIONING OF WORSHIP LEADERS

INTRODUCTION

Worship Leaders are persons appointed, according to the provisions of Standing Orders, to take a leading and significant role in the conduct of worship in a local church. The service which follows is primarily intended as a commissioning service for newly-accredited Worship Leaders, though it may be adapted for use as an annual commissioning service for all Worship Leaders within a local church.

NOTE

The Commissioning of Worship Leaders should normally take place after the sermon during a celebration of ***Holy Communion***.

---

1 This or some other prayer:

Almighty God,
your Son has opened for us
a new and living way into your presence.
Give us new hearts and constant wills
to worship you in spirit and in truth;
through Jesus Christ our Lord. **Amen.**

THE PREFACE

2 The minister says:

Today we commission *those* who *offer themselves* for service as *Worship Leaders* in the Methodist Church.

We are the Body of Christ:

each of us is a member of it.

There is one ministry of Christ:

in this ministry we all share.

There are different ways of serving God:

it is the same Lord whom we serve.

Those who offer themselves for service as Worship Leaders within the Methodist Church are trained and tested before they are commissioned. *N and N (N) have* completed a course of training and the Church Council, having consulted the Circuit Local Preachers' Meeting, has appointed *them* as *Worship Leaders.* We are now to commission *them* for this task.

THE COMMISSIONING

3 *Those* to be commissioned *move* to the front of the church as *their names are* read. The minister then says:

N and N (N), do you believe that you are called by God through the Church to serve as *Worship Leaders*?

Answer: I do so believe.

Will you be diligent in preparation and continue to equip yourself for this ministry?

Answer: With God's help, I will.

In your daily life and in your leadership of worship, will you seek to promote, not your own glory, but the glory of the Lord?

Answer: With God's help, I will.

The minister says:

Let us pray.

We thank you, gracious God,
for those whom you have called
to lead your people in worship.
Guide and inspire them by your Holy Spirit
that they may fulfil this ministry
to the honour and glory of your name;
through Jesus Christ our Lord. **Amen.**

4 The people stand. The minister says to them:

Members of the Body of Christ, will you encourage *these* Worship *Leaders* in *their* ministry and support *them* with your prayers?

With God's help, we will.

5 The minister gives the hand of fellowship to each Worship Leader.

6 The service continues.

THE RECEPTION OF CHRISTIANS OF OTHER COMMUNIONS INTO THE MEMBERSHIP OF THE METHODIST CHURCH

NOTES

1 This service is for the reception into the membership of the Methodist Church of baptized persons who have been confirmed and/or been members of other Christian communions.

2 The reception should take place during a celebration of ***Holy Communion***.

3 If the reception takes place during a celebration of Holy Communion other than one which includes Baptism and/or Confirmation and Reception into Membership, it should immediately precede the prayers of intercession.

4 If the reception takes place during a service of ***Baptism*** and/or ***Confirmation and Reception into Membership***, it should immediately follow the Promise of the People.

---

1 *Those* who *are* to be received into the membership of the Methodist Church *stand*. The minister says to *them*:

N and N (N), you have been *members* of *other communions* within the Church of Christ. Do you now wish to be *members* of the Methodist Church?

Answer: I do.

2 The minister says to *them*:

N and N (N), we receive and welcome you as *members* of the Methodist Church and of the church in this place.

May the Lord bless you with his grace
and fill you with his peace. **Amen.**

3 The minister and a representative of the local church extend the hand of fellowship to *those* who *have* been welcomed.

4 The following questions may be asked:

N and N (N), I ask you now to respond to God's love and grace by making these promises.

Do you commit yourself with us to the Christian life of worship and service, and to be open to the renewing power of God?

Answer: I do.

Will you continue to seek the strength of God's Spirit as you follow Jesus Christ in your daily life?

Answer: With God's help I will.

Will you witness, by word and deed, to the Good News of God in Christ, and so bring glory to God?

Answer: With God's help I will.

5 The people stand. The minister says to them:

Members of the body of Christ, we rejoice to welcome *these* our *sisters and brothers.*

Will you maintain the Church's life of worship and service and build each other up in love as we follow Christ our Lord?

With God's help we will.

6 The service continues.

THE WELCOME OF MINISTERS, DEACONS AND PROBATIONERS

INTRODUCTION

Methodist ministers (presbyters), deacons and probationers are stationed by the Conference to circuits and other appointments. For this reason, this service is regarded as a service of welcome, rather than one of induction.

NOTES

1 The presiding minister may invite other people, including representatives of ecumenical partners, to read readings, preach the sermon and lead the prayers of intercession.

2 The first form of the Presentation, Promises and Welcome should be used for presbyters and probationers for presbyteral ministry; the second form should be used for deacons and probationers for diaconal ministry.

3 If a minister already stationed in the circuit has now been appointed by the Conference as the Superintendent, the form of Welcome set out in the Appendix on pages 365-366 may be used at the beginning of the Presentation, Promises and Welcome.

4 If *a* Lay *Worker is* to be commissioned during a Welcome Service, nos. 10 and 11 of ***The Commissioning of Lay Workers*** are inserted immediately before no. 18 of the Welcome Service.

THE GATHERING OF THE PEOPLE OF GOD

1 Grace and peace to you from God our Father
and the Lord Jesus Christ. **Amen.**

2 Hymn

3 Let us pray.

God of truth,
you are worthy of higher praise than we can offer,
and of purer worship than we can imagine.
By your Holy Spirit,
assist us in our prayers
and draw us to yourself,
so that what is lacking
in our thoughts and actions
and in our words and music,
may be supplied by your overflowing love;
through Jesus Christ our Lord. **Amen.**

Silence

4 Gracious God,
when we do not listen for your word in the words of others,
forgive and renew us.

When we do not use the gifts you have bestowed on us,
forgive and renew us.

When we do not love one another as sisters and brothers in Christ,
forgive and renew us.

When we do not serve our neighbours in their need,
forgive and renew us.

When we do not share the Good News with those around us,
forgive and renew us.

Silence

God calls us to serve,
forgives us in Christ,
and renews us by the Spirit.
Amen. Thanks be to God.

5 God of all grace,
you call your Church to be a holy people
to the praise of your name.
In the power of your Spirit,
fill our hearts with your love
and our lives with your glory;
through Jesus Christ our Lord. **Amen.**

6 Hymn

THE MINISTRY OF THE WORD

7 The Old Testament reading for the day, or Isaiah 61:1-3, or one of the following:

Isaiah 42:1-9
Isaiah 52:7-10

8 A Psalm or portion of a Psalm may be said or sung.

9 The Epistle for the day, or Ephesians 4:1-16, or one of the following:

Acts 2:42-47
Romans 12:1-13
2 Corinthians 4:1-6
Philippians 2:1-11

10 Hymn

11 A reading from the Gospel according to . . .

Hear the Gospel of Christ.
Glory to Christ our Saviour.

The Gospel for the day is read, or John 13:12-20, or one of the following:

Matthew 10:24-42
Luke 4:16-21
John 21:15-19

This is the Gospel of Christ.
Praise to Christ our Lord.

12 Sermon

THE PRESENTATION, PROMISES AND WELCOME

Nos. 13 and 14 (and, when appropriate, no. 15) are used for presbyters.
Nos. 13 and 14 are used for probationers for presbyteral ministry.
Nos. 16 and 17 are used for deacons or probationers for diaconal ministry.

FOR PRESBYTERS AND PROBATIONERS FOR PRESBYTERAL MINISTRY

13 All stand.

The presiding minister says to the people:

Sisters and brothers, I present to you *N*, whom the Conference has appointed to serve in this Circuit.

14 The presiding minister says to the newly-appointed *presbyter or probationer* for presbyteral ministry:

N,
will you hold before us
the story of God's love and mercy,
above all, the Gospel of our Saviour Jesus Christ,
and will you be among us
as one who preaches the word of God,
administers Baptism,
presides at the Lord's Supper,
teaches the faith,
and cares for the flock?

Answer: I will.
I ask God to help me,
and I invite you all to join with me
in proclaiming the Gospel of life and hope.

Through Christ, we have Good News to share.

(* This line is omitted for a probationer unless the Conference has granted an Authorisation to preside at the Lord's Supper. When necessary, this question is put separately to such a probationer.)

Will you hold before us
God's call to holy living
and be among us
as one who awakens the careless
and strengthens the faithful?

Answer: I will.
I ask God to help me,
and I invite you all to join with me
in commitment to the way of Christ.

May we reveal Christ's way
through our words and example.

Will you hold before us
God's commitment to human community,
to our neighbourhoods
and all who live within them,
and to the world that God has made?

Answer: I will.
I ask God to help me,
and I invite you all to join with me
in sharing God's all-embracing love.

May we respond to Christ in all we meet.

15 If a newly-appointed presbyter is the new Superintendent, the presiding minister says to her/him:

N, to you is committed the responsibility
for the life and work of this Circuit.
Will you, with your colleagues, lay and ordained,
care for its people,
inspire its witness
and watch over its life
in the name of Christ?

The new Superintendent replies:

I will, and I ask God to help me.

FOR DEACONS AND PROBATIONERS FOR DIACONAL MINISTRY

16 All stand.

The presiding minister says to the people:

Sisters and brothers, I present to you *N*, whom the Conference has appointed to serve in this Circuit.

17 The presiding minister says to the newly-appointed *deacon or probationer* for diaconal ministry:

N,
will you hold before us
the story of God's love and mercy,
above all, the Gospel of our Saviour Jesus Christ,
and will you be among us
as one who makes known the Good News,
by deeds of loving service?

Answer: I will.
I ask God to help me,
and I invite you all to join with me
in proclaiming the Gospel of life and hope.

Through Christ, we have Good News to share.

Will you hold before us
God's call to serve the needs of others
and be among us
as one who ministers Christ's love and compassion?

Answer: I will.
I ask God to help me,
and I invite you all to join with me
in commitment to the way of Christ.

May we reveal Christ's way
through our words and example.

Will you hold before us
God's commitment to human community,
to our neighbourhoods
and all who live within them,
and to the world that God has made?

Answer: I will.
I ask God to help me,
and I invite you all to join with me
in sharing God's all-embracing love.

May we respond to Christ in all we meet.

---

18 A Circuit Steward says to the people:

Sisters and brothers,
will you welcome *N*
and will you offer *her/him*
your friendship, support and prayers
as we join together in the work
to which God has called us?

With God's help, we will.

19 Welcomes may then be given by circuit and ecumenical representatives, civic leaders, and other appropriate persons.

Each newly-appointed presbyter, deacon or probationer may reply briefly in her/his own words and/or as follows:

I thank you for your welcome.
I will work with you and pray for you.

20 Hymn

21 These or some other prayers of intercession:

Let us pray.

In faith we pray to God,
who is more ready to hear than we are to ask.

Let us pray for the whole Church of God,
that, rejoicing in our richness and variety,
we may seek peace and unity
and be constantly renewed for mission and service.

Silence

The Lord hears our prayer.
Thanks be to God.

Let us pray for the churches of our Circuit and District
and for other churches in this area,
that, rejoicing in our common heritage,
we may strengthen each other and be built up in love.

Silence

The Lord hears our prayer.
Thanks be to God.

Let us pray for the life of the world,
that, rejoicing in our common humanity,
we may reject the ways of war and conflict
and work together for justice and peace.

Silence

The Lord hears our prayer.
Thanks be to God.

Let us rejoice in the communion of saints,
that, strengthened by their faithful example,
we may follow the way of Christ
and live to God's praise and glory.

Silence

The Lord hears our prayer.
Thanks be to God.

Give us wisdom, Lord, to know your will,
and courage to do it.
May our words declare your love
and may our compassion give substance to our words;
through Jesus Christ our Lord. **Amen.**

22 The Lord's Prayer

EITHER

We say together the prayer that Jesus gave us:

Our Father in heaven,
hallowed be your Name,
your kingdom come,
your will be done,
on earth as in heaven.
Give us today our daily bread.
Forgive us our sins
as we forgive those who sin against us.
Save us from the time of trial
and deliver us from evil.
For the kingdom, the power and the glory are yours,
now and for ever. Amen.

OR

As our Saviour taught his disciples, we pray:

Our Father, who art in heaven,
hallowed be thy Name;
thy kingdom come;
thy will be done;
on earth as it is in heaven.
Give us this day our daily bread.
And forgive us our trespasses,
as we forgive those who trespass against us.
And lead us not into temptation;
but deliver us from evil.
For thine is the kingdom, the power, and the glory,
for ever and ever. Amen.

23 The Peace

All stand.

We are the Body of Christ.

**In the one Spirit
we were all baptized into one body.
Let us therefore keep the unity of the Spirit
in the bond of peace.**

The peace of the Lord be always with you.
And also with you.

The people may greet one another in the name of Christ.

24 When the Lord's Supper follows, the service continues from the Preparation of the Gifts. Any appropriate order may be used, but that for ***The Day of Pentecost and Times of Renewal in the Life of the Church*** (page 174) is especially suitable.

If the Lord's Supper is not celebrated, the service concludes as follows:

25 Offering and prayer of dedication

26 This or some other prayer of thanksgiving:

Let us pray.

Gracious God,
we thank you that in every generation
you reveal your love for the world,
and set before your people
your word of life and hope.

We thank you for Jesus Christ your Son,
in whom you have made known
your way of perfect love,
and in whose dying and rising
we see your final purpose.

We thank you for your Holy Spirit,
who leads your people into all truth;
for the service and witness of your Church;
and for the preaching of the word
and the celebration of the sacraments,
through which you renew and strengthen us.

All honour and glory be yours,
in the Church and in the world,
in time and in eternity;
through Jesus Christ our Lord. Amen.

27 Hymn

28 The presiding minister says:

May the God of love
stir up in us the gifts of his grace
and sustain each of us
in our discipleship and service;
and the blessing of God,
the Father, the Son and the Holy Spirit,
remain with *you/us* for ever. **Amen.**

APPENDIX

The Welcome of a Minister already stationed in a Circuit and now appointed as the Superintendent

1 The presiding minister says to the people:

Sisters and brothers, I present to you *N*, who serves as a minister in this Circuit. The Circuit Meeting has shown its confidence in *her/his* ministry by inviting *her/him* to serve as Superintendent, and the Conference has so appointed *her/him.*

2 The presiding minister says to the new Superintendent:

N, to you is committed the responsibility
for the life and work of this Circuit.
Will you, with your colleagues, lay and ordained,
care for its people,
inspire its witness
and watch over its life
in the name of Christ?

The new Superintendent replies:

I will, and I ask God to help me.

The people say to the new Superintendent:

We receive you as our Superintendent.
We pray that God's blessing will rest upon you. Amen.

MARRIAGE AND THE BLESSING OF A MARRIAGE

INTRODUCTION

A marriage ceremony is a formal occasion when a solemn, legal contract is made between a man and a woman. In a Christian context, it is also an act of worship in which marriage is celebrated as a gift of God and the joy of the couple is shared and their commitment to each other is witnessed by family and friends. ***The Marriage Service***'s themes of love, hope, faithfulness, sacrifice and trust are at the heart of the Christian gospel.

The Blessing of a Marriage Previously Solemnized also gives expression to these themes. It is intended for those whose marriage was solemnized in a civil ceremony and who later desire the blessing of that marriage in an act of Christian worship.

THE MARRIAGE SERVICE

NOTES

1 At the time of publication, it is required by law in England and Wales that the words of declaration at no. 5 and the words of contract at no. 13 (or the permitted alternative forms, set out in the Appendix on page 384) should be said in the presence of the Authorized Person (or the Registrar) and two witnesses. The full names of the parties should be used.

2 When this service is used in Scotland, the Channel Islands, the Isle of Man, Northern Ireland, the Republic of Ireland, or any other jurisdiction whose marriage legislation is different from that of England and Wales, the minister should ensure that the service complies with the legal requirements of that jurisdiction. Appropriate substitutions should be made at nos. 5 and 13 if necessary.

THE PREPARATION

1 The people stand as the bridal or marriage party enters the church. The persons to be married stand together before the minister, the woman on the left of the man.

The minister may welcome the congregation.

The minister says:

We meet together in the presence of God
to witness the marriage of *A* and *C*,
to ask God's blessing upon them,
to support them with our prayers
and to share their joy.

2 Hymn

3 The people remain standing. The minister says:

Let us pray.

Gracious God, your generous love surrounds us,
and everything we enjoy comes from you.
We confess our ingratitude for your goodness
and our selfishness in using your gifts.
Forgive and renew us,
and fill us with your Spirit
that in true thankfulness
we may bear witness to your love;
through Jesus Christ our Lord. **Amen.**

4 The minister says:

A and *C*, with your families and friends,
we thank God on this day
for the gift of marriage.

It is the will of God that, in marriage,
husband and wife should experience
a life-long unity of heart, body and mind;
comfort and companionship;
enrichment and encouragement;
tenderness and trust.

It is the will of God that marriage
should be honoured as a way of life,
in which we may know the security of love and care,
and grow towards maturity.
Through such marriage,
children may be nurtured,
family life strengthened,
and human society enriched.

No one should enter into this lightly or selfishly,
for marriage involves the giving
of a man and a woman
wholeheartedly to each other.
Christ in his self-giving comes to our help,
for he loves us and gave himself for us.

A and *C*, you are now to share this way of life
which God has created
and, in Christ, has blessed.
Today we pray that the Holy Spirit
will guide and strengthen you
that you may fulfil God's purposes
for the rest of your lives.

5 The Legal Declarations

The minister says to the people:

A and *C* are now to make the declarations which the law requires.

The minister says to the man:

Are you, *AB*, free lawfully to marry *CD*?

The man answers: I am.

The minister says to the woman:

Are you, *CD*, free lawfully to marry *AB*?

The woman answers: I am.

6 The minister says to the man and the woman:

You have made the declarations required by law. I ask you now to affirm, in the presence of us all, your intention to marry each other.

The minister says to the man:

A, are you willing to give yourself in marriage to *C*?

The man answers: I am.

The minister says to the man:

Will you love her, comfort and honour her, be her companion through all the joys and sorrows of life, and be faithful to her as long as you both shall live?

The man answers: With God's help, I will.

The minister says to the woman:

C, are you willing to give yourself in marriage to *A*?

The woman answers: I am.

The minister says to the woman:

Will you love him, comfort and honour him, be his companion through all the joys and sorrows of life, and be faithful to him as long as you both shall live?

The woman answers: With God's help, I will.

THE MINISTRY OF THE WORD

The whole of the Ministry of the Word may occur here or at no. 18, or the scripture readings may be read here and the sermon may be preached at no. 18.

7 All sit. At least one passage of scripture is read. If Holy Communion is to be celebrated, a passage from the Gospels always concludes the readings.

Many waters cannot quench love, neither can floods drown it. If one offered for love all the wealth of one's house, it would be utterly scorned.

Song of Solomon 8:7

Love is patient; love is kind; love is not envious or boastful or arrogant or rude. It does not insist on its own way; it is not irritable or resentful; it does not rejoice in wrongdoing, but rejoices in the truth. It bears all things, believes all things, hopes all things, endures all things. Love never ends.

And now faith, hope, and love abide, these three; and the greatest of these is love.

1 Corinthians 13:4-8*a*, 13

For this reason I bow my knees before the Father, from whom every family in heaven and on earth takes its name. I pray that, according to the riches of his glory, he may grant that you may be strengthened in your inner being with power through his Spirit, and that Christ may dwell in your hearts through faith, as you are being rooted and grounded in love.
I pray that you may have the power to comprehend, with all the saints, what is the breadth and length and height and depth, and to know the love of Christ that surpasses knowledge, so that you may be filled with all the fullness of God.

Ephesians 3:14-19

As God's chosen ones, holy and beloved, clothe yourselves with compassion, kindness, humility, meekness, and patience. Bear with one another and, if anyone has a complaint against another, forgive each other; just as the Lord has forgiven you, so you also must forgive. Above all, clothe yourselves with love, which binds everything together in perfect harmony. And let the peace of Christ rule in your hearts, to which indeed you were called in the one body. And be thankful. Let the word of Christ dwell in you richly; teach and admonish one another in all wisdom; and with gratitude in your hearts sing psalms, hymns and spiritual songs to God. And whatever you do, in word or deed, do everything in the name of the Lord Jesus, giving thanks to God the Father through him.

Colossians 3:12-17

Jesus said: 'From the beginning of creation, "God made them male and female." "For this reason a man shall leave his father and mother and be joined to his wife, and the two shall become one flesh." So they are no longer two, but one flesh. Therefore what God has joined together, let no one separate.'

Mark 10:6-9

Jesus said: 'As the Father has loved me, so I have loved you; abide in my love. If you keep my commandments, you will abide in my love, just as I have kept my Father's commandments and abide in his love. I have said these things to you so that my joy may be in you, and that your joy may be complete. This is my commandment, that you love one another as I have loved you.'

John 15:9-12

Additional scripture readings are listed on page 398.

8 Sermon

9 Hymn

THE MARRIAGE

10 All stand. The minister may say to the people:

I ask you, the families and friends of *A* and *C*:

Will you do all in your power to support and encourage them in their marriage?

The people answer:

With God's help, we will.

11 If the woman has a relative or friend presenting her for marriage, the minister says:

Who presents *C* to be married to *A*?

The woman's relative or friend answers: I do.

If the man has a relative or friend presenting him for marriage, the minister says:

Who presents *A* to be married to *C*?

The man's relative or friend answers: I do.

12 The minister says:

Gracious God,
as you have brought *A* and *C* together in love and trust,
enable them through the power of your Holy Spirit
to make and keep their vows;
through Jesus Christ our Lord. **Amen.**

13 The Vows

The man takes the woman's right hand in his and says to her:

I, *AB*, take you, *CD*, to be my wedded wife,
for better, for worse,
for richer, for poorer,
in sickness and in health,
to love and to cherish,
from this day forward,
until we are parted by death;
and this is my solemn vow.

They loose hands.

The woman takes the man's right hand in hers and says to him:

I, *CD*, take you, *AB*, to be my wedded husband,
for better, for worse,
for richer, for poorer,
in sickness and in health,
to love and to cherish,
from this day forward,
until we are parted by death;
and this is my solemn vow.

They loose hands.

14 The Giving of the Ring(s)

IF TWO RINGS ARE BEING GIVEN

The minister receives the rings on the book, and says:

Eternal God,
bless these rings
that they may be
symbols of the love and trust
between *A* and *C*. **Amen.**

EITHER

The man places a ring on the woman's ring finger, and says:

I give you this ring
as a sign of our marriage.
With my body I honour you,
all that I am I give to you,
and all that I have
I share with you,
within the love of God,
Father, Son and Holy Spirit.

The woman places a ring on the man's ring finger, and says:

I give you this ring
as a sign of our marriage.
With my body I honour you,
all that I am I give to you,
and all that I have
I share with you,
within the love of God,
Father, Son and Holy Spirit.

IF ONLY ONE RING IS BEING GIVEN

The minister receives the ring on the book, and says:

Eternal God,
bless this ring,
that it may be
a symbol of the love and trust
between *A* and *C*. **Amen.**

EITHER

The man places the ring on the woman's ring finger, and says:

I give you this ring
as a sign of our marriage.
With my body I honour you,
all that I am I give to you,
and all that I have
I share with you,
within the love of God,
Father, Son and Holy Spirit.

The woman says:

I receive this ring
as a sign of our marriage.
With my body I honour you,
all that I am I give to you,
and all that I have
I share with you,
within the love of God,
Father, Son and Holy Spirit.

OR

After the rings have been given and received, the man and the woman say together:

With these rings
we pledge ourselves
to each other,
in the Name of the Father,
and of the Son,
and of the Holy Spirit.

OR

After the ring has been given and received, the man and the woman say together:

With this ring
we pledge ourselves
to each other,
in the Name of the Father,
and of the Son,
and of the Holy Spirit.

15 The minister joins the right hands of the man and the woman. The minister may wrap her/his stole around, and/or place her/his hand on their joined hands.

The minister says to the man and the woman:

A and *C*, God so join you together
that none shall ever part you.

The minister says to the people:

Before God and in the presence of us all,
A and *C* have exchanged vows,
joined their hands,
and given and received *rings/a ring*,
binding themselves to each other
in the covenant of marriage.
I therefore proclaim
that they are now husband and wife.

16 A hymn may be sung here or after no. 17.

17 The people remain standing. The husband and wife may kneel and the minister may lay hands upon their heads.

The minister says:

A and *C*,
the blessing of God the Father,
God the Son, and God the Holy Spirit,
be upon you and remain with you always.
May God be your protection and your wisdom,
your guide and your peace,
your joy, your comfort, and your eternal rest. **Amen.**

18 The whole of the Ministry of the Word follows, if it has not occurred earlier. If the sermon has been deferred, it is preached here.

THE PRAYERS

19 These or some other prayers of intercession:

Let us pray.

God of grace, source of all love,
we pray for *A* and *C*
that they may live together in love and faithfulness
to the end of their lives.

Lord of life,
hear us in your love.

Enrich their friendship,
that each may be for the other
a companion in joy and a comforter in sorrow.

Lord of life,
hear us in your love.

Help *A* and *C* to be patient, gentle and forgiving,
that their marriage may reflect Christ's love for all people.

Lord of life,
hear us in your love.

Enable them to make their home
a place of welcome and friendship,
that their life together
may be a source of strength to others.

Lord of life,
hear us in your love.

Other intercessions may be included.

May we, who have witnessed these vows today,
be signs of your love in the world;
through Jesus Christ our Lord. **Amen.**

20 The Lord's Prayer

EITHER

We say together the prayer that Jesus gave us:

**Our Father in heaven,
hallowed be your Name,
your kingdom come,
your will be done,
on earth as in heaven.
Give us today our daily bread.
Forgive us our sins
as we forgive those who sin against us.
Save us from the time of trial
and deliver us from evil.
For the kingdom, the power and the glory are yours,
now and for ever. Amen.**

OR

As our Saviour taught his disciples, we pray:

**Our Father, who art in heaven,
hallowed be thy Name;
thy kingdom come;
thy will be done;
on earth as it is in heaven.
Give us this day our daily bread.
And forgive us our trespasses,
as we forgive those who trespass against us.
And lead us not into temptation;
but deliver us from evil.
For thine is the kingdom, the power, and the glory,
for ever and ever. Amen.**

21 If Holy Communion is to be celebrated, the service continues from no. 25.

If Holy Communion is not celebrated, the service continues as follows:

22 All stand.

The minister says this prayer, or gives thanks in her/his own words:

Praise God,
who is the source of joy and celebration,
pleasure and delight, love and friendship.

Praise God,
who, in the life and victory of Jesus Christ,
reveals to us the glory of self-giving love.

Praise God,
who sends the Holy Spirit to be our helper
and to guide us into the way of perfect love.

Praise God, Father, Son, and Holy Spirit. Amen.

23 Hymn

24 The minister says to all present:

God the Father, God the Son,
and God the Holy Spirit,
make *you/us* strong in faith
and guide *you/us* in truth and love.

EITHER

The Lord bless you
and keep you;
the Lord make his face to shine on you
and be gracious to you;
the Lord look on you with kindness
and give you peace. **Amen.**

OR

May God be gracious to us
and bless us,
and make his face to shine
upon us. **Amen.**

HOLY COMMUNION

25 The Peace

All stand.

The peace of the Lord be always with you.
And also with you.

The people may greet one another in the name of Christ.

THE PREPARATION OF THE GIFTS

26 Bread and wine are brought to the table by the husband and wife or other members of the congregation (or if already on the table are uncovered). The presiding minister takes the bread and wine and prepares them for use.

THE THANKSGIVING

27 All stand.

The presiding minister leads the great prayer of thanksgiving:

The Lord be with you.
And also with you.

Lift up your hearts.
We lift them to the Lord.

Let us give thanks to the Lord our God.
It is right to give our thanks and praise.

We praise you, gracious God,
creator and sustainer of all things.

From the beginning
you made man and woman
for yourself and for each other,
and you call us to reflect your faithfulness
in lives of love and service.

You gave yourself to us in your Son, Jesus Christ,
the Lord of heaven and earth,
and entrusted him to the care of a human family.
In his life, death and resurrection,
you revealed the power of self-giving love,
rescued us from sin and selfishness,
and made us a new family through your grace.

You give yourself to us today,
and by your Holy Spirit
you promise to be with us always
as our companion and our guide.

And so, with all your people on earth and in heaven,
we give you thanks and praise:

Holy, holy, holy Lord,
God of power and might,
heaven and earth are full of your glory.
Hosanna in the highest.
Blessèd is he who comes in the name of the Lord.
Hosanna in the highest.

Holy God, we praise you
that on the night in which he was betrayed
our Saviour Christ took bread
and gave you thanks.
He broke it, and gave it to his disciples, saying,
'Take, eat. This is my body, given for you.
Do this in remembrance of me.'

After supper, he took the cup of wine,
gave thanks, and gave it to them, saying,
'Drink this, all of you.
This is my blood of the new covenant,
poured out for all people for the forgiveness of sins.
Do this in remembrance of me.'

And so, gracious God, we remember and celebrate
all that Christ has done for us.
We offer ourselves to you in humble thanksgiving.

Send your Holy Spirit
that these gifts of bread and wine
may be for us the body and blood of Christ.
Together with all your people,
may we have life in all its fullness,
live in the power of love,
and fill creation with a song of endless praise.

**Through Christ, with Christ, and in Christ,
in the unity of the Holy Spirit,
all glory is yours, God most holy,
now and for ever. Amen.**

THE BREAKING OF THE BREAD

28 The presiding minister breaks the bread in the sight of the people in silence, or saying:

The bread we break is a sharing in the body of Christ.

The presiding minister may lift the cup in silence, or saying:

The cup we bless is a sharing in the blood of Christ.

29 Silence, all seated or kneeling

THE SHARING OF THE BREAD AND WINE

30 The presiding minister receives, then, beginning with the husband and wife and their families, the people, according to local custom.

31 Words such as the following are said during the distribution:

The body of Christ. **Amen.**

The blood of Christ. **Amen.**

32 During the distribution there may be appropriate music.

33 The elements that remain are covered with a white cloth.

PRAYERS AND DISMISSAL

34 Let us pray.

**We thank you, Lord,
that you have fed us in this sacrament,
united us with Christ,
and given us a foretaste of the heavenly banquet
prepared for all people. Amen.**

35 Hymn

36 The presiding minister says to all present:

God the Father, God the Son,
and God the Holy Spirit,
make *you/us* strong in faith
and guide *you/us* in truth and love.

EITHER

The Lord bless you
and keep you;
the Lord make his face to shine on you
and be gracious to you;
the Lord look on you with kindness
and give you peace. **Amen.**

OR

May God be gracious to us
and bless us,
and make his face to shine
upon us. **Amen.**

APPENDIX

1 As an alternative to the questions and answers in no. 5, the persons contracting the marriage may make the declaration required by law by saying:

EITHER

A **I do solemnly declare**
that I know not
of any lawful impediment
why I, *AB/CD,***
may not be joined in matrimony
to *CD/AB.*

OR

B **I declare that I know of no legal reason why I,**
AB/CD, **may not be joined in marriage to *CD/AB.***

2 As an alternative to the words of contract set out in no. 13,

EITHER

A the persons to be married may say:

I call upon these persons here present
to witness that I, *AB/CD,*
do take thee, *CD/AB,* *
to be my lawful wedded *wife/husband,*
for better, for worse,
for richer, for poorer,
in sickness and in health,
to love and to cherish,
from this day forward,
until we are parted by death;
and this is my solemn vow.

OR

B the persons to be married may say to each other:

I, *AB/CD,* **take thee, *CD/AB,***
to be my wedded *wife/husband,*
for better, for worse,
for richer, for poorer,
in sickness and in health,
to love and to cherish,
from this day forward,
until we are parted by death;
and this is my solemn vow.

(* The full names of the parties must be used.)

THE BLESSING OF A MARRIAGE PREVIOUSLY SOLEMNIZED

NOTES

1 This form of service must not be used for the solemnization of a marriage.

2 This form of service is not suitable for those who wish to reaffirm or renew marriage vows.

3 This service should normally be conducted by the minister with pastoral charge of the church in which it takes place. It can be used either as a private ceremony or with a congregation of family and friends.

THE PREPARATION

1 The persons whose marriage is to be blessed stand together before the minister, the wife on the left of her husband.

The minister may welcome the congregation.

The minister says:

We meet together in the presence of God
to join with *A* and *C*,
in asking God's blessing upon their marriage.

2 Hymn

3 The minister says:

A and *C*, with your families and friends,
we thank God on this day
for the gift of marriage.

It is the will of God that, in marriage,
husband and wife should experience
a life-long unity of heart, body and mind;
comfort and companionship;
enrichment and encouragement;
tenderness and trust.

It is the will of God that marriage
should be honoured as a way of life,
in which we may know the security of love and care,
and grow towards maturity.
Through such marriage,
children may be nurtured,
family life strengthened,
and human society enriched.

No one should enter into this lightly or selfishly,
for marriage involves the giving
of a man and a woman
wholeheartedly to each other.
Christ in his self-giving comes to our help,
for he loves us and gave himself for us.

A and *C*,
you have already entered this way of life
which God has created
and, in Christ, has blessed.
Today we pray that the Holy Spirit
will guide and strengthen you
that you may fulfil God's purposes
for the rest of your lives.

THE MINISTRY OF THE WORD

The whole of the Ministry of the Word may occur here or at no. 13, or the scripture readings may be read here and the sermon may be preached at no. 13.

4 All sit. At least one passage of scripture is read. If Holy Communion is to be celebrated, a passage from the Gospels always concludes the readings.

Many waters cannot quench love, neither can floods drown it. If one offered for love all the wealth of one's house, it would be utterly scorned.

Song of Solomon 8:7

Love is patient; love is kind; love is not envious or boastful or arrogant or rude. It does not insist on its own way; it is not irritable or resentful; it does not rejoice in wrongdoing, but rejoices in the truth. It bears all things, believes all things, hopes all things, endures all things. Love never ends.

And now faith, hope, and love abide, these three; and the greatest of these is love.

1 Corinthians 13:4-8*a*, 13

For this reason I bow my knees before the Father, from whom every family in heaven and on earth takes its name. I pray that, according to the riches of his glory, he may grant that you may be strengthened in your inner being with power through his Spirit, and that Christ may dwell in your hearts through faith, as you are being rooted and grounded in love.
I pray that you may have the power to comprehend, with all the saints, what is the breadth and length and height and depth, and to know the love of Christ that surpasses knowledge, so that you may be filled with all the fullness of God.

Ephesians 3:14-19

As God's chosen ones, holy and beloved, clothe yourselves with compassion, kindness, humility, meekness, and patience. Bear with one another and, if anyone has a complaint against another, forgive each other; just as the Lord has forgiven you, so you also must forgive. Above all, clothe yourselves with love, which binds everything together in perfect harmony. And let the peace of Christ rule in your hearts, to which indeed you were called in the one body. And be thankful. Let the word of Christ dwell in you richly; teach and admonish one another in all wisdom; and with gratitude in your hearts sing psalms, hymns and spiritual songs to God. And whatever you do, in word or deed, do everything in the name of the Lord Jesus, giving thanks to God the Father through him.

Colossians 3:12-17

Jesus said: 'From the beginning of creation, "God made them male and female." "For this reason a man shall leave his father and mother and be joined to his wife, and the two shall become one flesh." So they are no longer two, but one flesh. Therefore what God has joined together, let no one separate.'

Mark 10:6-9

Jesus said: 'As the Father has loved me, so I have loved you; abide in my love. If you keep my commandments, you will abide in my love, just as I have kept my Father's commandments and abide in his love. I have said these things to you so that my joy may be in you, and that your joy may be complete. This is my commandment, that you love one another as I have loved you.'

John 15:9-12

Additional scripture readings are listed on page 398.

5 Sermon

6 Hymn

THE BLESSING OF THE MARRIAGE

7 All stand. The minister says:

Gracious God,
you have brought *A* and *C* together in love and trust.

By the power of your Holy Spirit,
may they receive your blessing upon their marriage;
through Jesus Christ our Lord. **Amen.**

8 The minister says to the husband:

A, you have come here as *C*'s husband
seeking God's blessing upon your marriage,
and desiring to live according to God's will.

I ask you, therefore:
will you love her, comfort and honour her,
be her companion
through all the joys and sorrows of life,
and be faithful to her
as long as you both shall live?

The husband answers:

With God's help, I will.

The minister says to the wife:

C, you have come here as *A's* wife
seeking God's blessing upon your marriage,
and desiring to live according to God's will.

I ask you, therefore:
will you love him, comfort and honour him,
be his companion
through all the joys and sorrows of life,
and be faithful to him
as long as you both shall live?

The wife answers:

With God's help, I will.

9 The husband and wife join their ring hands. The minister places a hand on their joined hands, and says:

Eternal God,
bless *these rings/this ring,*
symbols/a symbol of the love and trust
between *A* and *C*. **Amen.**

10 The minister may wrap her/his stole around their joined hands. The husband and wife say together:

Within the love of God,
Father, Son, and Holy Spirit,
I am bound to you in marriage
for better, for worse,
for richer, for poorer,
in sickness and in health,
to love and to cherish,
until we are parted by death.

11 The people remain standing. The husband and wife may kneel, and the minister may lay hands upon their heads.

The minister says:

A and *C*,
the blessing of God the Father,
God the Son, and God the Holy Spirit,
be upon you and remain with you always.
May God be your protection and your wisdom,
your guide and your peace,
your joy, your comfort, and your eternal rest. **Amen.**

12 Hymn

13 The whole of the Ministry of the Word follows, if it has not occurred earlier. If the sermon has been deferred, it is preached here.

THE PRAYERS

14 All sit.

These or some other prayers of intercession:

Let us pray.

God of grace, source of all love,
we pray for *A* and *C*
that they may live together in love and faithfulness
to the end of their lives.

Lord of life,
hear us in your love.

Enrich their friendship,
that each may be for the other
a companion in joy and a comforter in sorrow.

Lord of life,
hear us in your love.

Help *A* and *C* to be patient, gentle, and forgiving,
that their marriage may reflect Christ's love for all people.

Lord of life,
hear us in your love.

Enable them to make their home
a place of welcome and friendship,
that their life together
may be a source of strength to others.

Lord of life,
hear us in your love.

Other intercessions may be included.

May we, who have witnessed their promises today,
be signs of your love in the world;
through Jesus Christ our Lord. **Amen.**

15 The Lord's Prayer

EITHER

We say together the prayer that Jesus gave us:

**Our Father in heaven,
hallowed be your Name,
your kingdom come,
your will be done,
on earth as in heaven.
Give us today our daily bread.
Forgive us our sins
as we forgive those who sin against us.
Save us from the time of trial
and deliver us from evil.
For the kingdom, the power and the glory are yours,
now and for ever. Amen.**

OR

As our Saviour taught his disciples, we pray:

**Our Father, who art in heaven,
hallowed be thy Name;
thy kingdom come;
thy will be done;
on earth as it is in heaven.
Give us this day our daily bread.
And forgive us our trespasses,
as we forgive those who trespass against us.
And lead us not into temptation;
but deliver us from evil.
For thine is the kingdom, the power, and the glory,
for ever and ever. Amen.**

16 If Holy Communion is to be celebrated, the service continues from no. 20.

If Holy Communion is not celebrated, the service continues as follows:

17 All stand.

The minister says this prayer, or gives thanks in her/his own words:

Praise God,
who is the source of joy and celebration,
pleasure and delight, love and friendship.

Praise God,
who, in the life and victory of Jesus Christ,
reveals to us the glory of self-giving love.

Praise God,
who sends the Holy Spirit to be our helper
and to guide us into the way of perfect love.

Praise God, Father, Son, and Holy Spirit. Amen.

18 Hymn

19 The minister says to all present:

God the Father, God the Son,
and God the Holy Spirit,
make *you/us* strong in faith
and guide *you/us* in truth and love.

EITHER

The Lord bless you
and keep you;
the Lord make his face to shine on you
and be gracious to you;
the Lord look on you with kindness
and give you peace. **Amen.**

OR

May God be gracious to us
and bless us,
and make his face to shine upon us. **Amen.**

HOLY COMMUNION

20 The Peace

All stand.

The peace of the Lord be always with you.
And also with you.

The people may greet one another in the name of Christ.

THE PREPARATION OF THE GIFTS

21 Bread and wine are brought to the table by the husband and wife or other members of the congregation (or if already on the table are uncovered). The presiding minister takes the bread and wine and prepares them for use.

THE THANKSGIVING

22 All stand.

The presiding minister leads the great prayer of thanksgiving:

The Lord be with you.
And also with you.

Lift up your hearts.
We lift them to the Lord.

Let us give thanks to the Lord our God.
It is right to give our thanks and praise.

We praise you, gracious God,
creator and sustainer of all things.

From the beginning
you made man and woman
for yourself and for each other,
and you call us to reflect your faithfulness
in lives of love and service.

You gave yourself to us in your Son, Jesus Christ,
the Lord of heaven and earth,
and entrusted him to the care of a human family.
In his life, death and resurrection,
you revealed the power of self-giving love,
rescued us from sin and selfishness
and made us a new family through your grace.

You give yourself to us today,
and by your Holy Spirit
you promise to be with us always
as our companion and our guide.

And so with all your people on earth and in heaven
we give you thanks and praise:

Holy, holy, holy Lord,
God of power and might,
heaven and earth are full of your glory.
Hosanna in the highest.
Blessèd is he who comes in the name of the Lord.
Hosanna in the highest.

Holy God, we praise you
that on the night in which he was betrayed
our Saviour Christ took bread
and gave you thanks.
He broke it, and gave it to his disciples, saying,
'Take, eat. This is my body, given for you.
Do this in remembrance of me.'

After supper, he took the cup of wine,
gave thanks, and gave it to them, saying,
'Drink this, all of you.
This is my blood of the new covenant,
poured out for all people for the forgiveness of sins.
Do this in remembrance of me.'

And so, gracious God, we remember and celebrate
all that Christ has done for us.
We offer ourselves to you in humble thanksgiving.

Send your Holy Spirit
that these gifts of bread and wine
may be for us the body and blood of Christ.
Together with all your people,
may we have life in all its fullness,
live in the power of love,
and fill creation with a song of endless praise.

Through Christ, with Christ, and in Christ,
in the unity of the Holy Spirit,
all glory is yours, God most holy,
now and for ever. Amen.

THE BREAKING OF THE BREAD

23 The presiding minister breaks the bread in the sight of the people in silence, or saying:

The bread we break is a sharing in the body of Christ.

The presiding minister may lift the cup in silence, or saying:

The cup we bless is a sharing in the blood of Christ.

24 Silence, all seated or kneeling

THE SHARING OF THE BREAD AND WINE

25 The presiding minister receives, then, beginning with the husband and wife and their families, the people, according to local custom.

26 Words such as the following are said during the distribution:

The body of Christ. **Amen.**

The blood of Christ. **Amen.**

27 During the distribution there may be appropriate music.

28 The elements that remain are covered with a white cloth.

PRAYERS AND DISMISSAL

29 Let us pray.

**We thank you, Lord,
that you have fed us in this sacrament,
united us with Christ,
and given us a foretaste of the heavenly banquet
prepared for all people. Amen.**

30 Hymn

31 The presiding minister says to all present:

God the Father, God the Son,
and God the Holy Spirit,
make *you/us* strong in faith
and guide *you/us* in truth and love.

EITHER

The Lord bless you
  and keep you;
the Lord make his face to
  shine on you
and be gracious to you;
the Lord look on you with
  kindness
and give you peace. **Amen.**

OR

May God be gracious to us
  and bless us,
and make his face to shine
  upon us. **Amen.**

ADDITIONAL SCRIPTURE READINGS

Old Testament

Genesis 1:26-29*a*, 31*a*	Man and woman created in God's image
Genesis 2:4-9, 15-24	A husband and wife become one flesh
Song of Solomon 1:15 - 2:4	A love song
Isaiah 61:10; 62:3-5	Wedded to God

Psalms

Psalm 23	The Lord our shepherd
Psalm 121	The Lord's protection and blessing
Psalm 127 *or* 128	The gift of a family

Epistle

Romans 12:1-2, 9-13	Love in practice
Ephesians 5:21-31	Husband and wife in Christian marriage
Philippians 1:9-11	Growing into a rich love
Philippians 2:1-11	The example of Jesus
1 John 3:18-24	Love in practice
1 John 4:7-12, 15-17	Love one another
Revelation 19:6-9	The wedding feast of the Lamb of God

Gospel

Matthew 5:1-10	The Beatitudes
Matthew 7:21, 24-27	Hearing and doing
Matthew 22:35-40	The greatest commandment
John 2:1-11	Jesus at a wedding

PASTORAL SERVICES

AN ACT OF THANKSGIVING AFTER THE BIRTH OR ADOPTION OF A CHILD

INTRODUCTION

In the Methodist tradition, the children of Christian parents are normally brought for Baptism, but there are occasions when ***An Act of Thanksgiving*** may be helpful, either suggested by the minister or requested by the *parents*. Prior to a child's Baptism, the *parents* may have some particular reason for wishing to give thanks for her/his arrival. Newly-adopted children may already have been baptized, and ***An Act of Thanksgiving*** serves to welcome the child into the local congregation. Some *parents* may have reservations about the Baptism of young children, while still desiring to give thanks for *their* child's arrival and to dedicate themselves for *their* new task.

The themes of the service are thanksgiving to God for the gift of children, assurance of God's love for all, and our need of God's blessing and help in the nurturing of our families.

NOTE

It is appropriate that this ***Act of Thanksgiving*** should follow the sermon, but it may be used before the Ministry of the Word.

1 The *parents stand* in front of the minister.

2 Let us pray.

Heavenly Father,
who entrusted your Son, Jesus Christ,
to the protection of Mary and Joseph:
bless us on this day of thanksgiving
with the gifts of your grace,
that *this child* and *her/his parents*
may always be united to you
and to each other;
through Jesus Christ our Lord. **Amen.**

3 The following passages of scripture are read:

Hear, O Israel: The Lord is our God, the Lord alone. You shall love the Lord your God with all your heart, and with all your soul, and with all your might. Keep these words that I am commanding you today in your heart. Recite them to your children and talk about them when you are at home and when you are away, when you lie down and when you rise.

Deuteronomy 6:4-7

Jesus took a little child and put it among them; and taking it in his arms, he said to them, 'Whoever welcomes one such child in my name welcomes me, and whoever welcomes me welcomes not me but the one who sent me.'

Mark 9:36-37

4 The minister asks the *names* of the *child.*

5 All stand.

Let us give thanks to the Lord our God.
It is right to give our thanks and praise.

We praise you, O God,
for creating all things
and for making us in your own image.

We thank you that while we were yet sinners
you gave your only Son, Jesus Christ,
to be born of Mary,
to live as one of us,
to suffer death on the cross,
and to rise again for our salvation.

And especially today
we give you thanks and praise
for the gift of a *daughter/son* to *A and B (A)*
and we pray that you will bless *N* by your grace
and through the love of *her/his parents.*

May *she/he* come to know you
and to share with all your people
the life of the baptized,
the bread of heaven,
and the joys of your kingdom;
through Jesus Christ our Lord. **Amen.**

6 The minister says to the *parents*:

A and B (A),
do you thankfully receive *N* as a gift from God,
and do you promise to love and care for *her/him*?

Answer: *We* do.

7 The minister may also say to the *parents*:

Will you share your faith with *N*
and help *her/him* to pray and worship
that you and *she/he* together
may cherish your place in the life of the Church?

Answer: With God's help, *we* will.

8 The minister says to the people:

Members of the body of Christ,
will you surround this family with your love,
and will you support them with your prayers?

With God's help, we will.

9 The minister may take each child in her/his arms.

The minister says:

God our Father,
bless *N* with your Holy Spirit
that *she/he* may come to believe in Christ
and glorify you for ever. **Amen.**

10 A Bible may be given to the *parents* or the *child.*

11 The minister says:

Let us pray.

Gracious God,
we pray for *N* and *her/his* family and friends
that they may be strengthened in their love for each other
and receive your gifts of wisdom and understanding.

The Lord hears our prayer.
Thanks be to God.

We pray that together we may follow Christ
and witness to your love in our homes and in our community.

The Lord hears our prayer.
Thanks be to God.

12 The Lord's Prayer, if it is not said at some other point in the service

EITHER

We say together the prayer that Jesus gave us:

**Our Father in heaven,
hallowed be your Name,
your kingdom come,
your will be done,
on earth as in heaven.
Give us today our daily bread.
Forgive us our sins
as we forgive those who sin against us.
Save us from the time of trial
and deliver us from evil.
For the kingdom, the power and the glory are yours,
now and for ever. Amen.**

OR

As our Saviour taught his disciples, we pray:

**Our Father, who art in heaven,
hallowed be thy Name;
thy kingdom come;
thy will be done;
on earth as it is in heaven.
Give us this day our daily bread.
And forgive us our trespasses,
as we forgive those who trespass against us.
And lead us not into temptation;
but deliver us from evil.
For thine is the kingdom, the power, and the glory,
for ever and ever. Amen.**

13 May the love of the Lord Jesus
draw us to himself;
may the power of the Lord Jesus
strengthen us in his service;
and may the joy of the Lord Jesus
fill our hearts, now and always. **Amen.**

14 The service continues.

A CELEBRATION OF CHRISTIAN RENEWAL

INTRODUCTION

From time to time a Christian may pass through an experience which strengthens her/his faith. This may be emergence from bereavement, for example, or a response to a call for deeper commitment, or the experience of beginning again with God after a lapse in the journey of faith. The use of ***A Celebration of Christian Renewal*** may be suggested by the minister or by the individual concerned.

Although this service marks and celebrates an individual's experience, to which personal testimony may well be given, it also recognizes God's gifts to the whole Christian community. The service looks forward to a continuing Christian life, firmly rooted in the total life of the Church's fellowship and worship.

NOTE

When ***A Celebration of Christian Renewal*** is used, it follows the sermon during a celebration of ***Holy Communion***. Any appropriate order for Holy Communion may be used, but that for ***The Day of Pentecost and Times of Renewal in the Life of the Church*** (page 174) is especially suitable.

---

1 The minister says:

The Lord has done great things for us and holy is his name.

N is here to give thanks for what the Lord has done for *her/him*; and to renew *her/his* commitment to the one God, Father, Son and Holy Spirit, in whose name *she/he* was baptized.

2 The minister may say to *N*:

N, do you believe in God, who is creator of the world and Father of our Lord Jesus Christ?

Answer: Yes, I do.

Do you confess Jesus Christ, the Son of God, who saves us from sin and renews the life of all who trust in him?

Answer: Yes, I do.

Do you know the power of God the Holy Spirit, whose fruit is love and whose gifts build up the Body of Christ?

Answer: Yes, I do.

Do you desire to love God with all your heart and soul and mind and strength, and your neighbour as yourself?

Answer: Yes, I do.

Do you promise to be faithful in prayer and in reading the Scriptures and in the worship and fellowship of the Church?

Answer: Yes, I do.

3 The minister may ask *N* to testify to God's renewing grace and to declare *her/his* commitment to Christ.

4 The minister says:

N, we rejoice with you in your experience of the grace of our Lord Jesus Christ, the love of God, and the fellowship of the Holy Spirit; and we pray for God's continued blessing on you.

5 The minister says:

May God, Father, Son and Holy Spirit,
bless you and keep you in eternal life. **Amen.**

This blessing may be accompanied by the laying on of hands.

6 EITHER the minister says:

Let us pray.

Father, we thank you
for what you have done in *N*'s life
through your Holy Spirit.
We pray that Christ may dwell
in *her/his* heart by faith,
and that *she/he* may be filled with all your fullness;
through Christ our Lord. **Amen.**

OR the minister prays in *her/his* own words.

7 The minister may invite others to commit their lives to Christ.

8 The minister says to the people:

Let us together renew our Christian commitment.

Almighty God,
in the power of your Spirit
we offer you our souls and bodies
to be a living sacrifice.
Strengthen us to serve you,
and gather us and all people
into your kingdom;
through Jesus Christ our Lord. Amen.

9 The service continues.

HEALING AND RECONCILIATION SERVICES

AN ORDER OF SERVICE FOR HEALING AND WHOLENESS

INTRODUCTION

Healing was central to the ministry of Jesus. It was a sign of God's kingdom, bringing renewal and wholeness of life to those who turned to God in their need. Jesus sent out his disciples with the commission to 'proclaim the kingdom of God and to heal' (Luke 9:2).

In every act of worship, the Church celebrates the grace of God who desires wholeness of body, mind and spirit for all people. At a service of healing, we focus on that aspect of God's character. We bring to God our own frailty and brokenness – felt not just in physical illness, but in guilt, anxiety, and all the burdens which weigh us down. We also bring our concerns for others and for the world. Above all, we come to the God who knows our needs before we ask, and whose love revealed in Jesus Christ is stronger than suffering and death.

The most appropriate setting for this service is ***Holy Communion***, where the risen Christ is present in the sacrament to heal and renew our lives. The laying on of hands and/or anointing with oil together with prayer for others, as practised by the early Church, may also form part of the service.

NOTES

1 Before the service begins, guidance should be given about the arrangements for receiving the laying on of hands and/or anointing with oil.

2 If the service includes the laying on of hands, hands should be laid on the person's head. If the service includes anointing with oil, the oil should be applied to the forehead.

3 This service may also be used for a person at home or in hospital. Whenever possible, family, friends and representatives of the church should also be present.

4 The basic elements of the service are marked by the symbol . Other sections may be omitted.

THE GATHERING OF THE PEOPLE OF GOD

1 One or more of the following sentences may be said:

Jesus said: 'Come to me, all you that are weary and are carrying heavy burdens, and I will give you rest. Take my yoke upon you, and learn from me; for I am gentle and humble in heart, and you will find rest for your souls.'

Jesus said: 'I have come that you may have life, and may have it in all its fullness.'

Confess your sins to one another and pray for one another, so that you may be healed. The prayer of the righteous is powerful and effective.

2 Hymn

3 Loving God,
in whom all things are made whole,
you sent your Son our Saviour
to heal a broken world.
Visit us with your salvation,
that we may be blessed
in body, mind and spirit;
through Jesus Christ our Lord. **Amen.**

* 4 Our Lord Jesus Christ said:
'Anyone who comes to me I will never turn away.'

In the presence of God, let us confess our sins.

Silence

Lord Jesus, you came to reconcile us to God and to one another.

Lord, have mercy.
Lord, have mercy.

Lord Jesus, you heal the wounds of sin and division.

Christ, have mercy.
Christ, have mercy.

Lord Jesus, you offer us a new beginning.

Lord, have mercy.
Lord, have mercy.

Silence

God is love.
Through Jesus our sins are forgiven.
Let us live in the power of the Spirit. **Amen.**

* 5 The collect of the day or this or some other prayer:

Holy God,
you give life to all;
you meet us in our need
and bring hope to those who look to you.
Give peace to our hearts and minds
as we pray to you with confidence;
through Jesus Christ our Lord. **Amen.**

6 If anointing is to take place, this prayer is said over the oil:

Heavenly Father, giver of life and salvation,
bless this oil for the healing of the sick.
May those who receive this ministry
be made whole by the power of the Holy Spirit;
through our Lord and Saviour Jesus Christ. **Amen.**

7 Hymn

THE MINISTRY OF THE WORD

8 The Old Testament reading for the day, or one of the following:

Isaiah 35:1-10
Isaiah 40:1-11
Isaiah 53:4-12
Isaiah 54:7-10
Ezekiel 47:1-12

9 The Psalm for the day, or one of the following:

Psalms 23, 27, 30, 46, 91, 103 *or* 121

10 The Epistle for the day, or one of the following:

Acts 3:1-16
Acts 28:7-10
Romans 8:18-27
2 Corinthians 4:16 - 5:5
James 5:13-16

11 Hymn

*12 A reading from the Gospel according to . . .

Hear the Gospel of Christ.
Glory to Christ our Saviour.

The Gospel for the day is read, or one of the following:

Matthew 5:1-12
Matthew 6:25-34
Mark 1:21-34
Mark 9:14-29
Luke 7:18-23
Luke 9:1-6
Luke 10:1-9, 38-42
Luke 11:5-13

John 9:1-41
John 14:12-27

This is the Gospel of Christ.
Praise to Christ our Lord.

*13 Sermon

14 Hymn

*15 Prayers for the healing of the Church, the nations and individuals may be offered, concluding with this or some other prayer:

Christ our Saviour, born for us,
bring healing and peace to all people.

Lord, have mercy.
Christ, have mercy.

Christ, baptized in the Jordan,
give hope to all who come to you.

Lord, have mercy.
Christ, have mercy.

Christ, tested in the desert,
give courage to those who are tempted.

Lord, have mercy.
Christ, have mercy.

Christ, who comforted and healed,
bring wholeness to all who are broken.

Lord, have mercy.
Christ, have mercy.

Christ, who hung in agony on the cross,
bring strength to those who suffer.

Lord, have mercy.
Christ, have mercy.

Christ, who died to save us,
give peace to all who face death.

Lord, have mercy.
Christ, have mercy.

Christ, raised from the tomb,
bring light and life to all the world.

Lord, have mercy.
Christ, have mercy.

Christ, present among your disciples,
unite all your people in love.

Lord, have mercy.
Christ, have mercy.

Silence

The grace of Christ attend us,
the love of God surround us,
and the Holy Spirit keep us,
this day and for ever. **Amen.**

THE LAYING ON OF HANDS AND/OR ANOINTING WITH OIL

16 If the Lord's Supper is to be celebrated, the laying on of hands and/or the anointing with oil may take place here, or at no. 29.

If the Lord's Supper is not to be celebrated, the laying on of hands and/or the anointing with oil takes place here.

Before the people receive the laying on of hands and/or anointing with oil, those exercising this ministry may receive it from one another.

One of the following sentences may be said at either the laying on of hands or the anointing with oil:

EITHER

A Father,
send your Spirit of life and health on your servant, *N*;
in the Name of Christ. **Amen.**

OR

B *N*, the grace of Christ bring you wholeness
and give you peace. **Amen.**

OR

C May the Spirit of the living God,
present with us now,
heal you of all that harms you,
in body, mind, or spirit;
in the Name of Jesus Christ. **Amen.**

17 The Peace

All stand.

Christ is our peace.
He breaks down the walls that divide us.

The peace of the Lord be always with you.
And also with you.

The people may greet one another in the name of Christ.

---

18 If the Lord's Supper is not to be celebrated, the service continues from no. 36.

THE LORD'S SUPPER

THE PREPARATION OF THE GIFTS

19 Hymn

*20 The offerings of the people are presented. Bread and wine are brought to the table (or if already on the table are uncovered). The presiding minister takes the bread and wine and prepares them for use.

THE THANKSGIVING

*21 All stand.

The presiding minister leads the great prayer of thanksgiving:

The Lord be with you.
And also with you.

Lift up your hearts.
We lift them to the Lord.

Let us give thanks to the Lord our God.
It is right to give our thanks and praise.

Gracious God,
you have loved us from the beginning of time
and remembered us when we were in trouble.
Your mercy endures for ever.

Redeeming God,
you have come to us in Jesus Christ,
to save us from our sins.
Your mercy endures for ever.

Holy God,
you have sent us your Spirit,
to comfort us and lead us into all truth.
Your mercy endures for ever.

And so we praise you
with the faithful of every time and place,
joining with choirs of angels in the eternal hymn:

Holy, holy, holy Lord,
God of power and might,
heaven and earth are full of your glory.
Hosanna in the highest.
Blessèd is he who comes in the name of the Lord.
Hosanna in the highest.

On the night before he died,
Jesus had supper with his disciples.
He took bread, gave thanks, broke it,
and gave it to them, saying,
'Take this and eat it.
This is my body given for you.
Do this in remembrance of me.'

After supper he took the cup of wine,
gave thanks, and gave it to them, saying,
'Drink from it all of you.
This is my blood of the new covenant,
shed for you and for all people
for the forgiveness of sins.
Do this in remembrance of me.'

Remembering, therefore, his death and resurrection,
we proclaim his eternal sacrifice,
and declare the mystery of faith:

Dying, you destroyed our death.
Rising, you restored our life.
Lord Jesus, come in glory.

Father, pour out your Holy Spirit
that these gifts of bread and wine
may be for us the body and blood of Christ.

In union with him, we offer ourselves to you
that, strengthened by the Spirit,
we may be signs of your life and love,
as we await the coming of his kingdom of justice and peace.

Through Christ, with Christ, in Christ,
in the unity of the Holy Spirit,
all glory is yours, Father most holy,
now and for ever. Amen.

*22 The Lord's Prayer

EITHER

We say together the prayer that Jesus gave us:

Our Father in heaven,
hallowed be your Name,
your kingdom come,
your will be done,
on earth as in heaven.
Give us today our daily bread.
Forgive us our sins
as we forgive those who sin against us.
Save us from the time of trial
and deliver us from evil.
For the kingdom, the power and the glory are yours,
now and for ever. Amen.

OR

As our Saviour taught his disciples, we pray:

Our Father, who art in heaven,
hallowed be thy Name;
thy kingdom come;
thy will be done;
on earth as it is in heaven.
Give us this day our daily bread.
And forgive us our trespasses,
as we forgive those who trespass against us.
And lead us not into temptation;
but deliver us from evil.
For thine is the kingdom, the power, and the glory,
for ever and ever. Amen.

THE BREAKING OF THE BREAD

*23 The presiding minister breaks the bread in the sight of the people in silence, or saying:

We break this bread to share in the body of Christ.
Though we are many, we are one body,
because we all share in one bread.

The presiding minister may lift the cup in silence, or saying:

We lift up the cup of salvation.
And call on the name of the Lord.

*24 Silence, all seated or kneeling

*25 Jesus is the Lamb of God
who takes away the sins of the world.
Happy are those who are called to his supper.

Lord, I am not worthy to receive you,
but only say the word, and I shall be healed.

THE SHARING OF THE BREAD AND WINE

*26 The presiding minister, those assisting with the distribution and the people receive, according to local custom.

Appropriate words of invitation may be said.

*27 Words such as the following are said during the distribution:

The body of Christ keep you in eternal life. **Amen.**

The blood of Christ keep you in eternal life. **Amen.**

28 During the distribution there may be appropriate music.

29 If the laying on of hands and/or the anointing with oil has not taken place at no. 16, it takes place here.

*30 The elements that remain are covered with a white cloth.

PRAYERS AND DISMISSAL

31 Silence

32 Let us pray.

**Gracious God,
we thank you
that you have nourished us
with the bread of life and the cup of salvation.
Renew us day by day
until, with all your people on earth and in heaven,
we come to fullness of life in your kingdom;
through Jesus Christ our Lord. Amen.**

33 Hymn

34 The presiding minister says:

EITHER

The Lord bless you and keep you;
the Lord make his face to shine on you
and be gracious to you;
the Lord look on you with kindness
and give you peace. **Amen.**

OR

God be gracious to us and bless us;
and make his face to shine upon us. **Amen.**

*35 The presiding minister says:

Go in peace
to rejoice in God's love
and to reflect his glory.

Thanks be to God. Amen.

If there is no celebration of the Lord's Supper, the service continues as follows after no. 17:

36 Prayers of thanksgiving

We thank you, gracious God.
You have loved us from the beginning of time
and remembered us when we were in trouble.
Your mercy endures for ever.

We thank you, redeeming God.
You have come to us in Jesus Christ,
to save us from our sins.
Your mercy endures for ever.

We thank you, holy God.
You have sent us your Spirit,
to comfort us and lead us into all truth.
Your mercy endures for ever.

Gracious, redeeming and holy God,
glory and praise be yours, now and for ever.
Amen.

37 The Lord's Prayer

EITHER

We say together the prayer that Jesus gave us:

**Our Father in heaven,
hallowed be your Name,
your kingdom come,
your will be done,
on earth as in heaven.
Give us today our daily bread.
Forgive us our sins
as we forgive those who sin against us.
Save us from the time of trial
and deliver us from evil.
For the kingdom, the power and the glory are yours,
now and for ever. Amen.**

OR

As our Saviour taught his disciples, we pray:

**Our Father, who art in heaven,
hallowed be thy Name;
thy kingdom come;
thy will be done;
on earth as it is in heaven.
Give us this day our daily bread.
And forgive us our trespasses,
as we forgive those who trespass against us.
And lead us not into temptation;
but deliver us from evil.
For thine is the kingdom, the power, and the glory,
for ever and ever. Amen.**

38 **Almighty God,
you have made us for yourself
and our hearts are restless
till they find their rest in you.
Teach us to offer ourselves to your service,
that here we may have your peace,
and in the world to come may see you face to face;
through Jesus Christ our Lord,
who lives and reigns with you and the Holy Spirit,
one God, now and for ever. Amen.**

THE DISMISSAL

39 Hymn

40 EITHER

The Lord bless you and
keep you;
the Lord make his face to
shine on you
and be gracious to you;
the Lord look on you with
kindness
and give you peace. **Amen.**

OR

God be gracious to us and
bless us;
and make his face to
shine upon us. **Amen.**

41 Go in peace
to rejoice in God's love
and to reflect his glory.

Thanks be to God. Amen.

A SERVICE OF REPENTANCE AND RECONCILIATION

INTRODUCTION

The ministry of reconciliation is one of God's gifts to the Church. According to the Gospel of John, on the evening of Easter Day, Jesus breathed on his disciples and said, 'Receive the Holy Spirit. If you forgive the sins of any, they are forgiven them; if you retain the sins of any, they are retained' (John 20:22-23). In response to this gift, the Church recognizes that an act of confession and declaration of forgiveness may be an important step towards reconciliation, spiritual growth and wholeness.

An act of repentance and reconciliation usually contains four elements: (i) we acknowledge our sins; (ii) we repent of sin and turn to God; (iii) we are assured of God's forgiveness; and (iv) we declare our intention to lead a new life.

NOTES

1 The penitent person may find it helpful to prepare a written confession. After the declaration of forgiveness this must be burnt or otherwise destroyed.

2 When guidance or counsel is given, it may include the recommendation of prayer, biblical or devotional reading, and other suitable acts.

3 Proper confidentiality must be maintained in respect of all that is disclosed in the context of this service.

---

1 The Lord be with you.
And also with you.

2 EITHER

We say together the prayer that Jesus gave us:

**Our Father in heaven,
hallowed be your Name,
your kingdom come,
your will be done,
on earth as in heaven.
Give us today our daily bread.
Forgive us our sins
as we forgive those who sin against us.
Save us from the time of trial
and deliver us from evil.
For the kingdom, the power and the glory are yours,
now and for ever. Amen.**

OR

As our Saviour taught his disciples, we pray:

**Our Father, who art in heaven,
hallowed be thy Name;
thy kingdom come;
thy will be done;
on earth as it is in heaven.
Give us this day our daily bread.
And forgive us our trespasses,
as we forgive those who trespass against us.
And lead us not into temptation;
but deliver us from evil.
For thine is the kingdom, the power, and the glory,
for ever and ever. Amen.**

THE MINISTRY OF THE WORD

3 1 John 1:8-9

If we say that we have no sin, we deceive ourselves, and the truth is not in us. If we confess our sins, he who is faithful and just will forgive us our sins and cleanse us from all unrighteousness.

One of the following may also be read:

Deuteronomy 30:15-16, 19
Psalm 32:3-5
Psalm 51
Psalm 103:8-14
Jeremiah 31:31-34

Ezekiel 11:19-20
Mark 1:14-15
Luke 6:36-37
Luke 15:8-10
John 8:31*b*-32, 34-36
Romans 5:8-9
Colossians 1:12-14
James 5:16
1 Peter 1:18-21

THE ACT OF REPENTANCE AND RECONCILIATION

4 May the Lord be in your heart and on your lips
that you may truly and humbly confess your sins.

5 The penitent person says these or similar words:

I confess to almighty God,
before you and all the company of heaven,
that I have sinned through my own fault
in what I have thought, said and done,
and in what I have failed to do.
In particular I confess . . .

These are the sins which I remember.
I ask God's forgiveness for them and for all my sins.

6 Appropriate guidance or counsel may be given.

7 The penitent person says:

Gracious and merciful God,
I am truly sorry and repent of all my sins.
Forgive me all that is past,
help me to amend what I am,
and direct what I shall be,
that I may delight in your will
and walk in your ways,
to the praise and glory of your name;
through Jesus Christ our Lord. **Amen.**

8 The minister may place her/his hand on the penitent's head or trace the sign of the cross on the penitent's forehead, saying:

God, the Father of all mercies,
through Jesus Christ his Son,
forgives all who truly repent and believe in him.

By the ministry of reconciliation
given by Christ to his Church,
I declare that your sins are forgiven,
in the name of the Father, and of the Son,
and of the Holy Spirit. **Amen.**

9 Go in peace,
pray for me, a sinner,
and remember the mercy of God. **Amen.**

PRAYER WITH THE DYING

INTRODUCTION

Prayer with the Dying may be part of the process of reconciliation with God. There is no more fitting way to spend the final moments of our life than in prayer to God who brought us into being and into whose arms we will pass. This is a service of readings and prayers which may be used either near or at the point of death. The words, 'Go forth upon your journey . . .', have traditionally been said either before or shortly after death.

NOTE

The way in which this service is used will depend greatly on the condition of the one who is dying. Even if the dying person cannot register a response it is still appropriate to pray with her or him. If necessary, the words printed in **bold** type may be said by the leader alone.

---

1 One or both of the following sentences:

Peace be to this house and all who dwell in it.

The grace of our Lord Jesus Christ,
and the love of God,
and the fellowship of the Holy Spirit,
be with you all. **Amen.**

2 One or both of the following may be said:

Saint Paul said: 'The Lord is near; do not be anxious, but in everything make your requests known to God in prayer and petition with thanksgiving. Then the peace of God, which is beyond all understanding, will guard your hearts and your thoughts in Christ Jesus.'

Jesus said: 'Come to me, all you that are weary and are carrying heavy burdens, and I will give you rest.'

3 Let us pray.

Heavenly Father,
bless *N* in this time of weakness,
and comfort *her/him*
with the promise of eternal life,
given in the resurrection of your Son,
Jesus Christ our Lord. **Amen.**

4 EITHER

The Lord is my shepherd, I shall not want.
He makes me lie down in green pastures;
he leads me besides still waters;
he restores my soul.
He leads me in right paths
for his name's sake.

Even though I walk through the darkest valley,
I fear no evil;
for you are with me;
your rod and your staff –
they comfort me.

You prepare a table before me
in the presence of my enemies;
you anoint my head with oil;
my cup overflows.
Surely goodness and mercy shall follow me
all the days of my life,
and I shall dwell in the house of the Lord
my whole life long.

Glory to the Father, and to the Son,
and to the Holy Spirit;
as it was in the beginning, is now,
and shall be for ever. Amen.

Psalm 23

OR

I lift up my eyes to the hills –
from where will my help come?
My help comes from the Lord,
who made heaven and earth.
He will not let your foot be moved;
he who keeps you will not slumber.
He who keeps Israel
will neither slumber nor sleep.
The Lord is your keeper;
the Lord is your shade at your right hand.
The sun shall not strike you by day,
nor the moon by night.
The Lord will keep you from all evil;
he will keep your life.
The Lord will keep your going out and your coming in
from this time on and for evermore.

Glory to the Father, and to the Son,
and to the Holy Spirit:
as it was in the beginning, is now,
and shall be for ever. Amen.

Psalm 121

OR

O Lord, my heart is not lifted up,
my eyes are not raised too high;
I do not occupy myself with things
too great and too marvellous for me.
But I have calmed and quieted my soul.

Glory to the Father, and to the Son,
and to the Holy Spirit:
as it was in the beginning, is now,
and shall be for ever. Amen.

Psalm 131:1-2*a*

5 Let us in silence confess our sins to God.

Silence

EITHER

A Lord, have mercy.
Lord, have mercy.

Christ, have mercy.
Christ, have mercy.

Lord, have mercy.
Lord, have mercy.

OR

B **Almighty God, our heavenly Father,**
we have sinned against you
and against our neighbours,
in thought and word and deed,
in the evil we have done
and in the good we have not done,
through ignorance, through weakness,
through our own deliberate fault.
We are truly sorry and repent of all our sins.
For the sake of your Son, Jesus Christ,
who died for us,
forgive us all that is past;
and grant that we may serve you
in newness of life;
to the glory of your name. Amen.

Christ Jesus came into the world to save sinners.

To all who truly repent
this is his gracious word:
'Your sins are forgiven.'

Amen. Thanks be to God.

6 Now, Lord, you let your servant go in peace:
your word has been fulfilled.
My own eyes have seen the salvation
which you have prepared in the sight of every people:
a light to reveal you to the nations
and the glory of your people Israel.

Glory to the Father, and to the Son,
and to the Holy Spirit:
as it was in the beginning, is now,
and shall be for ever. Amen.

7 One or both of the following prayers may be said, or the minister may pray in her/his own words:

Remember, O Lord,
those who are sick or suffer pain
and those who are close to death,
especially our *sister/ brother N.*
Comfort us with your presence,
sustain us by your promises,
and grant us your peace;
in the name of Jesus Christ. **Amen.**

God of glory,
make bright with your presence
the path of those who walk in the valley of darkness.
Deliver *N*'s family and friends from anxiety and fear,
that they may live in peace and be at one with you;
through Christ our Lord. **Amen.**

8 The Lord's Prayer

EITHER

We say together the prayer that Jesus gave us:

Our Father in heaven,
hallowed be your Name,
your kingdom come,
your will be done,
on earth as in heaven.
Give us today our daily bread.
Forgive us our sins
as we forgive those who sin against us.
Save us from the time of trial
and deliver us from evil.
For the kingdom, the power and the glory are yours,
now and for ever. Amen.

OR

As our Saviour taught his disciples, we pray:

Our Father, who art in heaven,
hallowed be thy Name;
thy kingdom come;
thy will be done;
on earth as it is in heaven.
Give us this day our daily bread.
And forgive us our trespasses,
as we forgive those who trespass against us.
And lead us not into temptation;
but deliver us from evil.
For thine is the kingdom, the power, and the glory,
for ever and ever. Amen.

9 EITHER

A Go forth upon your journey, Christian soul,
in the name of God the Father
who created you;
in the name of Jesus Christ
who suffered for you;
in the name of the Holy Spirit
who strengthens you;
in communion with the blessèd saints,
with angels and archangels
and with all the heavenly host.
May you rest in peace
and may the City of God
be your eternal dwelling. **Amen.**

OR

B May God the Father,
who created you,
have mercy on you.
May God the Son, Jesus Christ,
who conquered death for you,
have mercy on you.
May God the Holy Spirit,
who sanctifies you,
have mercy on you.
May God almighty,
the Father, the Son and the Holy Spirit,
grant you eternal rest and peace. **Amen.**

OR

C Mighty God,
we commend your *daughter/son N*
to your everlasting love and mercy.
Give *her/him* joy and gladness in your presence;
give *her/him* the assurance of your forgiveness and love;
give *her/him* your peace, now and for ever. **Amen.**

10 The peace of God,
which passes all understanding,
keep *your/our* hearts and minds
in the knowledge and love of God
and of his Son, Jesus Christ our Lord;
and the blessing of God,
the Father, the Son and the Holy Spirit,
remain with *you/us* always. **Amen.**

FUNERAL AND RELATED SERVICES

INTRODUCTION

Christians believe that the death and resurrection of Jesus Christ give them hope and cause for thanksgiving in the face of death. In this faith, we entrust those who have died to the infinite mercy and love of God. Rites used on these occasions need to reflect local traditions and culture. These services provide a broad range of material for use when a person has died.

A Vigil is an ancient Christian rite, which is an important part of the funeral customs in some places.

Two patterns of funeral service are provided. The first begins in a church, a crematorium, or a cemetery chapel, and ends with the Committal. The second service begins with a Service of Committal at a crematorium or cemetery, followed by a Service of Thanksgiving in church. While the second part of this service may follow on the same day, it is possible for it to follow at a later date.

A funeral service for a child and another for a stillborn child are provided. The latter may also be used, with adaptation, after a miscarriage or a neo-natal death.

The service for the burial of ashes provides for the final disposal of cremated remains.

PRAYERS IN THE HOME OR HOSPITAL AFTER A DEATH

NOTE

These prayers are suitable for use by the minister or a pastoral visitor on the first pastoral visit to the home or hospital after a death.

---

1 In this moment of sorrow the Lord is with us. He consoles us with these words: 'Blessèd are those who mourn; they shall be comforted.'

Let us be silent and make our own prayers.

Silence

2 *This or some other passage of scripture may be read:*

Jesus said: 'Do not let your hearts be troubled. Believe in God, believe also in me. In my Father's house there are many dwelling-places. If it were not so, would I have told you that I go to prepare a place for you? And if I go and prepare a place for you, I will come again and will take you to myself, so that where I am, there you may be also. And you know the way to the place where I am going.' Thomas said to him, 'Lord, we do not know where you are going. How can we know the way?' Jesus said to him, 'I am the way, and the truth, and the life. No one comes to the Father except through me.'

'Peace I leave with you; my peace I give to you. I do not give to you as the world gives. Do not let your hearts be troubled, and do not let them be afraid.'

John 14:1-6, 27

3 The Lord's Prayer

EITHER

We say together the prayer that Jesus gave us:

Our Father in heaven,
hallowed be your Name,
your kingdom come,
your will be done,
on earth as in heaven.
Give us today our daily bread.
Forgive us our sins
as we forgive those who sin against us.
Save us from the time of trial
and deliver us from evil.
For the kingdom, the power and the glory are yours,
now and for ever. Amen.

OR

As our Saviour taught his disciples, we pray:

Our Father, who art in heaven,
hallowed be thy Name;
thy kingdom come;
thy will be done;
on earth as it is in heaven.
Give us this day our daily bread.
And forgive us our trespasses,
as we forgive those who trespass against us.
And lead us not into temptation;
but deliver us from evil.
For thine is the kingdom, the power, and the glory,
for ever and ever. Amen.

4 One or more of the following prayers may be said, and the sign of the cross may be made on the forehead of the person who has died.

A Father of mercies and God of all comfort,
you embrace us with the arms of love.
In the shadow of death your light shines on us.
We remember before you our *sister/brother N.*
May we, with *her/him,*
inherit your eternal kingdom,
and rest with you in light and peace.
This we ask through Jesus Christ our Lord. **Amen.**

B Give rest, O Christ,
to your servant with your saints,
where sorrow and pain are no more,
neither sighing, but life everlasting.

You only are immortal,
the creator and maker of all;
and we are mortal, formed of the earth,
and to earth we shall return.
For so did you ordain when you created us, saying,
'You are dust and to dust you shall return.'

All of us go down to the dust;
yet even at the grave we make our song:
Alleluia, alleluia, alleluia.

Give rest, O Christ,
to your servant with your saints,
where sorrow and pain are no more,
neither sighing, but life everlasting. **Amen.**

C God of all grace,
we pray for one another,
especially for . . .
In our loss and sorrow
be our refuge and strength,
and enfold us in your everlasting arms;
through Jesus Christ our Lord. **Amen.**

5 The peace of God
which passes all understanding,
keep *your/our* hearts and minds
in the knowledge and love of God
and of his Son, Jesus Christ our Lord;
and the blessing of God,
the Father, the Son and the Holy Spirit,
remain with *you/us* always. **Amen.**

AN OFFICE OF COMMENDATION

NOTE

This Office may be used on hearing of a death or on the day of the funeral by those not able to be present. It is particularly appropriate when a person dies abroad and the immediate family is not able to attend the funeral service.

---

1 Christ your light shall rise in the darkness,
and your healing shall spring up like the dawn.

The light and peace of Jesus Christ be with you.
And also with you.

The trumpet shall sound and the dead will rise immortal,
and the mortal will be clothed with immortality.

2 One of the following, or another prayer may be said:

A God of love,
who brought us to birth
and in whose arms we die:
in our grief and shock,
contain and comfort us,
give us hope in our confusion
and embrace us with your love;
through Jesus Christ. **Amen.**

B God of mercy,
from whom we come,
by whose grace we live,
in whose love we are held at the last:
surround us with your presence
that in our grief and loss
we may find assurance and hope
in the One who died for us and rose again,
even your Son, Jesus Christ our Lord. **Amen.**

3 Hymn

4 One of the following, or some other Psalm may be read: Psalms 23, 42, 43, 121, 130 *or* 139.

5 One of the following, or some other passage of scripture may be read:

John 11:21-27
John 14:1-3
Romans 6:3-9
Philippians 1:20-26

6 Memories of the person who has died may be shared.

7 Gracious God,
we praise you for creating us in your own image,
and calling each one of us
to love and serve you.
We thank you for *N*
and for all we treasure
and remember with gratitude about *her/him.*
As memories fill our minds,
assure us of your forgiveness
for things said or done which we regret;
for things we longed to do, but never did;
longed to say, but never said.
Give us the strength and courage
to leave *N* in your keeping,
trusting in your everlasting goodness;
through Jesus Christ our Lord. **Amen.**

8 God of mercy,
as *N* has journeyed beyond our sight,
we commend *her/him* to you.

Silence

God of all consolation,
in your unending love and mercy
you turn the darkness of death
into the dawn of new life.
Your Son, by dying for us, conquered death
and, by rising again, restored to us eternal life.

May we go forward eagerly to meet our Redeemer
and, after our life on earth,
be reunited with all our sisters and brothers
in that place where every tear is wiped away
and all things are made new;
through Jesus Christ our Saviour. **Amen.**

9 The Lord's Prayer

EITHER

We say together the prayer that Jesus gave us:

**Our Father in heaven,
hallowed be your Name,
your kingdom come,
your will be done,
on earth as in heaven.
Give us today our daily bread.
Forgive us our sins
as we forgive those who sin against us.
Save us from the time of trial
and deliver us from evil.
For the kingdom, the power and the glory are yours,
now and for ever. Amen.**

OR

As our Saviour taught his disciples, we pray:

**Our Father, who art in heaven,
hallowed be thy Name;
thy kingdom come;
thy will be done;
on earth as it is in heaven.
Give us this day our daily bread.
And forgive us our trespasses,
as we forgive those who trespass against us.
And lead us not into temptation;
but deliver us from evil.
For thine is the kingdom, the power, and the glory,
for ever and ever. Amen.**

10 EITHER

A Magnified and sanctified
be the great name of God
in the world created according to his will.
May God establish his kingdom
in your life and in your days,
and in the lifetime of all his people:
quickly and speedily may it come.
Let us say, Amen:

Amen. Blessèd be God for ever!

Blessèd, praised and glorified,
exalted, extolled and honoured,
magnified and lauded
be the name of the Holy One.
Let us say, Amen:

Amen. Blessèd be God for ever!

Though God be high above all the blessings
and hymns, praises and consolations,
which are uttered in the world,
let us say, Amen:

Amen. Blessèd be God for ever!

May there be abundant peace from heaven
and life for us and for all people.
Let us say, Amen:

Amen. Blessèd be God for ever!

OR

B Now to the one who is able to keep us from falling
and set us in the presence of the divine glory,
to the only God our Saviour
be glory and majesty, dominion and praise,
now and for ever. **Amen.**

11 The peace of God
which passes all understanding,
keep *your/our* hearts and minds
in the knowledge and love of God
and of his Son, Jesus Christ our Lord;
and the blessing of God,
the Father, the Son and the Holy Spirit,
remain with *you/us* always. **Amen.**

A VIGIL

NOTE

This service may take place on the evening before the funeral service, in the home, in a church or in a chapel of rest, whether or not the body is present.

GREETING

1 The God of hope grant us peace,
now and in all our days. **Amen.**

Sisters and brothers in Christ,
at this time of death and parting
we are confident that God knows us and is with us.
Let us pray in silence
as we remember our *sister/brother N.*

Silence

2 Gracious God,
your love holds in its embrace
your children in this world and the next.
Neither life nor death
can separate those who trust in you.
Unite us to yourself,
together with our *sister/brother N*,
that in our fellowship with you
we may be one with those we love.
Give us courage, constancy and hope,
through Jesus Christ,
who died and rose again for us. **Amen.**

THE MINISTRY OF THE WORD

3 One or more of the following passages of scripture may be read, followed by a time of silence:

The Lord is my light and my salvation:
whom shall I fear?
The Lord is the stronghold of my life;
of whom shall I be afraid?

One thing I asked of the Lord,
that will I seek after:
to live in the house of the Lord
all the days of my life,
to behold the beauty of the Lord,
and to inquire in his temple.

For he will hide me in his shelter
in the day of trouble;
he will conceal me under the cover of his tent;
he will set me high on a rock.

Hear, O Lord, when I cry aloud,
be gracious to me and answer me!
'Come,' my heart says, 'seek his face!'
Your face, Lord, do I seek.
Do not hide your face from me.

Do not turn your servant away in anger,
you who have been my help.
Do not cast me off, do not forsake me,
O God of my salvation!
If my father and mother forsake me,
the Lord will take me up.

I believe that I shall see the goodness of the Lord
in the land of the living.
Wait for the Lord;
be strong, and let your heart take courage;
wait for the Lord!

Psalm 27:1, 4-5, 7-10, 13-14

We know that if the earthly tent we live in is destroyed, we have a building from God, a house not made with hands, eternal in the heavens.

So we are always confident; even though we know that while we are at home in the body we are away from the Lord – for we walk by faith, not by sight. Yes, we do have confidence, and we would rather be away from the body and at home with the Lord. So whether we are at home or away, we make it our aim to please him. For all of us must appear before the judgement seat of Christ, so that each may receive recompense for what has been done in the body, whether good or evil.

2 Corinthians 5:1, 6-10

When Jesus arrived, he found that Lazarus had already been in the tomb for four days. Now Bethany was near Jerusalem, some two miles away, and many of the Jews had come to Martha and Mary to console them about their brother. When Martha heard that Jesus was coming, she went and met him, while Mary stayed at home. Martha said to Jesus, 'Lord, if you had been here, my brother would not have died. But even now I know that God will give you whatever you ask of him.' Jesus said to her, 'Your brother will rise again.' Martha said to him, 'I know that he will rise again in the resurrection on the last day.' Jesus said to her, 'I am the resurrection and the life. Those who believe in me, even though they die, will live, and everyone who lives and believes in me will never die.'

John 11:17-26*a*

PRAYERS

4 Let us pray.

Crucified Saviour,
save us from the fear of death:

Lord, have mercy.
Christ, have mercy.

Risen Lord,
raise us to glory:

Lord, have mercy.
Christ, have mercy.

Gentle Shepherd,
bring rest to our souls:

Lord, have mercy.
Christ, have mercy.

Lamb of God,
grant us with *N* your peace for ever:

Lord, have mercy.
Christ, have mercy.

Son of Mary,
bless those who mourn:

Lord, have mercy.
Christ, have mercy.

5 The Lord's Prayer

EITHER

We say together the prayer that Jesus gave us:

**Our Father in heaven,
hallowed be your Name,
your kingdom come,
your will be done,
on earth as in heaven.
Give us today our daily bread.
Forgive us our sins
as we forgive those who sin against us.
Save us from the time of trial
and deliver us from evil.
For the kingdom, the power and the glory are yours,
now and for ever. Amen.**

OR

As our Saviour taught his disciples, we pray:

**Our Father, who art in heaven,
hallowed be thy Name;
thy kingdom come;
thy will be done;
on earth as it is in heaven.
Give us this day our daily bread.
And forgive us our trespasses,
as we forgive those who trespass against us.
And lead us not into temptation;
but deliver us from evil.
For thine is the kingdom, the power, and the glory,
for ever and ever. Amen.**

6 One of the following prayers, or another prayer:

A **Christ be with me, Christ within me,
Christ behind me, Christ before me,
Christ beside me, Christ to win me,
Christ to comfort and restore me.**

**Christ beneath me, Christ above me,
Christ in quiet, Christ in danger,
Christ in hearts of all that love me,
Christ in mouth of friend and stranger. Amen.**

B Lord Jesus Christ,
you willingly gave yourself up to death
so that we might be saved
and pass from death to life.
We ask that you will receive *N*
into the arms of your mercy
and comfort *her/his* family in their grief.
Grant to *N* a place of light and joy in your presence for ever.
In Christ's name we ask it. **Amen.**

7 EITHER

A **The grace of our Lord Jesus Christ,
and the love of God,
and the fellowship of the Holy Spirit,
be with us all evermore. Amen.**

OR

B The peace of God
which passes all understanding,
keep *your/our* hearts and minds
in the knowledge and love of God
and of his Son, Jesus Christ our Lord;
and the blessing of God,
the Father, the Son and the Holy Spirit,
remain with *you/us* always. **Amen.**

A FUNERAL SERVICE IN A CHURCH, A CREMATORIUM, OR A CEMETERY, LEADING TO COMMITTAL

GATHERING

1 Either at the entrance to the church, crematorium or cemetery chapel, or at the graveside, the minister says:

'I am the resurrection and the life,' says the Lord. 'Those who believe in me, even though they die, will live, and everyone who lives and believes in me will never die.'

2 The minister, going before the body, may say one or more of the following sentences, the people standing:

Blessèd are those who mourn, for they will be comforted.

God so loved the world that he gave his only Son, so that everyone who believes in him may not perish but may have eternal life.

The steadfast love of the Lord never ceases, his mercies never come to an end; they are new every morning.

In the world you have tribulation; but be of good cheer, I have overcome the world.

God is our refuge and strength, a very present help in trouble.

3 Hymn

4 Let us pray.

EITHER

A God our comforter,
you are our refuge and strength,
a helper close at hand in times of trouble.
Help us so to hear your word
that our fear may be dispelled,

our loneliness eased,
and our hope reawakened.
May your Holy Spirit lift us above our sorrow,
to the peace and light of your constant love;
through Jesus Christ our Lord. **Amen.**

OR

B Loving God, who brought us to birth,
help us to live as those who are prepared for death.
Enable us to hear your message
of death overcome and life renewed,
that as we face the mystery of death
we may see the light of eternity;
through Christ our risen Saviour. **Amen.**

THE MINISTRY OF THE WORD

5 The minister may say:

We meet in this solemn moment to worship God;
to give thanks for the life of our *sister/brother N;*
to commend *her/him* to God's loving and faithful care;
and to pray for all who mourn.

In the presence of death,
Christ offers us sure ground
for hope and confidence and even for joy,
because he shared our human life and death,
was raised again triumphant
and lives for evermore.
In him his people find eternal life.

Let us then hear the words of Holy Scripture,
that from them we may draw comfort and strength.

6 One of the following Psalms, or another Psalm:

Out of the depths I cry to you, O Lord.
Lord, hear my voice!
Let your ears be attentive
to the voice of my supplications!

If you, O Lord, should mark iniquities,
Lord, who could stand?
But there is forgiveness with you,
so that you may be revered.

I wait for the Lord, my soul waits,
and in his word I hope;
my soul waits for the Lord
more than those who watch for the morning,
more than those who watch for the morning.

O Israel, hope in the Lord!
For with the Lord there is steadfast love,
and with him is great power to redeem.
It is he who will redeem Israel
from all its iniquities.

Psalm 130

The Lord is my shepherd, I shall not want.
He makes me lie down in green pastures;
he leads me besides still waters;
he restores my soul.
He leads me in right paths
for his name's sake.

Even though I walk through the darkest valley,
I fear no evil;
for you are with me;
your rod and your staff –
they comfort me.

You prepare a table before me
in the presence of my enemies;
you anoint my head with oil;
my cup overflows.
Surely goodness and mercy shall follow me
all the days of my life,
and I shall dwell in the house of the Lord
my whole life long.

Psalm 23

The Lord is merciful and gracious,
slow to anger and abounding in steadfast love.
He will not always accuse,
nor will he keep his anger for ever.
He does not deal with us according to our sins,
nor repay us according to our iniquities.
For as the heavens are high above the earth,
so great is his steadfast love towards those who fear him;
as far as the east is from the west,
so far he removes our transgressions from us.
As a father has compassion for his children,
so the Lord has compassion for those who fear him.
For he knows how we were made;
he remembers that we are dust.

As for mortals, their days are like grass;
they flourish like a flower of the field;
for the wind passes over it, and it is gone,
and its place knows it no more.
But the steadfast love of the Lord
is from everlasting to everlasting on those who fear him,
and his righteousness to children's children,
to those who keep his covenant
and remember to do his commandments.

Psalm 103:8-18

7 One of the following, or some other passage from the Gospels, is read:

Jesus said: 'Do not let your hearts be troubled. Believe in God, believe also in me. In my Father's house there are many dwelling-places. If it were not so, would I have told you that I go to prepare a place for you? And if I go and prepare a place for you, I will come again and will take you to myself, so that where I am, there you may be also. And you know the way to the place where I am going.' Thomas said to him, 'Lord, we do not know where you are going. How can we know the way?' Jesus said to him, 'I am the way, and the truth, and the life. No one comes to the Father except through me.'

'Peace I leave with you; my peace I give to you. I do not give to you as the world gives. Do not let your hearts be troubled, and do not let them be afraid.'

John 14:1-6, 27

Jesus said: 'I am the bread of life. Whoever comes to me will never be hungry, and whoever believes in me will never be thirsty. But I said to you that you have seen me and yet do not believe. Everything that the Father gives me will come to me, and anyone who comes to me I will never drive away; for I have come down from heaven, not to do my own will, but the will of him who sent me. And this is the will of him who sent me, that I should lose nothing of all that he has given me, but raise it up on the last day. This is indeed the will of my Father, that all who see the Son and believe in him may have eternal life; and I will raise them up on the last day.'

John 6:35-40

8 One or more of the following passages of scripture, or of the passages listed on pages 501-502, may also be read:

I handed on to you as of first importance what I in turn had received: that Christ died for our sins in accordance with the scriptures, and that he was buried, and that he was raised on the third day in accordance with the scriptures, and that he appeared to Cephas, then to the twelve.

1 Corinthians 15:3-5

Christ has been raised from the dead, the first fruits of those who have died. For since death came through a human being, the resurrection of the dead has also come through a human being; for as all die in Adam, so all will be made alive in Christ. But each in his own order: Christ the first fruits, then at his coming those who belong to Christ.

Then comes the end, when he hands over the kingdom to God the Father, after he has destroyed every ruler and every authority and power.

1 Corinthians 15:20-24

Blessed be the God and Father of our Lord Jesus Christ! By his great mercy he has given us a new birth into a living hope through the resurrection of Jesus Christ from the dead, and into an inheritance that is imperishable, undefiled, and unfading, kept in heaven for you, who are being protected by the power of God through faith for a salvation ready to be revealed in the last time. In this you rejoice, even if now for a little while you have had to suffer trials, so that the genuineness of your faith – being more precious than gold that, though perishable, is tested by fire – may be found to result in praise and glory and honour when Jesus Christ is revealed. Although you have not seen him, you love him; and even though you do not see him now, you believe in him and rejoice with an indescribable and glorious joy, for you are receiving the outcome of your faith, the salvation of your souls.

1 Peter 1:3-9

We know that all things work together for good for those who love God, who are called according to his purpose.

If God is for us, who is against us? He who did not withhold his own Son, but gave him up for all of us, will he not with him also give us everything else? Who will bring any charge against God's elect? It is God who justifies. Who is to condemn? It is Christ Jesus, who died, yes, who was raised, who is at the right hand of God, who indeed intercedes for us. Who will separate us from the love of Christ? Will hardship, or distress, or persecution, or famine, or nakedness, or peril, or sword?

No, in all these things we are more than conquerors through him who loved us. For I am convinced that neither death, nor life, nor angels, nor rulers, nor things present, nor things to come, nor powers, nor height, nor depth, nor anything else in all creation, will be able to separate us from the love of God in Christ Jesus our Lord.

Romans 8:28, 31*b*-35, 37-39

9 Sermon

RESPONSE

10 Let us pray.

Glory and thanks be given to you,
almighty God, our Father,
because in your great love for the world
you gave your Son to be our Saviour.
He lived our life, bore our griefs,
and died our death upon the Cross.

We thank you that you have brought him back from death
with power and great glory,
that he has conquered sin and death,
and opened the kingdom of heaven to all believers.

We praise you for the great company of the faithful,
whom Christ has brought through death to behold your face in glory,
who join with us in worship, prayer and service.

For your full, perfect and sufficient gift of life in Christ,
all praise and thanks be given to you
for ever and ever. **Amen.**

Eternal God, in your wisdom and grace
you have given us joy
through the lives of your departed servants.
We thank you for *N*
and for our memories of *her/him.*

We praise you for your goodness and mercy
that followed *her/him* all the days of *her/his* life,
and for *her/his* faithfulness
in the tasks to which you called *her/him.*

We thank you that for *N*
the tribulations of this world are over and death is past,
and we pray that you will bring us with *her/him*
to the joy of your perfect kingdom;
through Jesus Christ our Lord. **Amen.**

Almighty God,
Father of all mercies and giver of all comfort,
deal graciously with those who mourn,
that they may cast every care on you
and know the consolation of your love;
through Jesus Christ our Lord. **Amen.**

11 Hymn

COMMENDATION

12 All stand.

Let us commend *N* to God.

EITHER

A Into your keeping, O merciful God,
we commend your servant *N*.
Receive *her/him* into the arms of your mercy,
into the joy of everlasting peace,
and into the glorious company of the saints in light;
through Christ our Lord. **Amen.**

OR

B Loving God,
we commend *N* to your perfect mercy and wisdom,
for in you alone we put our trust. **Amen.**

13 The Lord's Prayer

EITHER

We say together the prayer that Jesus gave us:

**Our Father in heaven,
hallowed be your Name,
your kingdom come,
your will be done,
on earth as in heaven.
Give us today our daily bread.
Forgive us our sins
as we forgive those who sin against us.
Save us from the time of trial
and deliver us from evil.
For the kingdom, the power and the glory are yours,
now and for ever. Amen.**

OR

As our Saviour taught his disciples, we pray:

**Our Father, who art in heaven,
hallowed be thy Name;
thy kingdom come;
thy will be done;
on earth as it is in heaven.
Give us this day our daily bread.
And forgive us our trespasses,
as we forgive those who trespass against us.
And lead us not into temptation;
but deliver us from evil.
For thine is the kingdom, the power, and the glory,
for ever and ever. Amen.**

14 When the whole service takes place in a crematorium chapel or at the graveside, the service continues from no. 17.

15 Otherwise the minister says:

The peace of God
which passes all understanding,
keep *your/our* hearts and minds
in the knowledge and love of God
and of his Son, Jesus Christ our Lord;
and the blessing of God,
the Father, the Son and the Holy Spirit,
remain with *you/us* always. **Amen.**

---

16 The minister, going before the body into the crematorium, or to the grave, may say one or more of these sentences:

As a father pities his children, so the Lord pities those who fear him. For he knows our frame; he remembers that we are dust.

Blessèd be the God and Father of our Lord Jesus Christ, the Father of mercies and God of all comfort, who comforts us in all our affliction.

To this end Christ died and lived again, that he might be Lord both of the dead and of the living.

COMMITTAL

17 All stand. The minister says:

EITHER

A Since the earthly life of *N* has come to an end,
we commit *her/his* body
to be cremated/to the elements/to be buried,
earth to earth, ashes to ashes, dust to dust;
in sure and certain hope
of the resurrection to eternal life
through our Lord Jesus Christ;
to whom be glory for ever and ever. **Amen.**

OR

B God alone is holy and just and good.
In this certainty we have commended *N* to God.
We therefore commit *her/his* body
to be cremated/to the elements/to be buried,
earth to earth, ashes to ashes, dust to dust;
trusting in the infinite mercy of God,
through Jesus Christ our Lord. **Amen.**

18 The minister may say:

Blessèd are the dead who die in the Lord;
for they rest from their labours.

PRAYERS

19 One or more of the following prayers may be said:

A Father of all,
we pray for those whom we love, but see no longer.
Grant them your peace;
let light perpetual shine upon them;
and in your loving wisdom and almighty power
work in them the good purpose of your perfect will;
through Jesus Christ our Lord. **Amen.**

B Father of mercies and God of all comfort,
you have made nothing in vain
and you love all that you have made.
Look in tender mercy on your bereaved servants,
and help them by your grace
to find in you their refuge and their strength. **Amen.**

C Grant us, O God,
in all our duties your help,
in all our perplexities your guidance,
in all our dangers your protection,
and in all our sorrows your peace;
through Jesus Christ our Lord. **Amen.**

D Support us, O Lord, all the day long,
until the shadows lengthen, the evening comes,
the busy world is hushed,
the fever of life is over and our work done.
Then, in your mercy, grant us a safe lodging,
a holy rest, and peace at the last;
through Jesus Christ our Lord. **Amen.**

E Bring us, Lord our God,
at our last awakening,
into the house and gate of heaven,
to enter into that gate,
and dwell in that house,
where there shall be
no darkness nor dazzling,
but one equal light;
no noise nor silence,
but one equal music;
no fears nor hopes,
but one equal possession;
no ends nor beginnings,
but one equal eternity;
in the habitation of your glory and dominion,
world without end. **Amen.**

20 The minister says:

EITHER

A God grant to the living, grace;
to the departed, rest;
to the world, peace;
and to us and all the faithful, life everlasting;
and the blessing of God,
the Father, the Son and the Holy Spirit,
be with *you/us* now and for ever. **Amen**.

OR

B May God in his infinite love and mercy
bring the whole Church,
living and departed in the Lord Jesus,
to a joyful resurrection
and the fulfilment of his eternal kingdom;
and the blessing of God,
the Father, the Son and the Holy Spirit,
remain with *you/us* always. **Amen.**

A FUNERAL AT A CREMATORIUM OR CEMETERY, FOLLOWED BY A SERVICE OF THANKSGIVING IN CHURCH

AT THE CREMATORIUM OR CEMETERY

GATHERING

1 Either at the entrance to the crematorium or cemetery chapel or at the graveside the minister may say:

'I am the resurrection and the life,' says the Lord. 'Those who believe in me, even though they die, will live, and everyone who lives and believes in me will never die.'

2 The minister, going before the body, may say one or more of the following sentences, the people standing:

Blessèd are those who mourn, for they will be comforted.

God so loved the world that he gave his only Son, so that everyone who believes in him may not perish but may have eternal life.

The steadfast love of the Lord never ceases, his mercies never come to an end; they are new every morning.

Jesus says: 'I am the Good Shepherd. . . . My sheep hear my voice and I know them . . . and no one shall snatch them out of my hand.'

God is our refuge and strength, a very present help in trouble.

Our Saviour Christ Jesus abolished death and brought life and immortality to light through the gospel.

3 Hymn

4 Let us pray.

EITHER

A Heavenly Father,
whose love is everlasting,
you can turn the shadow of death
into the light of morning.
Speak to us your gracious promise,
that we may be lifted above our distress
into the light and peace of your presence;
through Jesus Christ our Lord. **Amen.**

OR

B Loving God, who brought us to birth,
help us to live as those who are prepared for death.
Enable us to hear your message
of death overcome and life renewed,
that as we face the mystery of death
we may see the light of eternity;
through Christ our risen Saviour. **Amen.**

THE MINISTRY OF THE WORD

5 The minister says:

We meet in this solemn moment to worship God;
to give thanks for the life of our *sister/brother N*;
to commend *her/him* to God's loving and faithful care;
and to pray for those who mourn.

In the presence of death
Christ offers us sure ground
for hope and confidence and even for joy,
because he shared our human life and death,
was raised again triumphant
and lives for evermore.
In him his people find eternal life.

Let us then hear the words of Holy Scripture,
that from them we may draw comfort and strength.

6 One of the following Psalms, or another Psalm:

Out of the depths I cry to you, O Lord.
Lord, hear my voice!
Let your ears be attentive
to the voice of my supplications!

If you, O Lord, should mark iniquities,
Lord, who could stand?
But there is forgiveness with you,
so that you may be revered.

I wait for the Lord, my soul waits,
and in his word I hope;
my soul waits for the Lord
more than those who watch for the morning,
more than those who watch for the morning.

O Israel, hope in the Lord!
For with the Lord there is steadfast love,
and with him is great power to redeem.
It is he who will redeem Israel
from all its iniquities.

Psalm 130

The Lord is my shepherd, I shall not want.
He makes me lie down in green pastures;
he leads me besides still waters;
he restores my soul.
He leads me in right paths
for his name's sake.

Even though I walk through the darkest valley,
I fear no evil;
for you are with me;
your rod and your staff –
they comfort me.

You prepare a table before me
in the presence of my enemies;
you anoint my head with oil;
my cup overflows.
Surely goodness and mercy shall follow me
all the days of my life,
and I shall dwell in the house of the Lord
my whole life long.

Psalm 23

The Lord is merciful and gracious,
slow to anger and abounding in steadfast love.
He will not always accuse,
nor will he keep his anger for ever.
He does not deal with us according to our sins,
nor repay us according to our iniquities.
For as the heavens are high above the earth,
so great is his steadfast love towards those who fear him;
as far as the east is from the west,
so far he removes our transgressions from us.
As a father has compassion for his children,
so the Lord has compassion for those who fear him.
For he knows how we were made;
he remembers that we are dust.
As for mortals, their days are like grass;
they flourish like a flower of the field;
for the wind passes over it, and it is gone,
and its place knows it no more.
But the steadfast love of the Lord
is from everlasting to everlasting on those who fear him,
and his righteousness to children's children,
to those who keep his covenant
and remember to do his commandments.

Psalm 103:8-18

7 One of the following, or some other passage from the Gospels, is read:

Jesus said: 'Do not let your hearts be troubled. Believe in God, believe also in me. In my Father's house there are many dwelling-places. If it were not so, would I have told you that I go to prepare a place for you? And if I go and prepare a place for you, I will come again and will take you to myself, so that where I am, there you may be also. And you know the way to the place where I am going.' Thomas said to him, 'Lord, we do not know where you are going. How can we know the way?' Jesus said to him, 'I am the way, and the truth, and the life. No one comes to the Father except through me.'

'Peace I leave with you; my peace I give to you. I do not give to you as the world gives. Do not let your hearts be troubled, and do not let them be afraid.'

John 14:1-6, 27

Jesus said: 'I am the bread of life. Whoever comes to me will never be hungry, and whoever believes in me will never be thirsty. But I said to you that you have seen me and yet do not believe. Everything that the Father gives me will come to me, and anyone who comes to me I will never drive away; for I have come down from heaven, not to do my own will, but the will of him who sent me. And this is the will of him who sent me, that I should lose nothing of all that he has given me, but raise it up on the last day. This is indeed the will of my Father, that all who see the Son and believe in him may have eternal life; and I will raise them up on the last day.'

John 6:35-40

8 One or more of the following passages of scripture, or of the passages listed on pages 501-502, may also be read:

I handed on to you as of first importance what I in turn had received: that Christ died for our sins in accordance with the scriptures, and that he was buried, and that he was raised on the third day in accordance with the scriptures, and that he appeared to Cephas, then to the twelve.

1 Corinthians 15:3-5

Christ has been raised from the dead, the first fruits of those who have died. For since death came through a human being, the resurrection of the dead has also come through a human being; for as all die in Adam, so all will be made alive in Christ. But each in his own order: Christ the first fruits, then at his coming those who belong to Christ.

Then comes the end, when he hands over the kingdom to God the Father, after he has destroyed every ruler and every authority and power.

1 Corinthians 15:20-24

Blessed be the God and Father of our Lord Jesus Christ! By his great mercy he has given us a new birth into a living hope through the resurrection of Jesus Christ from the dead, and into an inheritance that is imperishable, undefiled, and unfading, kept in heaven for you, who are being protected by the power of God through faith for a salvation ready to be revealed in the last time. In this you rejoice, even if now for a little while you have had to suffer trials, so that the genuineness of your faith – being more precious than gold that, though perishable, is tested by fire – may be found to result in praise and glory and honour when Jesus Christ is revealed. Although you have not seen him, you love him; and even though you do not see him now, you believe in him and rejoice with an indescribable and glorious joy, for you are receiving the outcome of your faith, the salvation of your souls.

1 Peter 1:3-9

We know that all things work together for good for those who love God, who are called according to his purpose.

If God is for us, who is against us? He who did not withhold his own Son, but gave him up for all of us, will he not with him also give us everything else? Who will bring any charge against God's elect? It is God who justifies. Who is to condemn? It is Christ Jesus, who died, yes, who was raised, who is at the right hand of God, who indeed intercedes for us. Who will separate us from the love of Christ? Will hardship, or distress, or persecution, or famine, or nakedness, or peril, or sword?

No, in all these things we are more than conquerors through him who loved us. For I am convinced that neither death, nor life, nor angels, nor rulers, nor things present, nor things to come, nor powers, nor height, nor depth, nor anything else in all creation, will be able to separate us from the love of God in Christ Jesus our Lord.

Romans 8:28, 31*b*-35, 37-39

9 A short address or reflection

COMMENDATION

10 The people stand.

Merciful God,
we praise you that we are made in your image and
likeness.
We thank you
for the life of your *daughter/son N*,
and for the love and mercy
she/he received from you and showed among us.
We rejoice in your gracious promise
to all your servants, living and departed,
that we shall rise again to be with Christ.
We ask that at the last we may come with *N*
to share in your glory;
through Jesus Christ our Lord. **Amen.**

11 Let us commend *N* to God.

EITHER

A Into your keeping, O merciful God,
we commend your servant *N*.
Receive *her/him* into the arms of your mercy,
into the joy of everlasting peace,
and into the glorious company of the saints in light;
through Christ our Lord. **Amen.**

OR

B Loving God,
we commend *N* to your perfect mercy and wisdom,
for in you alone we put our trust. **Amen.**

---

12 If the service has been held in a cemetery chapel, the coffin is taken to the graveside. The minister goes before the body to the grave and may read appropriate scripture sentences not used previously in the service.

COMMITTAL

13 All stand. The minister says:

EITHER

A Since the earthly life of *N* has come to an end,
we commit *her/his* body
to be cremated/to the elements/to be buried,
earth to earth, ashes to ashes, dust to dust;
in sure and certain hope
of the resurrection to eternal life
through our Lord Jesus Christ;
to whom be glory for ever and ever. **Amen.**

OR

B God alone is holy and just and good.
In this certainty we have commended *N* to God.
We therefore commit *her/his* body
to be cremated/to the elements/to be buried,
earth to earth, ashes to ashes, dust to dust;
trusting in the infinite mercy of God,
through Jesus Christ our Lord. **Amen.**

14 The minister may say:

Blessèd are the dead who die in the Lord;
for they rest from their labours.

15 Hymn

PRAYERS

16 One or more of the following prayers may be said:

A Father of all,
we pray for those whom we love, but see no longer.
Grant them your peace;
let light perpetual shine upon them;
and in your loving wisdom and almighty power
work in them the good purpose of your perfect will;
through Jesus Christ our Lord. **Amen.**

B Almighty God,
Father of all mercies and giver of all comfort,
deal graciously with those who mourn,
that they may cast every care on you
and know the consolation of your love;
through Jesus Christ our Lord. **Amen.**

C Father of mercies and God of all comfort,
you have made nothing in vain
and you love all that you have made.
Look in tender mercy on your bereaved servants,
and help them by your grace
to find in you their refuge and their strength. **Amen.**

D Grant us, O God,
in all our duties your help,
in all our perplexities your guidance,
in all our dangers your protection,
and in all our sorrows your peace;
through Jesus Christ our Lord. **Amen.**

E Support us, O Lord, all the day long,
until the shadows lengthen, the evening comes,
the busy world is hushed,
the fever of life is over and our work done.
Then, in your mercy, grant us a safe lodging,
a holy rest, and peace at the last;
through Jesus Christ our Lord. **Amen.**

F Bring us, Lord our God,
at our last awakening,
into the house and gate of heaven,
to enter into that gate,
and dwell in that house,
where there shall be
no darkness nor dazzling,
but one equal light;
no noise nor silence,
but one equal music;
no fears nor hopes,
but one equal possession;
no ends nor beginnings,
but one equal eternity;
in the habitation of your glory and dominion,
world without end. **Amen.**

17 The Lord's Prayer

EITHER

We say together the prayer that Jesus gave us:

**Our Father in heaven,
hallowed be your Name,
your kingdom come,
your will be done,
on earth as in heaven.
Give us today our daily bread.
Forgive us our sins
as we forgive those who sin against us.
Save us from the time of trial
and deliver us from evil.
For the kingdom, the power and the glory are yours,
now and for ever. Amen.**

OR

As our Saviour taught his disciples, we pray:

**Our Father, who art in heaven,
hallowed be thy Name;
thy kingdom come;
thy will be done;
on earth as it is in heaven.
Give us this day our daily bread.
And forgive us our trespasses,
as we forgive those who trespass against us.
And lead us not into temptation;
but deliver us from evil.
For thine is the kingdom, the power, and the glory,
for ever and ever. Amen.**

18 EITHER

A The peace of God,
which passes all understanding,
keep *your/our* hearts and minds
in the knowledge and love of God
and of his Son, Jesus Christ our Lord;
and the blessing of God,
the Father, the Son and the Holy Spirit,
remain with *you/us* always. **Amen.**

OR

B May God in his infinite love and mercy
bring the whole Church,
living and departed in the Lord Jesus,
to a joyful resurrection
and the fulfilment of his eternal kingdom;
and the blessing of God,
the Father, the Son and the Holy Spirit,
remain with *you/us* always. **Amen.**

---

19 The service continues in church either on the same day or at a later date.

AT THE CHURCH

20 If the urn or casket containing the ashes is brought into church, it should be placed on a table which has been covered with a white cloth, in front of the communion table.

GATHERING

21 Praise be to the God and Father of our Lord Jesus Christ! In his great mercy by the resurrection of Jesus Christ from the dead, he gave us new birth into a living hope, the hope of an inheritance, reserved in heaven for you, which nothing can destroy or spoil or wither.

22 Hymn

23 The minister says:

EITHER

A Blessèd are you, Sovereign God,
ruler and judge of all;
to you be praise and glory for ever.
In the darkness of this age that is passing away
may the glory of your kingdom,
which the saints enjoy,
surround our steps as we journey on.
May we reflect the light of your glory this day
and so be made ready to come into your presence,
Father, Son and Holy Spirit.

Blessèd be God for ever.

OR

B Lord of all life and power,
who through the mighty resurrection of your Son
overcame the old order of sin and death
to make all things new in him:
grant that we, being dead to sin
and alive to you in Jesus Christ,
may reign with him in glory;
to whom with you in the unity of the Holy Spirit
be praise and honour, glory and might,
now and in all eternity. **Amen.**

THE MINISTRY OF THE WORD

24 Sisters and brothers in Christ,
we meet as the community of faith to worship God
as we proclaim our resurrection faith;
to give thanks for our *sister/brother N*;
to remember *her/his* life among us;
and to uphold and support those who mourn.

25 A Psalm may be read or sung.

Other passages of scripture are read. If the service in church occurs on the same day as the Committal these should be different from those used at that service.

26 Sermon

27 Hymn

RESPONSE

28 Let us praise God in Christ our Lord.

**You, Christ, are the king of glory,
the eternal Son of the Father.
When you took our flesh to set us free
you humbly chose the Virgin's womb.
You overcame the sting of death
and opened the kingdom of heaven to all believers.
You are seated at God's right hand in glory.
We believe that you will come to be our judge.
Come then, Lord, and help your people,
bought with the price of your own blood,
and bring us with your saints to glory everlasting.
Amen.**

Let us pray.

Holy God, we thank you
for the life and witness of the Church on earth . . .

Grant to us, who are still on our pilgrimage,
that your Holy Spirit may lead us,
as we walk by faith,
in holiness and righteousness all our days.

Lord, in your mercy,
hear our prayer.

Holy God, we thank you
for the love and care we receive in times of sorrow.
Grant to all who mourn
a sure confidence in your loving care . . .
May they have strength to meet the days ahead
in the comfort of a holy and certain hope,
and in the joyful expectation of eternal life with those they love.

Lord, in your mercy,
hear our prayer.

Holy God, we thank you
for the love and fellowship that we shared with *N.*

Members of the congregation may pray in silence or offer their prayers, ending with the words:

Lord, in your mercy,
hear our prayer.

Almighty God, we thank you
that you have joined together your faithful people
in one communion and fellowship
in the mystical body of your Son.
Give us grace so to follow your blessèd saints
in all virtuous and godly living,
that we may come to those inexpressible joys
which you have prepared for those who love you;
through Jesus Christ our Lord. **Amen.**

29 The Lord's Prayer

EITHER

We say together the prayer that Jesus gave us:

**Our Father in heaven,
hallowed be your Name,
your kingdom come,
your will be done,
on earth as in heaven.
Give us today our daily bread.
Forgive us our sins
as we forgive those who sin against us.
Save us from the time of trial
and deliver us from evil.
For the kingdom, the power and the glory are yours,
now and for ever. Amen.**

OR

As our Saviour taught his disciples, we pray:

**Our Father, who art in heaven,
hallowed be thy Name;
thy kingdom come;
thy will be done;
on earth as it is in heaven.
Give us this day our daily bread.
And forgive us our trespasses,
as we forgive those who trespass against us.
And lead us not into temptation;
but deliver us from evil.
For thine is the kingdom, the power, and the glory,
for ever and ever. Amen.**

30 Hymn

31 EITHER

A God grant to the living, grace;
to the departed, rest;
to the world, peace;
and to us and all the faithful, life everlasting;
and the blessing of God,
the Father, the Son and the Holy Spirit,
be with *you/us* now and for ever. **Amen.**

OR

B The peace of God,
which passes all understanding,
keep *your/our* hearts and minds
in the knowledge and love of God
and of his Son, Jesus Christ our Lord;
and the blessing of God,
the Father, the Son and the Holy Spirit,
remain with *you/us* always. **Amen.**

A FUNERAL SERVICE FOR A CHILD

GATHERING

1 One or more of the following sentences may be said:

'I am the resurrection and the life,' says the Lord. 'Those who believe in me, even though they die, will live, and everyone who lives and believes in me will never die.'

God is our refuge and strength, a very present help in trouble.

As a father has compassion on his children, so the Lord has compassion on those who fear him.

'As a mother comforts her child, so shall I myself comfort you,' says the Lord.

Blessèd are those who mourn, for they will be comforted.

Jesus said: 'Let the children come to me; do not try to stop them; for the kingdom of God belongs to such as these.'

Jesus said: 'Set your troubled hearts at rest. Trust in God always; trust also in me.'

Nothing in all creation can separate us from the love of God in Christ Jesus our Lord.

2 Hymn

3 The minister says:

We meet in God's loving presence
to give thanks for the life of *N*,
the *daughter/son* of *A and B (A)*;
to commend *her/him* to God;
and to uphold and support those who mourn.

4 Let us pray.

As we seek the strength and comfort of God,
let us in silence bring our confusion and sorrow,
our anger and pain,
and lay them before God.

Silence

EITHER

A Eternal God, the Lord of life,
you are our help in every time of trouble;
comfort us who mourn.
Give us grace, in the presence of death,
to worship you,
that we may have sure hope of eternal life.
Enable us to put our whole trust
in your goodness and mercy;
through Jesus Christ our Lord. **Amen.**

OR

B Father in heaven,
you gave your Son Jesus Christ
to suffer and to die on the cross,
and raised him to life in glory.
Grant us faith and patience in time of darkness,
and strengthen our hearts with the knowledge of your love;
through Jesus Christ our Lord. **Amen.**

THE MINISTRY OF THE WORD

5 Let us hear the words of Holy Scripture,
that from them we may draw comfort and strength.

One or more of the following, or one or more other passages of scripture:

The Lord is my shepherd, I shall not want.
He makes me lie down in green pastures;
he leads me besides still waters;
he restores my soul.
He leads me in right paths
for his name's sake.

Even though I walk through the darkest valley,
I fear no evil;
for you are with me;
your rod and your staff –
they comfort me.

You prepare a table before me
in the presence of my enemies;
you anoint my head with oil;
my cup overflows.
Surely goodness and mercy shall follow me
all the days of my life,
and I shall dwell in the house of the Lord
my whole life long.

Psalm 23

People were bringing little children to Jesus in order that he might touch them; and the disciples spoke sternly to them. But when Jesus saw this, he was indignant and said to them, 'Let the little children come to me; do not stop them; for it is to such as these that the kingdom of God belongs. Truly I tell you, whoever does not receive the kingdom of God as a little child will never enter it.' And he took them up in his arms, laid his hands on them, and blessed them.

Mark 10:13-16

Jesus said: 'Do not let your hearts be troubled. Believe in God, believe also in me. In my Father's house there are many dwelling-places. If it were not so, would I have told you that I go to prepare a place for you? And if I go and prepare a place for you, I will come again and will take you to myself, so that where I am, there you may be also. And you know the way to the place where I am going.'

Thomas said to him, 'Lord, we do not know where you are going. How can we know the way?' Jesus said to him, 'I am the way, and the truth, and the life. No one comes to the Father except through me.'

'Peace I leave with you; my peace I give to you. I do not give to you as the world gives. Do not let your hearts be troubled, and do not let them be afraid.'

John 14:1-6, 27

I saw a new heaven and a new earth; for the first heaven and the first earth had passed away, and the sea was no more. And I saw the holy city, the new Jerusalem, coming down out of heaven from God, prepared as a bride adorned for her husband. And I heard a loud voice from the throne saying,
'See, the home of God is among mortals.
He will dwell with them;
and they will be his peoples,
and God himself will be with them;
he will wipe every tear from their eyes.
Death will be no more;
mourning and crying and pain will be no more,
for the first things have passed away'.
And the one who was seated on the throne said,
'See, I am making all things new'.

Revelation 21:1-5*a*

6 Sermon

COMMENDATION

7 The minister may say such parts of the following prayer as are appropriate, or some other prayer.

Loving heavenly Father,
you have made us in your own image and likeness.
We thank you for *N*,
for the richness of *her/his* personality,
for the pleasure and love,
laughter and tears
that we shared together.
We thank you that *she/he*
is free from pain and suffering,
and is at peace with you.

God of all comfort,
we give you thanks
that Jesus took children in his arms and blessed them.
Help us to know that Jesus has welcomed *N*
into the kingdom of heaven.
We make our prayers through Jesus Christ our Saviour.
Amen.

8 All stand.

Let us commend *N* to God.

EITHER

A Into your keeping, O merciful God,
we commend your servant *N*.
Receive *her/him* into the arms of your mercy,
into the joy of everlasting peace,
and into the glorious company of the saints in light;
through Christ our Lord. **Amen.**

OR

B Loving God,
we commend *N* to your perfect mercy and wisdom,
for in you alone we put our trust. **Amen.**

9 When the whole service takes place in a crematorium or at the graveside, the service continues from no. 12.

10 Otherwise the minister says:

The peace of God,
which passes all understanding,
keep *your/our* hearts and minds
in the knowledge and love of God
and of his Son, Jesus Christ our Lord;
and the blessing of God,
the Father, the Son and the Holy Spirit,
remain with *you/us* always. **Amen.**

---

11 The minister, going before the body into the crematorium, or to the grave, may say one or more of these sentences:

Blessèd be the God and Father of our Lord Jesus Christ, the Father of mercies and God of all comfort, who comforts us in all our affliction.

'As a mother comforts her child, so shall I myself comfort you,' says the Lord.

Like a shepherd he will tend his flock and with his arms keep them together.

COMMITTAL

12 All stand. The minister says:

Gracious God,
you have made nothing in vain
and love all that you have made.
We therefore commit *N*'s body
to be cremated/to the elements/to be buried,
earth to earth, ashes to ashes, dust to dust;
in sure and certain hope
of the resurrection to eternal life,
through our Lord Jesus Christ;
to whom be glory for ever and ever. **Amen.**

Christ, the Good Shepherd,
will lead *N* to springs of living water;
and God will wipe away every tear from *her/his* eyes.

13 Silence

14 Hymn

PRAYERS

15 The minister may say such parts of the following prayer as are appropriate, or some other prayer.

Let us pray.

God of all compassion,
we remember that Jesus wept
at the grave of Lazarus.
Look with tender love
upon those who grieve and sorrow,
especially . . . *(parents, family and close friends)*.

Silence

Be our support and strength;
shield us with your arms,
enfold us in the shadow of your wings,
and hold us close to you.

Lord, in your mercy,
hear our prayer.

God of all forgiveness,
we remember how Jesus laid his hands
on those who were distressed in mind and spirit.
Take from us any burden of guilt,
and heal within us those memories which now bring pain.

Silence

Pardon our sins,
and reveal to us, as forgiven people,
the new life offered to us in Christ.

Lord, in your mercy,
hear our prayer.

God of all comfort,
we remember how Mary stood at the cross
and watched her own Son die.
Help all who grieve at the death of a child
to know the strength of your presence.

Silence

Comfort and uphold us
in this dark and lonely hour,
that we may find new confidence
through our faith in the risen Christ.

Lord, in your mercy,
hear our prayer.

God of love,
you hold all things together.
Bind . . . *(parents, family and close friends)*
as one in mutual love and care,
that in the face of *N*'s death
they may find unity and strength.

Silence

Support us, as we commit ourselves to your providence and care,
that, in your good time,
we may be united with all your children
in the brightness of your glory;
through Jesus Christ our Lord. **Amen.**

16 One or more of these prayers may be said:

A God of infinite compassion,
look in love and pity on those who mourn.
Be their support and strength
that they may trust in you
and be delivered out of their distress;
through Jesus Christ our Lord. **Amen.**

B Lord, listen to our prayers for this family who put their trust in you.
In their sorrow
may they find hope in your infinite love;
through Jesus Christ our Lord. **Amen.**

C Grant us, O God,
in all our duties your help,
in all our perplexities your guidance,
in all our dangers your protection,
and in all our sorrows your peace;
through Jesus Christ our Lord. **Amen.**

17 The Lord's Prayer

EITHER

We say together the prayer that Jesus gave us:

**Our Father in heaven,
hallowed be your Name,
your kingdom come,
your will be done,
on earth as in heaven.
Give us today our daily bread.
Forgive us our sins
as we forgive those who sin against us.
Save us from the time of trial
and deliver us from evil.
For the kingdom, the power and the glory are yours,
now and for ever. Amen.**

OR

As our Saviour taught his disciples, we pray:

**Our Father, who art in heaven,
hallowed be thy Name;
thy kingdom come;
thy will be done;
on earth as it is in heaven.
Give us this day our daily bread.
And forgive us our trespasses,
as we forgive those who trespass against us.
And lead us not into temptation;
but deliver us from evil.
For thine is the kingdom, the power, and the glory,
for ever and ever. Amen.**

18 **Christ be with me, Christ within me,
Christ behind me, Christ before me,
Christ beside me, Christ to win me,
Christ to comfort and restore me.**

**Christ beneath me, Christ above me,
Christ in quiet, Christ in danger,
Christ in hearts of all that love me,
Christ in mouth of friend and stranger. Amen.**

19 EITHER

A The Lord bless you and keep you;
the Lord make his face to shine on you
and be gracious to you;
the Lord look on you with kindness
and give you peace. **Amen.**

OR

B Christ the Good Shepherd
enfold *you/us* with love,
fill *you/us* with peace,
and lead *you/us* in hope,
this day and all *your/our* days;
and the blessing of God,
the Father, the Son and the Holy Spirit,
be with *you/us* evermore. **Amen.**

A FUNERAL SERVICE FOR A STILLBORN CHILD

NOTES

1 This service can be adapted for use after a miscarriage or neo-natal death.

2 If the child has been given a name this should be used; otherwise it is appropriate to say 'this child'.

3 If there is a coffin it may be brought into the building before the service.

GATHERING

1 The minister says:

We meet in God's loving presence
to acknowledge our loss of one so young.
God knows and loves this child
(whose *parents, A and B (A),*
have given *her/him* the name *N).*
We ask for God's grace
that in our pain we may find comfort;
in our sorrow, hope;
in our questioning, understanding;
and in the experience of death, resurrection.

2 Let us be silent and make our own prayers.

Silence

Lord, you love us and watch over us;
you have known us from the very beginning;
and nothing is hidden from you.

Help us now as we entrust *N* to you,
knowing that *she/he* is safe in your care;
in Jesus' name. **Amen.**

THE MINISTRY OF THE WORD

3 Let us hear the words of Holy Scripture,
that from them we may draw comfort and strength.

One or both of the following Psalms may be read.

The Lord is my shepherd, I shall not want.
He makes me lie down in green pastures;
he leads me besides still waters;
he restores my soul.
He leads me in right paths
for his name's sake.

Even though I walk through the darkest valley,
I fear no evil;
for you are with me;
your rod and your staff –
they comfort me.

You prepare a table before me
in the presence of my enemies;
you anoint my head with oil;
my cup overflows.
Surely goodness and mercy shall follow me
all the days of my life,
and I shall dwell in the house of the Lord
my whole life long.

Psalm 23

O Lord, you have searched me and known me.

For it was you who formed my inward parts;
you knit me together in my mother's womb.
I praise you, for I am fearfully and wonderfully made.

Wonderful are your works;
that I know very well.
My frame was not hidden from you,
when I was being made in secret,
intricately woven in the depths of the earth.
Your eyes beheld my unformed substance.
In your book were written all the days that were formed for
me,
when none of them as yet existed.
How weighty to me are your thoughts, O God!
How vast is the sum of them.
I try to count them – they are more than the sand;
I come to the end – I am still with you.

Psalm 139:1, 13-18

4 One or more of the following, or one or more other passages of scripture:

The disciples came to Jesus and asked, 'Who is the greatest in the kingdom of Heaven?' He called a child, whom he put among them, and said, 'Truly I tell you, unless you change and become like children, you will never enter the kingdom of heaven. Whoever becomes humble like this child is the greatest in the kingdom of heaven. Whoever welcomes one such child in my name welcomes me.'

Matthew 18:1-5

Jesus said: 'All things have been handed over to me by my Father; and no one knows the Son except the Father, and no one knows the Father except the Son and anyone to whom the Son chooses to reveal him.

'Come to me, all you that are weary and are carrying heavy burdens, and I will give you rest. Take my yoke upon you, and learn from me; for I am gentle and humble in heart, and you will find rest for your souls. For my yoke is easy, and my burden is light.'

Matthew 11:27-30

Blessed be the God and Father of our Lord Jesus Christ, the Father of mercies and the God of all consolation, who consoles us in all our affliction, so that we may be able to console those who are in any affliction with the consolation with which we ourselves are consoled by God. For just as the sufferings of Christ are abundant for us, so also our consolation is abundant through Christ. If we are being afflicted, it is for your consolation and salvation; if we are being consoled, it is for your consolation, which you experience when you patiently endure the same sufferings that we are also suffering. Our hope for you is unshaken; for we know that as you share in our sufferings, so also you share in our consolation.

2 Corinthians 1:3-7

5 A short address or reflection

COMMENDATION

6 Let us pray.

Silence

Loving God,
we praise and thank you that *N* is, like us,
an heir to all your promises;
sharing with us in the humanity
that you have redeemed in Christ,
and in the eternal life revealed to us through him. **Amen.**

7 All stand.

Let us commend *N* to God.

Heavenly Father,
we thank you for *N*,
and commend *her/him* to your perfect mercy and wisdom,
for in you alone we put our trust. **Amen.**

8 When the whole service takes place in a crematorium or at the graveside, the service continues from no. 11. When there is to be no Committal the service continues from no. 12.

9 Otherwise the minister says:

The grace of our Lord Jesus Christ,
and the love of God,
and the fellowship of the Holy Spirit,
be with us all evermore. **Amen.**

---

10 The minister, going before the body into the crematorium or to the grave, may say one or more of these sentences:

Blessèd be the God and Father of our Lord Jesus Christ, the Father of mercies and God of all comfort, who comforts us in all our affliction.

'As a mother comforts her child, so shall I myself comfort you,' says the Lord.

Like a shepherd he will tend his flock and with his arm keep them together.

COMMITTAL

11 All stand. The minister says:

Gracious God,
you have made nothing in vain
and love all that you have made.
We therefore commit *N's* body
to be cremated/to the elements/to be buried,
earth to earth, ashes to ashes, dust to dust;
in sure and certain hope
of the resurrection to eternal life,
through our Lord Jesus Christ;
to whom be glory for ever and ever. **Amen.**

PRAYERS

12 The minister may say such parts of the following prayers as are appropriate, or some other prayers.

A Holy God,
you are like a loving parent to all your children.
Although the burdens of life overwhelm us,
we still put our trust in you,
knowing that you are with us always;
through Jesus Christ our Lord. **Amen.**

B God and Father of all,
comfort *A and B (A)*,
together with *their families*,
in *their* grief,
and uphold *them* with your love;
through Jesus Christ our Saviour. **Amen.**

C Gracious God,
may your loving arms enfold us in our grief.
Support *N*'s mother *B*,
who with love has carried *her/him* to birth.
Uphold *N*'s father *A*,
who has watched and waited.
Be with them now
in their emptiness and pain;
through him who bears our griefs
and carries our sorrows,
Jesus Christ our Lord. **Amen.**

D Grant us, O God,
in all our duties your help,
in all our perplexities your guidance,
in all our dangers your protection,
and in all our sorrows your peace;
through Jesus Christ our Lord. **Amen.**

13 The Lord's Prayer

EITHER

We say together the prayer that Jesus gave us:

Our Father in heaven,
hallowed be your Name,
your kingdom come,
your will be done,
on earth as in heaven.
Give us today our daily bread.
Forgive us our sins
as we forgive those who sin against us.
Save us from the time of trial
and deliver us from evil.
For the kingdom, the power and the glory are yours,
now and for ever. Amen.

OR

As our Saviour taught his disciples, we pray:

Our Father, who art in heaven,
hallowed be thy Name;
thy kingdom come;
thy will be done;
on earth as it is in heaven.
Give us this day our daily bread.
And forgive us our trespasses,
as we forgive those who trespass against us.
And lead us not into temptation;
but deliver us from evil.
For thine is the kingdom, the power, and the glory,
for ever and ever. Amen.

14 EITHER

A The peace of God
which passes all understanding,
keep *your/our* hearts and minds
in the knowledge and love of God
and of his Son, Jesus Christ our Lord;
and the blessing of God,
the Father, the Son and the Holy Spirit,
remain with *you/us* always. **Amen.**

OR

B Christ the Good Shepherd
enfold *you/us* with love,
fill *you/us* with peace,
and lead *you/us* in hope,
this day and all *your/our* days;
and the blessing of God,
the Father, the Son and the Holy Spirit,
be with *you/us* evermore. **Amen.**

A SERVICE FOR THE BURIAL OF ASHES

NOTE

If the ashes are to be scattered, this service should be adapted appropriately.

GATHERING

1 The people gather at the place of burial.

2 The minister says:

We meet together to bury the ashes of our *sister/brother N.*

As we gather in faith we remember that, although our bodies return to dust, we shall be raised with Christ in glory. Let us rejoice in this promise as we hear the words of Holy Scripture.

THE MINISTRY OF THE WORD

3 One or more of the following, or one or more other passages of scripture:

If we have died with Christ, we believe that we will also live with him. We know that Christ, being raised from the dead, will never die again.

Romans 6:8-9*a*

We know that if the earthly tent we live in is destroyed, we have a building from God, a house not made with hands, eternal in the heavens.

2 Corinthians 5:1

The Lamb at the centre of the throne will be their shepherd, and he will guide them to springs of the water of life, and God will wipe away every tear from their eyes.

Revelation 7:17

4 Let us pray.

God of all consolation,
in your unending love and mercy
you turn the darkness of death
into the dawn of new life.
Show us your compassion
and be our refuge and our strength.
Lift us from the darkness of grief
into the light of your presence.
This we ask in the name of the risen Christ. **Amen.**

BURIAL

5 As the ashes are lowered into the ground the minister says:

We have commended our *sister/brother N*
to God's everlasting love and care.
We now return to the earth
the ashes of *her/his* mortal body.
May *she/he* rest in peace and rise in glory. **Amen.**

6 One or more of the following prayers may be said:

A Father of all,
we pray for those whom we love, but see no longer.
Grant them your peace;
let light perpetual shine upon them;
and in your loving wisdom and almighty power
work in them the good purpose of your perfect will;
through Jesus Christ our Lord. **Amen.**

B Almighty God,
grant that we, with all who have trusted in you,
may be united in the full knowledge of your love
and the unclouded vision of your glory;
through Jesus Christ our Lord. **Amen.**

C God of all consolation,
our refuge and strength in sorrow;
we rejoice that by dying,
our Lord Jesus Christ conquered death;
and that by rising from the grave,
he restored us to life.
When our life on earth is ended,
unite us in your heavenly kingdom with all who love him.
We ask this in his name and for his sake. **Amen.**

7 The Lord's Prayer

EITHER

We say together the prayer that Jesus gave us:

**Our Father in heaven,
hallowed be your Name,
your kingdom come,
your will be done,
on earth as in heaven.
Give us today our daily bread.
Forgive us our sins
as we forgive those who sin against us.
Save us from the time of trial
and deliver us from evil.
For the kingdom, the power and the glory are yours,
now and for ever. Amen.**

OR

As our Saviour taught his disciples, we pray:

**Our Father, who art in heaven,
hallowed be thy Name;
thy kingdom come;
thy will be done;
on earth as it is in heaven.
Give us this day our daily bread.
And forgive us our trespasses,
as we forgive those who trespass against us.
And lead us not into temptation;
but deliver us from evil.
For thine is the kingdom, the power, and the glory,
for ever and ever. Amen.**

DISMISSAL AND BLESSING

8 EITHER

A We go in the name of Christ.
Let us turn from this place as we journey on,
to seek new life on earth
as we rejoice over new life in heaven.
May the Spirit of the living Christ be with *you/us.*

The blessing of God,
the Father, the Son and the Holy Spirit,
be with *you/us* evermore. **Amen.**

OR

B Go out into the world
in the power of the Holy Spirit;
in all things and at all times
remember Christ is with you;
and the blessing of God,
the Father, the Son and the Holy Spirit,
be with *you/us* evermore. **Amen.**

ADDITIONAL SCRIPTURE READINGS

Job 19:1, 21-27*a*	Job answered, 'Pity me, have pity on me.'
Psalms 8; 16; 27; 30; 42:1-8; 43:3-5; 46; 90; 103; 116; 118:14-21, 28-29; 121; 138; 139:1-14, 17-18, 23	
Isaiah 25:6-9	God will wipe away tears
Isaiah 40:1-6, 8-11, 28-31	Comfort my people
Isaiah 43:1-3*a*, 5-7, 13, 15, 18-19, 25	Behold, I am doing a new thing
Isaiah 44:6, 8*a*	I am the first and I am the last
Isaiah 55:1-3, 6-13	Hear that your soul may live
Isaiah 61:1-3	Bind up the broken hearted
Lamentations 3:17-26, 31-33	The steadfast love of the Lord never ceases
Ecclesiastes 3:1-15	For everything its season
Luke 24:13-35	The Lord has risen indeed
John 5:19-25	The Father raises the dead and gives them life
John 6:35-40	I am the bread of life
John 11:1-6, 17-27, 32-35, 38-44	There was a man named Lazarus
2 Corinthians 4:16 - 5:10	In the body we are exiles from the Lord

Ephesians 1:15-23	Now that I have heard of your faith
Ephesians 2:1, 4-10	You once were dead because of your sins
Philippians 3:10-21	My one desire is to know Christ
1 Thessalonians 4:13-18	We believe that Jesus died and rose again
2 Timothy 2:8-12*a*	If we die with him we shall live with him
1 John 3:1-2	We are now God's children
1 John 4:7-18*a*	My dear friends, let us love one another
Revelation 7:9-17	Victory to our God who sits on the throne
Revelation 21:1-7	I saw a new heaven and a new earth
Revelation 21:22-27	The Lamb's book of life
Revelation 22:1-5	The Lord God will give them light

BLESSING AND DEDICATION SERVICES

INTRODUCTION

Throughout these services there runs the common theme that, for Christians, buildings can be places of celebration and light, of beauty, hope and joy.

An Order for the Blessing of a Home
Christians believe that in Jesus Christ, God comes to share and bless our daily life. Christians, and Jews before them, have always recognized the importance of the home in fostering and expressing faith. This service affirms that the home is a symbol of God's loving care to those who live within it and to those who enjoy their hospitality.

An Order for the Laying of a Foundation Stone* and *An Order for the Dedication of a Church Building and its Furnishings
From early days, Christians have set apart particular areas or buildings and dedicated them to the glory of God and for the use of God's people. It is a practice which is rooted in the Bible. The Temple in Jerusalem offers us the clearest example of a place specially built for worship, but we also see how the site of Jacob's dream at Bethel, the tent of meeting, and the synagogue are all 'sacred space'. At the same time, the Bible offers words of caution. God's presence is not confined to any building, nor should God's people presume that the provision of a sanctuary guarantees God's blessing and protection; faithful and obedient living is required.

Christians use a variety of buildings to help them as they worship and share in God's mission. Both these services may need adaptation to local circumstances and should always be used in ways which reflect the contribution of many skilled and devoted people to the realization of a building project.

AN ORDER FOR THE BLESSING OF A HOME

1 The person leading the service, members of the household, and friends assemble at the home.

2 Peace be to this home and to all who dwell in it. **Amen.**

3 Let us pray.

God of truth and love, you make your home in our hearts and shelter us in the shadow of your wings. Be present with us as we ask your blessing upon this home. Assist our prayers and unite us in peace. Grant that *those* who *make their* home here may walk each day by the light of your Holy Spirit. Make this a place of joy, security and peace; through Jesus Christ our Lord. **Amen.**

4 One or more of the following Psalms may be read or sung:

Psalm 23
Psalm 95:1-7

5 One or more of the following passages of scripture:

Genesis 18:1-8
Matthew 6:25-34
Luke 10:38-42
Luke 12:28-34
1 John 4:11-21
Revelation 21:1-7

THE PRAYERS

6 Lord, bless this *house* and *N and N (N)* who *make* it *their* home. Defend it with your heavenly grace, and create within its walls a place of warmth, love and safety.

Lord, in your mercy,
hear our prayer.

May all who share the life of this household grow in wisdom and grace, and learn to love whatever is good and to rejoice in your creation.

Lord, in your mercy,
hear our prayer.

May all who enter this home find a welcome. May old friendships be strengthened and new friendships blossom and grow.

Lord, in your mercy,
hear our prayer.

Comfort and sustain *N and N (N)* in times of stress or illness and give *them* patience and strength when trouble comes.

Lord, in your mercy,
hear our prayer.

Let your presence fill this home. May it be a place of prayer and thanksgiving and a sign of your love in this neighbourhood.

Lord, in your mercy,
hear our prayer.

God of all, whose Son our Saviour made his home among us: grant that we may know his presence in our daily life together. We ask this in his name. **Amen.**

7 The Lord's Prayer

EITHER

We say together the prayer that Jesus gave us:

Our Father in heaven,
hallowed be your Name,
your kingdom come,
your will be done,
on earth as in heaven.
Give us today our daily bread.
Forgive us our sins
as we forgive those who sin against us.
Save us from the time of trial
and deliver us from evil.
For the kingdom, the power and the glory are yours,
now and for ever. Amen.

OR

As our Saviour taught his disciples, we pray:

Our Father, who art in heaven,
hallowed be thy Name;
thy kingdom come;
thy will be done;
on earth as it is in heaven.
Give us this day our daily bread.
And forgive us our trespasses,
as we forgive those who trespass against us.
And lead us not into temptation;
but deliver us from evil.
For thine is the kingdom, the power, and the glory,
for ever and ever. Amen.

8 Here some symbolic act may be made, such as the giving and receiving of a gift for the home, the lighting of a candle or lamp, or, if there is a garden, the planting of a tree or shrub. Further prayers may be said in particular rooms.

9 **The grace of our Lord Jesus Christ,**
and the love of God,
and the fellowship of the Holy Spirit,
be with us all evermore. Amen.

AN ORDER FOR THE LAYING OF A FOUNDATION STONE

NOTES

1 It is appropriate to invite representatives of the wider connexion, of the local Christian community, and of other religious traditions to attend this service.

2 This order will need to be adapted at the places indicated by *italics* when it is used in respect of a building other than a place of worship.

---

1 The grace of the Lord Jesus Christ,
and the love of God,
and the fellowship of the Holy Spirit,
be with you all. **Amen.**

2 A welcome is given.

3 The minister or a representative of the congregation briefly describes the circumstances which led to the commitment to build on the site, and affirms the belief that the congregation is acting in obedience to God's will.

4 One or more of the following passages of scripture:

Ezra 3:10-11
Psalm 43:3-5
1 Corinthians 3:9-11
Ephesians 2:14-22
1 Peter 2:4-6
Luke 6:46-49

5 A sermon may be preached.

6 The person appointed lays the foundation stone, saying:

In faith, hope and trust we begin the building of *N Church* by laying this foundation stone in the Name of the Father, and of the Son, and of the Holy Spirit. **Amen.**

7 The minister says:

Almighty God,
ruler of all things in heaven and on earth,
giver of every good gift,
inspire the building of this *church*
and give us the wisdom and courage to complete it.
Guide and protect all who will labour to construct this *church,*
and grant that they may honour you in their work.
May we be faithful stewards of everything you have entrusted to us,
that this *church* may be a sign of your love to all the world,
in the name of Jesus Christ,
the chief corner stone of all things in heaven and on earth.
Amen.

8 The Lord's Prayer

EITHER

We say together the prayer that Jesus gave us:

**Our Father in heaven,
hallowed be your Name,
your kingdom come,
your will be done,
on earth as in heaven.
Give us today our daily bread.
Forgive us our sins
as we forgive those who sin against us.
Save us from the time of trial**

OR

As our Saviour taught his disciples, we pray:

**Our Father, who art in heaven,
hallowed be thy Name;
thy kingdom come;
thy will be done;
on earth as it is in heaven.
Give us this day our daily bread.
And forgive us our trespasses,
as we forgive those who trespass against us.**

and deliver us from evil. **For the kingdom, the** **power and the glory** **are yours,** **now and for ever. Amen.**	**And lead us not into** **temptation;** **but deliver us from evil.** **For thine is the kingdom,** **the power, and the** **glory,** **for ever and ever. Amen.**

9 This or some other appropriate act of commitment:

In the name of Jesus Christ,
we commit ourselves to the building of this *church*,
and we pledge our support and encouragement
to all who labour for its completion.
As we pray and work together,
we offer all we do to the glory of God,
for the service of the Church and the world,
and for the coming of the kingdom.

All things come from you, O Lord.

And of your own do we give you.

Blessèd be the name of the Lord.

The Lord's name be praised.

10 The blessing of God,
the Father, the Son and the Holy Spirit,
remain with *you/us* always. **Amen.**

11 Go in peace to love and serve the Lord.

In the name of Christ. Amen.

AN ORDER FOR THE DEDICATION OF A CHURCH BUILDING AND ITS FURNISHINGS

NOTES

1 It is fitting that, when a building is set apart for holy use, the word of God should be preached and the Lord's Supper celebrated. If it is not considered practicable to include the Lord's Supper, it is desirable that this sacrament should be celebrated on the Sunday following.

2 The people may gather at some place outside the building and may move in procession to the building singing appropriate hymns, songs or psalms (Psalm 84 is especially appropriate for such a procession). Whether or not there is a procession, the people (or a group consisting of representative members of the local church, the presiding minister and other ministers and those involved with the planning, construction, and furnishing of the building) may assemble at the church door.

---

1 At the church door the following may be said:

Cry out to the Lord, all the earth;
serve the Lord with gladness;
come into his presence with songs of joy.

**Be assured that the Lord is God;
he has made us for himself.
We are his own, his people,
the sheep who feed on his pasture.**

Come into his gates with thanksgiving,
enter his courts with praise;
give thanks to him and bless his name.

Truly the Lord is good:
his love endures for ever,
and from age to age he is faithful.

Glory to the Father, and to the Son,
and to the Holy Spirit:
as it was in the beginning, is now,
and shall be for ever. Amen.

2 We have come here today to dedicate this building for the worship and service of God in this community.

3 Let us pray.

Eternal God,
to whose glory we dedicate this church:
grant that all who enter here
may find it to be none other
than the house of God and the gate of heaven;
through Jesus Christ our Lord. **Amen.**

THE PRESENTATION OF THE BUILDING

4 One of those involved with the planning, construction, and furnishing of the building presents the key to a representative of the local church, saying:

We present to you this church building to be dedicated.

The representative replies:

We receive this church building to be dedicated to the glory of God and for the use of this community.

The presiding minister may say:

By what name is this church to be called?

The minister or another designated person answers with the name of the church.

5 Let the door(s) of this church be open!
May the love of Christ dwell within this house
and may all who enter here find peace. **Amen.**

6 Hymn

If the people have assembled outside the building, they enter and take their places.

Any who have assembled at the church door take their places in the building.

THE MINISTRY OF THE WORD

7 One of the following or the Old Testament reading for the day is read:

Genesis 28:10-17
1 Kings 8:22-30
1 Chronicles 29:10-14
Jeremiah 7:1-7

8 One of the following or the Psalm for the day is read:

Psalm 24:1-10
Psalm 48:1-3, 9-14
Psalm 93:1-5
Psalm 122:1-9

9 One of the following or the Epistle for the day is read:

1 Corinthians 3:9-13, 16-17
Ephesians 2:14-22
Hebrews 10:19-25
Revelation 21:1-7, 22-26

10 Hymn

11 One of the following or the Gospel for the day is read:

Matthew 7:24-27
Matthew 16:13-18
Matthew 21:10-14
Luke 11:1-13
John 4:19-26

12 Sermon

13 Hymn

THE DEDICATION

14 The people stand. This or some other appropriate prayer is said:

Generous God, of your great goodness you have given your people the vision and skill to build this house of prayer. Bless this church. Here may the Gospel of Jesus Christ be proclaimed and made known in service and in fellowship. Here may the sacraments be celebrated with joy and reverence, and your people nurtured and strengthened in faith and hope and love. Here may the seeker find faith, the weak find courage, and the grieving find comfort. Lord, hear us when we pray to you in this house. May it be a place of peace to all who enter; a fortress against all hatred, envy, and pride; and a beacon to all who seek your presence.

In the Name of God the Father,
who formed us in love and calls us by grace,

we dedicate this church.

In the Name of Jesus Christ our Lord,
who draws us together in unity,

we dedicate this church.

In the Name of the Holy Spirit,
who speaks in our hearts the words of eternal life,

we dedicate this church.

Generous God, of your great goodness you renew your people in their daily living. Bless this congregation. Empower us, on this day of dedication, for fresh ventures in faith, greater commitment to worship, and new acts of service.

In the Name of God the Father, God the Son, and God the Holy Spirit we dedicate ourselves in service and praise. Amen.

15 The following prayers are said:

At the font or baptistry:

Living God, through water and the Spirit you give new birth to your people. Grant that all who are brought to the waters of Baptism may be reborn by the Holy Spirit and live the risen life of Jesus Christ our Saviour. **Amen.**

At the pulpit or reading desk:

Heavenly Father, in your great mercy you have given us your holy Word. Grant that, in the reading of the Scriptures, the preaching of the word, and the prayers of your people, all who worship you in this church may hear your voice and respond to your love; through Jesus Christ our Lord. **Amen.**

At the communion table:

Father of all, whose Son Jesus Christ was born among us, and lived and died for our salvation: grant that all who are fed at this holy table may live in communion with him and each other and, at the last, share with all the saints in your heavenly banquet; through Jesus Christ our Lord. **Amen.**

16 One or more of the following may also be said after the prayer at the font or baptistry:

At the organ or other musical instrument(s):

Holy God, you have given us the gift of music that we may sing your praises and tune our hearts to the beauty of your love. Bless those who play and hear *this instrument* and grant that at the sound of *its* music we may worship you with joy and glorify your name; through Jesus Christ our Lord. **Amen.**

Other furnishings:

Lord our God, we thank you for all that you have given us to use in your service. In the faith of Jesus Christ we dedicate *this N . . .*, to the glory of your name. **Amen.**

17 Litany

Let us pray to God our Father through Jesus Christ our Lord in the power of the Holy Spirit.

We pray that God's presence may always be found in this place by all who turn to him:

When here we share our daily common life,

Lord, have mercy.
Lord, hear us.

When your people gather here
to seek your face
and offer praise and prayer,

Lord, have mercy.
Lord, hear us.

When here we celebrate new life
in Baptism, in the breaking of bread,
and in the faithful hearing of your word,

Lord, have mercy.
Lord, hear us.

When vows and commitments are made here
in marriage
and in our life of faith and service,

Lord, have mercy.
Lord, hear us.

When here we commend your servants
into your hands,
to pass through death to you,

Lord, have mercy.
Lord, hear us.

When we seek forgiveness and grace here,
peace and reassurance,
strength and consolation,

Lord, have mercy.
Lord, hear us.

Silence

Father of unending goodness,
maker and builder of all,
sustain all that you have made.

Jesus Christ,
the sure foundation and cornerstone,
confirm our hope and trust in you.

Holy Spirit,
source of all skill and love and power,
inspire the work of our hands.

To the living God,
Father, Son and Holy Spirit
be all glory now and for ever. Amen.

Go before us, Lord, in all that we do,
with your most gracious favour,
and guide us with your continual help,
that in all our works,
begun, continued and ended in you,
we may glorify your holy name,
and finally by your mercy obtain everlasting life;
through Jesus Christ our Lord. **Amen.**

18 The Lord's Prayer

EITHER

We say together the prayer that Jesus gave us:

**Our Father in heaven,
hallowed be your Name,
your kingdom come,
your will be done,
on earth as in heaven.
Give us today our daily bread.
Forgive us our sins
as we forgive those who sin against us.
Save us from the time of trial
and deliver us from evil.
For the kingdom, the power and the glory are yours,
now and for ever. Amen.**

OR

As our Saviour taught his disciples, we pray:

**Our Father, who art in heaven,
hallowed be thy Name;
thy kingdom come;
thy will be done;
on earth as it is in heaven.
Give us this day our daily bread.
And forgive us our trespasses,
as we forgive those who trespass against us.
And lead us not into temptation;
but deliver us from evil.
For thine is the kingdom, the power, and the glory,
for ever and ever. Amen.**

19 When the Lord's Supper is celebrated, the service continues from the Preparation of the Gifts. Any appropriate order may be used, but that for ***The Day of Pentecost and Times of Renewal in the Life of the Church*** (page 174) is especially suitable.

If the Lord's Supper is not celebrated, the service continues as follows:

20 Prayer of thanksgiving

Praise God,
who has created us
and given us hearts to worship him.

Praise God,
who has sent us his Son, Jesus Christ,
and given us a Gospel to proclaim.

Praise God,
who has poured out the Holy Spirit upon us,
and given us voices to sing his praise.

Praise God, Father, Son and Holy Spirit. Amen.

21 Hymn

BLESSING AND DISMISSAL

22 The blessing of God,
the Father, the Son and the Holy Spirit,
remain with *you/us* always. **Amen.**

Go in peace in the power of the Spirit
to live and work to God's praise and glory.

Thanks be to God.

CALENDAR, COLLECTS AND LECTIONARY

INTRODUCTION

The Calendar (The Christian Year)

The observance of the Christian calendar is an ancient feature of the Church's life. It enables us, in an ordered way, to hear the great story of salvation, celebrate God's mighty acts and be led into a deeper knowledge and love of Christ.

The calendar begins with Advent, a season of penitence and preparation. This leads to Christmas and Epiphany when we celebrate the Incarnation, God's supreme self-revelation. After a period of 'Ordinary Time' comes the preparatory season of Lent, a period of forty weekdays which reflect the forty days which Jesus spent in the desert. Passiontide begins on the fifth Sunday of Lent and culminates in the commemoration of the crucifixion on Good Friday. The great fifty days of Easter are a celebration of Christ's resurrection. Following the chronology in Acts, the Ascension is celebrated on the fortieth day and the coming of the Holy Spirit on the fiftieth, the Day of Pentecost. The following Sunday has developed into Trinity Sunday, after which we return to Ordinary Time until Advent begins again.

Liturgical colours are used in many churches to recognize and reflect the movement and moods of the Christian Year. A scheme in common use is: violet for preparation and penitence; white or gold for celebration and rejoicing; red for the blood of Christ and the fire of the Spirit; green for Ordinary Time. To help those who use colours in this way, guidance is included with the lectionary.

The Collects

The collect is one of the oldest models of Christian Prayer in the Western tradition. It gathers together (collects) the prayers of the congregation and is preceded by a moment for silent reflection. The collect usually forms part of the opening prayers but may also be said at other times.

The traditional form of the prayer is short with a definite structure. In the oldest prayers, which go back to at least the seventh century, the collect was usually a single sentence. Thomas Cranmer developed the collect form and, through **The Book of Common Prayer**, collects have become part of Methodist spirituality; for example, there are many echoes of them in Charles Wesley's hymns. The collects throughout this book bear witness both to this long history and to a modern renaissance, drawing, like the householder in the parable, from 'treasures new and old'.

The traditional structure of the collect in itself offers a paradigm of petitionary prayer. This structure is as follows:

(a) address to God (*Almighty God*);

(b) a characteristic of God's nature (*to whom all hearts are open . . .*);

(c) a petition (*cleanse the thoughts of our hearts . . .*);

(d) the purpose of the petition (*that we may perfectly love you . . .*);

(e) conclusion (*through Christ our Lord*).

The simple ending may be filled out by a Trinitarian ascription of praise and glory (*who is alive and reigns with you, in the unity of the Holy Spirit, one God now and for ever*); and

(f) a final '**Amen**'.

At least two collects are offered here for each Sunday and some for other occasions. For certain days, when there may be a variety of services at different times, there is greater provision. The **NOTES** on page 523 indicate how the collects may be used.

The Lectionary

The lectionary for the Principal Service is derived from the ecumenical **Revised Common Lectionary (RCL)**, which has won widespread acceptance in most English-speaking countries. **RCL** operates on a three-year cycle. Most of the Gospel readings in Year A are from Matthew, in Year B from Mark and in Year C from Luke. Readings from John occur in all three years. Much of the lectionary is offered in a semi-continuous form, following a particular book from Sunday to Sunday. During the greater part of Ordinary Time, **RCL** offers two sets of readings. In one, described below as 'continuous', the Old Testament reading forms part of a semi-continuous series. In the other, described below as 'related', the Old Testament reading is linked with the Gospel.

The lectionary for a Second Service is derived from a lectionary authorised for use by the Church of England and designed to accompany **RCL**. Two readings are normally supplied in this lectionary, one from the Old Testament and one from the New Testament. If the New Testament reading is not from the Gospels, a third reading (from the Gospels) is provided, and this should always be read if the service is a celebration of ***Holy Communion***.

Readings are also supplied for special occasions, such as a Church Anniversary.

Finding the Collects and Readings

To find the appropriate readings for a given date, it is necessary first to identify the correct lectionary year by reference to the table on page 522. Then, if the date is between Advent Sunday and Epiphany (6 January), or between the Sunday before Lent and Trinity Sunday inclusive, the collect and readings for the Sunday or other day in the Church's calendar (for example, the Third Sunday of Easter) are used. For dates outside those periods, the collect and readings for the secular date (for example, the Sunday between 7 and 13 August) are used. Secular dates are stated inclusively.

MOVEABLE DATES TO THE YEAR 2025

YEAR	ADVENT SUNDAY	SUNDAY BEFORE LENT	ASH WEDNESDAY	EASTER	PENTECOST	TRINITY SUNDAY
A	29 November 1998	14 February 1999	17 February 1999	4 April 1999	23 May 1999	30 May 1999
B	28 November 1999	5 March 2000	8 March 2000	23 April 2000	11 June 2000	18 June 2000
C	3 December 2000	25 February 2001	28 February 2001	15 April 2001	3 June 2001	10 June 2001
A	2 December 2001	10 February 2002	13 February 2002	31 March 2002	19 May 2002	26 May 2002
B	1 December 2002	2 March 2003	5 March 2003	20 April 2003	8 June 2003	15 June 2003
C	30 November 2003	22 February 2004	25 February 2004	11 April 2004	30 May 2004	6 June 2004
A	28 November 2004	6 February 2005	9 February 2005	27 March 2005	15 May 2005	22 May 2005
B	27 November 2005	26 February 2006	1 March 2006	16 April 2006	4 June 2006	11 June 2006
C	3 December 2006	18 February 2007	21 February 2007	8 April 2007	27 May 2007	3 June 2007
A	2 December 2007	3 February 2008	6 February 2008	23 March 2008	11 May 2008	18 May 2008
B	30 November 2008	22 February 2009	25 February 2009	12 April 2009	31 May 2009	7 June 2009
C	29 November 2009	14 February 2010	17 February 2010	4 April 2010	23 May 2010	30 May 2010
A	28 November 2010	6 March 2011	9 March 2011	24 April 2011	12 June 2011	19 June 2011
B	27 November 2011	19 February 2012	22 February 2012	8 April 2012	27 May 2012	3 June 2012
C	2 December 2012	10 February 2013	13 February 2013	31 March 2013	19 May 2013	26 May 2013
A	1 December 2013	2 March 2014	5 March 2014	20 April 2014	8 June 2014	15 June 2014
B	30 November 2014	15 February 2015	18 February 2015	5 April 2015	24 May 2015	31 May 2015
C	29 November 2015	7 February 2016	10 February 2016	27 March 2016	15 May 2016	22 May 2016
A	27 November 2016	26 February 2017	1 March 2017	16 April 2017	4 June 2017	11 June 2017
B	3 December 2017	11 February 2018	14 February 2018	1 April 2018	20 May 2018	27 May 2018
C	2 December 2018	3 March 2019	6 March 2019	21 April 2019	9 June 2019	16 June 2019
A	1 December 2019	23 February 2020	26 February 2020	12 April 2020	31 May 2020	7 June 2020
B	29 November 2020	14 February 2021	.17 February 2021	4 April 2021	23 May 2021	30 May 2021
C	28 November 2021	27 February 2022	2 March 2022	17 April 2022	5 June 2022	12 June 2022
A	27 November 2022	19 February 2023	22 February 2023	9 April 2023	28 May 2023	4 June 2023
B	3 December 2023	11 February 2024	14 February 2024	31 March 2024	19 May 2024	26 May 2024
C	1 December 2024	2 March 2025	5 March 2025	20 April 2025	8 June 2025	15 June 2025

THE COLLECTS

NOTES

1 One of the collects provided for each day should normally be included in the opening section of the Principal Service. Another collect may be said at a Second Service or, when appropriate, at a different point in the Principal Service.

2 In Lent and Advent, the seasonal collect may be said after one of the collects of the day.

First Sunday of Advent

The first collect, the collect of the Advent season, may be said on any day in Advent in addition to the collect of the day.

Almighty God,
give us grace to cast away the works of darkness
and to put on the armour of light,
now in the time of this mortal life,
in which your Son Jesus Christ
came to us in great humility:
that, on the last day,
when he shall come again in his glorious majesty
to judge the living and the dead,
we may rise to the life immortal;
through him who is alive and reigns with you,
in the unity of the Holy Spirit,
one God, now and for ever. **Amen.** 5*

Lord our God,
keep us your servants alert and watchful
as we await the return of Christ your Son,
so that when he comes and knocks at the door
he may find us vigilant in prayer,
with songs of praise on our lips.

We ask this through Jesus Christ our Lord,
who is alive and reigns with you,
in the unity of the Holy Spirit,
one God, now and for ever. **Amen.** 16

Second Sunday of Advent

God of all holiness,
your promises stand unshaken through all generations
and you lift up all who are burdened and brought low:
renew our hope in you,
as we wait for the coming in glory of Jesus Christ,
our Judge and our Saviour,
who is alive and reigns with you,
in the unity of the Holy Spirit,
one God, world without end. **Amen.** 27*

God of all time and space,
who are we, that you should come to us?
Yet you have visited your people
and redeemed us in your Son.
As we prepare to celebrate his birth,
make our hearts leap for joy at the sound of your word
and move us by your Spirit
to bless your wonderful works.
We ask this through him whose coming is certain,
whose day draws near,
even your Son, Jesus Christ our Saviour. **Amen.** 15*

The collect for Bible Sunday (page 561) may also be said.

Third Sunday of Advent

God for whom we wait and watch,
you sent your servant John the Baptist
to prepare your people for the coming of the Messiah.
Inspire the ministers and stewards of your truth
to turn our disobedient hearts to you;
that, when Christ shall come again in glory to be our judge,
we may stand with confidence before him,
who is alive and reigns with you,
in the unity of the Holy Spirit,
one God, world without end. **Amen.** 3*

God of mercy and power,
whose Son rules over all,
grant us so to live in obedience to your holy will,
that at his appearing
we may be raised to eternal life;
through Jesus Christ our Lord,
who is alive and reigns with you,
in the unity of the Holy Spirit,
one God, now and for ever. **Amen.**

Fourth Sunday of Advent

God our Redeemer,
you chose the Virgin Mary,
to be the mother of our Lord and Saviour.
Fill us with your grace
that in all things we may embrace your holy will
and with her rejoice in your salvation;
through Jesus Christ our Lord
who is alive and reigns with you,
in the unity of the Holy Spirit,
one God, now and for ever. **Amen.** 10*

All-powerful God,
let the splendour of your glory
rise in our hearts like the dawn,
that the darkness of the night may be scattered
and the coming of your only Son may reveal us
as children of the light.
We ask this through Jesus Christ our Lord,
who is alive and reigns with you,
in the unity of the Holy Spirit,
one God, now and for ever. **Amen.** 16

Christmas Eve

God, faithful and true,
make us eager in expectation,
as we look for the fulfilment of your promise
in Jesus Christ our Saviour. **Amen.** 21

Almighty God,
you make us glad with the yearly remembrance
of the birth of your Son Jesus Christ.
Grant that, as we joyfully receive him as our redeemer,
so we may with sure confidence behold him
when he shall come to be our judge;
who is alive and reigns with you,
in the unity of the Holy Spirit,
one God, now and for ever. **Amen.** 1*

Christmas Day (Midnight)

Eternal God, who made this most holy night to shine
with the brightness of your one true light:
bring us, who have known the revelation of that light on earth,
to see the radiance of your heavenly glory;
through Jesus Christ our Lord,
who is alive and reigns with you,
in the unity of the Holy Spirit,
one God, now and for ever. **Amen.** 12

God of light and hope,
of stars and surprises:
open our eyes to your glory
and our hearts to your presence,
that we may respond with joy to the angel song;
through Jesus Christ our Lord,
who is alive and reigns with you,
in the unity of the Holy Spirit,
one God, now and for ever. **Amen.** 22*

Christmas Day

Almighty God,
you have given us your only-begotten Son
to take our nature upon him
and as at this time to be born of a pure virgin.
Grant that we, who have been born again
and made your children by adoption and grace,
may daily be renewed by your Holy Spirit;

through Jesus Christ our Lord,
who is alive and reigns with you,
in the unity of the Holy Spirit,
one God, now and for ever. **Amen.** 5*

Ever-living God,
whose glory was revealed
in the Word made flesh:
may we, who have seen such splendour
in the coming of your Son,
be true witnesses to your self-giving love in the world;
through Jesus Christ our Lord,
who is alive and reigns with you,
in the unity of the Holy Spirit,
one God, now and for ever. **Amen.**

First Sunday of Christmas (26 to 31 December inclusive)

God of glory,
who wonderfully created us in your own image
and yet more wonderfully restored us
in your Son Jesus Christ:
grant that, as he came to share in our humanity,
so we may share in the life of his divinity;
who is alive and reigns with you,
in the unity of the Holy Spirit,
one God, now and for ever. **Amen.** 12*

Radiant God,
in Jesus Christ your light shines in our darkness,
giving joy in our sorrow
and revealing your presence in our loneliness.
Fill our hearts with your light
that in the darkness of this world
our lives may shine with your eternal splendour;
through Jesus Christ our Lord. **Amen.** 25*

Second Sunday of Christmas (1 to 5 January inclusive)

God of power and life,
the glory of all who believe in you;
fill the world with your splendour
and show the nations the light of your truth;
through Jesus Christ your Son our Lord,
who is alive and reigns with you,
in the unity of the Holy Spirit,
one God, now and for ever. **Amen.** 3*

God of beauty and light,
with the appearing of your Son
you have brought us into your new creation.
Renew in us your image and likeness
that our lives may reflect your glory;
through Jesus Christ our Lord,
who is alive and reigns with you,
in the unity of the Holy Spirit,
one God, now and for ever. **Amen.** 24*

The Epiphany (6 January) – or the preceding Sunday

Eternal God,
by a star you led wise men to the worship of your Son.
Guide by your light the nations of the earth,
that the whole world may see your glory;
through Jesus Christ our Lord,
who is alive and reigns with you,
in the unity of the Holy Spirit,
one God, now and for ever. **Amen.** 12*

Almighty God,
your Son our Saviour Jesus Christ
is the light of the world.
May your people
shine with the radiance of his glory,
that he may be known, worshipped and obeyed
to the ends of the earth;
who is alive and reigns with you,
in the unity of the Holy Spirit,
one God, now and for ever. **Amen.** 27*

Sunday between 7 and 13 January inclusive – Sunday after Epiphany and the First Sunday in Ordinary Time

God our Redeemer,
through Jesus Christ
you have assured your children of eternal life
and in Baptism have made us one in him.
Deliver us from the death of sin
and raise us to new life in Christ;
for he is alive and reigns with you,
in the unity of the Holy Spirit,
one God, now and for ever. **Amen.** 12

Eternal Father,
at the Baptism of Jesus
you revealed him to be your Son
and anointed him with the Holy Spirit.
Keep all who are born of water and the Spirit
faithful to their calling as your people;
through Jesus Christ our Lord. **Amen.** 4

Sunday between 14 and 20 January inclusive – Second Sunday in Ordinary Time

Living God,
in Christ you make all things new.
Transform the poverty of our nature
by the riches of your grace,
and in the renewal of our lives
make known your heavenly glory;
through Jesus Christ our Lord. **Amen.** 8

Almighty God,
by whose grace alone we are accepted
and called to your service,
strengthen us by your Spirit,
and make us worthy of our calling;
through Jesus Christ our Lord. **Amen.** 12

Sunday between 21 and 27 January inclusive – Third Sunday in Ordinary Time

Loving God,
through your Son you have called us to repent of our sin,
to believe the good news,
and to celebrate the coming of your kingdom.
Grant that we may hear the call to discipleship
and gladly proclaim the gospel to a waiting world;
through Jesus Christ our Lord. **Amen.**

Almighty God,
whose Son revealed in signs and miracles
the wonder of your saving love:
renew all your people with your heavenly grace,
and in all our weakness
sustain us by your mighty power;
through Jesus Christ our Lord. **Amen.** 12

Sunday between 28 January and 3 February inclusive – Fourth Sunday in Ordinary Time (unless it is the Sunday before Lent).

God of heaven and earth,
whose power is made fully known
in your pardoning mercy:
ever fill us with your grace,
that, entering more fully into your promises,
we may come to share in the good things of heaven;
through Jesus Christ our Lord. **Amen.**

Lord, you have taught us
that all our doings without love are worth nothing.
Send your Holy Spirit,
and pour into our hearts that most excellent gift of love,
the true bond of peace and of all virtues;
through Jesus Christ our Lord. **Amen.** 5*

Sunday between 4 and 10 February inclusive – Fifth Sunday in Ordinary Time (unless it is the Sunday before Lent or falls in Lent)

Loving God,
the light of the minds that know you,
the life of the souls that love you,
and the strength of the wills that serve you:
help us so to know you
that we may truly love you,
and so to love you
that we may truly serve you,
whom to serve is perfect freedom;
through Jesus Christ our Lord. **Amen.** 27*

God our Father,
whose Word has come among us:
may the light of faith, kindled in our hearts,
shine in our words and deeds;
through him who is Christ the Lord,
who is alive and reigns with you,
in the unity of the Holy Spirit,
one God, now and for ever. **Amen.** 3*

Sunday between 11 and 17 February inclusive – Sixth Sunday in Ordinary Time (unless it is the Sunday before Lent or falls in Lent)

O God,
forasmuch as without you we are not able to please you;
mercifully grant that your Holy Spirit
may in all things direct and rule our hearts;
through Jesus Christ our Lord. **Amen.** 5*

You alone, O God,
can satisfy our deepest hunger,
and protect us from the lure of wealth and power.
Teach us to seek your kingdom above all else,
that we may know the security and joy
of those who put their trust in you;
through Jesus Christ our Lord. **Amen.** 16*

Sunday between 18 and 24 February inclusive – Seventh Sunday in Ordinary Time (unless it is the Sunday before Lent or falls in Lent)

God of infinite mercy,
grant that we who know your pity
may rejoice in your forgiveness
and gladly forgive others,
for the sake of Jesus Christ our Saviour. **Amen.** 21

God of pardon and deliverance,
your forgiving love, revealed in Christ,
has brought to birth a new creation.
Raise us from our sins to walk in your ways,
that we may witness to your power
which makes all things new,
in Jesus Christ our Lord. **Amen.** 16

Sunday between 25 and 29 February inclusive – Eighth Sunday in Ordinary Time (unless it is the Sunday before Lent or falls in Lent)

Grant to us, Lord, we pray,
the spirit to think and do always those things that are right;
that we, who can do no good thing without you,
may by you be enabled to live according to your will;
through Jesus Christ our Lord. **Amen.** 5*

God of tenderness and compassion,
you led your people into the desert,
and embraced them there in love and faithfulness.
By word and sacrament
renew in us your covenant love,
that we may rejoice in your gift of new life;
through Jesus Christ our Lord. **Amen.** 16

Sunday before Lent

God of life and light,
your Son was revealed in majesty
before he suffered death on the cross.

Give us grace to perceive his glory,
that we may be strengthened to follow him
and be changed into his likeness, from glory to glory;
who is alive and reigns with you,
in the unity of the Holy Spirit,
one God, now and for ever. **Amen.** 7*

Lord God,
whose glory shines upon us
in the face of Jesus Christ,
and whose nature is made known to us
in the mystery of the cross:
number us, we pray,
among his faithful followers
for whom nothing matters
but the doing of your will;
through Jesus Christ our Lord. **Amen.** 26

Ash Wednesday

Almighty and everlasting God,
you hate nothing that you have made,
and forgive the sins of all those who are penitent.
Create and make in us new and contrite hearts,
that we, worthily lamenting our sins
and acknowledging our wretchedness,
may receive from you, the God of all mercy,
perfect remission and forgiveness;
through the merits of Jesus Christ,
our only mediator and advocate. **Amen.** 5*

OR

Almighty and merciful God,
you hate nothing that you have made,
and forgive the sins of all who are penitent.
Create in us new and contrite hearts,
so that when we turn to you and confess our sins
we may receive your full and perfect forgiveness;
through Jesus Christ our Lord. **Amen.** 21*

One of the above alternative versions of the collect for Lent may be said in addition to the collect of the day until the Fifth Sunday in Lent.

An additional collect for Ash Wednesday:

Remember, O Lord, what you have wrought in us,
and not what we deserve;
and as you have called us to your service,
make us worthy of our calling;
through Jesus Christ our Lord. **Amen.** 7*

First Sunday in Lent

Almighty God,
whose Son Jesus Christ
fasted forty days in the wilderness,
and was tempted as we are, yet without sin:
give us grace to discipline ourselves
in obedience to your Spirit;
and, as you know our weakness,
so may we know your power to save;
through Jesus Christ our Lord. **Amen.** 12

Gracious Father,
your blessèd Son Jesus Christ came from heaven
to be the true bread which gives life to the world.
Evermore give us this bread,
that he may live in us, and we in him;
through Jesus Christ our Lord. **Amen.** 3*

Second Sunday in Lent

Christ, Son of the living God,
who for a season laid aside the divine glory
and learned obedience through suffering:
teach us in all our afflictions
to raise our eyes to the place of your mercy
and to find in you our peace and deliverance.
We make our prayer in your name. **Amen.** 18*

Merciful Lord,
grant your people grace to withstand the temptations
of the world, the flesh and the devil,
and with pure hearts and minds to follow you,
the only God;
through Jesus Christ our Lord. **Amen.** 5*

Third Sunday in Lent

Almighty God,
whose most dear Son went not up to joy
but first he suffered pain,
and entered not into glory before he was crucified:
mercifully grant that we, walking in the way of the cross,
may find it none other than the way of life and peace;
through Jesus Christ our Lord. **Amen.** 2

Almighty God,
you see that we have no power of ourselves to help ourselves.
Keep us both outwardly in our bodies and inwardly in our souls,
that we may be defended from all adversities
which may happen to the body,
and from all evil thoughts
which may assault and hurt the soul;
through Jesus Christ our Lord. **Amen.** 5*

Fourth Sunday in Lent

Lord God,
whose blessèd Son our Saviour
gave his back to those who struck him
and did not hide his face from shame:
give us grace to endure
the sufferings of this present time
with sure confidence in the glory that shall be revealed;
through the same Jesus Christ our Lord. **Amen.** 6*

O God, rich in mercy,
you so loved the world
that, when we were dead in our sins,
you sent your only Son for our deliverance.
Lifted up from the earth,
he is light and life;
exalted upon the cross,
he is truth and salvation.
Raise us up with Christ
that we may walk as children of light.
We ask this through Christ,
who is alive and reigns with you
in the unity of the Holy Spirit,
holy and mighty God, for ever and for ever. **Amen.** 16*

Mothering Sunday

God of compassion,
whose Son Jesus Christ, the child of Mary,
shared the life of a home in Nazareth:
strengthen us each day,
that in joy and sorrow
we may know your presence;
through Jesus Christ our Lord. **Amen.** 23*

Fifth Sunday in Lent (First Sunday of the Passion)

Most merciful God,
who by the death and resurrection of your Son Jesus Christ
delivered and saved the world:
grant that by faith in him who suffered on the cross,
we may triumph in the power of his victory;
through Jesus Christ our Lord,
who is alive and reigns with you,
in the unity of the Holy Spirit,
one God, now and for ever. **Amen.** 12

Almighty God,
your Son came into the world
to free us all from sin and death.
Breathe upon us with the power of your Spirit,
that we may be raised to new life in Christ,
and serve you in holiness and righteousness all our days;
through the same Jesus Christ our Lord. **Amen.** 4

Sixth Sunday in Lent (Second Sunday of the Passion or Palm Sunday)

Eternal God,
in your tender love towards the human race
you sent your Son our Saviour Jesus Christ
to take our flesh and to suffer death upon a cross.
Grant that we may follow the example of his great humility,
and share in the glory of his resurrection;
through the same Jesus Christ our Lord. **Amen.** 5*

God of all-redeeming grace,
in your great love you gave your only Son
to die for the sins of the whole world.
Help us by your Holy Spirit
to worship you with reverence,
and to enter with joy
into the celebration of those mighty acts
whereby you bring us life and immortality;
through Jesus Christ our Lord. **Amen.** 4*

Maundy Thursday

God our Father,
you have invited us to share in the supper
which your Son gave to his Church.
Nourish us, we pray, by his presence,
and unite us in his love;
who is alive and reigns with you,
in the unity of the Holy Spirit,
one God, now and for ever. **Amen.** 17*

Gracious God,
we thank you for the gift of this sacrament
in which we remember Jesus Christ your Son.
May we who revere this sacred mystery
know and reveal in our lives
the fruits of his redemption;
who is alive and reigns with you,
in the unity of the Holy Spirit,
one God, now and for ever. **Amen.** 1*

Gracious God,
your Son Jesus Christ girded himself with a towel
and washed the feet of his disciples.
Give us the will to be the servants of others
as he was the servant of all,
who gave up his life and died for us,
yet lives and reigns with you and the Holy Spirit,
one God, now and for ever. **Amen.** 21

Good Friday

Gracious and eternal God,
look with mercy on this your family,
for which our Lord Jesus Christ
was content to be betrayed
and given up into the hands of sinners
and to suffer death upon the cross;
who is alive and glorified with you,
in the unity of the Holy Spirit,
one God, now and for ever. **Amen.** 5*

Almighty God,
your Son Jesus Christ
endured the cross for our sake.
Remove from us all coldness and cowardice of heart,
and give us courage
to take up our cross and follow him;
through the same Jesus Christ our Lord. **Amen.** 4

Almighty and everlasting God,
by your Spirit the whole body of the Church
is governed and sanctified.
Hear the prayers we offer for all your faithful people,
that in their vocation and ministry
each may serve you in holiness and truth,
to the glory of your name;
through Jesus Christ our Saviour. **Amen.** 1*

Eternal God,
bless all who look to Abraham
as the father of faith.
Set us free from prejudice, blindness,
and hardness of heart,
that in accordance with your will and guided by your truth
our life together may be for the glory of your name;
we ask this through Jesus Christ our Lord. **Amen.**

Holy Saturday

Grant, Lord,
that we who are baptized into the death
of your Son our Saviour Jesus Christ
may continually put to death our evil desires
and be buried with him;
that through the grave and gate of death
we may pass to our joyful resurrection;
through the merits of him
who died and was buried and rose again for us,
your Son Jesus Christ our Lord. **Amen.** 1*

Easter Day (Services after sunset until Easter Dawn)

God of glory,
you have filled this night with the radiance of Christ.
Renew in us our Baptism,
and bring us through the waters to the promised land;
through Jesus Christ our Redeemer,
who is alive and reigns with you,
in the unity of the Holy Spirit,
one God, now and for ever. **Amen.** 21*

Eternal God, giver of life and light,
you make this holy night shine
with the radiance of the risen Christ.
Renew your Church
with the joy and gladness of his presence,
that we may shine as lights in the world;
through Jesus Christ our Lord,
who is alive and reigns with you,
in the unity of the Holy Spirit,
one God, now and for ever. **Amen.** 4*

Easter Day (Services after dawn)

Lord of all life and power,
who through the mighty resurrection of your Son
overcame the old order of sin and death
to make all things new in him:
grant that we, being dead to sin
and alive to you in Jesus Christ,
may reign with him in glory;
to whom with you in the unity of the Holy Spirit
be praise and honour, glory and might,
now and in all eternity. **Amen.** 12

Most glorious God,
who on this day delivered us
by the mighty resurrection of your Son, Jesus Christ,
and made your whole creation new:
grant that we who celebrate with joy
his rising from the dead
may be raised from the death of sin
to the life of righteousness;
through him who is alive and reigns with you,
in the unity of the Holy Spirit,
one God, now and for ever. **Amen.** 21*

Second Sunday of Easter

Faithful God,
the strength of all who believe
and the hope of those who doubt;
may we, who have not seen, have faith
and receive the fullness of Christ's blessing;
who is alive and reigns with you,
in the unity of the Holy Spirit,
one God, now and for ever. **Amen.** 3

God of the prophets,
you fulfilled your promise
that Christ would suffer and rise to glory.
Open our minds to understand the scriptures
that we may be his witnesses to the ends of the earth.
We ask this through Jesus Christ our Lord,
who is alive and reigns with you,
in the unity of the Holy Spirit,
one God, world without end. **Amen.** 16

Third Sunday of Easter

God of life and love,
your Son made himself known to his disciples
in the breaking of the bread.
Open our eyes that we may see him
in his redeeming work;
who is alive and reigns with you,
in the unity of the Holy Spirit,
one God, now and for ever. **Amen.** 3*

Christ our friend,
you ask for our love
in spite of our betrayal.
Give us courage to embrace forgiveness,
know you again,
and trust ourselves in you;
we pray in your name. **Amen.** 20

Fourth Sunday of Easter

God of peace,
who brought again from the dead our Lord Jesus Christ,
that great Shepherd of the sheep,
with the blood of the eternal covenant:
make us perfect in every good work to do your will,
and work in us that which is well-pleasing in your sight;
through Jesus Christ our Lord,
who is alive and reigns with you,
in the unity of the Holy Spirit,
one God, now and for ever. **Amen.** 12*

Good Shepherd of the sheep,
by whom the lost are sought
and guided into the fold:
feed us and we shall be satisfied;
heal us and we shall be made whole;
and lead us, that we may be with you;
for you are alive and reign,
with the Father and the Holy Spirit,
one God, now and for ever. **Amen.** 21*

Fifth Sunday of Easter

Eternal God,
whose Son Jesus Christ
is the way, the truth and the life:
grant us to walk in his way,
to rejoice in his truth,
and to share his risen life;
who is alive and reigns with you,
in the unity of the Holy Spirit,
one God, now and for ever. **Amen.** 12*

Loving and eternal God,
through the resurrection of your Son,
help us to face the future
with courage and assurance,

knowing that nothing in life or death
can ever part us from your love for us
in Jesus Christ our Saviour;
who is alive and reigns with you,
in the unity of the Holy Spirit,
one God, now and for ever. **Amen.** 21*

Sixth Sunday of Easter

God of mercy,
as we rejoice in the resurrection of your Son,
the Bread of Life,
feed us with your plenty
and increase in us compassion for the hungry;
through Jesus Christ our Lord,
who is alive and reigns with you,
in the unity of the Holy Spirit,
one God, now and for ever. **Amen.**

Almighty and everlasting God,
you are always more ready to hear than we to pray,
and give more than either we desire or deserve.
Pour down upon us the abundance of your mercy,
forgiving us those things
of which our conscience is afraid
and giving us those good things
which we are not worthy to ask
save through the merits and mediation
of Jesus Christ your Son our Lord;
who is alive and reigns with you,
in the unity of the Holy Spirit,
one God, now and for ever. **Amen.** 12

Ascension Day

Eternal and gracious God,
grant that as we believe your Son,
our Saviour Jesus Christ,
to have ascended with triumph
into your kingdom in heaven,
so may we also in heart and mind ascend to where he is
and with him continually dwell;
who is alive and reigns with you,
in the unity of the Holy Spirit,
one God, now and for ever. **Amen.** 5*

Almighty and everlasting Father,
you raised our Lord Jesus Christ
to your right hand on high.
As we rejoice in his exaltation,
fill us with his Spirit,
that we may go into all the world
and faithfully proclaim the gospel.
This we ask through Jesus Christ our Lord,
who is alive and reigns with you,
in the unity of the Holy Spirit,
one God, for ever and ever. **Amen.** 27*

Seventh Sunday of Easter (Sunday in Ascensiontide)

Lord of Hosts,
purify our hearts
that the King of Glory may come in,
even your Son, Jesus our Redeemer;
for he is alive and reigns with you,
in the unity of the Holy Spirit,
one God, now and for ever. **Amen.** 9

Eternal God,
you have given all authority in heaven and on earth
to your Son, our Saviour Jesus Christ.
Grant that we may never lose
the vision of your kingdom
but serve you with hope and joy;

through him who lives and reigns with you,
in the unity of the Holy Spirit,
one God, now and for ever. **Amen.** 21*

or the collect for Ascension Day may be said.

Pentecost

God, who at this time
taught the hearts of your faithful people
by sending to them the light of your Holy Spirit:
grant us by the same Spirit
to have a right judgement in all things
and evermore to rejoice in his holy comfort;
through the merits of Christ Jesus our Saviour,
who is alive and reigns with you,
in the unity of the Holy Spirit,
one God, now and for ever. **Amen.** 12

Almighty God,
who on the day of Pentecost
sent your Holy Spirit on the disciples
with the wind from heaven and with tongues of flame,
filling them with joy and boldness to preach the gospel:
send us out in the power of the same Spirit
to witness to your truth
and to draw everyone to the fire of your love;
through Jesus Christ our Lord. **Amen.** 12*

Faithful God,
you fulfilled the promise of Easter
by sending your Holy Spirit
and opening the way of eternal life
to all the human race.
Keep us in the unity of your Spirit,
that every tongue may tell of your glory;
through Jesus Christ our Lord,
who is alive and reigns with you,
in the unity of the Holy Spirit,
one God, now and for ever. **Amen.** 3*

Trinity Sunday

Almighty and everlasting God,
you have given your servants grace,
by the confession of a true faith,
to acknowledge the glory of the eternal Trinity
and in the power of the divine majesty to worship the Unity.
Keep us steadfast in this faith,
that we may evermore be defended from all adversities;
through Jesus Christ our Lord,
who is alive and reigns with you,
in the unity of the Holy Spirit,
one God, now and for ever. **Amen.** 5*

Father God,
you have created all things
and through Christ revealed your salvation
in all the world.
Give us a vision of your glory
and by your Holy Spirit fill us with life and love
that we may praise and serve you
through Jesus Christ our Lord,
who is alive and reigns with you,
in the unity of the Holy Spirit,
one God, for ever and ever. **Amen.**

Sunday between 24 and 28 May
(if after Trinity Sunday) – Eighth Sunday in Ordinary Time

Grant to us, Lord, we pray,
the spirit to think and do always those things that are right;
that we, who can do no good thing without you,
may by you be enabled to live according to your will;
through Jesus Christ our Lord. **Amen.** 5*

God of tenderness and compassion,
you led your people into the desert,
and made them your own in love and faithfulness.
By word and sacrament
renew in us your covenant love,

that we may rejoice in your gift of new life;
through Jesus Christ our Lord. **Amen.** 16

Sunday between 29 May and 4 June inclusive
(if after Trinity Sunday) – Ninth Sunday in Ordinary Time

Almighty God,
you have built your Church
on the foundation of the apostles and prophets,
Jesus Christ himself being the chief cornerstone.
Join us together in unity of spirit by their teaching,
that we may become a holy temple, acceptable to you;
through Jesus Christ our Lord. **Amen.** 5*

Faithful God,
whose covenant love is new every morning:
open our eyes to your wisdom
and give us grace to keep faith with all your creation;
through Christ our Lord. **Amen.**

Sunday between 5 and 11 June inclusive
(if after Trinity Sunday) – Tenth Sunday in Ordinary Time

God, faithful and true,
you call every generation to make a pilgrim journey.
Guide our feet along the road of faith,
that we may put our whole trust in you;
through Jesus Christ our Lord. **Amen.**

Ever-loving God,
your Son Jesus Christ healed the sick
and restored them to wholeness of life.
Look with compassion on the anguish of the world,
and by your power make whole both people and nations;
through Jesus Christ our Lord. **Amen.** 12*

Sunday between 12 and 18 June inclusive
(if after Trinity Sunday) – Eleventh Sunday in Ordinary Time

Your glory, O God, fills heaven and earth
and all creation resounds with your praise.
As we rejoice in your presence,
may we know your power to save
and praise you for your faithfulness,
now and for ever;
through Jesus Christ our Lord. **Amen.**

Generous God,
you gather your people
and lavish your gifts upon us, day by day.
Grant that each experience of your pardon
may enlarge our own love,
until it meets the measure of your extravagant forgiveness,
through Jesus Christ our Lord. **Amen.** 16*

Sunday between 19 and 25 June inclusive
(if after Trinity Sunday) – Twelfth Sunday in Ordinary Time

Creator God,
in the beginning
your word subdued the chaos
and in the fullness of time
you sent Jesus, your Son,
to rebuke the forces of evil
and to make all things new.
By that same power
transform our fear into faith
that we may have courage to follow
in the way of your kingdom;
through the same Jesus Christ our Lord. **Amen.** 16*

God of all power and truth and grace,
you call your Church to love and praise.
Inspire us with zeal for your gospel,
and grant us boldness to proclaim your word,
that we and all the world may praise your name;
through Jesus Christ our Lord. **Amen.** 9*

Sunday between 26 June and 2 July inclusive – Thirteenth Sunday in Ordinary Time

Lord of heaven and earth,
you sent your Holy Spirit
to be the life and power of your Church.
Sow in our hearts the seeds of your grace
that we may bear the fruit of the Spirit,
in love and joy and peace;
through Jesus Christ our Lord. **Amen.** 12*

Merciful God,
out of the depths we cry to you
and you hear our prayer.
Make us attentive to the voice of your Son
that we may rise from the death of sin
and take our place in the new creation.
We make our prayer through Jesus Christ,
who lives and reigns with you,
in the unity of the Holy Spirit,
one God for ever and ever. **Amen.**

Sunday between 3 and 9 July inclusive – Fourteenth Sunday in Ordinary Time

Servant Lord,
grant us both the opportunity and the will
to serve you day by day.
May all that we do
and how we bear each other's burdens
be our offering of love and service
to the glory of your name. **Amen.** 21*

Boundless, O God, is your saving power;
your harvest reaches to the ends of the earth.
Set our hearts on fire for your kingdom
and put on our lips the good news of peace.
Grant us perseverance as heralds of your Gospel
and joy as disciples of your Son,
Jesus Christ our Lord;
who lives and reigns with you,
in the unity of the Holy Spirit,
one God for ever and ever. **Amen.** 16*

Sunday between 10 and 16 July inclusive – Fifteenth Sunday in Ordinary Time

Give us, we pray, gentle God,
a mind forgetful of past injury,
a will to seek the good of others
and a heart of love,
that we may learn to live
in the way of your Son, Jesus Christ,
through whom we pray. **Amen.** 21*

Eternal God, giver of love and peace,
you call your children to live together as one family.
Give us grace to learn your ways
and to do your will,
that we may bring justice and peace to all people,
in the name of Jesus Christ. **Amen.** 21

Sunday between 17 and 23 July inclusive – Sixteenth Sunday in Ordinary Time

Grant us, Lord,
not to be anxious about earthly things,
but to love things heavenly;
and even now,
while we are placed among things that are passing away,
to hold fast to those things which last for ever;
through Jesus Christ our Lord. **Amen.** 27*

Eternal God,
in Christ you make yourself our guest.
Amid all our cares and concerns
make us attentive to your voice
and alert to your presence,
that we may prize your word above all else;
through Jesus Christ our Lord. **Amen.** 16*

Sunday between 24 and 30 July inclusive – Seventeenth Sunday in Ordinary Time

Gracious God,
your Son Jesus Christ fed the hungry
with the bread of life
and the word of your kingdom.
Renew your people with your heavenly grace,
and in all our weakness
sustain us by your true and living bread,
even Jesus Christ our Lord. **Amen.** 3*

God, you have poured the Spirit of your Son into our hearts
so that we call you Father.
Give us grace to devote our freedom to your service
that we and all creation may be brought
into the glorious liberty of the children of God.
For the kingdom, the power, and the glory are yours,
now and for ever. **Amen.** 12*

Sunday between 31 July and 6 August inclusive – Eighteenth Sunday in Ordinary Time

Lord and giver of life,
you alone nourish and sustain your people,
through Christ, the bread of life.
Feed our hunger and quench our thirst,
that we may no longer work for what fails to satisfy,
but do what you require, in obedience and faith;
through Jesus Christ our Lord. **Amen.** 16*

Almighty God,
your Son has opened for us
a new and living way into your presence.
Give us new hearts and constant wills
to worship you in spirit and in truth;
through Jesus Christ our Lord. **Amen.** 12*

Sunday between 7 and 13 August inclusive – Nineteenth Sunday in Ordinary Time

Living God,
you have placed in the hearts of your children
a longing for your word and a hunger for your truth.
Grant that, believing in the One whom you have sent,
we may know him to be the true bread of heaven,
your Son, Jesus Christ our Lord. **Amen.** 27*

O God, the protector of all who trust in you,
without whom nothing is strong, nothing is holy:
increase and multiply upon us your mercy
that with you as our ruler and guide,
we may so pass through things temporal
that we finally lose not the things eternal;
grant this, heavenly Father,
for the sake of Jesus Christ our Lord. **Amen.** 5*

Sunday between 14 and 20 August inclusive – Twentieth Sunday in Ordinary Time

God of the nations,
to whose table all are invited
and in whose kingdom no one is a stranger:
hear the cries of the hungry
and mercifully extend to all the peoples on earth
the joy of your salvation;
through Jesus Christ our Lord. **Amen.** 16

To set the earth ablaze, O God,
your Son submitted to death on the cross,
and from his cup of suffering
you call the Church to drink.
When we are tempted
give us strength to run the race that lies before us,
and to keep our eyes fixed on Jesus;
who is alive and reigns with you,
in the unity of the Holy Spirit,
one God, now and for ever. **Amen.** 16

Sunday between 21 and 27 August inclusive – Twenty-first Sunday in Ordinary Time

Holy God,
you liberate the oppressed
and make a way of salvation.
Unite us with all who cry for justice,
and lead us together into freedom;
through our Lord and Liberator, Jesus Christ. **Amen.**

Merciful God,
grant that your Church,
being gathered by your Holy Spirit into one,
may reveal your glory among all peoples,
to the honour of your name;
through Jesus Christ our Lord. **Amen.** 4*

Sunday between 28 August and 3 September inclusive – Twenty-second Sunday in Ordinary Time

Redeemer God,
you heard the cry of your people
and sent Moses your servant
to lead them out of slavery.
Free us from the tyranny of sin and death
and, by the leading of your Spirit,
bring us to our promised land;
through Jesus Christ our Lord. **Amen.** 21*

God of all creation,
you call all peoples of the earth into your kingdom.
Grant that we, with young and old of all nations,
may boldly confess Jesus Christ as Lord;
to whom, with you and the Holy Spirit,
be all honour and praise, now and for ever. **Amen.** 27*

Sunday between 4 and 10 September inclusive – Twenty-third Sunday in Ordinary Time

O God, you bear your people ever on your heart and mind.
Watch over us in your protecting love,
that, strengthened by your grace
and led by your Spirit,
we may not miss your way for us
but enter into your glory,
made ready for all in Christ our Lord. **Amen.**

Go before us, Lord, in all that we do,
with your most gracious favour,
and guide us with your continual help,
that in all our works,
begun, continued and ended in you,
we may glorify your holy name,
and finally by your mercy obtain everlasting life;
through Jesus Christ our Lord. **Amen.** 5*

Sunday between 11 and 17 September inclusive – Twenty-fourth Sunday in Ordinary Time

God our Redeemer,
who called your Church to witness
that you were in Christ
reconciling the world to yourself:
help us so to proclaim the good news of your love
that all who hear it may be reconciled to you;
through Jesus Christ our Lord. **Amen.** 12*

Gracious God,
like a mother you give us new life,
and make us your children in Jesus Christ.
Look on us in your love,
and bring us to the inheritance which you promised.
Grant this through Jesus Christ, your Son. **Amen.** 27*

Sunday between 18 and 24 September inclusive – Twenty-fifth Sunday in Ordinary Time

Merciful God,
you have prepared for those who love you
such good things as pass our understanding.
Pour into our hearts such love towards you
that we, loving you above all things,
may obtain your promises,
which exceed all that we can desire;
through Jesus Christ our Lord. **Amen.** 12*

O God, surer than the breaking of the day,
in the morning, fill us with your love,
and in the evening, as the dew falls,
refresh us with your mercy,
that we may live according to your promises;
through Jesus Christ our Lord. **Amen.**

Sunday between 25 September and 1 October inclusive – Twenty-sixth Sunday in Ordinary Time

Gracious God,
you give the water of eternal life
through Jesus Christ your Son.
May we always turn to you,
the spring of life and source of goodness;
through the same Jesus Christ our Lord. **Amen.** 4*

Father of all,
you gave your only Son,
to take upon himself the form of a servant
and to be obedient even to death on a cross.
Give us the same mind that was in Christ Jesus
that, sharing in his humility,
we may come to be with him in his glory;
for he lives and reigns with you,
in the unity of the Holy Spirit,
one God, now and for ever. **Amen.** 12*

Sunday between 2 and 8 October inclusive – Twenty-seventh Sunday in Ordinary Time

Blessèd are you, O Lord,
and blessèd are those who observe and keep your law.
Help us to seek you with our whole heart,
to delight in your commandments
and to walk in the glorious liberty
given us by your Son, Jesus Christ,
in whose name we make our prayer. **Amen.** 9*

Almighty and everlasting God,
mercifully look upon our infirmities,
and in all our dangers and necessities
stretch out your hand to help and defend us;
through Jesus Christ our Lord. **Amen.** 5*

Sunday between 9 and 15 October inclusive – Twenty-eighth Sunday in Ordinary Time

Lord, in your goodness,
open our eyes to your light,
and so fill our hearts with your glory
that we may always acknowledge Jesus as Saviour,
and hold fast to his word in sincerity and truth.
We make our prayer
through Jesus Christ our Lord. **Amen.** 13

God of all power and might,
the author and giver of all good things,
graft in our hearts the love of your name,
increase in us true religion,
nourish in us all goodness
and of your great mercy keep us in the same;
through Jesus Christ our Lord. **Amen.** 12*

Sunday between 16 and 22 October inclusive – Twenty-ninth Sunday in Ordinary Time

Lord Jesus Christ,
you have taught us
that what we do for the least of our brothers and sisters,
we do also for you.
Give us the will to be the servants of others
as you were the servant of all;
for you gave up your life and died for us,
but live and reign with the Father and the Holy Spirit,
one God, now and for ever. **Amen.** 12*

Almighty God,
you have created the heavens and the earth
and formed us in your own image.
Teach us to discern your hand in all your works,
and to serve you with reverence and thanksgiving;
through Jesus Christ our Lord,
who reigns, with you and the Holy Spirit,
supreme over all creation,
now and for ever. **Amen.** 12*

Sunday between 23 and 29 October inclusive – Thirtieth Sunday in Ordinary Time

Eternal God, giver of love and peace,
you call your children to live together as one family.
Give us grace to learn your ways
and to do your will,
that we may bring justice and peace to all people,
in the name of Jesus Christ. **Amen.** 21

Lord of creation,
you give new strength to our faith.
Grant that we may recognise your presence
in all life and history,
and face our trials with serenity and peace.
We ask this through our Lord Jesus Christ. **Amen.** 27*

All Saints (1 November) – or the Sunday between 30 October and 5 November inclusive

Almighty God,
you have knit together your chosen people
in one communion and fellowship
in the mystical body of your Son Christ our Lord.
Give us grace so to follow your blessèd saints
in all virtuous and godly living
that we may come to those inexpressible joys
which you have prepared for those who love you;
through Jesus Christ our Lord. **Amen.** 9*

Holy God,
you have called witnesses from every nation
and revealed your glory in their lives.
Grant to us the same faith and love
that, following their example,
we may be sustained by their fellowship
and rejoice in their triumph;
through Jesus Christ our Lord. **Amen.**

Sunday between 30 October and 5 November inclusive – Thirty-first Sunday in Ordinary Time

Merciful Lord,
you have taught us through your Son
that love is the fulfilling of the law.
Grant that we may love you with our whole heart
and our neighbours as ourselves;
through Jesus Christ our Lord. **Amen.** 12*

All-embracing God,
your care for us surpasses
even a mother's tender love.
Through your word and sacrament
renew our trust in your providence,
that we may abandon all anxiety
and seek first your kingdom.
We make our prayer
through Jesus Christ our Lord. **Amen.** 16*

Sunday between 6 and 12 November inclusive – Thirty-second Sunday in Ordinary Time

Eternal God,
in whose perfect realm
no sword is drawn but the sword of justice,
and no strength known but the strength of love:
guide and inspire all who seek your kingdom,
that peoples and nations may find their security
in the love which casts out fear;
through Jesus Christ our Saviour. **Amen.** 9*

God of peace,
whose will is to restore all things
in your beloved Son, the King of all:
govern the hearts and minds of those in authority,
and bring the families of the nations,
divided and torn apart by the ravages of sin,
to be subject to his just and gentle rule;
who is alive and reigns with you,
in the unity of the Holy Spirit,
one God, now and for ever. **Amen.** 12*

Sunday between 13 and 19 November inclusive – Thirty-third Sunday in Ordinary Time

Eternal God,
from whom all thoughts of truth and peace proceed:
kindle, we pray, in every heart the true love of peace,
and guide with your pure and peaceable wisdom
those who take counsel for the nations of the earth;
that in justice and peace your kingdom may go forward,
till the earth is filled with the knowledge of your love;
through Jesus Christ our Lord. **Amen.** 7*

Almighty God,
you sent your Son Jesus Christ
to be the light of the world.
Free us from all that darkens and ensnares us,
and bring us to eternal light and joy;
through the power of him
who is alive and reigns with you,
in the unity of the Holy Spirit,
one God, now and for ever. **Amen.** 4

Sunday between 20 and 26 November inclusive – Sunday before Advent

Eternal Father,
whose Son Jesus Christ ascended to the throne of heaven
that he might rule over all things as Lord:
keep the Church in the unity of the Spirit
and in the bond of peace,
and bring the whole created order to worship at his feet;
who is alive and reigns with you and the Holy Spirit,
one God, now and for ever. **Amen.** 12

Stir up, O Lord,
the wills of your faithful people,
that they, bringing forth the fruit of good works,
may by you be richly rewarded;
through Jesus Christ our Lord. **Amen.** 5*

COLLECTS FOR SPECIAL OCCASIONS

Bible Sunday

Blessèd Lord,
who caused all holy scriptures to be written for our learning:
help us so to hear them,
read, mark, learn and inwardly digest them,
that through patience and the comfort of your holy word
we may embrace and ever hold fast
the hope of everlasting life,
which you have given us
in our Saviour Jesus Christ. **Amen.** 5*

Christian Unity

Lord God, we thank you for calling us
into the company of those who trust in Christ
and seek to obey his will.
May your Spirit guide and strengthen us
in mission and service to your world;
for we are strangers no longer
but pilgrims together on the way to your kingdom;
through Jesus Christ our Lord. **Amen.** 11

God of all,
through the gift of your Spirit
you have united your people
in the confession of your name.
Lead us, by the same Spirit,
to show to the whole earth
one mind in faith
and one faith for justice;
through Jesus Christ our Lord. **Amen.** 4*

Church Anniversary

Almighty God,
to whose glory we celebrate the anniversary of this church:
we thank you for the fellowship
of those who have worshipped here,
and we pray that all who seek you here may find you,
and, being filled with the Holy Spirit,
may become a living temple,
a dwelling place for your life-giving presence in the world.
We ask it through Jesus Christ our Lord. **Amen.** 14*

Harvest Thanksgiving

Bountiful God,
you entrust your creation to our care.
Grant us grace so to order our common life
that we may use your gifts to your glory,
for the relief of those in need
and for our own well-being;
through Jesus Christ our Lord. **Amen.** 1*

John and Charles Wesley

Almighty God,
you raised up your servants, John and Charles Wesley,
to proclaim anew the gift of redemption
and the life of holiness.
Pour out your Spirit,
and revive your work among us;
that inspired by the same faith,
and upheld by the same grace in word and sacrament,
we and all your children may be made one
in the unity of your Church on earth,
even as in heaven we are made one in you;
through Jesus Christ our Lord. **Amen.** 19*

God of mercy,
who inspired John and Charles Wesley
with zeal for your gospel:
grant that all your people may boldly proclaim your word
and evermore rejoice in singing your praises;
through Jesus Christ our Lord. **Amen.** 9*

New Year: Watchnight

Lord of history,
to whom a thousand years are as a day:
renew us by your Holy Spirit,
that, while we have life and breath,
we may serve you with courage and hope;
through the grace of your Son,
our Saviour Jesus Christ. **Amen.**

Eternal God,
you sent your Son to be born among us
that we might be born again to newness of life.
Fill us with the gladness of your great redemption,
that as we begin this new year with your blessing,
we may continue it in your favour,
and live all our days as your children
in the name of Jesus Christ our Lord;
who is alive and reigns with you and the Holy Spirit,
one God, now and for ever. **Amen.** 4*

Remembrance Sunday

Eternal God,
in whose perfect realm
no sword is drawn but the sword of justice,
and no strength known but the strength of love:
guide and inspire all who seek your kingdom,
that peoples and nations may find their security
in the love which casts out fear;
through Jesus Christ our Saviour. **Amen.** 9*

THE LECTIONARY

NOTES

1 Verses are stated inclusively. The letter *a* indicates the first part of a verse, *b* the second and, occasionally, *c* the third part.

2 Parts of a passage shown in brackets may be omitted.

3 When a reading begins with a personal pronoun (for example, '*He*'), the reader should substitute the appropriate name (for example, '*Jesus*'). When a reading begins with a direct quotation (for example, when a gospel reading starts with the words of Jesus) the reader should begin, for example, '*Jesus said*'.

4 Bible references are to **The New Revised Standard Version (Anglicized Edition)**. Adaptations may be needed when other translations are used.

THE LECTIONARY

	Year A Beginning on the First Sunday of Advent in 1998, 2001, 2004, 2007, 2010, 2013, 2016, 2019, 2022, 2025, 2028	Year B Beginning on the First Sunday of Advent in 1999, 2002, 2005, 2008, 2011, 2014, 2017, 2020, 2023, 2026, 2029	Year C Beginning on the First Sunday of Advent in 2000, 2003, 2006, 2009, 2012, 2015, 2018, 2021, 2024, 2027, 2030
First Sunday of Advent (Violet)	**Principal Service** Isaiah 2:1-5 Psalm 122 Romans 13:11-14 Matthew 24:36-44	**Principal Service** Isaiah 64:1-9 Psalm 80:1-7, 17-19 1 Corinthians 1:3-9 Mark 13:24-37	**Principal Service** Jeremiah 33:14-16 Psalm 25:1-10 1 Thessalonians 3:9-13 Luke 21:25-36
	Second Service Isaiah 52:1-12 Psalm 9:1-8 (9-20) Matthew 24:15-28	**Second Service** Isaiah 1:1-20 Psalm 25:1-10 (11-22) Matthew 21:1-13	**Second Service** Joel 3:9-21 Psalm 9:1-8 (9-20) Revelation 14:13 - 15:4 John 3:1-17
Second Sunday of Advent (Violet)	**Principal Service** Isaiah 11:1-10 Psalm 72:1-7, 18-19 Romans 15:4-13 Matthew 3:1-12	**Principal Service** Isaiah 40:1-11 Psalm 85:1-2, 8-13 2 Peter 3:8-15*a* Mark 1:1-8	**Principal Service** Baruch 5:1-9 *or* Malachi 3:1-4 *Canticle:* Benedictus (Luke 1:68-79) Philippians 1:3-11 Luke 3:1-6
	Second Service 1 Kings 18:17-39 Psalm 11 John 1:19-28	**Second Service** 1 Kings 22:1-28 Psalm 40: (1-10) 11-17 Romans 15:4-13 Matthew 11:2-11	**Second Service** Isaiah 40:1-11 Psalm 75 Luke 1:1-25

Third Sunday of Advent (Violet)	**Principal Service** Isaiah 35:1-10 Psalm 146:5-10 *or Canticle:* Magnificat (Luke 1:46*b*-55) James 5:7-10 Matthew 11:2-11	**Principal Service** Isaiah 61:1-4, 8-11 Psalm 126 *or Canticle:* Magnificat (Luke 1:46*b*-55) 1 Thessalonians 5:16-24 John 1:6-8, 19-28	**Principal Service** Zephaniah 3:14-20 *Canticle:* Isaiah 12:2-6 Philippians 4:4-7 Luke 3:7-18
	Second Service Isaiah 5:8-30 Psalm 12 Acts 13:13-41 John 5:31-40	**Second Service** Malachi 3:1-4; 4:1-6 Psalm 68:1-8 (9-20) Philippians 4:4-7 Matthew 14:1-12	**Second Service** Isaiah 35:1-10 Psalm 50:1-6 Luke 1:57-66 (67-80)
Fourth Sunday of Advent (Violet)	**Principal Service** Isaiah 7:10-16 Psalm 80:1-7, 17-19 Romans 1:1-7 Matthew 1:18-25	**Principal Service** 2 Samuel 7:1-11, 16 *Canticle:* Magnificat (Luke 1:46*b*-55) *or* Psalm 89:1-4, 19-26 Romans 16:25-27 Luke 1:26-38	**Principal Service** Micah 5:2-5*a* *Canticle:* Magnificat (Luke 1:46*b*-55) *or* Psalm 80:1-7 Hebrews 10:5-10 Luke 1:39-45 (46-55)
	Second Service 1 Samuel 1:1-20 Psalm 113 Revelation 22:6-21 Luke 1:39-45	**Second Service** Zechariah 2:10-13 Psalm 113 Luke 1:39-55	**Second Service** Isaiah 10:33 - 11:10 Psalm 123 Matthew 1:18-25

Christmas Day
(White *or* Gold)

Any of the following sets of readings may be used on the evening of Christmas Eve and on Christmas Day. Set III should be used at some service during the celebration.

I Isaiah 9:2-7; Psalm 96; Titus 2:11-14; Luke 2:1-14 (15-20)
II Isaiah 62:6-12; Psalm 97; Titus 3:4-7; Luke 2:(1-7) 8-20
III Isaiah 52:7-10; Psalm 98; Hebrews 1:1-4 (5-12); John 1:1-14

	Year A	Year B	Year C
First Sunday of Christmas *(26 to 31 December inclusive)* (White *or* Gold)	**Principal Service** Isaiah 63:7-9 Psalm 148 Hebrews 2:10-18 Matthew 2:13-23	**Principal Service** Isaiah 61:10 - 62:3 Psalm 148 Galatians 4:4-7 Luke 2:22-40	**Principal Service** 1 Samuel 2:18-20, 26 Psalm 148 Colossians 3:12-17 Luke 2:41-52
	Second Service Isaiah 49:7-13 Psalm 132 Philippians 2:1-11 Luke 2:41-52	**Second Service** Isaiah 35:1-10 Psalm 132 Colossians 1:9-20 Luke 2:41-52	**Second Service** Isaiah 61:1-11 Psalm 132 Galatians 3:27 - 4:7 Luke 2:15-21

When Christmas Day falls on a Sunday, it is regarded as the First Sunday of the Christmas Season and the readings listed above are not required.

	Year A	Year B	Year C
Second Sunday of Christmas *(1 to 5 January inclusive)* (White *or* Gold)	**Principal Service** Jeremiah 31:7-14 Psalm 147:12-20 Ephesians 1:3-14 John 1:(1-9) 10-18 *or* Sirach/Ecclesiasticus 24:1-12 *Canticle*: Wisdom of Solomon 10:15-21 Ephesians 1:3-14 John 1:(1-9) 10-18	**Principal Service** Jeremiah 31:7-14 Psalm 147:12-20 Ephesians 1:3-14 John 1:(1-9) 10-18 *or* Sirach/Ecclesiasticus 24:1-12 *Canticle*: Wisdom of Solomon 10:15-21 Ephesians 1:3-14 John 1:(1-9) 10-18	**Principal Service** Jeremiah 31:7-14 Psalm 147:12-20 Ephesians 1:3-14 John 1:(1-9) 10-18 *or* Sirach/Ecclesiasticus 24:1-12 *Canticle:* Wisdom of Solomon 10:15-21 Ephesians 1:3-14 John 1:(1-9) 10-18

	Second Service Isaiah 41:21 - 42:4 Psalm 135:1-14 (15-21) Colossians 1:1-14 Matthew 2:13-23	**Second Service** Isaiah 46:3-13 Psalm 135:1-14 (15-21) Romans 12:1-8 Matthew 2:13-23	**Second Service** 1 Samuel 1:20-28 Psalm 135:1-14 (15-21) 1 John 4:7-16 Matthew 2:13-23

The Epiphany *(6 January)*
(White *or* Gold)

Principal Service: Isaiah 60:1-6; Psalm 72:1-7, 10-14; Ephesians 3:1-12; Matthew 2:1-12

Second Service: Baruch 4:36 - 5:9 *or* Isaiah 60:1-9; Psalms 98; 100; John 2:1-11

When 6 January is a weekday, these readings may replace those of the preceding Sunday.

Sunday between 7 and 13 January inclusive *– Sunday after Epiphany and the First Sunday in Ordinary Time* (White *or* Gold)	**Principal Service** Isaiah 42:1-9 Psalm 29 Acts 10:34-43 Matthew 3:13-17	**Principal Service** Genesis 1:1-5 Psalm 29 Acts 19:1-7 Mark 1:4-11	**Principal Service** Isaiah 43:1-7 Psalm 29 Acts 8:14-17 Luke 3:15-17, 21-22
	Second Service Joshua 3:1-8, 14-17 Psalm 46 Hebrews 1:1-12 Luke 3:15-22	**Second Service** Isaiah 42:1-9 Psalm 46 Ephesians 2:1-10 Matthew 3:13-17	**Second Service** Isaiah 55:1-11 Psalm 46 Romans 6:1-11 Mark 1:4-11

	Year A	Year B	Year C
Sunday between 14 and 20 January inclusive *– Second Sunday in Ordinary Time* (Green)	**Principal Service** Isaiah 49:1-7 Psalm 40:1-11 1 Corinthians 1:1-9 John 1:29-42	**Principal Service** 1 Samuel 3:1-10 (11-20) Psalm 139:1-6, 13-18 1 Corinthians 6:12-20 John 1:43-51	**Principal Service** Isaiah 62:1-5 Psalm 36:5-10 1 Corinthians 12:1-11 John 2:1-11
	Second Service Ezekiel 2:1 - 3:4 Psalm 96 Galatians 1:11-24 John 1:43-51	**Second Service** Isaiah 60:9-22 Psalm 96 Hebrews 6:17 - 7:10 Matthew 8:5-13	**Second Service** 1 Samuel 3:1-20 Psalm 96 Ephesians 4:1-16 John 1:29-42
Sunday between 21 and 27 January inclusive *– Third Sunday in Ordinary Time* (Green)	**Principal Service** Isaiah 9:1-4 Psalm 27:1, 4-9 1 Corinthians 1:10-18 Matthew 4:12-23	**Principal Service** Jonah 3:1-5, 10 Psalm 62:5-12 1 Corinthians 7:29-31 Mark 1:14-20	**Principal Service** Nehemiah 8:1-3, 5-6, 8-10 Psalm 19 1 Corinthians 12:12-31*a* Luke 4:14-21
	Second Service Ecclesiastes 3:1-11 Psalm 33:1-12 (13-22) 1 Peter 1:3-12 Luke 4:14-21	**Second Service** Jeremiah 3:21 - 4:2 Psalm 33:1-12 (13-22) Titus 2:1-8, 11-14 Matthew 4:12-23	**Second Service** Numbers 9:15-23 Psalm 33:1-12 (13-22) 1 Corinthians 7:17-24 Mark 1:21-28

Sunday between 28 January and 3 February inclusive* *– Fourth Sunday in Ordinary Time* (Green)	**Principal Service** Micah 6:1-8 Psalm 15 1 Corinthians 1:18-31 Matthew 5:1-12	**Principal Service** Deuteronomy 18:15-20 Psalm 111 1 Corinthians 8:1-13 Mark 1:21-28	**Principal Service** Jeremiah 1:4-10 Psalm 71:1-6 1 Corinthians 13:1-13 Luke 4:21-30
	Second Service Genesis 28:10-22 Psalm 34:1-10 (11-22) Philemon 1-16 Mark 1:21-28	**Second Service** 1 Samuel 3:1-20 Psalm 34:1-10 (11-22) 1 Corinthians 14:12-20 Matthew 13:10-17	**Second Service** 1 Chronicles 29:6-19 Psalm 34:1-10 (11-22) Acts 7:44-50 John 4:19-29*a*
Sunday between 4 and 10 February inclusive* *– Fifth Sunday in Ordinary Time* (Green)	**Principal Service** Isaiah 58:1-9*a* (9*b*-12) Psalm 112:1-9 (10) 1 Corinthians 2:1-12 (13-16) Matthew 5:13-20	**Principal Service** Isaiah 40:21-31 Psalm 147:1-11, 20*c* 1 Corinthians 9:16-23 Mark 1:29-39	**Principal Service** Isaiah 6:1-8 (9-13) Psalm 138 1 Corinthians 15:1-11 Luke 5:1-11
	Second Service Amos 2:4-16 Psalm 4 Ephesians 4:17-32 Mark 1:29-39	**Second Service** Numbers 13:1-2, 27-33 Psalm 5 Philippians 2:12-28 Luke 5:1-11	**Second Service** Wisdom of Solomon 6:1-21 *or* Hosea 1:1-11 Psalm 2 Colossians 3:1-22 Matthew 5:13-20

** Unless it is the Sunday before Lent or falls in Lent*

	Year A	Year B	Year C
Sunday between 11 and 17 February inclusive* *– Sixth Sunday in Ordinary Time* (Green)	**Principal Service** Deuteronomy 30:15-20 *or* Sirach/Ecclesiasticus 15:15-20 Psalm 119:1-8 1 Corinthians 3:1-9 Matthew 5:21-37	**Principal Service** 2 Kings 5:1-14 Psalm 30 1 Corinthians 9:24-27 Mark 1:40-45	**Principal Service** Jeremiah 17:5-10 Psalm 1 1 Corinthians 15:12-20 Luke 6:17-26
	Second Service Amos 3:1-8 Psalm 13 Ephesians 5:1-17 Mark 1:40-45	**Second Service** Numbers 20:2-13 Psalm 6 Philippians 3:7-21 Luke 6:17-26	**Second Service** Wisdom of Solomon 11:21 - 12:11 *or* Hosea 10:1-8, 12 Psalm 6 Galatians 4:8-20 Matthew 5:21-37
Sunday between 18 and 24 February inclusive* *– Seventh Sunday in Ordinary Time* (Green)	**Principal Service** Leviticus 19:1-2, 9-18 Psalm 119:33-40 1 Corinthians 3:10-11, 16-23 Matthew 5:38-48	**Principal Service** Isaiah 43:18-25 Psalm 41 2 Corinthians 1:18-22 Mark 2:1-12	**Principal Service** Genesis 45:3-11, 15 Psalm 37:1-11, 39-40 1 Corinthians 15:35-38, 42-50 Luke 6:27-38
	Second Service Amos 9:5-15 Psalm 18:1-19 *or* Psalm 18:20-29 Ephesians 6:1-20 Mark 2:1-12	**Second Service** Numbers 22:21 - 23:12 Psalm 10 Philippians 4:10-20 Luke 6:27-38	**Second Service** Hosea 14:1-9 Psalm 13 Galatians 5:2-10 Matthew 6:1-8

** Unless it is the Sunday before Lent or falls in Lent*

	Year A	Year B	Year C
Sunday between 25 and 29 February inclusive* *– Eighth Sunday in Ordinary Time* (Green)	**Principal Service** Isaiah 49:8-16*a* Psalm 131 1 Corinthians 4:1-5 Matthew 6:24-34	**Principal Service** Hosea 2:14-20 Psalm 103:1-13, 22 2 Corinthians 3:1-6 Mark 2:13-22	**Principal Service** Sirach/Ecclesiasticus 27:4-7 *or* Isaiah 55:10-13 Psalm 92:1-4, 12-15 1 Corinthians 15:51-58 Luke 6:39-49
	Second Service Proverbs 8:1, 22-31 Psalm 148 Revelation 4:1-11 Luke 12:16-31	**Second Service** Genesis 2:4*b*-25 Psalm 65 Luke 8:22-35	**Second Service** Genesis 1:1 - 2:3 Psalm 147:(1-11) 12-20 Matthew 6:25-34
Sunday before Lent (Green)	**Principal Service** Exodus 24:12-18 Psalm 2 *or* Psalm 99 2 Peter 1:16-21 Matthew 17:1-9	**Principal Service** 2 Kings 2:1-12 Psalm 50:1-6 2 Corinthians 4:3-6 Mark 9:2-9	**Principal Service** Exodus 34:29-35 Psalm 99 2 Corinthians 3:12 - 4:2 Luke 9:28-36 (37-43)
	Second Service Sirach/Ecclesiasticus 48:1-10 *or* 2 Kings 2:1-12 Psalm 84 Matthew 17:(1-8) 9-23	**Second Service** 1 Kings 19:1-16 Psalm 2 2 Peter 1:16-21 Mark 9:(2-8) 9-13	**Second Service** Exodus 3:1-6 Psalm 89:(1-4) 5-12 (13-18) John 12:27-36*a*
Ash Wednesday (Violet)	Joel 2:1-2, 12-17 *or* Isaiah 58:1-12; Psalm 51:1-17; 2 Corinthians 5:20*b* - 6:10; Matthew 6:1-6, 16-21		

** Unless it is the Sunday before Lent or falls in Lent*

	Year A	Year B	Year C
First Sunday in Lent (Violet)	**Principal Service** Genesis 2:15-17; 3:1-7 Psalm 32 Romans 5:12-19 Matthew 4:1-11	**Principal Service** Genesis 9:8-17 Psalm 25:1-10 1 Peter 3:18-22 Mark 1:9-15	**Principal Service** Deuteronomy 26:1-11 Psalm 91:1-2, 9-16 Romans 10:8*b*-13 Luke 4:1-13
	Second Service Deuteronomy 6:4-9, 16-25 Psalm 50:1-15 Luke 15:1-10	**Second Service** Genesis 2:15-17; 3:1-7 Psalm 119:17-32 Romans 5:12-19 Luke 13:31-35	**Second Service** Jonah 3:1-10 Psalm 119:73-88 Luke 18:9-14
Second Sunday in Lent (Violet)	**Principal Service** Genesis 12:1-4*a* Psalm 121 Romans 4:1-5, 13-17 John 3:1-17	**Principal Service** Genesis 17:1-7, 15-16 Psalm 22:23-31 Romans 4:13-25 Mark 8:31-38	**Principal Service** Genesis 15:1-12, 17-18 Psalm 27 Philippians 3:17 - 4:1 Luke 13:31-35
	Second Service Numbers 21:4-9 Psalm 135:1-14 (15-21) Luke 14:27-33	**Second Service** Genesis 12:1-9 Psalm 135:1-14 (15-21) Hebrews 11:1-3, 8-16	**Second Service** Jeremiah 22:1-9, 13-17 Psalm 135:1-14 (15-21) Luke 14:27-33
Third Sunday in Lent (Violet)	**Principal Service** Exodus 17:1-7 Psalm 95 Romans 5:1-11 John 4:5-42	**Principal Service** Exodus 20:1-17 Psalm 19 1 Corinthians 1:18-25 John 2:13-22	**Principal Service** Isaiah 55:1-9 Psalm 63:1-8 1 Corinthians 10:1-13 Luke 13:1-9

<table>
<tr><td></td><td>Second Service
Joshua 1:1-9
Psalm 40
Ephesians 6:10-20
John 2:13-22</td><td>Second Service
Exodus 5:1 - 6:1
Psalms 11; 12
Philippians 3:4b-14
Matthew 10:16-22</td><td>Second Service
Genesis 28:10-19a
Psalms 12; 13
John 1:35-51</td></tr>
<tr><td>Fourth Sunday in Lent
(Violet)</td><td>Principal Service
1 Samuel 16:1-13
Psalm 23
Ephesians 5:8-14
John 9:1-41</td><td>Principal Service
Numbers 21:4-9
Psalm 107:1-3, 17-22
Ephesians 2:1-10
John 3:14-21</td><td>Principal Service
Joshua 5:9-12
Psalm 32
2 Corinthians 5:16-21
Luke 15:1-3, 11b-32</td></tr>
<tr><td></td><td>Second Service
Micah 7:1-20
or Prayer of Manasseh 1-15
Psalm 31:1-8 (9-16)
James 5:1-20
John 3:14-21</td><td>Second Service
Exodus 6:2-13
Psalms 13; 14
Romans 5:1-11
John 12:1-8</td><td>Second Service
Prayer of Manasseh 1-15
or Isaiah 40:27 - 41:13
Psalm 30
2 Timothy 4:1-18
John 11:17-44</td></tr>
<tr><td>Or for Mothering Sunday
(Violet)</td><td colspan="3">Exodus 2:1-10 or 1 Samuel 1:20-28; Psalm 34:11-20 or Psalm 127:1-4; 2 Corinthians 1:3-7 or Colossians 3:12-17; Luke 2:33-35 or John 19:25-27</td></tr>
<tr><td>Fifth Sunday in Lent
(First Sunday of the Passion)
(Violet)</td><td>Principal Service
Ezekiel 37:1-14
Psalm 130
Romans 8:6-11
John 11:1-45</td><td>Principal Service
Jeremiah 31:31-34
Psalm 51:1-12
or Psalm 119:9-16
Hebrews 5:5-10
John 12:20-33</td><td>Principal Service
Isaiah 43:16-21
Psalm 126
Philippians 3:4b-14
John 12:1-8</td></tr>
</table>

	Year A	Year B	Year C
Fifth Sunday in Lent continued	**Second Service** Lamentations 3:19-33 Psalm 30 Matthew 20:17-34	**Second Service** Exodus 7:8-24 Psalm 34:1-10 (11-22) Romans 5:12-21 Luke 22:1-13	**Second Service** 2 Chronicles 35:1-6, 10-16 Psalm 35:1-9 (10-28) Luke 22:1-13
Sixth Sunday in Lent *(Second Sunday of the Passion or Palm Sunday)* (Violet *or* Red) **Entry into Jerusalem**	**Principal Service** Matthew 21:1-11 Psalm 118:1-2, 19-29	**Principal Service** Mark 11:1-11 *or* John 12:12-16 Psalm 118:1-2, 19-29	**Principal Service** Luke 19:28-40 Psalm 118:1-2, 19-29
The Passion	**Principal Service** Isaiah 50:4-9*a* Psalm 31:9-16 Philippians 2:5-11 Matthew 26:14 - 27:66 *or* Matthew 27:11-54	**Principal Service** Isaiah 50:4-9*a* Psalm 31:9-16 Philippians 2:5-11 Mark 14:1 - 15:47 *or* Mark 15:1-39 (40-47)	**Principal Service** Isaiah 50:4-9*a* Psalm 31:9-16 Philippians 2:5-11 Luke 22:14 - 23:56 *or* Luke 23:1-49
	Second Service Isaiah 5:1-7 Psalm 80 Matthew 21:33-46	**Second Service** Isaiah 5:1-7 Psalm 69:1-18 Mark 12:1-12	**Second Service** Isaiah 5:1-7 Psalm 69:1-18 Luke 20:9-19
Monday in Holy Week (Violet *or* Red)	Isaiah 42:1-9; Psalm 36:5-11; Hebrews 9:11-15; John 12:1-11		
Tuesday in Holy Week (Violet *or* Red)	Isaiah 49:1-7; Psalm 71:1-14; 1 Corinthians 1:18-31; John 12:20-36		

Wednesday in Holy Week
(Violet *or* Red)

Isaiah 50:4-9*a*; Psalm 70; Hebrews 12:1-3; John 13:21-32

Maundy Thursday
(White *or* Gold)

Exodus 12:1-4 (5-10) 11-14; Psalm 116:1-2, 12-19; 1 Corinthians 11:23-26; John 13:1-17, 31*b*-35

The readings for the Watch and the Vigil are given on pages 252 and 254.

Good Friday
(None *or* Red)

Isaiah 52:13 - 53:12; Psalm 22; Hebrews 10:16-25 *or* Hebrews 4:14-16; 5:7-9; John 18:1 - 19:42

Holy Saturday
(None)

Job 14:1-14 *or* Lamentations 3:1-9, 19-24; Psalm 31:1-4, 15-16; 1 Peter 4:1-8; Matthew 27:57-66 *or* John 19:38-42

The readings for the Easter Vigil are given in the text of the service which begins on page 265.

Easter Day
(White *or* Gold)

Principal Service
Acts 10:34-43
or Jeremiah 31:1-6
Psalm 118:1-2, 14-24
Colossians 3:1-4
or Acts 10:34-43
John 20:1-18
or Matthew 28:1-10

Second Service
Song of Solomon 3:2-5; 8:6-7
Psalms 114; 117
Revelation 1:12-18
John 20:11-18

Principal Service
Acts 10:34-43
or Isaiah 25:6-9
Psalm 118:1-2, 14-24
1 Corinthians 15:1-11
or Acts 10:34-43
John 20:1-18
or Mark 16:1-8

Second Service
Ezekiel 37:1-14
Psalms 114; 117
Luke 24:13-35

Principal Service
Acts 10:34-43
or Isaiah 65:17-25
Psalm 118:1-2, 14-24
1 Corinthians 15:19-26
or Acts 10:34-43
John 20:1-18
or Luke 24:1-12

Second Service
Isaiah 43:1-21
Psalms 66; 114; 117
1 Corinthians 15:1-11
John 20:19-23

	Year A	Year B	Year C
Second Sunday of Easter (White *or* Gold)	**Principal Service** Acts 2:14*a*, 22-32 Psalm 16 1 Peter 1:3-9 John 20:19-31 **Second Service** Daniel 6:(1-5) 6-23 Psalm 30:1-5 Mark 15:46 - 16:8	**Principal Service** Acts 4:32-35 Psalm 133 1 John 1:1 - 2:2 John 20:19-31 **Second Service** Isaiah 26:1-9, 19 Psalm 143:1-11 Luke 24:1-12	**Principal Service** Acts 5:27-32 Psalm 118:14-29 *or* Psalm 150 Revelation 1:4-8 John 20:19-31 **Second Service** Isaiah (52:13-15) 53:1-6 (7-8) 9-12 Psalm 16 Luke 24:13-35
Third Sunday of Easter (White *or* Gold)	**Principal Service** Acts 2:14*a*, 36-41 Psalm 116:1-4, 12-19 1 Peter 1:17-23 Luke 24:13-35 **Second Service** Haggai 1:13 - 2:9 Psalm 48 1 Corinthians 3:10-17 John 2:13-22	**Principal Service** Acts 3:12-19 Psalm 4 1 John 3:1-7 Luke 24:36*b*-48 **Second Service** Deuteronomy 7:7-13 Psalm 142 Revelation 2:1-11 Luke 16:19-31	**Principal Service** Acts 9:1-6 (7-20) Psalm 30 Revelation 5:11-14 John 21:1-19 **Second Service** Isaiah 38:9-20 Psalm 86 John 11:(17-26) 27-44
Fourth Sunday of Easter (White *or* Gold)	**Principal Service** Acts 2:42-47 Psalm 23 1 Peter 2:19-25 John 10:1-10	**Principal Service** Acts 4:5-12 Psalm 23 1 John 3:16-24 John 10:11-18	**Principal Service** Acts 9:36-43 Psalm 23 Revelation 7:9-17 John 10:22-30

	Second Service Ezra 3:1-13 Psalm 29:1-10 Ephesians 2:11-22 Luke 19:37-48	**Second Service** Exodus 16:4-15 Psalm 81:8-16 Revelation 2:12-17 John 6:30-40	**Second Service** Isaiah 63:7-14 Psalms 113; 114 Luke 24:36-49
Fifth Sunday of Easter (White *or* Gold)	**Principal Service** Acts 7:55-60 Psalm 31:1-5, 15-16 1 Peter 2:2-10 John 14:1-14	**Principal Service** Acts 8:26-40 Psalm 22:25-31 1 John 4:7-21 John 15:1-8	**Principal Service** Acts 11:1-18 Psalm 148 Revelation 21:1-6 John 13:31-35
	Second Service Zechariah 4:1-10 Psalm 147:1-11 Revelation 21:1-14 Luke 2:25-32 (33-38)	**Second Service** Isaiah 60:1-14 Psalm 96 Revelation 3:1-13 Mark 16:9-16	**Second Service** Daniel 6:(1-5) 6-23 Psalm 98 Mark 15:46 - 16:8
Sixth Sunday of Easter (White *or* Gold)	**Principal Service** Acts 17:22-31 Psalm 66:8-20 1 Peter 3:13-22 John 14:15-21	**Principal Service** Acts 10:44-48 Psalm 98 1 John 5:1-6 John 15:9-17	**Principal Service** Acts 16:9-15 Psalm 67 Revelation 21:10, 22 - 22:5 John 14:23-29 *or* John 5:1-9
	Second Service Zechariah 8:1-13 Psalms 36:5-10; 87 Revelation 21:22 - 22:5 John 21:1-14	**Second Service** Song of Solomon 4:16 - 5:2; 8:6-7 Psalm 45 Revelation 3:14-22 Luke 22:24-30	**Second Service** Zephaniah 3:14-20 Psalms 126; 127 Matthew 28:1-10, 16-20

	Year A	Year B	Year C
Ascension Day (White *or* Gold)	Acts 1:1-11; Psalm 47 *or* Psalm 93; Ephesians 1:15-23; Luke 24:44-53		
Seventh Sunday of Easter *(Sunday in Ascensiontide)* (White *or* Gold)	**Principal Service** Acts 1:6-14 Psalm 68:1-10, 32-35 1 Peter 4:12-14; 5:6-11 John 17:1-11	**Principal Service** Acts 1:15-17, 21-26 Psalm 1 1 John 5:9-13 John 17:6-19	**Principal Service** Acts 16:16-34 Psalm 97 Revelation 22:12-14, 16-17, 20-21 John 17:20-26
	Second Service 2 Samuel 23:1-5 Psalm 47 Ephesians 1:15-23 Mark 16:14-20	**Second Service** Isaiah 61:1-11 Psalm 147:1-11 Luke 4:14-21	**Second Service** Isaiah 44:1-8 Psalm 68:1-14 (15-18) 19-20 (21-35) Ephesians 4:7-16 Luke 24:44-53
Pentecost (Red)	**Principal Service** Acts 2:1-21 *or* Numbers 11:24-30 Psalm 104:24-34, 35*b* 1 Corinthians 12:3*b*-13 *or* Acts 2:1-21 John 20:19-23 *or* John 7:37-39	**Principal Service** Acts 2:1-21 *or* Ezekiel 37:1-14 Psalm 104:24-34, 35*b* Romans 8:22-27 *or* Acts 2:1-21 John 15:26-27; 16:4*b*-15	**Principal Service** Acts 2:1-21 *or* Genesis 11:1-9 Psalm 104:24-34, 35*b* Romans 8:14-17 *or* Acts 2:1-21 John 14:8-17 (25-27)

	Second Service Joel 2:21-32 Psalms 67; 133 Acts 2:14-21 (22-38) Luke 24:44-53	**Second Service** Ezekiel 36:22-28 Psalm 139:1-12 (13-18, 23-24) Acts 2:22-38 John 20:19-23	**Second Service** Exodus 33:7-20 Psalms 36:5-10; 150 2 Corinthians 3:4-18 John 16:4*b*-15
Trinity Sunday (White *or* Gold)	**Principal Service** Genesis 1:1 - 2:4*a* Psalm 8 2 Corinthians 13:11-13 Matthew 28:16-20 **Second Service** Isaiah 6:1-8 Psalms 93; 150 John 16:5-15	**Principal Service** Isaiah 6:1-8 Psalm 29 Romans 8:12-17 John 3:1-17 **Second Service** Ezekiel 1:4-10, 22-28*a* Psalm 104:1-9 Revelation 4:1-11 Mark 1:1-13	**Principal Service** Proverbs 8:1-4, 22-31 Psalm 8 Romans 5:1-5 John 16:12-15 **Second Service** Exodus 3:1-15 Psalm 73:1-3, 16-28 John 3:1-17
Sunday between 24 and 28 May inclusive *(if after Trinity Sunday) – Eighth Sunday in Ordinary Time* (Green)	**Principal Service** Isaiah 49:8-16*a* Psalm 131 1 Corinthians 4:1-5 Matthew 6:24-34 **Second Service** Proverbs 8:1, 22-31 Psalm 148 Revelation 4:1-11 Luke 12:16-31	**Principal Service** Hosea 2:14-20 Psalm 103:1-13, 22 2 Corinthians 3:1-6 Mark 2:13-22 **Second Service** Genesis 2:4*b*-25 Psalm 65 Luke 8:22-35	**Principal Service** Sirach/Ecclesiasticus 27:4-7 *or* Isaiah 55:10-13 Psalm 92:1-4, 12-15 1 Corinthians 15:51-58 Luke 6:39-49 **Second Service** Genesis 1:1 - 2:3 Psalm 147:(1-11) 12-20 Matthew 6:25-34

	Year A	Year B	Year C
Sunday between 29 May and 4 June inclusive *(if after Trinity Sunday) – Ninth Sunday in Ordinary Time* (Green)	**Principal Service** *Continuous* Genesis 6:9-22; 7:24; 8:14-19 Psalm 46 Romans 1:16-17; 3:22*b*-28 (29-31) Matthew 7:21-29	**Principal Service** *Continuous* 1 Samuel 3:1-10 (11-20) Psalm 139:1-6, 13-18 2 Corinthians 4:5-12 Mark 2:23 - 3:6	**Principal Service** *Continuous* 1 Kings 18:20-21 (22-29) 30-39 Psalm 96 Galatians 1:1-12 Luke 7:1-10
	Related Deuteronomy 11:18-21, 26-28 Psalm 31:1-5, 19-24 Romans 1:16-17; 3:22*b*-28 (29-31) Matthew 7:21-29	*Related* Deuteronomy 5:12-15 Psalm 81:1-10 2 Corinthians 4:5-12 Mark 2:23 - 3:6	*Related* 1 Kings 8:22-23, 41-43 Psalm 96:1-9 Galatians 1:1-12 Luke 7:1-10
	Second Service Ruth 2:1-20*a* Psalm 33:(1-12) 13-22 Luke 8:4-15	**Second Service** Jeremiah 5:1-19 Psalm 35:1-10 (11-28) Romans 7:7-25 Luke 7:1-10	**Second Service** Genesis 4:1-16 Psalm 39 Mark 3:7-19
Sunday between 5 and 11 June inclusive *(if after Trinity Sunday) – Tenth Sunday in Ordinary Time* (Green)	**Principal Service** *Continuous* Genesis 12:1-9 Psalm 33:1-12 Romans 4:13-25 Matthew 9:9-13, 18-26	**Principal Service** *Continuous* 1 Samuel 8:4-11 (12-15) 16-20 (11:14-15) Psalm 138 2 Corinthians 4:13 - 5:1 Mark 3:20-35	**Principal Service** *Continuous* 1 Kings 17:8-16 (17-24) Psalm 146 Galatians 1:11-24 Luke 7:11-17

	Related Hosea 5:15 - 6:6 Psalm 50:7-15 Romans 4:13-25 Matthew 9:9-13, 18-26	*Related* Genesis 3:8-15 Psalm 130 2 Corinthians 4:13 - 5:1 Mark 3:20-35	*Related* 1 Kings 17:17-24 Psalm 30 Galatians 1:11-24 Luke 7:11-17
	Second Service 1 Samuel 18:1-16 Psalm 41 Luke 8:41-56	**Second Service** Jeremiah 6:16-21 Psalm 37:1-11 (12-14) Romans 9:1-13 Luke 7:11-17	**Second Service** Genesis 8:15 - 9:17 Psalm 44:1-8 (9-26) Mark 4:1-20
Sunday between 12 and 18 June inclusive *(if after Trinity Sunday) – Eleventh Sunday in Ordinary Time* (Green)	**Principal Service** *Continuous* Genesis 18:1-15 (21:1-7) Psalm 116:1-2, 12-19 Romans 5:1-8 Matthew 9:35 - 10:8 (9-23)	**Principal Service** *Continuous* 1 Samuel 15:34 - 16:13 Psalm 20 2 Corinthians 5:6-10 (11-13) 14-17 Mark 4:26-34	**Principal Service** *Continuous* 1 Kings 21:1-10 (11-14) 15-21*a* Psalm 5:1-8 Galatians 2:15-21 Luke 7:36 - 8:3
	Related Exodus 19:2-8*a* Psalm 100 Romans 5:1-8 Matthew 9:35 - 10:8 (9-23)	*Related* Ezekiel 17:22-24 Psalm 92:1-4, 12-15 2 Corinthians 5:6-10 (11-13) 14-17 Mark 4:26-34	*Related* 2 Samuel 11:26 - 12:10, 13-15 Psalm 32 Galatians 2:15-21 Luke 7:36 - 8:3
	Second Service 1 Samuel 21:1-15 Psalm 43 Luke 11:14-28	**Second Service** Jeremiah 7:1-16 Psalm 39 Romans 9:14-26 Luke 7:36 - 8:3	**Second Service** Genesis 13:1-18 Psalm 52 Mark 4:21-41

	Year A	Year B	Year C
Sunday between 19 and 25 June inclusive *(if after Trinity Sunday) – Twelfth Sunday in Ordinary Time* (Green)	**Principal Service** *Continuous* Genesis 21:8-21 Psalm 86:1-10, 16-17 Romans 6:1*b*-11 Matthew 10:24-39	**Principal Service** *Continuous* 1 Samuel 17:(1*a*, 4-11, 19-23) 32-49 Psalm 9:9-20 *or* 1 Samuel 17:57 - 18:5, 10-16 Psalm 133 2 Corinthians 6:1-13 Mark 4:35-41	**Principal Service** *Continuous* 1 Kings 19:1-4 (5-7) 8-15*a* Psalms 42; 43 Galatians 3:23-29 Luke 8:26-39
	Related Jeremiah 20:7-13 Psalm 69:7-10 (11-15) 16-18 Romans 6:1*b*-11 Matthew 10:24-39	*Related* Job 38:1-11 Psalm 107:1-3, 23-32 2 Corinthians 6:1-13 Mark 4:35-41	*Related* Isaiah 65:1-9 Psalm 22:19-28 Galatians 3:23-29 Luke 8:26-39
	Second Service 1 Samuel 24:1-17 Psalm 46 Luke 14:12-24	**Second Service** Jeremiah 10:1-16 Psalm 49 Romans 11:25-36 Luke 8:26-39	**Second Service** Genesis 24:1-27 Psalm 57 Mark 5:21-43
Sunday between 26 June and 2 July inclusive *– Thirteenth Sunday in Ordinary Time* (Green)	**Principal Service** *Continuous* Genesis 22:1-14 Psalm 13 Romans 6:12-23 Matthew 10:40-42	**Principal Service** *Continuous* 2 Samuel 1:1, 17-27 Psalm 130 2 Corinthians 8:7-15 Mark 5:21-43	**Principal Service** *Continuous* 2 Kings 2:1-2, 6-14 Psalm 77:1-2, 11-20 Galatians 5:1, 13-25 Luke 9:51-62

	Related Jeremiah 28:5-9 Psalm 89:1-4, 15-18 Romans 6:12-23 Matthew 10:40-42	*Related* Wisdom of Solomon 1:13-15; 2:23-24 *or* Lamentations 3:23-33 Psalm 30 2 Corinthians 8:7-15 Mark 5:21-43	*Related* 1 Kings 19:15-16, 19-21 Psalm 16 Galatians 5:1, 13-25 Luke 9:51-62
	Second Service 1 Samuel 28:3-19 Psalm 50:1-15 (16-23) Luke 17:20-37	**Second Service** Jeremiah 11:1-14 Psalm 53 Romans 13:1-10 Luke 9:51-62	**Second Service** Genesis 27:1-40 Psalm 60 Mark 6:1-6
Sunday between 3 and 9 July inclusive *– Fourteenth Sunday in Ordinary Time* (Green)	**Principal Service** *Continuous* Genesis 24:34-38, 42-49, 58-67 Psalm 45:10-17 *or Canticle:* Song of Solomon 2:8-13 Romans 7:15-25*a* Matthew 11:16-19, 25-30	**Principal Service** *Continuous* 2 Samuel 5:1-5, 9-10 Psalm 48 2 Corinthians 12:2-10 Mark 6:1-13	**Principal Service** *Continuous* 2 Kings 5:1-14 Psalm 30 Galatians 6:(1-6) 7-16 Luke 10:1-11, 16-20
	Related Zechariah 9:9-12 Psalm 145:8-14 Romans 7:15-25*a* Matthew 11:16-19, 25-30	*Related* Ezekiel 2:1-5 Psalm 123 2 Corinthians 12:2-10 Mark 6:1-13	*Related* Isaiah 66:10-14 Psalm 66:1-9 Galatians 6:(1-6) 7-16 Luke 10:1-11, 16-20
	Second Service 2 Samuel 2:1-11; 3:1 Psalm 56 Luke 18:31 - 19:10	**Second Service** Jeremiah 20:1-11*a* Psalm 64 Romans 14:1-17 Luke 10:1-11, 16-20	**Second Service** Genesis 29:1-20 Psalm 65 Mark 6:7-29

	Year A	Year B	Year C
Sunday between 10 and 16 July inclusive *– Fifteenth Sunday in Ordinary Time* (Green)	**Principal Service** *Continuous* Genesis 25:19-34 Psalm 119:105-112 Romans 8:1-11 Matthew 13:1-9, 18-23 *Related* Isaiah 55:10-13 Psalm 65:(1-8) 9-13 Romans 8:1-11 Matthew 13:1-9, 18-23 **Second Service** 2 Samuel 7:18-29 Psalm 60 Luke 19:41 - 20:8	**Principal Service** *Continuous* 2 Samuel 6:1-5, 12*b*-19 Psalm 24 Ephesians 1:3-14 Mark 6:14-29 *Related* Amos 7:7-15 Psalm 85:8-13 Ephesians 1:3-14 Mark 6:14-29 **Second Service** Job 4:1; 5:6-27 *or* Sirach/Ecclesiasticus 4:11-31 Psalm 66:1-9 (10-20) Romans 15:14-29 Luke 10:25-37	**Principal Service** *Continuous* Amos 7:7-17 Psalm 82 Colossians 1:1-14 Luke 10:25-37 *Related* Deuteronomy 30:9-14 Psalm 25:1-10 Colossians 1:1-14 Luke 10:25-37 **Second Service** Genesis 32:9-30 Psalm 77:1-12 (13-20) Mark 7:1-23
Sunday between 17 and 23 July inclusive *– Sixteenth Sunday in Ordinary Time* (Green)	**Principal Service** *Continuous* Genesis 28:10-19*a* Psalm 139:1-12, 23-24 Romans 8:12-25 Matthew 13:24-30, 36-43	**Principal Service** *Continuous* 2 Samuel 7:1-14*a* Psalm 89:20-37 Ephesians 2:11-22 Mark 6:30-34, 53-56	**Principal Service** *Continuous* Amos 8:1-12 Psalm 52 Colossians 1:15-28 Luke 10:38-42

	Related Wisdom of Solomon 12:13, 16-19 *or* Isaiah 44:6-8 Psalm 86:11-17 Romans 8:12-25 Matthew 13:24-30, 36-43	*Related* Jeremiah 23:1-6 Psalm 23 Ephesians 2:11-22 Mark 6:30-34, 53-56	*Related* Genesis 18:1-10*a* Psalm 15 Colossians 1:15-28 Luke 10:38-42
	Second Service 1 Kings 2:10-12; 3:16-28 Psalm 67 Acts 4:1-22 Mark 6:30-34, 53-56	**Second Service** Job 13:13 - 14:6 *or* Sirach/Ecclesiasticus 18:1-14 Psalm 73:(1-20) 21-28 Hebrews 2:5-18 Luke 10:38-42	**Second Service** Genesis 41:1-16, 25-37 Psalm 81 1 Corinthians 4:8-13 John 4:31-35
Sunday between 24 and 30 July inclusive *– Seventeenth Sunday in Ordinary Time* (Green)	**Principal Service** *Continuous* Genesis 29:15-28 Psalm 105:1-11, 45*b* *or* Psalm 128 Romans 8:26-39 Matthew 13:31-33, 44-52	**Principal Service** *Continuous* 2 Samuel 11:1-15 Psalm 14 Ephesians 3:14-21 John 6:1-21	**Principal Service** *Continuous* Hosea 1:2-10 Psalm 85 Colossians 2:6-15 (16-19) Luke 11:1-13
	Related 1 Kings 3:5-12 Psalm 119:129-136 Romans 8:26-39 Matthew 13:31-33, 44-52	*Related* 2 Kings 4:42-44 Psalm 145:10-18 Ephesians 3:14-21 John 6:1-21	*Related* Genesis 18:20-32 Psalm 138 Colossians 2:6-15 (16-19) Luke 11:1-13

	Year A	Year B	Year C
Sunday between 24 and 30 July continued	**Second Service** 1 Kings 6:11-14, 23-38 Psalm 75 Acts 12:1-17 John 6:1-21	**Second Service** Job 19:1-27*a* *or* Sirach/Ecclesiasticus 38:24-34 Psalm 74:(1-11) 12-17 (18-23) Hebrews 8:1-13 Luke 11:1-13	**Second Service** Genesis 42:1-25 Psalm 88:1-9 (10-18) 1 Corinthians 10:1-24 Matthew 13:24-30 (31-43)
Sunday between 31 July and 6 August inclusive *– Eighteenth Sunday in Ordinary Time* (Green)	**Principal Service** *Continuous* Genesis 32:22-31 Psalm 17:1-7, 15 Romans 9:1-5 Matthew 14:13-21	**Principal Service** *Continuous* 2 Samuel 11:26 - 12:13*a* Psalm 51:1-12 Ephesians 4:1-16 John 6:24-35	**Principal Service** *Continuous* Hosea 11:1-11 Psalm 107:1-9, 43 Colossians 3:1-11 Luke 12:13-21
	Related Isaiah 55:1-5 Psalm 145:8-9, 14-21 Romans 9:1-5 Matthew 14:13-21	*Related* Exodus 16:2-4, 9-15 Psalm 78:23-29 Ephesians 4:1-16 John 6:24-35	*Related* Ecclesiastes 1:2, 12-14; 2:18-23 Psalm 49:1-12 Colossians 3:1-11 Luke 12:13-21
	Second Service 1 Kings 10:1-13 Psalm 80:1-7 (8-19) Acts 13:1-13 John 6:24-35	**Second Service** Job 28:1-28 *or* Sirach/Ecclesiasticus 42:15-25 Psalm 88:1-9 (10-18) Hebrews 11:17-31 Luke 12:13-21	**Second Service** Genesis 50:4-26 Psalm 107:1-12 (13-32) 1 Corinthians 14:1-19 Mark 6:45-52

Sunday between 7 and 13 August inclusive *– Nineteenth Sunday in Ordinary Time* (Green)	**Principal Service** *Continuous* Genesis 37:1-4, 12-28 Psalm 105:1-6, 16-22, 45*b* Romans 10:5-15 Matthew 14:22-33 *Related* 1 Kings 19:9-18 Psalm 85:8-13 Romans 10:5-15 Matthew 14:22-33 **Second Service** 1 Kings 11:41 - 12:20 Psalm 86 Acts 14:8-20 John 6:35, 41-51	**Principal Service** *Continuous* 2 Samuel 18:5-9, 15, 31-33 Psalm 130 Ephesians 4:25 - 5:2 John 6:35, 41-51 *Related* 1 Kings 19:4-8 Psalm 34:1-8 Ephesians 4:25 - 5:2 John 6:35, 41-51 **Second Service** Job 39:1 - 40:4 *or* Sirach/Ecclesiasticus 43:13-33 Psalm 91:1-12 (13-16) Hebrews 12:1-17 Luke 12:32-40	**Principal Service** *Continuous* Isaiah 1:1, 10-20 Psalm 50:1-8, 22-23 Hebrews 11:1-3, 8-16 Luke 12:32-40 *Related* Genesis 15:1-6 Psalm 33:12-22 Hebrews 11:1-3, 8-16 Luke 12:32-40 **Second Service** Isaiah 11:10 - 12:6 Psalm 108 2 Corinthians 1:1-22 Mark 7:24-30
Sunday between 14 and 20 August inclusive *– Twentieth Sunday in Ordinary Time* (Green)	**Principal Service** *Continuous* Genesis 45:1-15 Psalm 133 Romans 11:1-2*a*, 29-32 Matthew 15:(10-20) 21-28 *Related* Isaiah 56:1, 6-8 Psalm 67 Romans 11:1-2*a*, 29-32 Matthew 15:(10-20) 21-28	**Principal Service** *Continuous* 1 Kings 2:10-12; 3:3-14 Psalm 111 Ephesians 5:15-20 John 6:51-58 *Related* Proverbs 9:1-6 Psalm 34:9-14 Ephesians 5:15-20 John 6:51-58	**Principal Service** *Continuous* Isaiah 5:1-7 Psalm 80:1-2, 8-19 Hebrews 11:29 - 12:2 Luke 12:49-56 *Related* Jeremiah 23:23-29 Psalm 82 Hebrews 11:29 - 12:2 Luke 12:49-56

	Year A	Year B	Year C
Sunday between 14 and 20 August continued	**Second Service** 2 Kings 4:1-37 Psalm 90:1-12 (13-17) Acts 16:1-15 John 6:51-58	**Second Service** Exodus 2:23 - 3:10 Psalm 100 Hebrews 13:1-15 Luke 12:49-56	**Second Service** Isaiah 28:9-22 Psalm 119:17-24 (25-32) 2 Corinthians 8:1-9 Matthew 20:1-16
Sunday between 21 and 27 August inclusive *– Twenty-first Sunday in Ordinary Time* (Green)	**Principal Service** *Continuous* Exodus 1:8 - 2:10 Psalm 124 Romans 12:1-8 Matthew 16:13-20	**Principal Service** *Continuous* 1 Kings 8:(1, 6, 10-11) 22-30, 41-43 Psalm 84 Ephesians 6:10-20 John 6:56-69	**Principal Service** *Continuous* Jeremiah 1:4-10 Psalm 71:1-6 Hebrews 12:18-29 Luke 13:10-17
	Related Isaiah 51:1-6 Psalm 138 Romans 12:1-8 Matthew 16:13-20	*Related* Joshua 24:1-2*a*, 14-18 Psalm 34:15-22 Ephesians 6:10-20 John 6:56-69	*Related* Isaiah 58:9*b*-14 Psalm 103:1-8 Hebrews 12:18-29 Luke 13:10-17
	Second Service 2 Kings 6:8-23 Psalm 95 Acts 17:15-34 John 6:56-69	**Second Service** Exodus 4:27 - 5:1 Psalm 116:(1-11) 12-19 Hebrews 13:16-21 Luke 13:10-17	**Second Service** Isaiah 30:8-21 Psalm 119:49-56 (57-72) 2 Corinthians 9:1-15 Matthew 21:28-32

Sunday between 28 August and 3 September inclusive *– Twenty-second Sunday in Ordinary Time* (Green)	**Principal Service** *Continuous* Exodus 3:1-15 Psalm 105:1-6, 23-26, 45*c* Romans 12:9-21 Matthew 16:21-28 *Related* Jeremiah 15:15-21 Psalm 26:1-8 Romans 12:9-21 Matthew 16:21-28	**Principal Service** *Continuous* Song of Solomon 2:8-13 Psalm 45:1-2, 6-9 James 1:17-27 Mark 7:1-8, 14-15, 21-23 *Related* Deuteronomy 4:1-2, 6-9 Psalm 15 James 1:17-27 Mark 7:1-8, 14-15, 21-23	**Principal Service** *Continuous* Jeremiah 2:4-13 Psalm 81:1, 10-16 Hebrews 13:1-8, 15-16 Luke 14:1, 7-14 *Related* Sirach/Ecclesiasticus 10:12-18 *or* Proverbs 25:6-7 Psalm 112 Hebrews 13:1-8, 15-16 Luke 14:1, 7-14
	Second Service 2 Kings 6:24-25; 7:3-20 Psalm 105:1-15 Acts 18:1-16 Mark 7:1-8, 14-15, 21-23	**Second Service** Exodus 12:21-27 Psalm 119:(1-8) 9-16 Matthew 4:23 - 5:20	**Second Service** Isaiah 33:13-22 Psalm 119:81-88 (89-96) John 3:22-36
Sunday between 4 and 10 September inclusive *– Twenty-third Sunday in Ordinary Time* (Green)	**Principal Service** *Continuous* Exodus 12:1-14 Psalm 149 Romans 13:8-14 Matthew 18:15-20 *Related* Ezekiel 33:7-11 Psalm 119:33-40 Romans 13:8-14 Matthew 18:15-20	**Principal Service** *Continuous* Proverbs 22:1-2, 8-9, 22-23 Psalm 125 James 2:1-10 (11-13) 14-17 Mark 7:24-37 *Related* Isaiah 35:4-7*a* Psalm 146 James 2:1-10 (11-13) 14-17 Mark 7:24-37	**Principal Service** *Continuous* Jeremiah 18:1-11 Psalm 139:1-6, 13-18 Philemon 1-21 Luke 14:25-33 *Related* Deuteronomy 30:15-20 Psalm 1 Philemon 1-21 Luke 14:25-33

	Year A	Year B	Year C
Sunday between 4 and 10 September continued	**Second Service** Ezekiel 12:21 - 13:16 Psalm 108 Acts 19:1-20 Mark 7:24-37	**Second Service** Exodus 14:5-31 Psalm 119:(41-48) 49-56 Matthew 6:1-18	**Second Service** Isaiah 43:14 - 44:5 Psalm 121 John 5:30-47
Sunday between 11 and 17 September inclusive *– Twenty-fourth Sunday in Ordinary Time* (Green)	**Principal Service** *Continuous* Exodus 14:19-31 Psalm 114 *or Canticle:* Exodus 15:1*b*-11, 20-21 Romans 14:1-12 Matthew 18:21-35	**Principal Service** *Continuous* Proverbs 1:20-33 Psalm 19 *or Canticle:* Wisdom of Solomon 7:26 - 8:1 James 3:1-12 Mark 8:27-38	**Principal Service** *Continuous* Jeremiah 4:11-12, 22-28 Psalm 14 1 Timothy 1:12-17 Luke 15:1-10
	Related Genesis 50:15-21 Psalm 103:(1-7) 8-13 Romans 14:1-12 Matthew 18:21-35	*Related* Isaiah 50:4-9*a* Psalm 116:1-9 James 3:1-12 Mark 8:27-38	*Related* Exodus 32:7-14 Psalm 51:1-10 1 Timothy 1:12-17 Luke 15:1-10
	Second Service Ezekiel 20:1-8, 33-44 Psalm 119:41-48 (49-64) Acts 20:17-38 Mark 8:27-38	**Second Service** Exodus 18:13-26 Psalm 119:73-80 (81-88) Matthew 7:1-14	**Second Service** Isaiah 60:1-22 Psalms 124; 125 John 6:51-69

Sunday between 18 and 24 September inclusive *– Twenty-fifth Sunday in Ordinary Time* (Green)	**Principal Service** *Continuous* Exodus 16:2-15 Psalm 105:1-6, 37-45 Philippians 1:21-30 Matthew 20:1-16	**Principal Service** *Continuous* Proverbs 31:10-31 Psalm 1 James 3:13 - 4:3, 7-8*a* Mark 9:30-37	**Principal Service** *Continuous* Jeremiah 8:18 - 9:1 Psalm 79:1-9 1 Timothy 2:1-7 Luke 16:1-13
	Related Jonah 3:10 - 4:11 Psalm 145:1-8 Philippians 1:21-30 Matthew 20:1-16	*Related* Wisdom of Solomon 1:16 - 2:1, 12-22 *or* Jeremiah 11:18-20 Psalm 54 James 3:13 - 4:3, 7-8*a* Mark 9:30-37	*Related* Amos 8:4-7 Psalm 113 1 Timothy 2:1-7 Luke 16:1-13
	Second Service Ezekiel 33:23, 30 - 34:10 Psalm 119:(113-120) 121-128 (129-136) Acts 26:1, 9-25 Mark 9:30-37	**Second Service** Exodus 19:10-25 Psalm 119:137-144 (145-152) Matthew 8:23-34	**Second Service** Ezra 1:1-11 Psalm 129 John 7:14-36
Sunday between 25 September and 1 October inclusive *– Twenty-sixth Sunday in Ordinary Time* (Green)	**Principal Service** *Continuous* Exodus 17:1-7 Psalm 78:1-4, 12-16 Philippians 2:1-13 Matthew 21:23-32	**Principal Service** *Continuous* Esther 7:1-6, 9-10; 9:20-22 Psalm 124 James 5:13-20 Mark 9:38-50	**Principal Service** *Continuous* Jeremiah 32:1-3*a*, 6-15 Psalm 91:1-6, 14-16 1 Timothy 6:6-19 Luke 16:19-31

	Year A	Year B	Year C
Sunday between 25 September and 1 October continued	*Related* Ezekiel 18:1-4, 25-32 Psalm 25:1-9 Philippians 2:1-13 Matthew 21:23-32	*Related* Numbers 11:4-6, 10-16, 24-29 Psalm 19:7-14 James 5:13-20 Mark 9:38-50	*Related* Amos 6:1*a*, 4-7 Psalm 146 1 Timothy 6:6-19 Luke 16:19-31
	Second Service Ezekiel 37:15-28 Psalm 124 1 John 2:22-29 Mark 9:38-50	**Second Service** Exodus 24:1-18 Psalms 120; 121 Matthew 9:1-8	**Second Service** Nehemiah 2:1-20 Psalm 135:1-14 (15-21) John 8:31-38, 48-59
Sunday between 2 and 8 October inclusive *– Twenty-seventh Sunday in Ordinary Time* (Green)	**Principal Service** *Continuous* Exodus 20:1-4, 7-9, 12-20 Psalm 19 Philippians 3:4*b*-14 Matthew 21:33-46	**Principal Service** *Continuous* Job 1:1; 2:1-10 Psalm 26 Hebrews 1:1-4; 2:5-12 Mark 10:2-16	**Principal Service** *Continuous* Lamentations 1:1-6 *Canticle:* Lamentations 3:19-26 *or* Psalm 137 2 Timothy 1:1-14 Luke 17:5-10
	Related Isaiah 5:1-7 Psalm 80:7-15 Philippians 3:4*b*-14 Matthew 21:33-46	*Related* Genesis 2:18-24 Psalm 8 Hebrews 1:1-4; 2:5-12 Mark 10:2-16	*Related* Habakkuk 1:1-4; 2:1-4 Psalm 37:1-9 2 Timothy 1:1-14 Luke 17:5-10
	Second Service Proverbs 2:1-11 Psalm 136:1-9 (10-26) 1 John 2:1-17 Mark 10:2-16	**Second Service** Joshua 3:7-17 Psalms 125; 126 Matthew 10:1-22	**Second Service** Nehemiah 5:1-13 Psalm 142 John 9:1-41

Sunday between 9 and 15 October inclusive *– Twenty-eighth Sunday in Ordinary Time* (Green)	**Principal Service** *Continuous* Exodus 32:1-14 Psalm 106:1-6, 19-23 Philippians 4:1-9 Matthew 22:1-14 *Related* Isaiah 25:1-9 Psalm 23 Philippians 4:1-9 Matthew 22:1-14 **Second Service** Proverbs 3:1-18 Psalm 139:1-12 (13-18) 1 John 3:1-15 Mark 10:17-31	**Principal Service** *Continuous* Job 23:1-9, 16-17 Psalm 22:1-15 Hebrews 4:12-16 Mark 10:17-31 *Related* Amos 5:6-7, 10-15 Psalm 90:12-17 Hebrews 4:12-16 Mark 10:17-31 **Second Service** Joshua 5:13 - 6:20 Psalm 127 Matthew 11:20-30	**Principal Service** *Continuous* Jeremiah 29:1, 4-7 Psalm 66:1-12 2 Timothy 2:8-15 Luke 17:11-19 *Related* 2 Kings 5:1-3, 7-15*b* Psalm 111 2 Timothy 2:8-15 Luke 17:11-19 **Second Service** Nehemiah 6:1-16 Psalm 144 John 15:12-27
Sunday between 16 and 22 October inclusive *– Twenty-ninth Sunday in Ordinary Time* (Green)	**Principal Service** *Continuous* Exodus 33:12-23 Psalm 99 1 Thessalonians 1:1-10 Matthew 22:15-22 *Related* Isaiah 45:1-7 Psalm 96:1-9 (10-13) 1 Thessalonians 1:1-10 Matthew 22:15-22	**Principal Service** *Continuous* Job 38:1-7 (34-41) Psalm 104:1-9, 24, 35*c* Hebrews 5:1-10 Mark 10:35-45 *Related* Isaiah 53:4-12 Psalm 91:9-16 Hebrews 5:1-10 Mark 10:35-45	**Principal Service** *Continuous* Jeremiah 31:27-34 Psalm 119:97-104 2 Timothy 3:14 - 4:5 Luke 18:1-8 *Related* Genesis 32:22-31 Psalm 121 2 Timothy 3:14 - 4:5 Luke 18:1-8

	Year A	Year B	Year C
Sunday between 16 and 22 October continued	**Second Service** Proverbs 4:1-18 Psalm 142 1 John 3:16 - 4:6 Mark 10:35-45	**Second Service** Joshua 14:6-14 Psalm 141 Matthew 12:1-21	**Second Service** Nehemiah 8:9-18 Psalm 149 John 16:1-11
Sunday between 23 and 29 October inclusive *– Thirtieth Sunday in Ordinary Time* (Green)	**Principal Service** *Continuous* Deuteronomy 34:1-12 Psalm 90:1-6, 13-17 1 Thessalonians 2:1-8 Matthew 22:34-46 *Related* Leviticus 19:1-2, 15-18 Psalm 1 1 Thessalonians 2:1-8 Matthew 22:34-46	**Principal Service** *Continuous* Job 42:1-6, 10-17 Psalm 34:1-8 (19-22) Hebrews 7:23-28 Mark 10:46-52 *Related* Jeremiah 31:7-9 Psalm 126 Hebrews 7:23-28 Mark 10:46-52	**Principal Service** *Continuous* Joel 2:23-32 Psalm 65 2 Timothy 4:6-8, 16-18 Luke 18:9-14 *Related* Sirach/Ecclesiasticus 35:12-17 *or* Jeremiah 14:7-10, 19-22 Psalm 84:1-7 2 Timothy 4:6-8, 16-18 Luke 18:9-14
	Second Service Ecclesiastes 11:1 - 12:14 Psalm 119:89-104 2 Timothy 2:1-7 Mark 12:28-34	**Second Service** Ecclesiastes 11:1 - 12:14 Psalm 119:121-136 2 Timothy 2:1-7 Luke 18:9-14	**Second Service** Ecclesiastes 11:1 - 12:14 Psalm 119:1-16 2 Timothy 2:1-7 Matthew 22:34-46

All Saints **(1 November)** (White *or* Gold)	**Principal Service** Revelation 7:9-17 Psalm 34:1-10, 22 1 John 3:1-3 Matthew 5:1-12	**Principal Service** Wisdom of Solomon 3:1-9 *or* Isaiah 25:6-9 Psalm 24 Revelation 21:1-6*a* John 11:32-44	**Principal Service** Daniel 7:1-3, 15-18 Psalm 149 Ephesians 1:11-23 Luke 6:20-31
	Second Service Sirach/Ecclesiasticus 44:1-15 *or* Isaiah 40:27-31 Psalms 1; 5 Revelation 19:6-10 John 11:20-27	**Second Service** Isaiah 65:17-25 Psalms 148; 150 Hebrews 11:32 - 12:2 Mark 8:34 - 9:1	**Second Service** Isaiah 35:1-9 Psalms 15; 84 Luke 9:18-27

When 1 November is a weekday, these readings may replace those of the Sunday between 30 October and 5 November inclusive.

Sunday between 30 October and 5 November inclusive *– Thirty-first Sunday in Ordinary Time* (Green)	**Principal Service** *Continuous* Joshua 3:7-17 Psalm 107:1-7, 33-37 1 Thessalonians 2:9-13 Matthew 23:1-12	**Principal Service** *Continuous* Ruth 1:1-18 Psalm 146 Hebrews 9:11-14 Mark 12:28-34	**Principal Service** *Continuous* Habakkuk 1:1-4; 2:1-4 Psalm 119:137-144 2 Thessalonians 1:1-4, 11-12 Luke 19:1-10
	Related Micah 3:5-12 Psalm 43 1 Thessalonians 2:9-13 Matthew 23:1-12	*Related* Deuteronomy 6:1-9 Psalm 119:1-8 Hebrews 9:11-14 Mark 12:28-34	*Related* Isaiah 1:10-18 Psalm 32:1-7 2 Thessalonians 1:1-4, 11-12 Luke 19:1-10
	Second Service Daniel 7:1-18 Psalms 111; 117 Luke 6:17-31	**Second Service** Daniel 2:1-11 (12-24) 25-48 Psalm 145:1-9 (10-21) Revelation 7:9-17 Matthew 5:1-12	**Second Service** Lamentations 3:22-33 Psalm 145:1-9 (10-21) John 11:(1-31) 32-44

	Year A	Year B	Year C
Sunday between 6 and 12 November inclusive *– Thirty-second Sunday in Ordinary Time* (Green)	**Principal Service** *Continuous* Joshua 24:1-3*a*, 14-25 Psalm 78:1-7 1 Thessalonians 4:13-18 Matthew 25:1-13	**Principal Service** *Continuous* Ruth 3:1-5; 4:13-17 Psalm 127 Hebrews 9:24-28 Mark 12:38-44	**Principal Service** *Continuous* Haggai 1:15*b* - 2:9 Psalm 145:1-5, 17-21 *or* Psalm 98 2 Thessalonians 2:1-5, 13-17 Luke 20:27-38
	Related Wisdom of Solomon 6:12-16 *or* Amos 5:18-24 *Canticle:* Wisdom of Solomon 6:17-20 *or* Psalm 70 1 Thessalonians 4:13-18 Matthew 25:1-13	*Related* 1 Kings 17:8-16 Psalm 146 Hebrews 9:24-28 Mark 12:38-44	*Related* Job 19:23-27*a* Psalm 17:1-9 2 Thessalonians 2:1-5, 13-17 Luke 20:27-38
	Second Service Judges 7:2-22 Psalm 82 John 15:9-17	**Second Service** Isaiah 10:33 - 11:9 Psalm 46 John 14:(1-22) 23-29	**Second Service** 1 Kings 3:1-15 Psalm 40 Romans 8:31-39 Matthew 22:15-22
Sunday between 13 and 19 November inclusive *– Thirty-third Sunday in Ordinary Time* (Green)	**Principal Service** *Continuous* Judges 4:1-7 Psalm 123 1 Thessalonians 5:1-11 Matthew 25:14-30	**Principal Service** *Continuous* 1 Samuel 1:4-20 *Canticle:* 1 Samuel 2:1-10 Hebrews 10:11-14 (15-18) 19-25 Mark 13:1-8	**Principal Service** *Continuous* Isaiah 65:17-25 *Canticle:* Isaiah 12:1-6 2 Thessalonians 3:6-13 Luke 21:5-19

Sunday between 13 and 19 November inclusive continued	*Related* Zephaniah 1:7, 12-18 Psalm 90:1-8 (9-11) 12 1 Thessalonians 5:1-11 Matthew 25:14-30	*Related* Daniel 12:1-3 Psalm 16 Hebrews 10:11-14 (15-18) 19-25 Mark 13:1-8	*Related* Malachi 4:1-2*a* Psalm 98 2 Thessalonians 3:6-13 Luke 21:5-19
	Second Service 1 Kings 1:(1-14) 15-40 Psalm 89:19-29 (30-37) Revelation 1:4-18 Luke 9:1-6	**Second Service** Daniel 3:(1-12) 13-30 Psalm 95 Matthew 13:24-30, 36-43	**Second Service** Daniel 6:1-28 Psalm 97 Matthew 13:1-9, 18-23
Sunday between 20 and 26 November inclusive *– Sunday before Advent* (White *or* Gold)	**Principal Service** *Continuous/Related* Ezekiel 34:11-16, 20-24 Psalm 95:1-7*a* *or* Psalm 100 Ephesians 1:15-23 Matthew 25:31-46	**Principal Service** *Continuous* 2 Samuel 23:1-7 Psalm 132:1-12 (13-18) Revelation 1:4*b*-8 John 18:33-37	**Principal Service** *Continuous/Related* Jeremiah 23:1-6 Psalm 46 *or Canticle:* Benedictus (Luke 1:68-79) Colossians 1:11-20 Luke 23:33-43
		Related Daniel 7:9-10, 13-14 Psalm 93 Revelation 1:4*b*-8 John 18:33-37	
	Second Service 2 Samuel 23:1-7 *or* 1 Maccabees 2:15-29 Psalm 93 Matthew 28:16-20	**Second Service** Daniel 5:1-31 Psalm 72:1-7 (8-20) John 6:1-15	**Second Service** 1 Samuel 8:4-20 Psalm 72:1-7 (8-20) John 18:33-37

Church Anniversary
(White *or* Gold)

Genesis 28:10-22 *or* 2 Chronicles 7:11-16; Psalm 84 *or* Psalm 122; Ephesians 2:19-22 *or* 1 Peter 2:1-5; Matthew 12:1-8 *or* John 4:19-26.

Covenant
(Red, *if in Ordinary Time*)

Exodus 24:3-11 *or* Deuteronomy 29:10-15; Jeremiah 31:31-34; Romans 12:1-2; John 15:1-10 *or* Mark 14:22-25. *Part of Psalm 51 is used in the service as a prayer.*

Harvest Thanksgiving
(Green)

Genesis 8:15-22 *or* Deuteronomy 26:1-11 *or* Ruth 2:1-23; Psalm 65; 1 Timothy 6:6-10 *or* Revelation 14:14-18; Matthew 6:25-33 *or* John 6:24-35.

John and Charles Wesley
(White *or* Gold)

Isaiah 12:1-6 *or* Isaiah 51:1-3,7-11; Psalm 130; Romans 5:1-11 *or* 2 Peter 1:1-11; Mark 12:28-37 *or* Luke 10:1-12, 17-20.

The readings are for use on Wesley Day (24 May), or on Aldersgate Sunday (24 May or the preceding Sunday), but should not normally be used at the Principal Service on Ascension Day, Pentecost, or Trinity Sunday.

New Year: Watchnight
(White *or* Gold)

Deuteronomy 8:1-20 *or* Ecclesiastes 3:1-15; Psalm 8 *or* Psalm 90; Revelation 21:1-6*a;* Matthew 25:31-46 *or* Luke 12:13-21 *or* Luke 12:35-50.

Remembrance Sunday
(Green)

Isaiah 25:1-9 *or* Isaiah 52:7-12 *or* Micah 4:1-8; Psalm 9:9-20 *or* Psalm 46; Romans 8:31-35, 37-39 *or* Revelation 22:1-5; Matthew 5:1-12 *or* Matthew 5:43-48 *or* John 15:9-17.

The related readings for the Sunday between 6 and 12 November may also be used; when Remembrance Sunday falls on 13 or 14 November, the related readings for the Sunday between 13 and 19 November may be used on the previous Sunday.

ACKNOWLEDGEMENTS

Every effort has been made to ensure that the following list of acknowledgements is as comprehensive as possible, but the experience of those involved in the preparation of **The Methodist Worship Book** is similar to that of the compilers of the **Book of Common Order** of the Church of Scotland, who state:

> Many sources have contributed to the compilation of this book, and not all of them are now traceable. Individual members of the Committee prepared drafts, which were revised more or less drastically by the Committee, often resulting in final versions which looked little like the original drafts. Among the casualties of this sometimes protracted process was the identity of many of the sources; they could not be recalled, nor did there seem to be any way to track them down. The Panel wishes to record at once both its indebtedness to any who may recognise in this book rhythms and patterns, expressions and phrases, ideas and images which are their own, and its regret that it became impossible to ask permission or seek consent for their inclusion . . .
>
> If, through inadvertence, copyright material has been used without permission or acknowledgement, the publisher will be grateful to be informed and will be pleased to make the necessary correction in subsequent editions.

The symbol * in the following paragraphs denotes that a text has been altered.

Except where indicated below, all psalms, scripture readings and scripture sentences are taken from **The New Revised Standard Version of the Bible (Anglicized Edition)**, © 1989, 1995 by the Division of Christian Education of the National Council of Churches of Christ in the United States of America, and are used by permission. All rights reserved.

Some scripture sentences are from **The Revised Standard Version**, © 1946 and 1952 by the Division of Christian Education of the National Council of Churches of Christ in the United States of America, and are used by permission. All rights reserved.

The texts of Psalm 134 on page 18, of Philippians 4:5b-7 on page 426 and of some scripture sentences are those of **The Revised English Bible**, © 1989 Oxford University Press and Cambridge University Press.

One scripture sentence comes from **The New Jerusalem Bible**, © 1985 Darton Longman & Todd and Doubleday & Co. Inc.

The text* of Psalm 51 on pages 143 and 286 appears in **A New Zealand Prayer Book - He Karakia Mihinare o Aotearoa**, © 1989 The Provincial Secretary, the Church of the Province of New Zealand. This book is also the source of one scripture sentence, the prayers of intercession* on pages 34f and 290f and the seasonal material* for Lent, Passiontide, Eastertide and All Saints on pages 55-57.

The texts of *Glory to God in the highest*, the Nicene Creed, the Apostles' Creed, *Sursum Corda*, *Sanctus*, *Benedictus Qui Venit*, *Gloria Patri*, *Te Deum Laudamus*, *Benedictus*, *Magnificat*, *Nunc Dimittis* and the left hand column version of the Lord's Prayer are from **Praying Together**, © 1988 by the English Language Liturgical Commission (ELLC).

The lectionary for the Principal Service is **The Revised Common Lectionary**, © 1992 The Consultation on Common Texts (CCT).

The lectionary for a Second Service (which forms part of the *Common Worship Lectionary* as published in **The Christian Year: Calendar, Lectionary and Collects**) is copyright © 1995, 1997 The Central Board of Finance of the Church of England. Reproduced by permission.

Prayer B on pages 27f, the introduction to the Peace on page 168, the prayer of confession* on page 241 and the prayers of intercession* on pages 244f are extracts from **Lent, Holy Week and Easter**, © 1984, 1986 The Central Board of Finance of the Church of England. Reproduced by permission.

Prayer A* on page 28, prayer A* on page 39, prayer B* on pages 40f, prayer A* on page 41, the address ('N and N, for you Jesus Christ came into the world . . .')* on pages 67f, 80f, 92f and 108, the prayer of confession* on page 330, the prayer on page 427, and prayers B and C on page 432 are from **Uniting in Worship**, © 1988 The Uniting Church in Australia Assembly Commission on Liturgy.

Prayer B on pages 28f and prayer A on pages 32f are from **Prayers for the Sunday Preaching Service**, Methodist Sacramental Fellowship, © 1987 C. Norman R. Wallwork.

Blessing B on page 38 is from the **Book of Common Order** of the Church of Scotland, © 1994 Panel on Worship of the Church of Scotland.

Prayer B* on page 39, prayer A* on page 437 and prayer A* on page 440 are from **Celebrating Common Prayer**, © 1992 The European Province of the Society of Saint Francis.

The structure and some of the text of prayer B on page 42 were inspired by a prayer in **The Iona Community Worship Book**, © 1991 Wild Goose Publications.

Prayer A on page 44 is from the **Supplemental Liturgical Resource No.1**, © The Presbyterian Church (USA).

Prayer A* on pages 45-47, the seasonal material* for Advent, Christmas and Epiphany, Ascensiontide, Pentecost and Trinity on pages 55-57, the seasonal introductions to the blessing* on pages 57-59 and 184, the prayer, 'We do not presume . . .', on pages 123, 157, 195, 227 and 233, the post-communion prayer on page 140, the preface for Trinity Sunday* on page 192, prayer B* on page 429 and one scripture sentence are extracts from **The Alternative Service Book 1980**, © 1980 The Central Board of Finance of the Church of England. Reproduced by permission.

The prayers* on pages 121f and the first part of the blessing* on page 128 are extracts from **The Promise of his Glory**, © 1990, 1991 The Central Board of Finance of the Church of England. Reproduced by permission.

The address* on pages 141f, the prayer over the ashes* on page 146 and the prayer over the palms* on page 237 are from **The Book of Common Prayer** of the Episcopal Church of the United States of America, 1979.

The act of penitence* on page 145f is from **The Book of Alternative Services**, © 1985 The General Synod of the Anglican Church of Canada.

Two lines of prayer B on page 172 are from David Silk, **Prayers for the Alternative Services**, Mowbray 1980, 1986.

The prayers* on pages 176f are from **A Book of Services**, © 1980 The United Reformed Church.

The prayer of confession* on pages 185f is from **The Daily Office Revised**, © 1978 The Joint Liturgical Group.

The preface for All Saints Day on page 193, the address on page 237 and the thanksgiving* on pages 275f are from **An Anglican Prayer Book 1989**, © 1989 The Provincial Trustees of the Church of the Province of Southern Africa.

The address* at no. 3 on page 230 is an extract from **Ministry to the Sick** © 1983 The Central Board of Finance of the Church of England. Reproduced by permission.

Prayer 19 B* on page 458, which also appears as prayer C on page 469, is from the **Book of Common Order** of the Church of Scotland, © 1940 Panel on Worship of the Church of Scotland.

Prayer C* on page 458, which also appears as prayer D on page 470 and prayer C on page 486, is from **Parish Prayers**, compiled and edited by Frank Colquhoun, 1964 Hodder and Stoughton.

The numbers shown against the collects on pages 523-563 refer to the following sources:

1 **The Alternative Service Book 1980**, © 1980 The Central Board of Finance of the Church of England

2 The American **Book of Common Prayer**, © 1928

3 **The Book of Alternative Services**, © 1985 The General Synod of the Anglican Church of Canada

4 **Book of Common Order** of the Church of Scotland, © 1994 Panel on Worship of the Church of Scotland

5 Extracts from **The Book of Common Prayer** (1662), the rights of which are vested in the Crown, reproduced by permission of the Crown's Patentee, Cambridge University Press

6 **The Book of Common Prayer** of the Episcopal Church of the United States of America, 1979

7 **The Book of Common Prayer with the Additions and Deviations Proposed in 1928**, © Central Board of Finance of the Church of England. Reproduced by permission

8 **The Book of Common Worship** of the Church of South India, © 1963 Oxford University Press

9 **Celebrating Common Prayer**, © 1992 The European Province of the Society of Saint Francis

10 Frank Colquhoun, ed., **Parish Prayers**, 1964 Hodder and Stoughton

11 The publishers are grateful to the Council of Churches for Britain and Ireland for permission to reproduce the *Pilgrim Prayer*, originally published in **The Next Steps Together in Pilgrimage**, BCC/CTS 1989, page 8

12 **The Daily Office Revised**, © 1978 The Joint Liturgical Group

13 **The Divine Office**, Volume 1, page 295, © 1974 Hierarchies of England and Wales. Reproduced by permission of A P Watt Ltd on behalf of the Liturgy Commission

14 Neil Dixon, ed., **Companion to the Lectionary: Volume 3**, © 1983 Epworth Press

15 International Commission on English in the Liturgy, © 1973

16 International Commission on English in the Liturgy, © 1993-94: Proposed Revision of the **Sacramentary**

17 **Lent, Holy Week and Easter**, © 1984, 1986 The Central Board of Finance of the Church of England

18 C. L. MacDonnell, in **Celebrating Common Prayer**

19 The Methodist Sacramental Fellowship

20 © Janet Morley, **All Desires Known**, SPCK 1992 (altered)

21 **A New Zealand Prayer Book - He Karakia Mihinare o Aotearoa**, © 1989 The Provincial Secretary, the Church of the Province of New Zealand

22 Gordon Nodwell, **Worship for all Seasons 1**, United Church of Canada

23 © 1993 (SPCK), Michael Perham, **Enriching the Christian Year**

24 Gail Ramshaw © 1988 : 7304 Boyer Street, Philadelphia PA19119

25 **Supplemental Liturgical Resources** © The Presbyterian Church (USA)

26 John V. Taylor, **Weep not for Me**, WCC Risk Books, 1986

27 **Uniting in Worship,** © 1988 The Uniting Church in Australia Assembly Commission on Liturgy